Translations of Power

Translations of Power

NARCISSISM AND THE UNCONSCIOUS

IN EPIC HISTORY

Elizabeth J. Bellamy

Cornell University Press

Ithaca and London

First published 1992 by Cornell University Press.

International Standard Book Number 0-8014-2698-7 (cloth)
International Standard Book Number 0-8014-9990-9 (paper)
Library of Congress Catalog Card Number 91-55549
Printed in the United States of America
*Librarians: Library of Congress cataloging information appears
on the last page of the book.*

⊗ The paper in this book meets the minimum requirements of the
American National Standard for Information Sciences–Permanence
of Paper for Printed Library Materials, ANSI Z39.48-1984.

For my parents

Contents

Acknowledgments

I thank both the Harvard University Andrew W. Mellon Faculty Fellowship Program in the Humanities for a year of research and writing, and the National Endowment for the Humanities, in particular for a NEH Summer Seminar at Princeton University directed by Thomas P. Roche, Jr. To him I owe a profound debt of gratitude for the scope and conception of this book.

The first section of Chapter 1, parts of the third section of Chapter 4, and the fourth section of Chapter 5 draw on essays that have appeared in *Bucknell Review, Comparative Literature Studies,* and *South Atlantic Quarterly.*

I thank the following friends and colleagues who have either read and commented on sections of the manuscript at various stages of its development or have lent their valuable moral support and encouragement: Albert Ascoli, Edwin Battistella, John Bernard, Elisabeth Bronfen, Jonathan Crewe, A. Leigh DeNeef, Margaret W. Ferguson, Valeria Finucci, Marjorie Garber, Kenneth Gross, Rachel Jacoff, Vassilis Lambropoulos, Artemis Leontis, Ada Long, Ellen Martin, David Lee Miller, Joy Potter, David Quint, Lawrence F. Rhu, Mary Beth Rose, and Sherry Sullivan. In addition, I thank Bernhard Kendler for his patience and editorial good judgment, the two anonymous readers for Cornell University Press, Kay Scheuer and Jessica Evans for their tireless copy-editing, and Judy Underhill for her help with the index. Tinker Dunbar of the Inter-Library Loan Department of Sterne Library at the University of Alabama at Birmingham unfailingly provided resources for me at a moment's no-

tice. Finally, a special thanks to Barbara, Jim, and Katie. The prover-
bial "without whom" formula of gratitude is inadequate to measure
their contributions to the completion of this book.

ELIZABETH J. BELLAMY
Boston, Massachusetts

Translations of Power

Principio muros obscuraque limina portae . . .
—*Aeneid* 11.752

Psychoanalyzing Epic History

Psychoanalyssance and the New Historicism

When Freud quotes from Jacob Burckhardt in his essay "The Moses of Michelangelo,"[1] the act invites us to ponder the larger question: what would constitute a meaningful convergence of psychoanalysis and the Renaissance (or a "psychoanalyssance," to coin a neologism)? Freud's fascination with the Renaissance is, of course, also revealed in his by now virtually canonical discussions of Shakespeare, but I propose that we turn brief attention to some of the specific implications of Freud's use of Burckhardt.[2] Certainly what is most intriguing is its embodiment of a symbolic convergence of two powerful epistemic moments in the history of ideas: "Renaissance humanism" as the "discovery" of modern individualism, and psy-

[1] Freud quotes Burckhardt's description of Michelangelo's Moses from his *Der Cicerone*: "'His form is animated by the inscription of a mighty movement and the physical strength with which he is endowed causes us to await it with fear and trembling'" (*The Standard Edition of the Complete Psychological Works of Sigmund Freud*, trans. James Strachey et al., ed. James Strachey [London: The Hogarth Press, 1953–74], 13:216). Freud uses Burckhardt's description to lend further evidence to his interpretation of Michelangelo's Moses as an embodiment of suppressed fury. (All references to the works of Freud are taken from *The Standard Edition*, hereafter abbreviated as *SE*.)

[2] Freud also quotes from Burckhardt in his essay on another titan of the Renaissance, Leonardo, in his essay "Leonardo da Vinci and a Memory of His Childhood" (*SE* 11:63). The essay on Leonardo is, of course, a key illustration of Freud's theory of sublimation, a topic I discuss in more detail in Chapter 4. In the specific context of Renaissance epic, Freud quotes from Tasso in his *Beyond the Pleasure Principle* in a passage I also discuss further in my fourth chapter.

choanalysis as the "discovery" that the individual is always subverted by an unconscious. If Burckhardt's *Civilization of the Renaissance in Italy* (1860) was instrumental in inaugurating what William
Kerrigan and Gordon Braden have referred to as an "inherited idea
of the Renaissance"[3] that has shaped our understanding of the development of modern consciousness, then Freud was responsible for
demonstrating how this process of self-recognition is always com-
promised through repression. The point of my observation is not to
suggest psychoanalysis as a "corrective" for the assumptions of Renaissance humanism, but rather to search for some ways in which we
can begin to conceive of how these two epistemes can mutually enrich one another. The two terms, one a period concept within political, cultural, and intellectual history, and the other a quasi-scientific
(and often biologistic) theory of (un)consciousness, are scarcely homologous in any way, but as monumental "epistemic moments"
they do share some crucial insights into the "fate" of the psyche and
its role in the formation of "subjecthood."

Both the "Renaissance" and "psychoanalysis" are, it goes without
saying, much larger than the figures of Burckhardt and Freud.[4] One
point of comparison between these two constructs is that neither
Freud nor Burckhardt problematized his respective model of consciousness and human endeavor by placing it in the perspective of
the sociocultural. Neither Burckhardt nor Freud experienced any
privileged insight into how his episteme suppressed, for example,
the truth of its bourgeois origins by divorcing his field of inquiry
from a complex matrix of socioeconomic and class factors—factors
whose absence have contributed to characterizations of psychoanalysis, in particular, as less a "master discourse" than, in the
words of V. N. Vološinov, "an abiding and profound expression of
certain crucial aspects of European bourgeois reality."[5] The insight of
the new historicism, then, takes on signal importance here, particularly its mandate that the Renaissance (and the Renaissance "subject") must be *contextualized* within the sociocultural. At the same
time, however, I will argue that psychoanalysis can serve as a useful
interpretive tool for Renaissance studies, but only if, ironically, we

[3]William Kerrigan and Gordon Braden, *The Idea of the Renaissance* (Baltimore: Johns
Hopkins University Press, 1989), xi.
[4]Here I should admit that I am taking some liberties in my analogy between Burckhardt and Freud. There was, of course, a "Renaissance" before Burckhardt; but there
was no "psychoanalysis" before Freud.
[5]V. N. Vološinov, *Freudianism: A Marxist Critique*, trans. I. R. Titunik, ed. I. R.
Titunik and Neal H. Bruss (New York: Academic Press, 1976), 8.

de-contextualize it from unfair generalizations that it is (like Burck-hardt's humanistic "Renaissance") merely a bourgeois praxis that is of little value in elucidating the role of the subject in history.

In its broadest scope my book suggests some ways in which we can forge a meaningful rapprochement between Renaissance litera-ture and psychoanalysis. In its particular focus, my book constitutes a psychoanalytic study of dynastic epic in the Renaissance, specifi-cally the conditions for the emergence of what could be termed an epic "subjecthood" throughout the literary history of dynastic epic that includes Virgil's *Aeneid*, Ariosto's *Orlando furioso*, Tasso's *Geru-salemme liberata*, and Spenser's *Faerie Queene*. Dynastic epic serves as a particularly intriguing locus of the intersection of psyche and his-tory, and I expand on my reasons for focusing on it later in this chapter. But at this point I should pose some of the general prob-lems inherent in any use of psychoanalysis for historical and literary figures.

Admittedly, such an endeavor, a psychoanalytic study of epic, al-ready runs the risk of begging the question: why epic *and* psycho-analysis? What do we stand to gain from a conjunction between these two divergent conceptual systems? Shoshana Felman has warned that a failure to forge a meaningful dialogue between litera-ture and psychoanalysis most often results in literature existing merely "to *serve* precisely the *desire* of psychoanalytical theory"; liter-ature is effaced by psychoanalysis and its ambitious "desire for mas-tery."[6] Such a project becomes even more complex when we con-sider that epic narrative also purports to be an account of *history*; and, as such, the specific question then arises, how can the "fictive" history of epic be reconciled with psychoanalysis?

Throughout this book I argue that the conjunction of epic and psychoanalysis can elude Felman's allegories of desire and mastery by offering some new insights into the difficult (and possibly unre-solvable) question of the mediation between subject (or psyche) and history. But before moving to the problematics of this mediation, I want to answer at length yet another question that naturally arises at this point: why is psychoanalysis more likely to accomplish a ne-gotiation between the epic subject and history than the perhaps more obvious path of the new historicism? As a kind of repository for national history, does not Renaissance epic logically lend itself to

---

[6]Shoshana Felman, "To Open the Question," in *Literature and Psychoanalysis: The Question of Reading: Otherwise*, ed. Shoshana Felman (Baltimore: Johns Hopkins Uni-versity Press, 1982), 6.

a critical methodology more explicitly "historicizing" than psycho-analysis?

Certainly any study of the Renaissance subject either in literature or in history must at least address itself to the successes of the new historicist project. As I mentioned earlier, under the influence of the new historicism, the "Renaissance" has for some time now been in the process of redefinition as less a cultural (or "period") concept than as a complex and problematized network of *socio*cultural codes, institutions, and practices. Accordingly, one of the results of the new historicism has been to place the concept of a Renaissance sub-ject under siege. The unity of the Renaissance subject is no longer assumed by new historicism, but is rather dispersed in the over-determinations of ideological appropriations of the subject. In Louis Montrose's conception, to cite only one influential example, Eliza-beth Tudor, the central "subject" of Spenser's *Faerie Queene*, was less a historical "person" than she was "the whole field of cultural mean-ings personified in her"—in short, the site of a "collective dis-course."[7] For new historicism then, the subject is of significance only insofar as he/she can be perceived as *sub-jected* to—embedded in—a network of cultural configurations and relations of power.

At this point, I wish to address a primary challenge: where can we situate psychoanalysis, as the formalized study of the "ego," in these new historicist repositionings of the subject? Why should and how can psychoanalysis be recuperated as a useful methodological tool in the field of Renaissance studies (and, in particular, the study of Renaissance epic), where increasingly the cry is, "Always histori-cize!"? The new historicism, though continuing to obscure its own methodology,[8] remains firmly opposed to psychoanalysis as a mean-ingful contributor to locating the place of the subject in/for/of the Renaissance. As the new historicism attempts to strengthen its hold over reconfiguring the Renaissance (and, in particular, the Renais-sance "subject"), psychoanalysis, implicitly or explicitly, finds itself marginalized. Stephen Greenblatt's essay "Psychoanalysis and Ren-aissance Culture" is to date the most explicit attempt to expunge psychoanalysis from the "narrative" of new historicism as *the* emer-

[7]Louis Montrose, "The Elizabethan Subject and the Spenserian Text," in *Literary Theory/Renaissance Texts*, ed. Patricia Parker and David Quint (Baltimore: Johns Hop-kins University Press, 1986), 303, 317.
[8]For an account of the new historicist's characteristic "reticence to discuss the the-ory that informs his practice," see Jean E. Howard's excellent overview, "The New Historicism in Renaissance Studies," *English Literary Renaissance* 16:1 (1986), esp. 35–43.

gent critical discipline of the discourse of the Renaissance subject. Greenblatt theorizes psychoanalysis out of Renaissance studies through a focus on the, for him, exemplary Renaissance subjectivity of Martin Guerre as "peripheral"—as "the *product* of relations, material objects, and judgments [in the legal struggle to determine his "real" identity] . . . rather than the *producer* of these relations, objects, and judgments";[9] and Greenblatt's argument throughout the essay constitutes the paradigmatic new historicist move whereby psychic experience disappears in the gaps of the subject's dispersal in the discursive formations of ideology.

I would argue that the new historicism, with its premature foreclosing on the unconscious, has allowed itself to be influenced by the recent objections to psychoanalysis that underwrite so much of current critical theory and, in the process, has recapitulated some of the same oversimplifications that plague these objections. Greenblatt's charge that psychoanalysis is "marginal"—and that it "can redeem its belatedness only when it historicizes its own procedures"[10] —can perhaps best be viewed as a microlevel reenactment of some of the current (non)receptions of psychoanalysis within the larger spectrum of post-Marxist cultural critique. Here, psychoanalysis (in either its clinical or its hermeneutic form) has for some time now been dismissed as a bourgeois praxis—perhaps, indeed, the last gasp of bourgeois, or even ironically Renaissance (or Burckhardtian), humanism—perpetuating obsolete emphases on the importance of the psychic history of the ego as an "object" of study. The de rigueur charge is that psychoanalysis does not sufficiently problematize the status of the subject—and the frequent conclusion seems to be that as the conventional notion of an "actual" subject goes, so goes psychoanalytic criticism.

A detailed consideration of Greenblatt's essay is essential for an understanding of how psychoanalysis can be used to problematize the very sociocultural codes that presumably render it belated. Greenblatt's focus, the story of Martin Guerre, is, on the surface, far removed from the concerns of Renaissance epic history. But through my analysis of his essay, it should become apparent that the unconscious must be factored into any discussion of the intersection of the subject and history.

Following a detailed summary of the historical record of the

<hr />

[9]Stephen Greenblatt, "Psychoanalysis and Renaissance Culture," in *Literary Theory/Renaissance Texts*, ed. Parker and Quint, 216.
[10]Ibid., 221.

strange case of Martin Guerre, in which Arnaud du Tilh, attempting to "usurp" his look-alike's identity, is sentenced as an impostor in a court of law, Greenblatt focuses on what must be determined as minimally inherent in the declaration of "selfhood." He argues that "what is at stake in this case is not psychic experience at all but rather a communal judgment that must, in extraordinary cases, be clarified and secured by legal authority."[11] The effect of declaring Martin Guerre to, in fact, *be* Martin Guerre is not his establishment as a subject complete with his own inalienable psychic history, but is rather a legal determination that has been shaped by a community consensus of what defines, in Greenblatt's words, "a complex system of possessions, kinship bonds, contractual relationships, customary rights, and ethical obligations."[12] The selfhood of the subject is constituted not within psychic experience, but within a matrix of sociocultural discourses, institutions, and practices, underwritten and validated by legal authority. "The move," continues Greenblatt, "is not from distinct physical traits to the complex life experience generated within, but outward to the community's determination that this particular body possesses by right a particular identity."[13] On this basis, then, Greenblatt concludes that psychoanalysis is belated—that it is "from this perspective, less the privileged explanatory key than the distant and distorted consequence of this cultural nexus."[14] Selfhood is not, as psychoanalysis would have it, "the very form of the human condition,"[15] but a belated act of self-fashioning made possible only after cultural and legal authority has defined the concept of "self."

Greenblatt envisions psychoanalysis as requiring the stable origin of a self as "a given upon which to construct interpretations"[16]—that psychoanalysis and its desire for mastery are disabled when the subject is seen as crisscrossed within a field of sociocultural codes and logics. But Greenblatt's argumentative move seems dependent on a peremptory foreclosure of the role of the unconscious in constituting the subject.[17] *The Return of Martin Guerre* might be subtitled, after

[11]Ibid., 215.
[12]Ibid., 216.
[13]Ibid.
[14]Ibid.
[15]Ibid.
[16]Ibid., 217.
[17]Here I should confess that Greenblatt's motives for his critique of psychoanalysis in this essay remain obscure to me. At times, he seems actually to be supporting the

Jacques Lacan, "The Subversion of the Subject and the Dialectic of Desire," because the more far-reaching issue at stake in this bizarre story of a purloined identity may be not the (legal or communal) constitution of the subject, but rather the *subversion* of the subject by the strange transferences that make up what we could term the mimetics of imposture—a subversion occurring long before legal authority intervenes to enunciate the subject. Greenblatt argues that Arnaud du Tilh "can manipulate appearances . . . but he cannot seize the other man's inner life."[18] But a well-known Lacanian axiom that can be readily invoked in any story of the uncanny double (whether in history or in literature) is that a subject is not simply a subject for another subject; rather the subject represents itself as a subject *for the other*—and that other is itself never a subject, but only another signifier. Or, as Lacan put it even more succinctly, the signifier represents the subject for another signifier.

Exactly how is it possible that Arnaud du Tilh can step in and *become* (imitate, assume the identity of) Martin Guerre? The question is so basic to the action of the story that its psychic complexities are easy to overlook. An analysis of such a mimetic gesture of imposture is facilitated by a presupposition that Martin Guerre the subject exists only as a collection of easily appropriated signifiers for Arnaud (the "signifying subject" as husband, son, nephew, father, heir to property, and so on), who, having earlier insinuated himself into his double's psychohistory, chooses to represent himself *as* Martin for the benefit of the other (of the wife Bertrande, of the uncle Pierre, and even of Jean de Coras, the judge in the case who was actually poised to rule in Arnaud's favor just before Martin's unexpected return). One of the more resonant speculations concerning this story

---

claims of psychoanalysis. Significant portions of his essay are given over to granting that "identity in Freud does not depend upon existential autonomy" (214); and there are times when it seems his impulse is to show that he understands Freud's project better than Freud himself. Moreover, surely in Greenblatt's earlier landmark study, *Renaissance Self-Fashioning*, we are justified in viewing his concept of "self-fashioning" as a brilliantly rich merger between the Renaissance and psychoanalysis, a reflection that his interest in Renaissance "selves" remains at least as strong as his interest in the larger networks of meaning that disperse these "selves." (Indeed, Greenblatt's account of Iago's "improvisations of power" over Othello rather uncannily resemble the erosions of Martin Guerre's identity by means of Arnaud du Tilh's improvisatory will.) Greenblatt's almost Oedipal ambivalence toward Freud is itself a major topic of interest and one that itself invites psychoanalytic speculation. In the meantime, his ambivalence makes for treacherous oversimplification when one claims that he *is* attacking psychoanalysis in his essay on Martin Guerre.

[18]"Psychoanalysis and Renaissance Culture," 214.

is the strong possibility that Martin's wife, Bertrande, knows that Arnaud is not her husband. To say this is by no means to make the absurd claim that Martin no longer exists; but her acceptance of this more tender and loving version of Martin as her surrogate husband enacts Bertrande's own fantasy of the other and is crucial to sustaining the allegory of Arnaud's representation of himself in his fantasy of being Martin—crucial to sustaining the allegory of signifiers representing the subject (Martin/Arnaud) for the other.

In such a scheme, "Arnaud du Tilh" is a signifier that represents Martin Guerre for another signifying subject—in this case, Bertrande. Arnaud's mimetics of imposture is enabled by a psychic allegory of intersubjective exchange that effaces Martin Guerre the subject, at the point at which Arnaud abandons his obscure life on the margins of society in favor of a "Martin Guerre" that is perhaps best conceptualized as a network of signifying positions (husband to Bertrande, nephew to Pierre, prosperous heir of property, and others)—a network ensuring that the subject is merely an "effect" of the other to which it seeks to represent itself. It is worthwhile to note here that, according to Natalie Zemon Davis, it is not known exactly *when* Arnaud began preparing for his usurping role as Martin.[19] Here we are confronted with a case of how the order of the signifier will often elude historical detective work. The ambiguous psychic moment when Arnaud takes on the "desire" of Martin (the other) as his own desire simply escapes historical documentation.

But the perhaps even more significant "other" story of the strange case of Martin Guerre is what happens when legal authority intervenes in this psychic field of signification to determine the integrity of the subject—the determination of what Greenblatt refers to as "a primal, creatural individuation" necessitated by the reappearance of the "other" Martin Guerre.[20] The sliding of the signifiers that make up the subject would seem to come to a halt in the lengthy trial in the court of law at Artigat, where the sentence finally passed by Jean de Coras, as recorded in the register of the Parlement, is that Arnaud is guilty of "imposture and false supposition of name and person and of adultery."[21] But a key question here is: what validates the

[19]Natalie Zemon Davis, *The Return of Martin Guerre* (Cambridge: Harvard University Press, 1983), 40.
[20]"Psychoanalysis and Renaissance Culture," 214. It is worth noting here that the motive for Martin's ill-tempered return seems more the intent to take revenge on his uncanny double than it does an admirable decision to reassume the burden of his abandoned responsibilities.
[21]Quoted in *The Return of Martin Guerre*, 86.

final authority of a legal speech act when it must intervene in psychic matters? As the judge in the case, Jean de Coras has the power to proclaim identity as a function of, in Greenblatt's words, "customary rights and ethical obligations," but that is not to say that this arbitrary declaration has power or authority over the signifier. To what extent can de Coras's court legislate against the "false suppositions" of the subject representing itself as a subject for the other? To what extent can it "discipline and punish" the dialectic of desire that constitutes every subject's encounter with the other in the order of the signifier?

The heart of the dilemma here is that the sociocultural and contractual field that Jean de Coras's court draws from to make a legal determination concerning who is allowed to *be* Martin Guerre (that is, husband, son, nephew, heir to property) is precisely the psychic field of the other that Arnaud appropriates for the successful representation of himself as Martin. When the Law becomes implicated in the "arresting" of the psychic other as the place of the signifier, it begins to lose its metaphysical grounding as the final arbiter of identity. One could say that Arnaud "knows" that his claim to be Martin resides in the "unarrested" and sliding chain of signifiers that constitutes his "dialectic of desire" to *be* Martin. In short, he seeks no higher authority beyond the other to ground his act of imposture. But the court at Artigat falls into the paradoxical trap of claiming that it *is* the "other" for the other, that it *is* the metaphysical grounding for the signifier. In effect, Jean de Coras validates the subjecthood of Martin Guerre through a matrix of social codes that shifts so freely (that is so psychically interchangeable) it can also sustain the subjecthood of what Louis Althusser would refer to as an "uninterpellated" man so marginalized that, as the signifier "Arnaud du Tilh," alias "Pansette," a "man of bad life from Sajas,"[22] he can scarcely be mapped by the communally agreed upon patrimonial coordinates of possessions, bonds, rights, and obligations. Or, to put it more simply, Arnaud has so insinuated himself into the psychohistory of Martin that he can without difficulty proclaim a rightful interpellation into the patrimonial codes of obligation that were unsuccessful in binding the latter to his legal "identity."

In this context, it is appropriate to consider Lacan's critique of metalanguage from his essay "The Subversion of the Subject" and its implications for Jean de Coras's sentencing of Arnaud.

[22]Ibid., 58.

Let us set out from the conception of the Other as the locus of the signifier. Any statement of authority has no other guarantee than its very enunciation, and it is pointless for it to seek it in another signifier, which could not appear outside this locus in any way. Which is what I mean when I say that no metalanguage can be spoken, or, more aphoristically, that there is no Other of the Other. And when the Legislator (he who claims to lay down the Law) presents himself to fill the gap, he does so as an imposter.[23]

Lacan's exposure of the metalinguistic impulse as an "imposter" has an uncanny resonance for Arnaud's trial of imposture. Jean de Coras rules against Arnaud, assuming the role of a legal *sujet supposé savoir* by using conventionally agreed upon cultural codes to "arrest" the signifiers of subjecthood. But if de Coras's legal enunciation concerning Martin's right to his own identity is directly dependent on bonds, rights, and obligations that are vulnerable to the psychic allegory of the other—if de Coras tries to "speak" (metalinguistically) as the (legal) other of the (psychic) other—to echo Lacan, he can do so, then, only as an imposter himself. Jean de Coras, then, attempting to pass legal sentence on Arnaud's imposture, doubles back mimetically as an imposter of the very other he seeks to delegitimize through legal enunciation. And the consequence is that Martin Guerre must "authorize" his freedom from imposture by a law that is itself an imposter. The "authority" of the legal utterance is questioned by Samuel Weber, who argues, "How, in general, can authority itself *take place*, if this place, as site of the Signifier, is not one that can ever be simply, or fully 'taken'?"[24] Weber's metaphors of positionality—his characterizations of the struggle for authority to find a "place" for itself—are crucial here, for they get us to the heart of what is wrong with what amounts to Greenblatt's "placing" of psychoanalysis. Greenblatt's argument is that the legally determined codes of the sociocultural "take (prior) place" over psychoanalysis

---

[23]Jacques Lacan, "The Subversion of the Subject and the Dialectic of Desire in the Freudian Unconscious," in *Écrits: A Selection*, trans. Alan Sheridan (New York: W. W. Norton, 1977), 309–10.

[24]Samuel Weber, "Psychoanalysis, Literary Criticism, and the Problem of Authority," in *Psychoanalysis and . . .* , ed. Richard Feldstein and Henry Sussman (New York: Routledge, 1990), 24. In his discussion of the current legal battle in Paris as to whether Lacan's Seminars constitute "works" by an author, Weber has constructed an intriguing critique of legal authority itself: "For what does it mean to 'assume' the authority of a law that necessarily remains without an author? Can we be sure that such a 'law' is itself legitimate? What if it were 'only' *powerful*, based on a more or less opaque force?" (23).

(over what Weber might refer to here as "the site of the Signifier"), which comes into being only as a belated effect of the establishing of subjecthood by the Law. But it can just as readily be demonstrated that the Law, seeking to establish (arbitrary) authority over the insistence of the signifier, must intervene to *dis*place psychoanalysis from the (always) already occupied site of the Signifier.

My point here is not to prioritize psychoanalysis as a discipline that renders the law belated, for such an argument merely puts psychoanalysis back in the undesirable "place" of striving, as it is often accused of doing, to be a master discourse.[25] But the easy reversibility of the "places" of psychoanalysis and the law in the story of Martin Guerre should lead us to suspect that the real issue at stake is how we are to interpret what we could view as the always shifting signifier of "psychoanalysis." When we invoke psychoanalysis to refute or support an argument, I would call for a heightened awareness of what we mean by "psychoanalysis." I would argue that the enabling strategy of Greenblatt's argument that psychoanalysis is belated is his marked tendency to interpret psychoanalysis as an orthodox Freudian endeavor—to view it in its almost monolithic incarnation as a kind of "ideological state apparatus" that can assume clinical operation only after the bourgeois subject has been defined (hence Greenblatt's allusion to Freud's celebrated Rat Man case to illustrate how psychoanalysis defines selfhood).[26]

Greenblatt's summarizing interpretation of the moral of the return of Martin Guerre as the securing of "proprietary rights to a name and a place in an increasingly mobile social world"[27] is surely well perceived, as is his articulation of the emerging conditions under which the (bourgeois) subject sees itself as "continuous" (and, implicitly, beginning to take shape for the analyst as a future "case history" that can respond to psychotherapy). But as part of his move

[25]I want to emphasize, too, that it is certainly not my point to privilege a Lacanian "return to Freud" as somehow better than a "Freudian return" to the return of Martin Guerre. My psychoanalytic explication in this book is not based on any choice between Freud or Lacan; I can discern no advantages in such a choice. Because of its greater emphasis on intersubjective relations, Lacanian psychoanalysis is often assumed to be of greater social value than Freud. However, as discussed in the next chapter, it is Freud's comprehensive studies of culture and repression that more fundamentally enable a psychoanalytic study of the Renaissance subject. It is my intention to read Freud and Lacan against each other, in the hopes of enriching our understanding of psychoanalytic theory by way of constantly shifting appositions, convergences, and refashionings of the theories of these two landmark figures.

[26]"Psychoanalysis and Renaissance Culture," 214.

[27]Ibid., 221.

to make psychoanalysis "belated," Greenblatt "places" it solely as a
bourgeois praxis, reducing its theoretical resonances and hermeneutic possibilities to, in effect, a disciplinary moment in the history of
the bourgeois subject—a history, for Greenblatt, beginning at some
point in the Renaissance and, perhaps, culminating somewhere
amid the bourgeois ills of Freud's clients, "'hystericalized,'" in the
words of Michael Schneider, "by the decline of the Austro-Hun-
garian monarchy."[28] Even as he (justifiably) calls for psychoanalysis
to historicize itself, Greenblatt (over) historicizes psychoanalysis as
an episteme conceived at a particular (bourgeois, capitalist) point in
the history of ideas, thus "placing" it as a belated effect of sociocultural codes already in place.[29] While continuing our awareness of
the clinical will to power of Freudian analysis and its complicities
with the Oedipal competitions that have been so instrumental in
shaping the suspect ethics of bourgeois capitalism, we must also
realize that "psychoanalysis" is as much a shifting signifier as the

[28]Michael Schneider, *Neurosis and Civilization: A Marxist/Freudian Synthesis*, trans.
Michael Roloff (New York: The Seabury Press, 1975), 70.
[29]In their introduction to a recent collection of essays on psychoanalysis, Richard
Feldstein and Henry Sussman call for a kind of "post-psychoanalysis," a kind of "hybrid form of psychoanalysis [that] could become decontextualized from the mirror of
clinical relations that has customarily supported its claims" (*Psychoanalysis and . . .*, ed.
Feldstein and Sussman, 1). A "decontextualized" psychoanalysis, we could affirm, is
better off for having no "proper place"—for being "dis-placed" from the shadowy
hegemony of bourgeois clinical practice. There is no question here that if psychoanalysis wishes to develop its "place" within post-Marxist culture critique, it will truly
have to become a post-psychoanalysis, giving up its place in bourgeois therapy (not
to mention its "fatal destiny" to cultivate an allegiance to a "master"), and giving itself
over to tracking the shifting rearticulations of the subject within the sociocultural. But
what, we should ask, *is* the cultural space of a psychoanalysis that, despite its presumed role as a "master discourse," has always been as shifting and unstable as the
subject it analyzes—in some sense, always already decontextualized, always constituted within someone else's discursive agenda?
    It would be difficult to write a history of psychoanalysis that would not be a story
of the multiple and contradictory invokings of its intentions. I have space for only a
brief sketch of some of the contradictions such a history might uncover. For Vološinov, for example, psychoanalysis became more bourgeois as it experienced increasing separation from its theoretical basis (8-9). But for Russell Jacoby, psychoanalysis
became more bourgeois at the point at which it became more "theoretical," losing its
originary political edge (as embodied by the likes of Helene Deutsch and Otto Fenichel) as it became more assimilated into the medical and clinical orthodoxies of
American psychoanalysis and the closed system of private therapy (*The Repression of
Psychoanalysis: Otto Fenichel and the Political Freudians* [New York: Basic Books, 1983],
17–19). It is certainly nothing new to hear that a concept has been reappropriated and
reshaped for any number of argumentative purposes, but it must be emphasized that
if psychoanalysis continues to be vulnerable to arbitrary decontextualization, then it
will become increasingly difficult to imagine what a post-psychoanalysis should be
called upon to do.

sociocultural codes that made the "Freudian moment" possible—
a signifier that must elude its reduction to merely a bourgeois "ideological state apparatus."

Let us, for the moment, broaden the scope of our discussion from
Greenblatt in particular to the goals of the new historicism in general
for the purposes of determining where we can "place" psychoanalysis as immanent in ideology critique. In its elucidation of the
complex dispersals of the subject within ideology, the new historicism has been careful to avoid making the subject disappear from
history entirely—careful to avoid making compensatory and over-
simplifying claims that the subject is merely the collective sum of its
sociocultural parts. Even as it successfully attacks the notion of the
"unified" bourgeois subject, the new historicism (at least the new
historicism that is not so inclined to accept a deterministic pervasiveness throughout society of power and domination) has always attempted to address the complexities of the interdependence of subject and structure and has even, for that matter, shown how the
individual subject-as-poet can create, fashion, and even to some extent control the operations of ideology.[30]

But these processes remain entirely on the level of consciousness.
In its call for (re)articulating the interdependence of subject and
structure, the new historicism has come up squarely against the
vexed and, by now, rather tired question of the tug-of-war between
the individual and the social that has plagued the critique of ideology since the Frankfurt School. I would argue that at the point at
which some hard questions must be asked of the exact nature of
these rearticulations, the new historicism and its assembling and re-
assembling of the subject within sociocultural formations flatten out
and threaten to lose their innovative edge. At what historical junctures (economic, political, social, cultural) is this interdependence
between subject and structure most likely to occur? What are the
conditions under which sociocultural structures are most likely to

---

[30]Louis Montrose, for example, argues that such a strategy of poetic fashioning is
particularly evident in Spenser's many representations of Queen Elizabeth: "In the
Spenserian text, and elsewhere, we can observe a mode of contestation at work
within the Elizabethan subject's very gestures of submission to the official fictions"
("The Elizabethan Subject," 331).

For an astute account of how this new historicist ideal of demonstrating how text
can actually influence context is "rarely achieved in current practice," see A. Leigh
DeNeef, "Of Dialogues and Historicisms," *South Atlantic Quarterly* 86:4 (1987), 502.
One of the implicit goals of my study is not only to show how the epic text influences
imperial context, but also to elucidate the role of the unconscious in such an intersection.

succeed in interpellating an individual subjectivity? Why can we reasonably conclude that not every subject is fully interpellated into the sociocultural? More particularly, why *does* a Martin Guerre seek to de-interpellate himself from legal and cultural codes, only to invoke the power of those codes over another site of de-interpellated subjectivity? What becomes of new historicist articulations of the intersection between subject and structure when we consider that the story of *The Return of Martin Guerre,* which, as we have seen, Greenblatt uses as a prooftext for his specifications of the conditions for the emergence of a bourgeois consciousness as an aftereffect of cultural codes, is also an account of an individual subject's refusal to "see" himself interpellated in the discourses of social bonds? In this direct abutting of subject and structure, what is the precise explanatory key that can make sense of *why* Martin leaves, only eventually to force a sociocultural articulation of his identity?

My argument is that the sociocultural overdeterminations that problematize the point of intersection between the subject and history are themselves overdetermined by the irruptions of the unconscious at perhaps unpredictable points in the constantly shifting rearticulations that make up the discontinuities of subject-positions. The new historicism forecloses on the unconscious just when it can help us in a further nuancing of the problematics of the subject within history. But it is possible to demonstrate that the unconscious works in history—that the unconscious is thoroughly implicated in historical specificity—and that a reconsideration of the operations of the unconscious can thereby offer us some new opportunities for rethinking the complex mediation between subject and history.

The Subject in/of/for Ideology

Interpreted in their broadest scope, both psychoanalysis and (post)Marxism are, among other things, involved in investigations of the problems inherent in recognizing oneself *as* a self. But this investigation raises such temporal questions as: In the intersection of subject and structure, which comes first? Or, reaching back even further, is it reasonable to assume that there are real temporal considerations involved as to when, in this juncture, an unconscious is formed? In short, what *causes* an unconscious?

Perhaps the best means of seeking further points of intersection between psychoanalysis and a critique of ideology—and their relevance for a study of the subject in the Renaissance—is first to focus on the Marxist concept of alienation. This concept has traditionally been invoked in a class context to refer to the worker's alienation from his own labor under capitalism. But, as Marx himself recognized, one consequence of this exploitation is that the subject is also alienated from his own mental life. The Marxist can justifiably insist on the necessity of making a rigorous distinction as to what it means for this "mental life" to be characteristically "proletarian" or "bourgeois"; but the concept of alienation nevertheless suggests that even within the economic tedium of class domination and exploitation of labor, there is an irreducibly psychic essence that can engender irruptions and discontinuities. Somewhere on the divide between false (class) consciousness and *un*consciousness lies this enigmatic, discontinuous alienation that is neither purely psychological nor purely reducible to the isolations of worker exploitation. Or, put more simply, alienation resides on that always stubbornly ill-defined and obscure threshold between the individual and the social.

The question then arises: just how "neurotic" is this privileged Marxist concept of alienation? A Marxist would argue that the question is irrelevant (or, even worse, irresponsibly bourgeois) because it moves in the direction of valorizing the psychohistory of the individual subject. Certainly this must be accepted as a fair accusation. But one is equally justified in pointing out that what has yet to be determined in the critique of ideology is the precise effect of alienation on psychosocial experience.

The charge that psychoanalysis does not sufficiently problematize the status of the subject (that is, the "placement" of psychoanalysis as a reflection of bourgeois European experience) must inevitably and to a large extent ignore the implications of Althusser's positive reception of Lacan and, in particular, the potentially rich analogies between the concepts of Althusserian "interpellation" and Lacanian *méconnaissance*—both of which seem to be meaningful extensions of the psychic implications of a Marxist alienation and serve as valuable starting points for any consideration of how ideology can actually be deformed by neurosis. Althusser's essay "Ideology and Ideological State Apparatuses" has long been perceived as relevant for the procedures of new historicism, but it is just as significant for its psychoanalytic nuancing of the intersection between subject and structure. Althusser claims that ideology operates "by constituting concrete subjects as subjects,"[31] which is to argue that a subject *becomes* a sub-

[31]Louis Althusser, "Ideology and Ideological State Apparatuses," in *Lenin and Philosophy and Other Essays*, trans. Ben Brewster (New York: Monthly Review Press, 1971), 173.

ject only when it can "recognize" itself within a given social formation—much as Martin Guerre is declared a subject only when legal
authority officially recognizes his interpellations as husband, father,
son, nephew, and heir. In such a scheme (the kind of scheme that
underwrites Greenblatt's argumentative strategy) the subject is always the (belated) *effect* of the expectations of ideology; but this retroactive entry of the subject into ideology ensures that there can be
no such entity as a unified (and fully "conscious") agency. The psychic edge inherent in Althusser's concept of interpellation, constituted by his landmark conception of ideology as a " 'representation' of
the imaginary relationship of individuals to their real conditions of
existence,"³² finds a model in the radical discontinuity between
Lacan's (by now rather hopelessly clichéd) rubrics of the Imaginary
and the Symbolic—a discontinuity in which the subject (like Arnaud
du Tilh) is fated to be forever caught in the trap of its own *méconnaissance*, such that it can never recognize itself as a *self*. For Althusser,
misrecognition ("ideological recognition") is "the 'Logos' meaning in
ideology,"³³ a false consciousness ensuring that the subject always
recognizes his place in ideological formations.

But, as we have touched upon earlier, what has yet to be determined in the critique of ideology is the extent to which the retroac-
tivity of the subject's entry into ideology may demarcate the space of
an unconscious, where the "real" subject is alienated and repressed
through its own (mis)representation of itself. The intersection between Althusser and Lacan is treacherous terrain indeed, where
again the goal must be to make sense of the highly refracted relationship between the subject and ideology. But what I want to emphasize here is the polemical implications of Althusser's conception
of ideology as an "imaginary representation," for it suggests that
ideology operates largely, and to an as yet unknown degree, on the
level of the unconscious.³⁴

³²Ibid., 162.
³³Ibid., 171.
³⁴In his recent book, *Discerning the Subject*, a rigorous articulation of the concept of
the "subject" within a variety of cultural codes, Paul Smith argues, "If anything
comes out as an injunction from the work done in the Freudian/Lacanian mode, it is
the necessity of taking into account the way in which human action, however defined
or to whatever social determinants it is said to be submitted, is *never not mediated by
the unconscious*" (*Discerning the Subject* [Minneapolis: University of Minnesota Press,
1988], 72–73; italics Smith's). Though by no means psychoanalytically oriented himself, Smith's observation clears the path for rethinking the operations of the unconscious within the sociocultural.

At the point at which we consider what Marxist alienation and Althusserian interpellation have in common, it is appropriate also to investigate the Lacanian unconscious and, specifically, the realm of the Symbolic as a crucial mediating site between psyche and ideology.[35] For Lacan, the unconscious is perceived not topographically, like the Freudian unconscious, but rather as an "edge" at which the subject is structured in relation to the Symbolic. In a process analogous to Althusserian interpellation, the Lacanian unconscious is not to be viewed as the *cause* of the subject, but emerges (retroactively) when the subject identifies itself as a "speaking" subject upon its entry into the Symbolic.[36] As the metaleptic trace-structure of this effect, the Lacanian subject (like Arnaud du Tilh) is always alienated from itself—always ex-centric, always *other* to itself—bound to recognize (only belatedly) that its other *was* where the subject itself *should be.* Thus, although we can argue that the subject experiences a

---

Althusser, of course, explicitly invokes Lacan in his essay "Freud and Lacan," where he defines the Lacanian "discourse of the Other" as that which "gives us a hold, a *conceptual* hold on the unconscious, which is in each human being the absolute place where his particular discourse seeks its own place, seeks, misses, and in missing, finds its own place, its own anchor to its place, in the imposition, imposture, complicity and denegation of its own imaginary fascinations" (*Lenin and Philosophy*, 212–13). For one of the earliest, post-Althusserian attempts to consider Lacan within the sociocultural, see Fredric Jameson, "Imaginary and Symbolic in Lacan: Marxism, Psychoanalytic Criticism, and the Problem of the Subject," in *Yale French Studies* 55/56 (1977), 338–95. For a more recent consideration of how a "critical theory of society must draw on psychoanalysis as an interpretive practice capable of generating a theory of subjectivity" (179), see John Brenkman's chapter "The Social Construction of Subjectivity," in his *Culture and Domination* (Ithaca: Cornell University Press, 1987). In his application of Lacan to Althusser, Slavoj Žižek discusses hysteria as an example of how the operations of the unconscious can result in what he calls a "failed interpellation" (*The Sublime Object of Ideology* [London: Verso, 1989], 113–17).

[35]It should be acknowledged here that Greenblatt concludes his attack on the ahistoricity of psychoanalysis by writing, "There are interesting signs of this historicizing—perhaps most radically in the school of Hegelian psychoanalysis associated with the work of Jacques Lacan, where identity is always revealed to be the identity of another" (221). Despite Greenblatt's slighting of Lacan, whose identity as a "strong father" in psychoanalysis is somewhat effaced in the broader rubric of "the school of Hegelian psychoanalysis," his own concept of self-fashioning (whereby subversion arises within the social order from a self that differs/defers from itself) is underwritten largely by the Lacanian subject as structured by the discourse of the other. (In his essay "The Death of the Modern: Gender and Desire in Marlowe's 'Hero and Leander,'" David Lee Miller has also observed that Greenblatt "has not come to terms with Lacan's pertinence to the new historicism" [*South Atlantic Quarterly*, 88:4 (1989), 760].)

[36]This process constitutes the temporally elusive "retroversion effect" by which, as Lacan writes, "the subject becomes at each stage what he was before and announces himself—he will have been—only in the future tense" ("Subversion of the Subject and the Dialectic of Desire," 306).

"fading" (an *aphanisis*) when it is interpellated in the dispersals of ideological formations (or, in a more Marxist scheme, when it becomes alienated within the structure of, say, worker exploitation),[37] it is by no means the case that sub-jection to the ideological or the sociohistorical diminishes the unconscious as a site of psychic resistance that renders the subject's entry into the Symbolic highly discontinuous. The unconscious, located on the Imaginary slope of an Althusserian interpellation, comes into being at the moment of the subject's *aphanisis*; and this process leaves in its wake a "lack" that marks the trace of the "real" self in what now survives only as a representation of the self to its-self.

Lacan's conception of the unconscious gets us very close to an understanding of how ideology can actually be deformed by neurosis. We could argue that it is this lack, this gap in self-representation, that renders the subject culturally as well as psychically alienated, unavailable for full appropriation into ideology.[38] In an Althusserian scheme, the subject must come to "recognize" itself in social formations; but the subject enters these formations under the spell of its own *méconnaissance* wherein the self still struggles with the impossibility of achieving its own self-recognition. Thus, if the subject is "overdetermined"—if it is unable to determine the nature of its own subjectivity—it is overdetermined as much because of the operations of the unconscious as by its dispersal in the sociocultural. And if the Foucaultian dramatis personae of ideology, the pervasive forces of surveillance, power, domination, and control, can be properly perceived as having their limits in that they tend to oversimplify

[37]Lacan defines *aphanisis* as the process whereby "the subject is this emergence which, just before, as subject, was nothing, but which, having scarcely appeared, solidifies into a signifier" ("From Love to the Libido," in *The Four Fundamental Concepts of Psycho-analysis*, ed. Jacques-Alain Miller, trans. Alan Sheridan [New York: W. W. Norton], 199).

[38]This Lacanian gap in the subject's self-representation such that full appropriation into ideology is not possible can perhaps be directly traced to Marx's concept of alienation through the mediating figure of Alexandre Kojève, who was almost single-handedly responsible for introducing Hegel's *Phenomenology of Spirit* into France. If Lacanian psychoanalysis is a distinctly Hegelian meditation on the dialectic between self and other, then Lacan's intimate familiarity with Kojève is one major reason. Kojève's interpretations of Hegel were, in turn, influenced by his exposure to the young Marx. This is the intellectual line of transmission, then, through which we might trace a direct link between Marx and Lacan. (For a brief assessment of Kojève's influence on Lacan, see Edward S. Casey and J. Melvin Woody, "Hegel, Heidegger, Lacan: The Dialectic of Desire," in *Interpreting Lacan*, ed. Joseph H. Smith and William Kerrigan [New Haven: Yale University Press, 1983], 75–112, and David Macey, *Lacan in Contexts* [London: Verso, 1988], 95–99).

ideology as monolithic, it may be because the unconscious, as a site of resistance within the sociocultural, exerts a more heterogeneous influence than has yet to be fully charted.

History/Psychoanalysis/Narrative

Thus far, I have focused on the complexities of what is entailed in a psychoanalytic nuancing of the subject and structure within history. With these complexities in mind, we can now turn to a perhaps even more difficult task—that of tracing the effects of the unconscious when this intersection of subject and structure takes place within a history that is refracted by narrative representation. At this point, several questions arise: In what ways can these previous discussions of the unconscious and its overdeterminations within the sociocultural be relevant to a subjecthood that is specifically *literary*? How do the belated formations of the unconscious become "manifest" when history is represented in narrative form? And, in particular, what does the previous discussion of the operations of the unconscious within ideology have to do with dynastic epic as the central "subject" of this book? As a narrative of national destiny whose characters are neither fully literary nor fully historical, dynastic epic is refracted by the intersection of history and fiction in ways that are particularly complex—and that can provide a particularly rich commentary on how any subject (literary or historical) is always the (belated) *effect* of the expectations of ideology. In such a study, psychoanalytic interpretations of the text prove to be indispensable. One of the major tasks of the new historicism has been, of course, to outline the complexities inherent in inserting the literary text into history. But again, I argue that any new historicist articulation of the relationship of fiction and history must take into account the influence of the unconscious and its unpredictable irruptions at the intersection of text and context.

In order to investigate further the implications of these questions, let us return, very briefly, to the story of Martin Guerre. One point of emphasis that should be made here is that the historical record of the case of Martin Guerre, whether it be in the form of a historical novel like Janet Lewis's *Wife of Martin Guerre*, or in the form of historical documentation like Natalie Zemon Davis's *Return of Martin Guerre*, has taken shape over centuries as a narrative. Though the case of Martin Guerre is, in one sense, a historical account of some

of the still not-fully-defined shifts from a feudalist to a capitalist society, it nevertheless has managed to take on a life of its own as a
story (as historical accounts so often do), shaped by a beginning, a
middle, and an end. If new historicism in general has concerned
itself with the insertion of the literary text into history, for Greenblatt, in particular, the "text" has often been widely interpreted as
historical narrative and anecdote—hence his fascination with the
historical record of Martin Guerre, where history and narrative converge.[39] And even as Greenblatt calls for an attention to the dispersal
of the subject within ideological formations, he continues to be irre-
sistibly drawn to the fate of the individual within narrative.

The critic, then, is left to negotiate a complex interpretive triangle
involving not just the intersection of the subject and history, but
also the portrayal of the subject within a history that is often explicitly narrative. The pertinent question, then, for any study of a subjecthood that is both literary and historical is: what is needed to
interpret the operations of the unconscious within narrative history?
Even if we reject the notion of a literary "character" as a fully constituted being in favor of a more Greimasian notion of "actants" who
are conceived in terms of modes of *participation* in narrative, we are
still left with the complex problem of the relationship between subject and narrative. Fredric Jameson has defined the concept of literary "character" not as a unified *cogito*, but rather as "that point in
the narrative text at which the problem of the insertion of the subject
into the Symbolic most acutely arises."[40] Thus, it follows that the
intersection of the subject with narrative also inherits all the complexities of the intersection of the subject with history—specifically,
the interpretive complexities that result from any consideration of
the unconscious as a site of psychic resistance within history.

It is at the level of narrative, then, that psychoanalysis can especially prove to be as useful in nuancing the intersection of subject
and history as the new historicism. It is my specific argument that

[39]For more on the natural complicity between new historicism and narrative, see
Alan Liu, "The Power of Formalism: The New Historicism," *English Literary History*
56:4 (1989), 721–77. Liu writes: "In essence, we may say, the New Historicism to date
has been a method preoccupied almost exclusively with the status not of annals imagination but of its narrative legitimation: variously legitimate or illegitimate subjects
who may only be recognized/discovered in story form. One way to approach the
problem of New Historicist 'paradigms' might thus be to recognize that they are first
and foremost highly sophisticated exercises in storytelling. Indeed, it often seems that
the most successful New Historicist works are those that form a sustained sequence
of tales akin to an updated hagiography" (767–55).
[40]Jameson, "Imaginary and Symbolic in Lacan," 301.

psychoanalysis and epic are naturally complicit in their endeavors because they are both so profoundly implicated in narrative. And although the genre of epic is intimately bound up with history, it is history (like the story of Martin Guerre) as heavily mediated through "fictive" narrative—a mediation that can be most successfully negotiated through psychoanalysis.

Jameson has described narrative provocatively and fundamentally as "the central function or *instance* of the human mind,"[41] while Peter Brooks has argued that "the structure of literature *is* in some sense the structure of mind."[42] What I find especially noteworthy here is that the works of Jameson, whose Marxist-informed imperative at the outset of *The Political Unconscious* is "Always historicize!," and of the psychoanalytically informed Brooks converge at the juncture of psychic and narrative structuration. This brief convergence of historical materialism and psychoanalysis affords us a valuable opportunity to pause and re-evaluate what happens to the concept of "subjecthood" when a literary character is seen as inhabiting this obscure coordinate between "mind" and narrative. The central concern of my book is: What happens when this juncture of psychic and narrative structuration takes place in history—specifically in history as represented within the narratives of dynastic epic? Jameson's criticism of psychoanalysis, so characteristic of its detractors, is that it "remains locked into the category of the individual subject."[43] But I argue that the category of the epic "subject," because it is, in some Jamesonian sense, always (already) historicized in the narrative of national destiny, offers a valuable site of mediation between psyche

[41]Fredric Jameson, *The Political Unconscious: Narrative as a Socially Symbolic Act* (Ithaca: Cornell University Press, 1981), 13.

[42]Peter Brooks, "The Idea of a Psychoanalytic Criticism," in *The Trial(s) of Psychoanalysis*, ed. Françoise Meltzer (Chicago: University of Chicago Press, 1987), 148.

[43]*The Political Unconscious*, 68. Despite his attacks on psychoanalysis, Jameson himself can actually serve as an ally in the psychoanalyzing of epic narrative because of the interpretive richness of his concept of the "political unconscious" and its reliance on the mechanisms of repression. Jameson has demonstrated that the often strange turns of narrative occur because narrative (under pressure, simply, to tell a story) must suppress or can no longer negotiate certain unresolvable political and social contradictions. I simply wish to stress that the effects of the political unconscious are as much unconscious (repressive) as they are political (suppressive); and if narrative is, as Brooks contends, "the structure of mind," it is such because narrative "unresolvability" is often structured on an obscure threshold between ideological (or historical) and psychic repression. The political unconscious, in other words, is not so historical that psychic experience (and its structuration in/of narrative) can be so readily occluded in social and ideological formations.

and history—a mediation that can transcend any reliance on a "unified" subject through an emphasis on the unconscious.

Epic and Its Romance Discontents

In an Althusserian scheme, as we have seen, the operations of ideology need subjects to fit their discursive formations, a process whereby the "social" subject is transformed, we could say, into a "grammatical" subject. Such a process is in accord with the Lacanian axiom that the unconscious is structured like a language. Lacan's Law of the Symbolic, which begins to operate as the subject is poised on the brink of interpellation, most fully manifests itself when the subject "names" itself. In the "linguistic" but alienating structuralism of the Symbolic, the "speaking" subject in effect receives a pronoun (a "he," a "she," a "theirs"—or, most traumatically, an "I," creating, under the guise of totality, an unconscious that alienates the subject from itself).[44] The speaking subject must, in other words, learn the pronominal and relational syntax of kinship systems (paternity, marriage, childhood) that await inscription in sociocultural formations.

It is at this point, then—at the juncture of the subject's entry into the Symbolic and of its unconscious (mis)recognition of the syntactical structures of the Symbolic—that we are justified in turning to the narrative of dynastic epic as the privileged representation of this matrix. Because narrative is inherently linguistic, it can be properly understood as itself structured by the discourse of the unconscious. And we could argue that dynastic epic, in particular, is the narrative par excellence of the process of the speaking subject's inscription into the sociocultural. All of which brings us to the effectiveness of psychoanalysis as an interpretive tool for epic. With its emphasis on filial piety, imperial intermarriages, and genealogical continuity—and its emphasis on moral conscience and ethical self-fashioning for its individual heroes—dynastic epic is perhaps *the* privileged narrative of the Symbolic.[45] But if the Law of the Symbolic, as we have

[44]In "The Subversion of the Subject and the Dialectic of Desire," Lacan writes, "Being of non-being, that is how *I* as subject comes on the scene, conjugated with the double aporia of a true survival that is abolished by knowledge of itself" (300).
[45]For a comprehensive discussion of "the rhetorical ideal" of the exemplary epic hero, see James Nohrnberg's chapter "The Institution of the Hero," in his *The Analogy of "The Faerie Queene"* (Princeton: Princeton University Press, 1976), 22–34.

seen, always entails a kind of primal repression, then epic logically provides its own conditions for the possibility of psychoanalytic interpretation. Psychoanalysis can reveal the extent to which the superstructures of epic narrative rest precariously on the unconscious as the retroactive residue of a resistance to imperial inscription.

To appreciate fully the precariousness of this narrative superstructure, we must first consider epic as a generic and discursive category, specifically its heavy investment in the Symbolic of imperial ideology.[46] Epic—and its ethical superstructure of *pietas*—is an explicitly ideological genre, and epic narrative is the aesthetic tool of imperialist ideology. As a literary mode of production, and indeed as a kind of ideological closure of a nascent imperial capitalism, epic is a textual commodity perhaps more dependent than other genres on the tacit social exchange between poet and reader, whose most dramatic and powerful embodiment is the glorified head of empire itself. When this tacit contract between poet and reader is observed, then the hegemonic will of imperial ideology is rendered invisible, and the (inter)textual production of epic as the recording of the *translatio imperii* proceeds smoothly.[47]

But what is at stake in the reliance of imperialist polemic on narrative representation—on the tacit complicity not only of poet and reader, but also of epic ideology and narrative? Can we speak, in short, of a "desire" of empire? Certainly we can argue that the *translatio imperii*, the "translation" of imperial power that structures epic narrative, is one of the more teleologically determined concepts in literary history, indeed a claim to be a totalizing history, an authoritative production of historical "truth" that contributed significantly to the exercise of an imperial will-to-power. As the informing structure of Western dynastic epic, the *translatio imperii* purports to be the final resting place of Aeneas's fragmented Trojan remnant, the point at which the interplay of history and (epic) literature celebrates the founding of the ultimate *imperium sine fine*, or "kingdom without

[46]For a discussion of the way in which epic ideology seeks to establish a moral superiority over what it perceives as "the dangerous excess of the East" (6), see David Quint, "Epic and Empire," *Comparative Literature* 41:1 (1989), 1–32. It is worth noting here that Ariosto's and Tasso's works, as representative "Western" epics, seem particularly, and problematically, concerned with understanding themselves against the pagan "other."

[47]Terry Eagleton neatly summarizes the process by which the complicity of writing and reading transforms literature into a mode of production: "Valuable text and valuable reader are reversible: in a mutual complicity, such a text writes its reader and such a reader writes the text" (*Criticism and Ideology: A Study in Marxist Literary Theory* [London: Verso, 1978], 164).

end," as promised to Aeneas by Jupiter in the first book of the *Aeneid*. The Trojan disaster becomes a kind of fortunate fall as the ruins
of Troy are happily reintegrated into the "fictive" history of (Roman,
Ferrarese, French, Portuguese, British) *imperium*. The *translatio imperii* is constituted within a vast temporality in which history ad-
vances teleologically from Troy as its posited origin to the inexo-
rable, providential fulfillment of empire in the current Royal House.
In such a temporally aggressive scheme, history becomes the-
matized. The unresolvable contradictions of historical contingency
are presented as the *iter durum*, the long, hard road, of epic destiny,
"redeemed" through a hermeneutics of empire; the *translatio imperii*
becomes, in effect, a metadiscourse that seeks to reveal the *imperium
sine fine* as virtually a theory of history itself.[48]

Such a programmatic complicity between ideology and narrative
(the very "desire" of empire) must give us pause as we consider the
ongoing methodological conundrum of how texts can be mean-
ingfully inserted into history.[49] Because the pseudohistorical invest-

---

[48]Dante's *De monarchia* is just such a meta-discursive document of a "theory" of
empire, what Frances Yates has referred to as "the most striking statement of imperialist theory in medieval times" (*Astraea: The Imperial Theme in the Sixteenth Century*
[London: Ark Paperbacks, 1985], 11). Yates also offers a discussion of Petrarch's efforts to proclaim a unified Italy as the continuation of the old Roman Empire (13).

[49]As I suggested earlier, the inaugural gesture of the new historicism was just such
an effort to join texts with history, thus Montrose's early chiastic presentations of its
project as the "historicity of texts" and the "textuality of history" ("Renaissance Literary Studies and the Subject of History," *English Literary Renaissance* 16:1 [1986], 8). But
one problematic tendency in the early stages of the new historicism was a "hyper-
textualizing" of history. A textual metaphysics of history is openly invoked when, in
a widely acknowledged precursor essay for the new historicism, Michael McCanles
argues that "the historicist can never rest finally with a text that interprets without
itself requiring interpretation" ("The Authentic Discourse of the Renaissance," *Diacritics* 10:1 [1980], 79). Similarly, David Carroll, in an explicitly deconstructionist move in
his early poststructuralist phase, writes that the "'real in itself' is always-already representation" and that history "is always *written*, consisting of repeated attempts to
reconstruct after the fact a present which necessarily escapes it" ("*Mimesis* Recon-
sidered: Literature, History, Ideology," *Diacritics* 5 [1975], 12). Thus, both McCanles
and Carroll early on problematized the status of the historical text as document or
cultural artifact, radically calling into question the positivist assumptions of the "old"
historicism. But the notion of history as never identical, never adequate to itself, is to
deprive history of its conflictual status within the Real. Thus, Jameson poses an alternative to poststructuralist accounts of history: "We would therefore propose the following revised formulation: that history is *not* a text, not a narrative, master or otherwise, but that, as an absent cause, it is inaccessible to us except in textual form, and
that our approach to it and to the Real itself necessarily passes through its prior
textualization, its narrativization in the political unconscious" (*The Political Unconscious*, 35).

ment of epic history is more ideological than historical, the telos of epic must be understood as structured by a gap between history and its representation. Epic poets, of course, were fully conscious of this gap between history and representation and sought to exploit its creative possibilities as the enabling move for the writing of epic history. In his *Discorsi dell'arte poetica*, for example, Tasso proclaims that the epic poet must use artistic skill in presenting history as "la sembianza della verità" ("the appearance of truth").[50] And Spenser, in his prefatory "Letter to Raleigh" revealing his overall design for *The Faerie Queene*, includes himself in a venerable line of "antique Poets historicall," even as he categorizes his own epic as "historicall fiction." Because epic narrative—as the generic and ontological elusiveness of "historicall fiction"—has no referent in the Real, then history in epic becomes, we could say, an "absent cause" that eludes full representation. The narrative that epic deploys to trace national history is structured on a political unconscious whereby epic "proph-

---

More recently, however, the intellectual historian Dominick LaCapra has "re-problematized" the situating of the text between history and literature by questioning Jameson's account of history as a unified totality and by suggesting the problem of the text as "precisely the sort of thing Jameson would like to resist" (*Rethinking Intellectual History: Texts, Contexts, and Language*) [Ithaca: Cornell University Press, 1983], 240). Thus, LaCapra, acknowledging, though by no means embracing, Derrida's claim that the text inhabits the very margins of Being, has articulated the complexities inherent in the project of inserting texts into history when he argues that "the very opposition between what is inside and what is outside texts is rendered problematic, and nothing is seen as being purely and simply inside or outside texts" (26). The point here is to emphasize the difficulties inherent in any investigation of epic, where history comes to us in its "prior textualization" in the specifically *literary* history of epic. (For a useful overview of the question of whether there even can be such a project as a poststructuralist history in the first place, see Peter De Bolla's essay "Disfiguring History," *Diacritics* 16:4 [1986], 49–58.)

[50]In his *Giudizio sovra la sua Gerusalemme da lui medesimo riformata* (1595), Tasso argues that the *Gerusalemme conquistata*, his carefully considered revision of the *Gerusalemme liberata*, is a superior work because it perfected his narration of historical truth: "se le cose vere fossero da me narrate con modo istorico, non meriterei laude alcuna di poeta; ma avendole io trattate con maniera poetica, e con l'eccesso della verità ricercata la maraviglia, in quelle cose nelle quali ho più conservata l'imagine dell'istoria, e quasi l'aspetto della verità, in quell'istesse ho meritata maggior lode di mirabile artificio poetico (if the true things had been narrated by me in a historical way, I should not merit any praise as a poet; but having treated them in a poetic manner, and having sought the marvelous through the excess of truth, in those things in which I have most completely preserved the image of history and as it were the aspect of truth, I have merited the greatest praise for admirable poetic artistry)" (quoted by Bernard Weinberg, *A History of Literary Criticism in the Italian Renaissance* [Chicago: University of Chicago Press, 1961], 2:1056.)

ecy," and its eschatological vision of providential fulfillment, is vulnerable to exposure as the consequences of an imperialist will-to-power disguised as aesthetic form.[51]

Moreover, as if the problems of the uneasy convergence between epic history and narrative were not complex enough, the hermeneutic problems posed by the possibility of a narrative unconscious for epic become even more mediated when we factor in the emergence of the individual epic subject and its positioning on the brink of receiving an imperial "name," a subjecthood proper to the Symbolic kinship systems of epic. The epic story, in effect, cannot be "told" until the hero has fulfilled himself through prophecy. Thus, the narrative of dynastic epic (and the tacit social exchange between poet and reader) inhabits an obscure threshold between psyche and history because of the unusually intense pressures that the chronicling of dynastic and imperial destinies exerts on the emerging epic subject (beginning with Aeneas's imperially ordained, but psychically disastrous, departure from Dido's Carthage and from his memories of the "old" Troy). As we shall see, one could argue that Renaissance epic history is really the story of how the unconscious *resists* interpellation into the ideology of epic.

Epic narrative, then, is structured at the juncture of a discontinuity inherent in representation itself. In the political unconscious of epic, the "absent cause" is not only history (History as the Real), but also the unconscious of its not-fully-interpellated subjects—both of which elude full representation in the manifest narrative. As a consequence, embedded in epic narrative are unresolved gaps that are the trace-structure not only of a political unconscious, but also of the unconscious of individual epic subjects, which intrudes to mark the limits of imperial ideology. A psychoanalytic focus on the operations of this epic unconscious might perhaps identify these narrative gaps as "psychologemes"—those irreducible points in the narrative

---

[51]Hayden White's concept of "metahistory" contends that history is as much shaped as discovered, with the effect of historical accounts being to assume the structure of plot or necessity. White demonstrates how historical events "are familiarized, not only because the reader now has more *information* about the events, but also because he has been shown how the data conform to an *icon* of a comprehensible finished process, a plot structure with which he is familiar as a part of his cultural endowment" (*Tropics of Discourse: Essays in Cultural Criticism* [Baltimore: Johns Hopkins University Press, 1978], 86). The concept of the *translatio imperii* is just such "an icon of a comprehensible finished process," whereby the historical data conform to the founding of empire because it is assumed by the "poets historicall" of the literary history of epic that historical truth is *intrinsically* epic.

(resistances such as Orlando's loss of his "wits"; Tancredi's pro-
tracted mourning for the uncanny Clorinda; Britomart's *méconnaissance* in Merlin's mirror of epic destiny, and so on), struggles against
an emerging epic consciousness as prophesied by the Symbolic formation of empire. Thus, we could argue that epic is the obscure
threshold where the representation of history through narrative
meets the (mis)representation of the subject to itself.

But even at that, the complications of locating and fully interpreting an epic unconscious do not end there. Surely one of the more
remarkable generic developments in literary history is the emergence of the epic romance—epic's hybrid incorporation of, or mod-
ulation into, the wandering deferrals of romance, specifically in the
form of the old Carolingian chivalric legends and their sagas of the
defense of Christendom against the infidels. The generic incom-
patibility of epic and romance, perhaps most dramatically demonstrated by Ariosto's lengthy *Orlando furioso* (itself a continuation of
Boiardo's sprawling *Orlando innamorato*), was a major preoccupation
of *cinquecento* Italian literary criticism, as has been amply docu-
mented in Bernard Weinberg's two-volume study, *A History of Literary Criticism in the Italian Renaissance*; in the massive critical debate
that ensued, the undisciplined meanderings of romance were felt to
be almost as threatening as the fierce infidels they described. That
critics saw in the *Innamorato* and the *Furioso* a strangeness, or new-
ness, was no doubt owing to their odd intersections of the individual and the sociocultural. And the generic discontinuities between
the disciplined architectonics of epic and the Protean sprawling of
the *romanzo* greatly complicate the task of interpreting the political
unconscious of the hybrid narrative seams of what became known
as epic romance. If we may claim that epic is, in some sense, the
historicization of fiction, then romance, as the fictionalization of history, may be said to have a historicity even more repressed than
epic.

Northrop Frye was perhaps the first great critic to be especially
attuned to the possibility of a romance unconscious. Frye has located in romance an essential "fictiveness" and, indeed, he goes so
far as to argue, "Romance is the structural core of all fiction."[52] In
Frye's conception, there is something that is recognizably human in
romance, something serving as "man's vision of his own life as a

---

[52]Northrop Frye, *The Secular Scripture: A Study of the Structure of Romance* (Cambridge: Harvard University Press, 1976), 15.

quest."[53] A key site of the generic discontinuity between epic and
romance (and a key insight into the nature of an epic unconscious)
may reside in the exact nature of this romance "quest." Again, Frye
makes an intriguing claim when he observes that "the quest-ro-
mance is the search of the libido or desiring self for a fulfillment that
will deliver it from the anxieties of reality."[54]

From Frye, then, we may perhaps advance by only a short step to
argue that romance, in its most fundamental sense, is the locus of
the unconscious, an indeterminate topography of thresholds that
suspends the subject, the questing "libido," on the verge—but only
on the verge—of identity and selfhood.[55] Like the unconscious, romance observes neither logic nor time. One thinks of the *Orlando
furioso*, where, like the structure of dreams, individual narratives terminate abruptly and without resolution, wandering aimlessly and
illogically into other narratives. A character like Logistilla, one of
Ariosto's rare pseudoallegorical embodiments of reason, can rescue
the truant Ruggiero from the temptations of Alcina's isle, but she is
powerless to prevent his relapse into errancy; and she seems to exist

[53]Ibid.

[54]Northrop Frye, *Anatomy of Criticism: Four Essays* (Princeton: Princeton University
Press, 1957), 193. Kevin Brownlee and Marina Scordilis Brownlee observe that romance "has no meaningful existence as a static category. Rather, it is a question of
genre as process" (*Romance: Generic Transformations from Chrétien de Troyes to Cervantes*,
ed. Brownlee and Brownlee [Hanover, N.H.: University Press of New England, 1985],
1). And to be sure, as much as any genre, the Protean shiftings of romance (and its
"anxieties of reality") intimately reflect changes in social codes, mixing as they do the
aristocratic *chansons de geste* with the *chansons d'avventura* of the lower classes. For that
matter, the aristocratic pretensions of the "magical narratives" of romance have been
explicitly described as enacting an allegory of class conflict by Jameson, who, in his
Political Unconscious, modifies Northrop Frye's transhistorical treatment of romance by
gesturing in the direction of a more historicized account of romance. It could be
added that in the specific case of epic romance, the regressive nostalgia of romance
chivalry may be viewed as creating a false consciousness that renders decidedly overdetermined the juncture between epic, as the ideology of a nascent capitalism, and of
romance (stemming from the older *chansons de geste*) as an aristocratic narrative seeking to foreclose on an increasingly socially mobile bourgeoisie.
    David Quint, however, assumes an implicitly anti-Jamesonian stance toward ro-
mance ideology in his essay, "The Boat of Romance and Renaissance Epic" (in *Romance*, ed. Brownlee and Brownlee). While granting that epic romance can reflect "an
ideology of class distinction" (178), Quint argues for epic as the heroic and aristocratic
genre of martial conquest, while romance reflects the commercial trading ventures of
the rising merchant class.

[55]Thomas Greene has written that in romance "one always senses the aimlessness
of the individual" (*The Descent from Heaven: A Study in Epic Continuity* [New Haven:
Yale University Press, 1963], 140). And Nohrnberg has observed of romance that "the
very vagabondage of its avatars implies a kind of release from the traumatic experience of a mass translation of rootedness or domain" (6).

as a reminder that epic can only attempt to serve as the "reason" of romance errancy and illogic. If epic expresses the urge to situate the hero in the cultural order of the Symbolic—if, in effect, epic is the denial of the unconscious—then romance seemingly remains suspended on the threshold of ego formation, at the point of the denial of castration, a denial of the responsibilities, passed on from fathers to sons, of a Virgilian *pietas*. The imperial ambition of epic seeks to trace the origins of national destiny, but the mental landscape of romance concerns itself with the "origin" of the ego in its own *méconnaissance*—which is why romance can never be but the narrative of wandering and "error."

Frye, as we have seen, perceives the questing hero as a "libido," and what his (perhaps not fully conscious) "return" to Freud so aptly identifies here is how epic romance is structured by a libidinal economy that undermines any vision of a unified epic subject.[56] Here we may properly view the libidinal, desiring self of romance as not so much structured on a Lacanian "lack"—so often viewed as the privileged term of structuration in psychoanalytic narration[57]—but rather as positioned on a "Real" divide between the somatic and psychic, where libido emerges as an "energic" or "quantitative" manifestation of desire, lying on the mental (or Imaginary) slope of sexuality.[58] For Freud, there is a moment in the development of the

[56]One of the more noteworthy misunderstandings of the nature of epic subjecthood can be found in Bakhtin's essay "Epic and Novel," where he describes the narrative space of the epic past as closed, absolute, and complete. "There is no place in the epic world," he argues, "for any openendedness, indecision, indeterminacy" (*The Dialogic Imagination*, ed. Michael Holquist, trans. Caryl Emerson and Michael Holquist [Austin: University of Texas Press, 1981], 16). Here, Bakhtin accurately assesses the Symbolic structure of epic. But he virtually denies the possibility of an unconscious for the epic hero when he writes that the "hero is a fully finished and completed being. . . . [H]e is all there, from beginning to end he coincides with himself, he is absolutely equal to himself" (34).

[57]For a study of "the discourse of the other" that constitutes a distinctly Lacanian narratology, see Robert Con Davis's essay "Lacan and Narration," in *Lacan and Narration: The Psychoanalytic Difference in Narrative Theory* (Baltimore: Johns Hopkins University Press, 1983), 848–59. For an account of a "lack" in Renaissance subjectivity within the distinctly non-narrative framework of the sonnet lyric, see Joel Fineman, *Shakespeare's Perjured Eye: The Invention of Poetic Subjectivity in the Sonnets* (Berkeley: University of California Press, 1986). In his introduction, Fineman argues that the sonnet poet, even in the process of articulating a "literary sense of self," nevertheless "experiences himself *as* his difference from himself" (25).

[58]Here more than anywhere we have a vivid illustration of Peter Brooks's assertion, quoted earlier in this chapter, that "the structure of literature *is* in some sense the structure of mind." In opposition to Brooks's argument, however, Jay Clayton, in his essay "Narrative and Theories of Desire" (*Critical Inquiry* 16:1 [1989]), brings up an

subject when the libido cathects its *own* ego—or, in some sense, "loves itself"—more than any external object or person. This is the precise stage of narcissism, where "self-love" is to be properly understood as a libidinal cathexis of the ego onto itself. Oscillating between the erotic and the egoistic, narcissism is the libidinal quest for the ego as its own object of desire; and when object-libido (a cathecting onto objects or persons from the outside) is suppressed in favor of ego-libido, we are at the very threshold of subject formation.[59] In his study "On Narcissism," Freud describes narcissism as an internal process resulting in a kind of "damming up of the libido."[60] Thus the "search of the libido or the desiring self" that Frye describes as inherent in romance is, more accurately, the narcissistic quest of the (ego) libido *for itself* as both the desiring and desired self.

Romance, then, is the narrative of narcissism as the locus of ego formation. But it is crucial to add that the narcissistic libido is not to be taken as a site of unity or of a unified agency, for the ego is

---

important criticism: "What do we do with the assertion that narrative is 'like' the psyche, other than admit that the parallel is intellectually interesting? Brooks is not arguing that one side of the analogy generates the other, that the form of the psyche creates or determines the form of narrative, because he does not want to engage in a genetic mode of psychoanalytic criticism. . . . What is gained by juxtaposing two patterns if neither is conceded to be fundamental and hence explanatory of the other?" (39). In response to Clayton, I would ask a question firmly rooted in the Real: If desire is the "motive force" of narrative, then what is the role of the somatic drives in "driving" the progress of narrative? In this sense, current psychoanalytic criticism has lost a great deal by "repressing" the origins of Freudian psychoanalysis in neuroscience and biology. It is not clear to me what Clayton means by a "genetic mode" of psychoanalytic criticism, but I agree with him that psychoanalytic studies of narrative are in need of a more detailed accounting of how a narrative unconscious links up with the often somatic origins of repression. This somatic emphasis would be one way to break us out of the prison-house of formalism within psychoanalytic criticism. (I attempt just such an investigation of the narrative complicity of "soma" and psyche in my concluding chapter, in the section "The 'Matter' of Life and Death in Epic.")

In this "somatic" context, we might also consider Jean Laplanche's assessment of narcissism as the enigmatic "node" of ego formation itself: "the passage from the ego as biological individual—as it appears precisely at the 'origin' of the 'ego-drives'—to the ego as an agency that can be the object of 'ego-libido' and the way station of that libido in its travels: such is the entire problematic of the *derivation of the psychoanalytic ego*" (*Life and Death in Psychoanalysis*, trans. Jeffrey Mehlman [Baltimore: Johns Hopkins University Press, 1976], 76; italics Laplanche's). The "way station of the libido in its travels" is no less than the narcissism that structures the questing libido of romance.

[59]In a more recent context, Paul Smith argues that "the subject/individual exists in a dialectic relationship with the social but also lives that relationship *alone* as much as interpersonally or as merely a factor within social formations" (*Discerning the Subject*, 6).

[60]*SE* 14:84.

inevitably formed through a process of identification with an other. Nor is this to contradict our earlier assertion that the narcissistic libido chooses only itself as an object. In Freud's conception, narcissism is structured as a dialectical process in which object-choice is modeled on the self—a self that can be constituted as such only through an identification with an "other" model, that is then aggressively incorporated back into the ego-libido. Narcissism is, simply, the dialectical process of loving oneself in the other.[61]

Whether the search is for a grail, a woman, or the identity of an unknown enemy, the "end" of the quest for ego formation by means of successful identification with, or appropriation of, the other is, in the narcissism of romance, endlessly deferred by the recuperation of the lost self (or Freud's *Verliebtheit*) back into the ego-libido—the "damming up of the libido." The dialectics of narcissism can be properly understood as inherently narrative—as inherently *romance*—enacting a kind of minimal, founding unit of narrative in the *fort/da* dialectic of loss and recuperation. Narcissism, then, in effect traces the ego's primal narrative of its own (mis)recognition of itself—which is perhaps why Frye, in the end, perceived romance as "the structural core of all fiction." As we have seen, in the gaps— the psychologemes—that inhabit the seams between epic and romance narrative lies the precarious intersection of the Imaginary and the Symbolic. And this intersection—where *méconnaissance* fails to "recognize" itself in ideological interpellation—may arise from the libidinal impulses of a narcissism that is "damming up" the subject and preventing its dispersal in history.

Translations of Power: Troy and the Narrative of Narcissism

The ego's (mis)recognition of itself, which constitutes the "primal scene" of narcissism, means that the appropriation of romance by epic can only be highly discontinuous and arbitrary. It is important to emphasize here that such a discontinuous appropriation can only result in a lack not simply in the individual psyche of the epic sub-

---

[61]Viewed in this context, we can perhaps now understand the full significance of Patricia Parker's description of the structure of romance as dialectical—a narrative of dilation and deviation that both posits and defers from its own end (*Inescapable Romance: Studies in the Poetics of a Mode* [Princeton: Princeton University Press, 1978], 3– 15). I would argue further that if the narrative of romance is "inescapable," it is because it is structured by the dialectic of narcissism itself.

ject, but, more significantly, within the epic narrative itself. In order for epic to tell its story—to fulfill its own prophecy as the ultimate destiny of that "translation" of power known as the *translatio imperii*—it must, in some sense, seek to repress the narcissistic impulses of romance. But such a description is not merely to posit some sort of one-on-one "confrontation" between epic and romance. Nor is it a simple matter of arguing that the *iter durum* of epic *causes* neurosis. The challenge posed by any interpretation of dynastic epic is to find more subtle ways of nuancing its complex intersections of psyche and history.

For such an endeavor, we might think of Freud's concept of the mechanics of condensation, an act of displacement in which a manifest element is seen as determined by a latent meaning. When we speak of epic romance as the intersection of two genres, we may more properly speak of an epic "condensation" of romance—the final consequence being not an "imperialist" appropriation of romance by epic, but rather a generic edge by means of which the aftereffects of a romance unconscious leave their repressed, but nonetheless observable, traces within the narrative of epic history. To return to the terms used earlier in my critique of Greenblatt, it is no mere bourgeois act of belatedness, then, to refer to the subject within epic history as "neurotic." The epic subject is "neurotic" because the libidinal impulses of romance have been left *unrepresented* within the manifest narrative of epic ideology—hence the lack that constitutes (retroactively) a narrative unconscious within epic history. What the ineffable edge between epic and romance demonstrates is that there will always be something in the unconscious that eludes full appropriation within and representation by the ideology of epic. In the hybrid genre of epic romance, we might properly view the "psychic structure" of epic prophecy, its ideological striving as the new *imperium sine fine*, as constituting itself out of the stratified layers of the more archaic and nostalgic (and narcissistic) elements of romance—layers that remain unrepresented in the prophetic superstructure of epic.[62]

---

[62]My metaphor of repressed layers has been influenced by Jean-Joseph Goux, who argues that, in an almost anthropological sense, the psychic structure of the individual subject is constituted not just by discrete events in the individual's psychohistory, but also, more phylogenetically, by the stratified layers or historically progressive stages of modes of production and exchange. In Goux's conception of the interrelationship between (un)consciousness and modes of production, when we speak of a lack in the psychic structure, it is not just the Lacanian *manque-à-être* that has so often been the target of the critique of ideology as too limited to the mechanics of merely

Thus, the story of the *translatio imperii* that is told by dynastic epic, even as it seeks to disperse its (romance) subject within the ideology of empire, also demarcates the space of a narrative unconscious within epic such that, as illustrated in the story of Martin Guerre, there can be *no* effective difference between the "ideological" subject (of epic) and the "neurotic" subject (of romance). It is not simply a case of the neuroses—the narcissistic impulses of romance—being dispersed and displaced within epic ideology; rather it is a case of these same neuroses themselves *displacing* ideology, leaving their residue of repressed traces in the generic seams and discontinuities inherent in epic romance. Neurosis, in short, becomes the deformation of epic ideology.

My book argues for dynastic epic as one of the more intriguing narrative sites of the complex intersection of psyche and history. I show how the narrative of imperial ideology becomes increasingly "neurotic" such that by the time we reach Spenser's *Faerie Queene*, the story of the *translatio imperii* has become the overdetermined site of narrative repressions too deep to be sufficiently "contained" within epic ideology. More specifically, I argue throughout my book that what makes the intersection of psyche and history in epic so overdetermined—what renders neurosis as the deformation of epic ideology—is the doomed city of Troy as the impossible "ego ideal" of epic history.

Larger than the fate of any individual participant or nation in epic history is the fate of Troy and its relationship to the narcissism of epic romance. My book addresses a central question: How does narcissism, as a structuring principle both for the psyche and for the narrative of romance, relate to Troy as the lost "origin" of the *translatio imperii*? As was discussed earlier in this chapter, the *translatio imperii*, as a "theory" of empire and its "translations" of power, purports to be the final resting place of Aeneas's fragmented Trojan remnant. But, in the end, the *translatio imperii* is structured on a paradox that exposes the desire of empire as inevitably narcissistic.

On an individual level, as we have seen, narcissism is the path to

---

individual desire, but a real, unrepresented absence of earlier forms of social consciousness: "The unconscious is built upon the traces of historically *outdated* symbolizations, in that the current mode of production and the current forms of consciousness that correspond to it and to which the subject must accede effectively supplant, and thus *repress*, these traces" (*Symbolic Economies: After Marx and Freud*, trans. Jennifer Curtiss Gage [Ithaca: Cornell University Press, 1990], 75). Where these phylogenetic forms of social consciousness are absented *to* is the unconscious. The subject is neurotic because something in the dominant socioeconomic mode is not being represented—hence the lack that "structures" an unconscious within history.

the other (as the ego ideal) that can reflect the ego as its own object of interest. But narcissism is also the precise point where epic history is overdetermined by the unconscious. The dialectical, narcissistic search for the other always results in the subject's exile from itself; at this point the narcissism of empire itself begins to exert its influence. For Virgil's Aeneas, haunted by the lost Troy as his "other," the exile from Troy becomes the origin of the narcissistic self in epic history. But Aeneas's personal history of his own exile from Troy also becomes the larger narcissistic origin of the *translatio imperii* itself. Tracing the westward movement of the signifying chain of empire, but, as we shall see, seeking always to recuperate Troy as its origin, the displacement of energy that constitutes the *translatio imperii* is the narcissism of empire—a displacement that represses and flees from the destruction of Troy, even as it nostalgically yearns to recuperate the tragic *Troiana fortuna* into a narcissistic re-vision of imperial "wholeness."[63]

Each individual epic that constitutes the signifying chain of the *translatio imperii* seeks to interpellate and disperse the subjects of its narrative within its particular configurations of imperial power. But if we consider the broader scope of epic throughout literary history, the exercise of imperial power known as the *translatio imperii* must be "translated" to another epic narrative (and another, and another)—and for this translation of power to occur, it must negotiate the ghost of Troy as the origin of its own narrative. These translations of power end up operating largely on the level of the unconscious, then, because ever since the trauma of Aeneas's confrontation with Dido's vivid murals of its destruction, Troy has been left unrepresented within the narrative of epic. Even as the literary history of epic translates its story of imperial power to another *imperium sine fine*, it is powerless to "end" its own strange transferences onto Troy as its narcissistic ego ideal. The "founding" premise of dynastic epic is the founding of a new city that can surpass the smoldering

[63]In his essay "Hippolytus among the Exiles: The Romance of Early Humanism" (in *Exile and Change in Renaissance Literature* [New Haven: Yale University Press, 1984]), A. Bartlett Giamatti writes: "The Renaissance, for all its assertive, expansive, cultural imperialism—its revival of the past, its new texts, institutions and perceptions—would never completely shake the sense that what it made was removed, not quite worthy of the original; if not second-rate, at least secondhand, just as beneath the oft-repeated boast of each people that their land had been colonized by a hero from Troy—Italy by Lusus, Britain by Brutus—there would be the constant awareness that Europe was founded by the losers, that the European people were colonists who, for all their glory, were exiled from the homeland, that in the Westering of culture, much had been gained but something had also been lost" (14).

ruins of Troy. But, as we shall see, Troy uncannily survives in the interstices of epic romance, such that the doomed city becomes transformed into the lack, the absent center, that constitutes (retroactively) a narrative unconscious within epic history.

It is in this sense, then, that Troy can be viewed as the subversive other of epic history. If Lacan is right in arguing that there can be no other of the other, then it is inherently impossible for the *translatio imperii* to fashion an *imperium sine fine* that can eliminate Troy as the Other of epic history. Like Jean de Coras's vain attempts in the court at Artigat to "arrest" the signifiers of Arnaud's imposture of Martin's subjecthood, the translations of power that make up the literary history of epic have no final authority over Troy as the "insistence" of the signifier that remains unrepresented in the prophetic superstructure of epic. As the narrative unconscious of the *translatio imperii*, the city of Troy guarantees that the intersection between psyche and epic history will remain persistently overdetermined by the unpredictable irruptions of the unconscious that deform epic ideology. The translations of power that constitute the literary history of epic are powerless to erase the aftereffects of an "untranslatable" *Troiana fortuna* in epic history. In a Lacanian scheme (as we saw in the discussion of Martin Guerre), the subject "disappears" in favor of the operations by which the signifier represents the subject for another signifier. Thus, we may argue that throughout the literary history of epic, the historical importance of any individual translation of imperial power disappears in favor of Troy, which signifies the narcissistic desire of epic for its own fictive (non)representations in successor epics.

The *translatio imperii* is inherently "neurotic," then, because its translations of power are dependent on an unrepresented Troy that persists in leaving its repressed traces in epic history. Even as the genre of romance eludes full appropriation within and representation by epic ideology, so also does Troy lurk not fully represented within epic narrative, refracted somewhere between the conflicting desires of romance and epic. But, even more specifically, the desire of the *translatio imperii*, more than simply "neurotic," is inherently narcissistic.[64] If narcissism is structured on a dialectical process in

---

[64]Norman O. Brown has written that Freud's "doctrine of the universal neurosis of mankind . . . compels us to entertain the hypothesis that the pattern of history exhibits a dialectic not hitherto recognized by historians, the dialectic of neurosis" (*Life against Death: The Psychoanalytical Meaning of History* [Middletown, Conn.: Wesleyan

which the self can be constituted as such only through an identification with an other that is then aggressively incorporated back into
the ego-libido, then the *translatio imperii* as a theory of empire can
only be narcissistic—attenuating its proleptic translations of power
by relying unwittingly on a repressed Troy to realize its "prophetic
moment." Troy, as the paradigmatic (but always retroactive) repression of the *translatio imperii*, is simply too overdetermined to be contained within the ideology of epic.

Throughout the literary history of epic, the point of intersection
between psyche and history is, simply, Troy as the repressed origin
of narrative. Viewed as a unified document within literary history,
the epics of Ariosto, Tasso, and Spenser, in "neurotic" competition
with the *Aeneid* as their precursor epic (itself in competition with
Homer's *Iliad*), constitute the "anxiety of influence" that is the *translatio imperii*, the will of empire both to allude to and occlude the
unrecuperable Troy. In my analysis of these epics, I have chosen to
focus on what I judge to be key moments within the literary history
of the *translatio imperii*—moments that serve as crucial intersections
between epic history and the individual subject's *méconnaissance* of
its place in that history. In particular, I have isolated for careful interpretation those key psychoanalytic moments—those "obscure
thresholds"—where the narrative of epic undoes its own storytelling
through its ambivalent relationship with Troy.[65] The *translatio imperii*,
even as it effects a sublation of the isolating narcissism of its own
epic participants, becomes implicated in its own narcissistic desire.
In the final analysis, the motivating force of epic, the recurring
transference that seeks a recuperation of Troy, becomes the very
narcissistic move that disables its own imperial operations.

I began this introductory chapter with a critique of new historicism and its foreclosure on the role of the unconscious within history. The interpretive (and still largely unspecified) methods of the
new historicism disable any understanding of the extent to which

---

University Press, 1959], 12). And if, as Laplanche argues, narcissism constitutes "the
entire problematic of the *derivation of the psychoanalytic ego*," then narcissism must be
reckoned with as residing at the heart of any mediation between psyche and history.

[65]The term "obscure thresholds" recurs throughout my book as a conscious echo of
Virgil's description of Aeneas's wife, Creusa, as she disappears within the *obscura
limina* of a burning Troy: "Principio muros obscuraque limina portae . . ." (*Aeneid*
II.752). The liminal concept of "obscure thresholds," then, is not only a direct echo of
the destruction of Troy, but is also an allusion to the failure of epic to move beyond
Troy—a failure that becomes the obscure threshold of *méconnaissance* that structures
epic history.

imperial ideology is as much a function of psychic experience as it is of history. In particular, new-historicist articulations of power cannot answer to the "power" of Troy and the extent to which epic history becomes as much a psychic allegory of its own intersubjective exchange with Troy as it does the exercise of imperial authority. New historicism can tell us very little about the extent to which the sociocultural and ideological field that dictates the story of epic becomes precisely the psychic field of Troy as the other for epic history. Even as the new historicism (rightly) guides us in the historicizing of our own critical procedures, so also is it just as valuable to perform a psychoanalyzing of the operations of epic history.

As a psychoanalyzing of epic history, my book can be viewed, in its broadest scope, as a renewal of the overarching project of certain members of the Frankfurt School and their commitment to historicizing Freud by a nuancing of the enigmatic links among neurosis, culture, and history. Herbert Marcuse's *Eros and Civilization*, for example, argues that what he calls "surplus repression" may always be inherent in culture and ideology. Perhaps a psychoanalytic study of epic is a way of reviving or casting in a new light some of Freud's own ambitious impulses to use psychoanalysis as a comprehensive critique of culture, developed in such monumental cultural documents as *Totem and Taboo*, *Civilization and Its Discontents*, and *Moses and Monotheism*. Certainly a psychoanalytic study of epic should vindicate one of Freud's more speculative arguments in *Civilization and Its Discontents* that culture is fundamentally built on repression. Such a study can reveal the not fully harmonious or satisfactory ways in which individual neuroses (and narcissism, in particular) are subsumed within larger historical processes.

A Disturbance of Memory
in Carthage

Rome Neuroses

In *Civilization and Its Discontents*, Freud explores the possibility of a pathology of cultural communities. If the development (or decline) of civilizations is analogous to the psychic history of the individual, then, Freud argues, "may we not be justified in reaching the diagnosis that, under the influence of cultural urges, some civilizations . . . have become 'neurotic'?"[1] Freud's diagnosis of civilizations as "neurotic" is not as tendentious as it may seem. In his specific conception of neurosis, symptoms arise as a result of psychic conflicts whose origins lie in the subject's childhood history. Thus neurosis may be viewed temporally as the site of an uneasy compromise between past history and the present. For Freud, the pathological case of Rome, of *Roma aeterna*, is just such a troubled site of compromise between past and present—the urban locus of neurosis itself. As he argues at the outset of *Civilization and Its Discontents*, may we not be justified in saying that Rome's ghostly ruins—those astounding strata where one could imagine "the palaces of the Caesars and the Septizonium of Septimius Severus would still be rising to their old height on the Palatine"[2]—afford the paradigmatic backdrop for the individual to perceive his own neuroses?

It was in the necromantic topography of a Rome in ruins that Ren-

[1] *SE* 21:144.
[2] Ibid., 70.

aissance humanism discovered its cultural past—and the psycho-analytic (or "neurotic") resonance of such an encounter must not go unexplored, for this collective discovery had its profound effect on the individual.[3] In 1553, Joachim Du Bellay, to focus on one such individual, was almost morbidly drawn to the antique fragments of a Rome that was no more. The result was his *Les antiquitez de Rome*, a poem, argues Thomas Greene, "not so much about the Roman ruins as about an individual responding to ruins."[4] What Greene suggests here is that such a meditative lament, in the form of a response to decline and decay, could occur only in a kind of (pre)Cartesian moment in which the subject realizes (belatedly) that he *exists* insofar as he is estranged from his past. *Cogito ergo eram.* Thus Du Bellay's poetic fetishizing of the fragmented and anachronistic cityscape of Roman ruins constitutes the quintessentially "neurotic" moment of compromise between the remembrance and forgetting of one's past history; and in Du Bellay's response to the ruins we can plot the coordinates of the psychic distance that in some sense demarcates the threshold of subjectivity itself. Du Bellay's experiencing of the strange transferences that can occur between Rome and its beholders demonstrates that the "selfhood" of Renaissance humanism is created (retroactively) by a self-conscious awareness of the unbridgeable distance between past and present. Or, more specifically, we can argue for an explicit link between Rome and subjectivity at the point at which Rome reveals the ghostly traces of its antiquity as an archaeology of *différance*—as a vestigial city that, like neurotic subjectivity, is never quite identical to itself. When Du Bellay writes that "Rome seule pouvoit à Rome ressembler (Rome alone can Rome resemble)" (*Antiquitez*, 6), he as much as asserts that Rome is both

---

[3]Renaissance humanism has traditionally been viewed as a kind of quest for identity; and the Renaissance, of course, becomes a particularly compelling site for a reinvestigation of psychoanalysis and the discourse of the subject because (admittedly at the risk of some oversimplification) it was Descartes who first made the "subject" his subject—the enclosed *cogito* whose own doubt inaugurates the individual as, in the words of Kerrigan and Braden, "the summation of consciousness" (*The Idea of the Renaissance*, 137). Perhaps it is in the era just prior to Descartes, then, that the nascent subject is most intriguing, from a psychohistorical perspective. If we juxtapose the performative clarity of the Cartesian injunction *cogito ergo sum* with Lacan's axiom of the (de)formation of the split subject ("I think of what I am wherever I do not think I am thinking" ["The Agency of the Letter in the Unconscious," *Écrits*, 164–65]), we can see the limitations of Cartesianism as, in the conception of Kerrigan and Braden, "the epoch's yearning for a positive version of the Narcissus myth" (147).

[4]For a detailed study of Du Bellay's years in Rome, see Greene's chapter "Du Bellay and the Disinterment of Rome," in *The Light in Troy: Imitation and Discovery in Renaissance Poetry* (New Haven: Yale University Press, 1982), 220–41.

the apotheosis of civic glory and the neurotic compromise of a forgotten history.[5]

Not coincidentally, it was Rome's necromantic topography that, in *Civilization and Its Discontents*, also offered Freud a useful mirror for the self—specifically, an analogy for his earlier "topographical" model of repression as buried in a "psychoarchaeology" of the conscious, the preconscious, and the unconscious. Du Bellay's hyper-awareness of the archaeological strata of Roman antiquity *as* antiquity—and his subsequent awareness of himself as a *self* alienated from his past—was reenacted by Freud, the theorist of the ego, for whom Rome was less a city than a "psychical entity," whose forgotten memory-traces uncannily mirror the self to its-self.[6] When Freud wrote of repression that "the raw material of memory-traces out of which it was forged remains unknown to us in its original form," he could easily have been thinking of Rome, a city that embodies both cultural continuity and the repressed memory-traces of ruin.[7] But Freud's own engagements with Rome, as much personal as theoretical, belie the simple ease of his analogy between psychoanalysis and archaeology. If civilizations, in Freud's conception, have become "neurotic," it may be because of a complex interplay between key cities of cultural history and the neurotic subject's narcissistic need to behold these cities as part of its process of self-discovery. If, as Norman O. Brown has argued, "the theory of neurosis must embrace a theory of history; and conversely a theory of history must embrace a theory of neurosis,"[8] then Rome may be seen as just such a site of the interplay between neurosis and history. As we shall see, Freud's "Rome neuroses" will eventually clear the path for an understanding of the ruins of Rome as a crucial site of mediation between psyche and history.

Long before the writing of his *Discontents*, Rome was a major preoccupation for Freud—not just as a psychic metaphor, but as a real historical city, a rich matrix of paganism, Catholicism, and imperialism. Freud sensed that surely Rome was the city where, no matter

---

[5]For an account of Rome as "belated," as "already a nostalgic and edited memory when it first appears" (53), see Marjorie Garber's chapter "A Rome of One's Own," in *Shakespeare's Ghost Writers: Literature as Uncanny Causality* (New York: Methuen, 1987), 52–73.

[6]*SE* 21:70.

[7]"Screen Memories," *SE* 3:322.

[8]*Life against Death*, 8.

how culturally exiled, one could discover his past.[9] He spent much of 1898, the year in which he was to become so frustrated in his efforts to complete *The Interpretation of Dreams*, almost obsessively studying the topography of Rome (as well as, perhaps, the glimpses it afforded into human neuroses). "I am not sufficiently collected, to be sure, to do anything in addition, other than possibly studying the topography of Rome," writes Freud to Fliess, "the yearning for which becomes ever more tormenting" (October, 1898).[10] Not surprisingly then, Rome became the subject of a number of his more vivid and memorable dreams, as if in anticipation of his future claim that the ghostly topography of Rome mimes the return of the repressed. In his first Rome dream, for example, an unknown figure leads Freud to the top of a hill, from which he views the awesome prospect of the city, "half-shrouded in mist," from a distance.[11] But surely what is most remarkable about this period in his career is that Freud, unlike that other exilic observer of Rome, Du Bellay, cultivated his fascination for Rome *only* at a distance. Between 1895 and 1898, he traveled to Italy no fewer than five times without ever reaching Rome, the "promised land,"[12] almost as if he were determined to preserve the metaphorical status of the city as an uncon-

[9]Worth noting at this point are the parallels between Freud's and E. R. Curtius's obsessions with Rome as the city of personal and professional discovery. In a lengthy passage from his Appendix to his *Essays on European Literature* (trans. Michael Kowal [Princeton: Princeton University Press, 1973]) in which he talks personally about his odyssey as a scholar, Curtius writes: "With this latter work [*The Civilization of France*, 1930] I felt that I had concluded my studies of modern France:—for inner reasons. A compelling psychological necessity drove me to seek a change in my field of research. I felt the need to return to older periods—metaphorically speaking I would say today, to more archaic strata of consciousness: in the first instance, the Romance Middle Ages. Beyond that I was seeking, without being precisely aware of it, the road to Rome. Ever since my first visit the city had become for me, not only on all its historical levels but rather in its spiritual essence, in other words in a sense that transcended history, the holy city; yet withal one not chosen but discovered, an ancestral homeland and a goal of pilgrimage. Every fresh sojourn in Rome strengthened this relation to my life. I knew myself bound to the *Roma aeterna*. In the course of years and decades I realized that this bond contained a secret with many layers of symbolic meaning. As my work moved away from France, a lock sprang open. The way was clear for the experience of Rome to flow into my research" (498). Curtius's emphasis on Rome as "a compelling psychological necessity," on his need for "more archaic strata of consciousness," and on the notion of being "bound" to Rome's "many layers of symbolic meaning," uncannily echoes Freud's metaphors of Rome as a kind of cultural unconsciousness in *Civilization and Its Discontents*. (I am grateful to Artemis Leontis for calling this passage in Curtius to my attention.)
[10]*The Complete Letters of Sigmund Freud to Wilhelm Fliess, 1887–1904*, trans. and ed. Jeffrey Moussaieff Masson (Cambridge: Harvard University Press, 1985), 332.
[11]*SE* 4:194.
[12]Ibid.

scious "psychical entity." During this period (when, not coincidentally, he also yearned for a professorship), Freud never beheld this
most "neurotic" city of history, but only dreamed of it, literally and
figuratively, from afar. "My longing for Rome," he admits to Fliess,
"is, by the way, deeply neurotic" (December, 1897).[13]

What neurosis was Freud working through in choosing never to
see Rome, this paradoxical city of ambition and decay, but only to
envision it as a "longing in my dreams"?[14] Freud confesses that he
had once turned back when he was only fifty miles from Rome, with
the later realization that "I had actually been following in Hannibal's
footsteps. Like him, I had been fated not to see Rome."[15] Taking a
cue from Freud's allusion to the Carthaginian general Hannibal, one
of his boyhood heroes, we can with little difficulty begin to see that
Freud's "quest" to view Rome, thwarted by enigmatic circumstances
over a period of years, begins to trace the narrative of an epic
quest—specifically of the *Aeneid*, where the long-deferred mission is
Aeneas's departure from Carthage to found Rome as the new *imperium sine fine*. Freud, of course, knew the *Aeneid* intimately, and the
parallels in the search for Rome did not escape him. Like Freud,
Aeneas never sees the city that Romulus will eventually found but
glimpses it only in a "dream," in the vision of future Augustan glory
granted him by Anchises in Book VI, just prior to the hero's leaving
Hades through the Ivory Gate of *falsa insomnia* (false dreams).

Indeed, we could argue that *The Interpretation of Dreams* becomes,
in effect, Freud's *Aeneid* because of its recurrent focus on "the matter
of Rome."[16] Like Virgil, Freud seems preoccupied with Rome as a
city of destiny, but his own self-fulfilling, counter-Virgilian prophecy is that, like Hannibal before him, he is "fated not to see Rome."
Carl Schorske has shown that Freud's use of Rome in this perhaps
greatest of his theoretical works was profoundly linked not only to
his ambivalences toward the ghosts of imperialism and political ambition, but also, much more personally, to his father, whose death in

[13]Masson, *The Complete Letters*, 285.
[14]*SE* 4:193.
[15]Ibid., 196. Peter Rudnytsky writes, "The most remarkable consequence of Freud's
youthful identification with Hannibal is that it largely explains his later inhibitions
about entering Rome" (*Freud and Oedipus* [New York: Columbia University Press,
1987], 40).
[16]For a valuable discussion of some of the parallels between *The Interpretation of
Dreams* and the *Aeneid*, see David Damrosch, "The Politics of Ethics: Freud and
Rome," in *Pragmatism's Freud: The Moral Disposition of Psychoanalysis*, ed. Joseph H.
Smith and William Kerrigan (Baltimore: Johns Hopkins University Press, 1986), 120–
21.

1896 was a crushing blow.[17] In the second edition of *The Interpretation of Dreams* (1908), Freud confesses: "For this book has a further subjective significance for me personally—a significance which I only grasped after I had completed it. It was, I found, a portion of my own self-analysis, my reaction to my father's death—that is to say, to the most important event, the most poignant loss, of a man's life."[18] We are now provided with a key insight into the connection between Freud's unsuccessful attempts to travel to Rome (his dreaming of Rome only from afar) and his subsequent difficulties in completing *The Interpretation of Dreams*—which he did not yet realize was, in effect, "a portion of my own self-analysis." Not just the historical site of imperial ambition, Rome also became, in Freud's dreams, the city where he was destined to confront the burdens of being a son.[19]

For both Virgil and Freud, then, Rome becomes the "neurotic" site of a complex, and indeed overdetermined, interplay of filial piety, Oedipal anxieties, and imperial (or professional) ambition. We can conclude here that it is, after all, this same overdetermined interplay that constitutes the deep structure of epic narrative itself. Epic is the most ambitious (perhaps the most pathological) of literary genres, not only because of its vast temporal scope, but also because of the epic poet's characteristic affliction with the "anxiety of influence," particularly evidenced in dynastic epic, his "neurotic" need to compete with and surpass his predecessors in an authoritative effort to legitimate his poetic celebration of the new *imperium sine fine*. In the *Aeneid*, then, Rome becomes the focus not only of the future imperial ambitions of Augustus, but also of Virgil's ambitions to surpass Homeric epic. And squarely in the midst of these imperial and literary ambitions is Aeneas's old father Anchises, who must be expunged from the narrative for both of these ambitions to be fulfilled. Old, weak, and obsolete, Anchises, and his link with past defeat, must make way for the ambitions of the newer, stronger Rome (as well as for the stronger son).

Thus it is in the Oedipal figure of the father that psychoanalysis

---

[17]Carl E. Schorske, "Politics and Patricide in Freud's *Interpretation of Dreams*," in *Fin-de-Siècle Vienna: Politics and Culture* (New York: Vintage Books, 1981).

[18]*SE* 4:26.

[19]For a discussion of the father as a central figure in epic, "whether he is called Jove or Priam or Anchises or Charlemagne or God" (2), see A. Bartlett Giamatti, "The Forms of Epic," in *Play of Double Senses: Spenser's "Faerie Queene"* (Englewood Cliffs, N.J.: Prentice-Hall, 1975), 17.

enters the literary history of epic.[20] The Oedipal narrative (like epic) traces the inevitability with which filial piety, the reluctance of the son to surpass the father, must give way to filial ambition. The fulfillment of imperial future awaits the totem-and-taboo narrative of the usurping of paternal authority. Thus the "neurotic" city of Rome, the city of patricidal impulses, is also the privileged locus of the juncture between psychoanalysis and epic. Like Aeneas, who delays his entry into Latium by accepting Anchises' misreading of the Delphian oracle that sidetracks the Trojans to Crete, Freud dreams of "this promised land from afar" but hesitates to enter it, because the city of imperial ambition embodies the paternal authority he is not ready to defy.

In his late autobiographical essay "A Disturbance of Memory on the Acropolis" (1936), Freud confesses that his longing to travel was no doubt related to his need to surpass the poverty and provinciality of his childhood. In an expression of what David Damrosch has called "the erotics of touristic conquest,"[21] Freud writes, "When first one catches sight of the sea, crosses the ocean and experiences as realities cities and lands which for so long had been distant, unattainable things of desire—one feels oneself like a hero who has performed deeds of improbable greatness."[22] But Freud's discovery of the "erotics of conquest" occurs, ironically, not in the context of his arrival in Rome but in Athens, a city whose repressed meaning for Freud is as a symptom of his uncanny near misses with the "neurotic" city of Rome over a three-year period. Freud evaluates the uneasy sense of guilt that overcame him after he had seen Athens for the first time: "There was something about it [the "erotic" satisfaction of seeing Athens] that was wrong, that from earliest times had been forbidden. . . . It seems as though the essence of success was to have got further than one's father, and as though to excel one's father was still something forbidden."[23] This confession, of course, presents an allegory of the Oedipal dangers of patricide. But for Freud the real Oedipal journey of the surpassing of the father is not from Vienna to Athens, but from Athens to Rome. In Athens, Freud can only be displaced. For it is only in Rome that Freud can

---

[20]For a discussion of the link between Rome and Freud's Oedipal struggle with his father, see Alexander Grinstein, *Sigmund Freud's Dreams* (New York: International Universities Press, 1980), 90–91.

[21]Damrosch, "The Politics of Ethics," 116.

[22]*SE* 22:246–47.

[23]*SE* 23:247–48.

transform the "erotics of conquest" experienced in Athens to a conquest of the father. The taboo surpassing of the father must reach its crisis point not in (Homeric) Greece but in (Virgilian) Italy, in a "neurotic" Rome where one's past history of filial piety is not readily reconciled with present (cultural, imperial, poetic, and professional) ambition.

In *The Interpretation of Dreams*, Freud describes his dream, occurring in 1898, of an event that takes place not in Rome but in his native Vienna. Finding himself standing on the platform of the train station next to an old blind man, Freud holds a urinal for this weak, debilitated figure, who, upon awakening, he realizes is his father.[24] The simple poignancy of this episode, in which the strong son gives aid to the weak father—and, in so doing, works through to a cathartic "beyond" that can transcend the anxieties of the Oedipal narrative—reenacts the drama of Aeneas's carrying of his old father out of the burning ruins of Troy. And both episodes experience, not coincidentally, the convergence of the child, the father, and the old man—the three actants in the Sphinx's riddle that Oedipus must solve. Helping the old father urinate in privacy in a busy public place, helping the old father "walk" through a charred and hostile terrain—these are the acts not of a vengeful counter-castration of the father, but of a kind of mourning of the father's loss just prior to the son's realization that he will surpass the father. Aeneas eventually sees Rome (if only in a dream), and, for that matter, himself attains the status of *pater*,[25] and Freud's dreams of Rome finally become a reality. In 1901, five years after his father's death, Freud enters Rome, and the city's Oedipal spell is broken.[26] Within this context of fathers and sons, it is worth mentioning at this point that in "Two Principles of Mental Functioning," Freud discusses a dream by a man who had nursed his father through a long and fatal illness: "in

---

[24]*SE* 5:431–35.

[25]David Quint notes that "Book 3 closes with the loss of the father—and his replacement by Aeneas who is called by the title of 'pater' as he ends his narration [to Dido]" ("Painful Memories: *Aeneid* 3 and the Problem of the Past," *Classical Journal* 78 [1982], 34).

[26]In his essay "The Metaphor of the Journey in *The Interpretation of Dreams*," in *Freud and His Self-Analysis, Downstate Psychoanalytic Institute Series*, I, ed. Mark Kanzer and Jules Glenn (New York: Jason Aronson, Inc., 1979), Leonard Shengold mentions a brief communication that Freud sent to Fliess. "It was a picture postcard from the temple of Neptune in Paestum, south of Rome. He had gone further south than Hannibal, was at the site of an archaeological treasure, was with the god of waters who could extinguish fire, and he separated himself from the father-figure with the one line message: 'cordial greetings from the culminating point of the journey'" (63).

the months following his father's death he had repeatedly dreamt that *his father was alive once more and that he was talking to him in his usual way. But he felt it exceedingly painful that his father had really died, only without knowing it.*"[27] Rome may be the one city in cultural history where fathers *do* come to know they are "dead."

Athens/Rome/Troy: The City Not Seen

Thus both Freudian psychoanalysis and Virgilian epic trace the Oedipal structure of the Symbolic itself, where subjecthood is in some sense constituted out of the son's (and the father's) realization that the father as phallic signifier is "dead." Given Freud's self-conscious awareness of the analogies between him and Aeneas, he might perhaps have chosen to declare that psychoanalysis enters epic at the point of realization that Rome is the city of sons. For that matter, Lacan also enacted the choice of Rome as a site of Oedipal anxiety (as a consequence of "patricide" and "neurosis"). In 1953, after his controversial, Oedipal break with the Société Psychanalytique de Paris, an attempt was made to bar Lacan from reading his soon-to-be-famous paper that became known as the "Discours de Rome" (or later, in English, as "The Function and Field of Speech and Language in Psychoanalysis"). In this essay, Lacan outlines the temporal illogic that haunts the formation of the split subject: "What is realized in my history is not the past definite of what was, since it is no more, or even the present perfect of what has been in what I am, but the future anterior of what I shall have been for what I am in the process of becoming."[28] It is significant that the "neurotic" city of Rome should serve as the backdrop for a theory of the *méconnaissance* that inevitably haunts one's personal history.

For Virgil and for Freud (and perhaps for Lacan, as well), the Oedipal narrative resolves itself in a city finally glimpsed only after a long deferral. But we must now consider the following question: What is the significance, for epic and for psychoanalysis, of cities of desire that remain unseen? Let us return momentarily to Freud's "A

[27]*SE* 12:225; italics Freud's. Lacan writes that "the symbolic Father is, in so far as he signifies [the] Law, the dead Father" ("On a Question Preliminary to Any Possible Treatment of Psychosis," *écrits*, 199). For an interesting interpretation of Freud's account of the dream of the dead father, see Jane Gallop's chapter "The Dream of the Dead Author," in her *Reading Lacan* (Ithaca: Cornell University Press, 1985).

[28]*Écrits*, 86.

Disturbance of Memory on the Acropolis," an essay of which Kerrigan has claimed, "No other paper gives itself so fully and beautifully . . . to the historical rhythms of Western culture."[29] In this short piece, Freud meditates on a trip he took to Athens in 1904 with his younger brother and, specifically, the feeling of surprise that overtook him when he actually gazed on the Acropolis for the first time: "'So all this really *does* exist, just as we learnt at school.'"[30] So amazed is he that the Acropolis is actually *there* before him that he confesses, "at the time I had (or might have had) a momentary feeling: '*What I see here is not real*': Such a feeling is known as a 'feeling of derealization.'"[31] Freud would seem to be admitting here that, through a process of "derealization," the historical reality of the city of Athens is somehow less "real" than its illusory, mimetic representation in his childhood imagination. In this counterpart to the phenomenon of *déjà vu*, the concept of "derealization" (or *Entfremdungsgefühl*) deconstructs Athens to the point that the city is most cherished only in its imaginative incarnation.

One implication of Freud's "disturbance of memory" is that the city *not* seen occupies an important place in cultural history. Consider, for example, the curious case of Johann Winckelmann and the city he never saw. Freud undoubtedly owed much of his interest in archaeology and antiquity to Winckelmann's renowned studies of classical archaeology and Greek art history (1755–64); and, in fact, the second edition of Carl Justi's biography of Winckelmann, *Winckelmann und seine Zeitgenossen*, was published in 1898, at the height of Freud's interest in archaeology. For much of his career, Winckelmann, like Freud a native of Vienna, resided in Rome; Schorske has written that it was essentially Winckelmann's Rome that Freud became so fascinated with.[32] In *The Interpretation of Dreams*, Freud writes: "I was in the act of making a plan to by-pass Rome next year and travel to Naples, when a sentence occurred to me which I must have read in one of our classical authors: 'Which of the two, it may be debated, walked up and down his study with the greater impatience after he had formed his plan of going to Rome—Winckelmann, the Vice-Principal, or Hannibal, the Commander-in-

[29]"What Freud Forgot: A Parable for Intellectuals," in *Pragmatism's Freud,*" 159.
[30]*SE* 22:241.
[31]Ibid., 244.
[32]Schorske, "Politics and Patricide," 192. For a discussion of the intriguing parallels between the careers of Winckelmann and Freud, see Damrosch, "The Politics of Ethics," 113–16.

Chief?' "[33] Freud's interest in the comparison between Hannibal and Winckelmann was perhaps more complex than he imagined. Freud, like Hannibal, had not yet seen Rome, but to what extent was Freud aware that Winckelmann had never seen Athens? What is so remarkable about Winckelmann's scholarly career is that his reconstructions of Greek antiquity were performed only derivatively through Roman copies; he refused to travel to Greece because he feared the journey was too dangerous.[34] Oddly, Winckelmann's studies of Greek antiquity were written in a Rome that Freud felt he was "fated not to see," while Freud ponders Oedipal anxieties in an Athens that Winckelmann was afraid to see. Thus the cultural trajectory between Greece and Rome (and the path of epic destiny as traced in the *Aeneid*) also traces the "royal road to the unconscious" where Freud's and Winckelmann's chiastic "neuroses" cultivate preoccupations with unseen cities that enrich their professional careers. Winckelmann's Rome served as a prominent Freudian model for psychic repression. But neither the founder of modern archaeology (as the science of physical strata) nor the founder of psychoanalysis (as the science of psychical strata) could readily convert their fascination with excavations and buried ghosts into a direct encounter with the cities that, for them, threatened a return of the repressed.

What Freud's "Rome neuroses" demonstrate, then, is the possibility that cities exert a fascination only insofar as they can be *imagined* (or derealized). And if the parallels between Freud and Aeneas as questers for Rome are compelling, we should also consider the uncanny similarity between another specialist of antiquity, Heinrich Schliemann, and Aeneas. One can hardly talk about archaeology during this period without mentioning Schliemann's dramatic excavations of perhaps the most haunting of derealized cities—ancient Troy. When Schliemann was only eight years old, he was given by his father a copy of Jerrer's *Universal History*, and he immediately became fascinated with an engraving of Troy in flames. Like Aeneas, standing spellbound before Dido's murals of the destruction of

---

[33]*SE* 4:196.

[34]In the eighteenth century, Greece was part of the Ottoman Empire, and Winckelmann's fears were perhaps partly rational. Indeed, centuries earlier, journeying to Greece proved fatal for Virgil. In 19 B.C. Virgil, working on revisions of his *Aeneid*, traveled to Greece, most likely in an effort to gain more knowledge about the particulars of Greek geography. But he caught a fever there and died shortly after his return to Italy. In this context, one also thinks of Freud's early "neurotic" fear of Rome: "for at the season of the year when it is possible for me to travel, residence in Rome must be avoided for reasons of health" (*SE* 4, 194).

Troy, the young Schliemann was enthralled by this lost city of history. At the age of twelve, he wrote his own pseudo-*Iliad*, an exercise that Schliemann himself later described as a "badly written Latin essay upon the principal events of the Trojan war,"[35] but which he nevertheless presented to his father as a Christmas gift. In this reciprocal exchange of gifts—a picture-book of Troy from father to son, and a child's *Iliad* from son to father—Troy becomes, perhaps even more than Rome, the primal, "neurotic" city of an Oedipal transference where fathers and sons recognize the origins of cultural (and psychic) history. Inspired by his father's gift, Schliemann eventually uncovered the key sites of a Greek preconscious—Mycenae, Tiryns, and, of course, Troy itself.

Not surprisingly, given his preoccupation with antiquity, Freud had read Schliemann's account of the Trojan digs, a narrative that mirrored to him his own psychoanalytic "excavations" of the unconscious.[36] And he must have viewed it as his good fortune that on one occasion, among those traveling with Freud to Athens (the city that prefigured his "Rome neuroses") was the prominent architect Wilhelm Dörpfeld, who had assisted Schliemann at Troy. Ernest Jones writes that "Freud gazed with awe at the man who had helped to discover ancient Troy, but he was too shy to approach him."[37] The uncharacteristically reticent Freud could only imagine how Dörpfeld might have entertained him with accounts of the buried Troy existing only as a stratified system of scarcely discernible layers, gradually and subtly teased into existence by meticulous architectural renderings of historical accounts, purely lucky hunches, and, finally, the scope of Schliemann's visual imagination. Schliemann's and Dörpfeld's accounts of the exhuming of Troy would surely have suggested to Freud his own process of psychic discovery—inferring the existence of the unconscious by way of the hypothetical guesswork

---

[35]Heinrich Schliemann, *Troy and Its Remains: A Narrative of Researches and Discoveries Made on the Site of Ilium, and in the Trojan Plain*, ed. Philip Smith (New York: Benjamin Blom, 1968), 3.

[36]In this context it should be noted that Freud was fascinated by the potential analogies between archaeological layers and the operations of repression. In a December 6, 1896, letter to Fliess, Freud wrote, "As you know, I am working on the assumption that our psychic mechanism has come into being by a process of stratification" (Masson, 207). And in his "Prefatory Remarks" to his "Fragment of an Analysis of a Case of Hysteria" (his celebrated analysis of "Dora"), Freud describes himself as a "conscientious archaeologist," bringing "to the light of day after their long burial the priceless though mutilated relics of antiquity" (*SE* 7:12).

[37]Ernest Jones, *The Life and Work of Sigmund Freud* (New York: Basic Books, 1953–57), 2:23–24.

(the process of derealization) required to bring its repressions to the surface. As Freud dreams of Rome in Homeric Athens, and Winckelmann "excavates" Athens from the vantage point of the Vatican Library in Rome, Schliemann is at work on a city that for centuries no one has seen. Thus Troy, this fascinating and elusive unseen city of antiquity, is the city most entangled in personal repressions and the unconscious—the city most derealized by the "neurotic" subject who imagines it.

Much more than the (merely) anachronistic cities of Rome or Athens, then, Troy is a city that exists only retroactively in the imaginations of belated observers like Aeneas and, centuries later, Schliemann—a city whose trace-structure must be carefully reconstructed by recourse only to the narrative or visual imagination. If Rome is the privileged city of the Symbolic, which can be entered only when sons learn to surpass their fathers, then Troy must be termed the city of the Imaginary, where the desire for a city not seen constitutes the very threshold of subjectivity.

In his use of Rome as a psychic metaphor in *Civilization and Its Discontents*, Freud may have uncovered more than he could possibly have anticipated. Taking as examples the careers of Winckelmann, Schliemann, and Freud—and their collective urban drama of missed encounters with their chosen "neurotic" cities—we could argue that a cultural history of the unconscious begins to take shape around key cities of antiquity that are not seen, but only desired, imagined, or reconstructed through representation. What is at stake in Freud's fascination with Rome is not a simple analogy between cities of antiquity and neurotic repression. Rather, Freud's "Rome neuroses" demonstrate that the city not seen is implicated within a mutual web of transference neuroses—an imaginary site where the beholder constitutes his subjectivity through the enactment of missed encounters with personal as well as cultural history. The unseen city of antiquity, then, becomes nothing less than a site of mediation between psyche and history. In such an urban drama, it is not simply a case of the subject being dispersed in history, but rather of (cultural) history as dispersed in the individual beholder of the city he chooses to imagine. As the careers of Schliemann and Freud demonstrate, somewhere between the buried stratigraphy of Troy and the vestigial ruins of Rome lies the threshold of a pre-Oedipal subjectivity itself. The city of antiquity, as a kind of trace-structure of the *enfance* of "neurotic" civilizations, becomes a site of mediation between psyche and history at the point at which it comes to embody the unconscious as a fear of the return of the repressed. Caught between past and present, Imaginary and Symbolic, the city of antiquity situates its observer *in* history, but in history as the history of exile.

To return to the terms with which I began this chapter, if Rome is the urban locus of neurosis, then Troy is the city of exile whose reality exists only in its dispossession. The experience of Aeneas (and, we could add, of Heinrich Schliemann) demonstrates that Troy can be represented only after it has been lost. If for Freud displacement was a fundamental psychic activity, an "energic" concept that renders inadequate the recovery of an origin, then the *translatio imperii*—the translation of power as a mode of geographic displacement—may be viewed as a kind of mimesis of the mechanics of the unconscious.

In its broadest scope, the *Aeneid* can be read as what Brooks Otis calls the "epic of the metropolis."[38] As such, the *Aeneid* finds itself suspended in the gap between Homer's Troy and Augustus's Rome. Whereas Odysseus's goal in the *Odyssey* is finally to return home to Ithaka, Aeneas can only leave Troy behind as the city of exile and push onward to a Rome he will never see. Moreover, it is in another key city of antiquity, in the emasculating luxury of Carthage, that Aeneas is granted a (retroactive) vision of a Troy in ruins that is meant to spur him on to his new destiny as the founder of Rome. It is in Carthage, then, future enemy of Rome, a city of antiquity that exists only insofar as it reveals Troy as the city of exile, that Virgil acts out his (urban) "anxiety of influence" with Homer.

Memory and Epic Origins

"Repressions that have failed," Freud observes provocatively, "will of course have more claim on our interest than those that may have been successful."[39] "Successful" repressions, as Freud argues throughout his *Civilization and Its Discontents*, are crucial for the foundations of culture—for the repressive conversion of aboriginal chaos into *civitas*. But what are the circumstances under which a culture comes to "remember" (or fail to repress) its previously "suc-

---

[38]Brooks Otis, *Virgil: A Study in Civilized Poetry* (Oxford: Clarendon Press, 1963), 3. As Otis writes, "Virgil was the first and only poet truly to recreate the heroic-age in an urban civilization" (2).

[39]*SE* 14: 153.

cessful" repressions? How does it achieve a "consciousness" that can open the flood-gates of cultural memory and create a past for itself? And how reliable is this cultural consciousness when it does remember its past? Northrop Frye has argued that it is every poet's function "primarily to remember";[40] and the literary genre most concerned with remembering (with the possible exception of elegy) is, of course, the epic. Epic is the story of culture bringers, and epic historiography is itself a mode of consciousness. But again, when a nation records its early legends and history, what determines what it remembers, and what it "successfully represses"? To what extent does historical memory have its "neurotic," as well as its ideological, consequences? The answers to these questions are themselves dependent on an understanding of the vexed question of "origins" and the role of memory in (re)constructing them. The faculty of memory and its mechanics of failed repression should, to echo Freud, stake a major "claim on our interest" because memory and origins have always had a problematic relationship. And if, as Freud argues in a letter to Fliess, "consciousness and memory are mutually exclusive" (December, 1896), then it is time to reexamine what it means when an epic poet, in Frye's simple terms, chooses to "remember."[41]

Throughout his professional career—from his "originary" neurological paradigms of memory as traced in the physiognomy of the brain in his *Project for a Scientific Psychology* (1896), to his consideration of the uses of the ruins of Rome to locate a discoverable past (a "primal scene" for civilization itself) in *Civilization and Its Discontents* (1930)—Freud was consistently engaged with the concept of memory and its exposing of the inevitably tropic nature of origins. One of the more magnificently failed repressions throughout the literary history of epic is, ironically, memory—specifically its belated attempts at recording history. As "theories" of the tracing of origins, Freudian psychoanalysis and the literary history of epic both privilege the faculty of memory and its representations of the past. But between the belated, *nachträglich* reconstructions of the fragile mnemic traces of the analysand searching for a primal scene and the retroactive, in medias res narratives of the epic hero searching for, in the words of Spenser's Arthur, his "name and nation," memory has revealed itself to be a notoriously unreliable mode of cognition for

---

[40] *Anatomy of Criticism*, 57.
[41] Masson, 208.

representations of the past.[42] Freud observes the shared mnemo-technics of psychoanalysis and of the epic in his "Case of Obsessional Neurosis," where he notes that the analysand's later consolidation of his childhood memories "involves a complicated process of remodelling, analogous in every way to the process by which a nation constructs legends about its early history."[43] Thus the (case) history of Freudian psychoanalysis and the (epic) history of the *translatio imperii* both reveal how problematic it is to undertake any representation of the past.[44]

I wish, at this point, to go back in time through epic history to discuss Virgil's Aeneas as the prototype for cultural heroes who *remember*, and the hero most responsible for making remembering the major mode of cognition for epic.[45] It is because of Aeneas that we can argue that the aetiology of epic lies in the primary process of memory—as though epic is always already remembering. First, I discuss how the attainment in the *Aeneid* of epic subjecthood itself is, in some sense, dependent on the faculty of memory—or, more accurately, on the obscure thresholds between memory and forgetting (the loci of "failed repression"). I then advance to a discussion of how the metaphor of the *translatio imperii* throughout the literary history of epic weaves a richly ambivalent tapestry of memory, repression, and forgetting that creates an unconscious for epic subjecthood throughout literary history. Arguing for Troy as the paradigmatic memory-trace for all of epic history, I demonstrate how the

[42]For a thorough account of Freud's struggles to provide psychoanalysis with a "primal scene," see Ned Lukacher, *Primal Scenes: Literature, Philosophy, Psychoanalysis* (Ithaca: Cornell University Press, 1986), especially his chapter "Primal Scenes: Freud and the Wolf-Man." See also Richard King, "Memory and Phantasy," *Modern Language Notes* 98:5 (1983), 1197–1213, and David Carroll, "Freud and the Myth of Origin," *New Literary History* 6:3 (1975), 513–28. For a discussion of Proust as the first great post-Freudian writer of a mnemonics that is "less a work of memory than a play of forgetfulness" (66), see Jerry Aline Flieger, "Proust, Freud, and the Art of Forgetting," *Sub-Stance* 29 (1981), 66–82.

[43]"A Case of Obsessional Neurosis," *SE* 10:206n1.

[44]In his article "Deconstructing Memory: On Representing the Past and Theorizing Culture in France since the Revolution" (*Diacritics* 15:4 [1985], 13–36), Richard Terdiman investigates the process by which the nineteenth century "theorized itself" by conceiving of memory as the self-conscious "stabilization and transmission" of history. Terdiman perceptively argues that in any study of memory, "What is at stake is nothing less than the way a culture imagines the representation of the past to be possible. For the problem of representing the past is really the representation problem itself" (19–20).

[45]My phrase is taken from Herbert Marcuse, who argues that memory is "a decisive mode of cognition" for psychoanalysis (*Eros and Civilization: A Philosophical Inquiry into Freud* [Boston: Beacon Press, 1955], 18).

unconscious, in the process of becoming implicated in Aeneas's narrative restructuring of his escape from Troy, results in a forgetting to remember that *is* the founding moment of dynastic epic.[46] My overarching purpose is to explore some of the ways in which psychoanalysis, both in its Freudian form and in its later (retroactive) Lacanian "return" to Freud, can provide some useful insights into what it means for epic history when Aeneas remembers Troy—insights that reveal how, within the operations of cultural memory, the past never survives intact.

Troy and the Return of the Repressed

Any history of memory in dynastic epic must begin with the first half of the *Aeneid*. Unlike the Troy of the *Iliad*, Virgil's Troy is a secondarily *narrated* entity, constituted only retroactively through its many reminiscences. No longer the (real) backdrop of the Homeric account of conflict between Greeks and Trojans, Virgil's Troy is the (imaginary) origin of the story of its own loss.

As the career of Schliemann demonstrates, there is something about the fall of Troy—something in its intimate association of narrative and memory—that has haunted our cultural imagination for centuries. Significantly, Schliemann, in the lengthy subtitle to his study *Troy and Its Remains: A Narrative of Researches and Discoveries Made on the Site of Ilium, and in the Trojan Plain*, specifically refers to his excavations of Troy as a "narrative." Shakespeare (even beyond the bounds of his own cynical saga of the Trojan War, *Troilus and Cressida*) seems to have been intrigued with its narrative resonances—its susceptibility to remembrance. In *The Rape of Lucrece*, one of the poet's more elaborate conceits is of a massive tapestry, an imaginary backdrop where Lucrece relives her own rape even as she "weeps Troy's painted woes" (1492). Similarly, in 2 *Henry VI*, the fall of Troy offers a rich source of analogy for Queen Margaret when she tells Henry:

> How often have I tempted Suffolk's tongue . . .
> To sit and witch me, as Ascanius did

---

[46]In his essay "Painful Memories," Quint has suggested that one of the major themes of the *Aeneid* is "the therapeutic effects of forgetting" (36), specifically the Trojans' need to forget Troy.

When he to madding Dido would unfold
His father's acts commenc'd in burning Troy!
(3.2.116–19)

And when Hamlet desires a performance from the players newly
arrived at Elsinore, he requests Aeneas's narration of Trojan slaughters to Dido in order to stir his imagination: "One speech in't I
chiefly lov'd, 'twas Aeneas' tale to Dido, and thereabout of it especially when he speaks of Priam's slaughter. If it live in your memory, begin at this line" (2.2.445–49). Finally, we can note that
Sidney, in his *Apology for Poetry*, suggests the fall of Troy as a kind of
mnemonic device for recalling exemplary courage: "Only let Aeneas
be worne in the tablet of your memory, how he governeth himselfe
in the ruine of his Countrey."

The fall of Troy, to paraphrase Hamlet, lived in Freud's memory,
as well. Freud's familiarity with the *Aeneid* dates at least from his
final high school examination, which tested him on it;[47] and, as I
suggested at the beginning of this chapter, it is intriguing to consider the extent to which Virgil's epic may have served as a significant cultural model for the development of Freudian psychoanalysis.
Not coincidentally, Troy "lived" in Freud's memory in his essay en-
titled "Screen Memories."[48] To lend emphasis to his argument that
even painful memories can be worth recalling, Freud isolates Aeneas's oft-quoted speech to his fellow Trojan exiles: "forsan et haec
olim meminisse iuuabit" ("Some day, perhaps, it will be a joy to
remember even these things" [I.203]).[49] Thus Freud uses Aeneas's
line as an eloquent affirmation of what he hoped would be the eventual successes of the "talking cure." And in *The Psychopathology of
Everyday Life*, Freud recounts the story of his conversation on the
train with a young Austrian Jew who, bemoaning the fate of Jews as
exiles, struggled to quote Dido's vengeful words after her abandonment by Aeneas: "Exoriare aliquis nostris ex ossibus ultor" ("Let
someone arise from my bones as an avenger" [IV.625]).[50] But Freud,

[47]This is pointed out by Jean Starobinski, "*Acheronta Movebo*," in *The Trial(s) of Psychoanalysis*, ed. Françoise Meltzer (Chicago: University of Chicago Press, 1988), 275.

[48]*SE* 3:317.

[49]All citations of the *Aeneid* are from *Vergili Maronis Opera*, ed. F. A. Hirtzel (1990;
reprint ed., Oxford: Oxford University Press, 1966). The English translation is Allen
Mandelbaum's *The Aeneid of Virgil* (New York: Bantam, 1971).

[50]As himself a Jew (and an exile from the medical community of Vienna), Freud
would have read much into Dido's vengeful prophecy. As Starobinski points out, the
abandonment of Dido, as a Phoenician or a "Semite," perhaps resulted in Freud's

pursuing his interest in slips of the tongue and the mechanics of imperfect memory, listens in fascination as the young man, omitting the *aliquis*, recites instead, "Exoriare ex nostris ossibus ultor."[51] Thus in this anecdote, the *Aeneid* is significantly linked by Freud with slight (but unconsciously motivated?) *imperfections* of memory (such as contaminate Aeneas's own recall of Troy, as we shall see later).[52] A final dramatic example of Freud's association of the *Aeneid* with repression appears on the title page of *The Interpretation of Dreams*, where we find Juno's curse prior to her unleashing of the suppressed fury of Allecto: "Flectere si nequeo superos, Acheronta movebo" ("If I cannot bend the higher powers, I shall stir up hell" [VII.312]). Freud himself wrote that Juno's curse "is intended to picture the efforts of the repressed instinctual impulses,"[53] thus suggesting an explicit link between Virgil's epic and the operations of repression.

As these examples from Freud illustrate, the association between the fall of Troy and the faculty of memory has become so conventional throughout cultural history that it is almost as if Troy existed only to the extent to which it was remembered. "Quis Troiae nesciat urbem?" ("Who knows not Troy?" [I.565]), asks Dido, hungry for Aeneas's narrative of its fall. But a tone of empty nostalgia pervades Dido's highly stylized rhetorical question, an elegiac evocation of Troy's absent presence that only emphasizes the belatedness of any attempt to reconstruct it. "Fuimus Troes, fuit Ilium" ("Troy has been" [II.325]) is the simple but resonant pronouncement of Panthus, priest of Apollo, in his effort to urge Aeneas to flee the burning city. But if Troy "has been" in the perfect tense, what does it mean that its fall still occupies so much of the narrative present tense of Virgil's epic?

In his chapter "Landino's Virgil" in his *Allegorical Epic*, Michael Murrin discusses the theme of perception in the *Aeneid*, specifically

---

"divided sympathies" between her and Aeneas (276).

[51]"The Forgetting of Foreign Words," *SE* 6:9.

[52]In this context of viewing the "history" of the *Aeneid* within the framework of psychoanalysis, it is interesting to note how Virgil's epic also serves as the backdrop for Lacan's correction of Poe's "memory" in his "Seminar on 'The Purloined Letter.'" In Poe's story, Dupin, criticizing the unknowing arrogance of the Minister who still believes he possesses the Queen's letter, claims that the Minister was premature to boast about his *facilis descensus Averni* (VI.126). In an editorial note, Lacan "corrects" Poe's incorrect grammar when quoting from the Sibyl's speech to Aeneas with the curt words, "Virgil's line reads: *facilis descensus Averno*" (*Yale French Studies: French Freud: Structural Studies in Psychoanalysis* 48 [1975], 68n40).

[53]*SE* 5:608n1.

as it evolved through the tradition of a "Platonized" Virgil (exemplified by commentators such as Servius, Fulgentius, Macrobius, Silvestris, Landino, and so on), and as it culminated in the skeptical epistemology of the Florentine Academy of Neoplatonists. Murrin examines the influence of, among others, the argument of Proclus, set forth in his commentary on Plato's *Republic*, that Troy "symbolizes man's sensual condition, what he must leave."[54] In the philosophy of the Florentine Platonists, true knowledge could not be discerned on earth. The uncanny shades of the *Aeneid*, inhabiting, in Murrin's words, "the vague region between sleep and waking," were oft-cited illustrations of the futility of sensory perception: "To support their skeptical epistemology, the philosophers of the New Academy stressed dreams and borderline cases, situations in which deception, illusion, and uncertainty bedevil the senses. And here they would have in the *Aeneid* an encyclopedia of such borderline cases. In a typical scene characters blunder about in the dark or guess uncertainly at objects by the light of the moon."[55] Even Anchises' subterranean revelation of the future Roman *imperium* concludes ambiguously with Aeneas's exit through the Ivory Gate of false dreams (*falsa insomnia*). Thus, many passages of the *Aeneid* prompted continual debate in the Florentine Academy as to the difficulty of distinguishing between false and true impressions (much as Freud dealt futilely with the vexed question of the "truth" or "falsehood" of his patients' memories). Not surprisingly, Freud was particularly fascinated by the phantasmagoric shades of Book VI, which, significantly, he reread while editing *The Interpretation of Dreams*.[56]

The shades, ghosts, and effigies of unburied, restless, and disturbed Trojans dominate Aeneas's exile in the first half of the *Aeneid*. It is the shade, the *infelix simulacrum* (II.772), of his vanished wife Creusa—all too easily and horribly lost in the *obscura limina* of a Troy in ruin—who returns to keep Aeneas's desperate memories alive, as does the hideously mangled body of Hector, who appears to Aeneas in a dream. Priam's headless corpse, his *ingens truncus*, is surely one of the more grisly images haunting Aeneas's memory. And it is the torn and bloody branch of Priam's son Polydorus (the progenitor of the topos of the bleeding branch throughout epic literary history) who warns Aeneas to flee from Thrace. Aeneas's journey to the Un-

[54] Michael Murrin, *The Allegorical Epic: Essays in Its Rise and Decline* (Chicago: University of Chicago Press, 1980), 31.
[55] Ibid., 34, 37.
[56] Starobinski, "*Acheronta Movebo*," 277.

derworld in Book VI constitutes a virtual theater of the return of the repressed, as a weird procession of forgotten shades, the *animas pallentis*, make their unanticipated reappearances: the ghost of the drowned Palinurus, the mangled and scarcely recognizable Deiphobus, the eerily silent and bitter shade of Dido who expected love and marriage in exchange for having worshipped Aeneas's Trojan past—in short, all the ghostly (dis)embodiments of the fragmented *Troiana fortuna*. These Trojan revenants constitute the very essence of the uncanny itself. Freud could easily have had the *Aeneid* in mind when, in "The Uncanny," he wrote, "Dismembered limbs, a severed head . . . all these have something peculiarly uncanny about them."[57] As ghosts they are not fully *heimlich* (literally, not fully "home-like," not fully *Trojan*), but as Trojans they are not fully *unheimlich* either, as to Aeneas they are immediately recognizable. As Freud argues, the uncanny "is in reality nothing new or alien, but something which is familiar and old-established in the mind and which has become alienated from it only through the process of repression."[58]

Early in Book I appears one of the *Aeneid*'s most oft-quoted lines: "Tantae molis erat Romanum condere gentem" ("It was so hard to found the race of Rome" [33]). Primarily, it is Troy's many returns of/from the repressed that render Jupiter's promise of a Roman *imperium sine fine* (1.279) such a difficult prophecy for Aeneas to fulfill. Although, early in the *Aeneid*, Aeneas urges his storm-tossed comrades to continue their push to Latium, he himself does not know the meaning of such a destiny, and the trauma of Troy's destruction festers unrecognized: "Premit altum corde dolorem" ("Its pain is held within, hidden" [1.209]). Indeed, the memory of Troy provides the very paradigm of the mechanics of repression. Throughout so much of the first half of Virgil's epic, Troy lurks somewhere between remembering and forgetting, "held within," a "hidden" representation in Aeneas's unconscious. This threshold of repression, then, comes to be the fullest meaning of the Virgilian state of *fato profugus* (or being "driven by fate"): Aeneas hovers between rejecting a Troy that must give way to Rome and resisting a Rome that cannot obliterate the memories of Troy. The inevitable result is exile.

Many of the *Aeneid*'s returns of the repressed, in particular, seem to inhabit this liminal boundary—almost a mental space—between

---

[57]*SE* 17:244.
[58]Ibid., 241.

Troy and Rome. Thus, the haunting shade of Creusa, sacrificed to a new Roman destiny, reappears to Aeneas in a vision, underscoring the *dolor* of Troy's destruction. Aeneas is warned to flee the defeated city not by Jupiter and his felicitous promise of an *imperium sine fine*, but by the mangled body of Hector who appears to him in a feverish and troubled dream. After his escape from Troy, Aeneas experiences no purposeful and direct progress to Latium, but is waylaid by a series of false effigies of Troy:[59] in Thrace at Aeneadae, in Pergamum, and, most remarkably, in the obsessive city of Buthrotum, where Priam's son Helenus rules over a simulacrum of Troy, a kind of *Troia recidiva* (bordered by a dried-up stream parodying the Xanthus), where Andromache, who fetishizes Trojan icons like the empty tomb of Hector, in her own confrontation with the return of the repressed faints when she sees Aeneas's Trojan armor.[60] And, indeed, Andromache's response to Aeneas constitutes the narrative space of the uncanny itself. Stiffening with fear and amazement at the sight of Aeneas, Andromache demands:

> Verane te facies, verus mihi nuntius adfers,
> Nate dea? Vivisne? aut, si lux alma recessit,
> Hector ubi est?
>
> (III.319–21)
>
> (Are you, born of a goddess, a true body,
> a real messenger who visits me?
> Are you alive? Or if the gracious light
> of life has left you, where is Hector?)

"Vivisne?" she demands to know. If, as Freud argues in "The Uncanny," one of the primary epistemological crises in perception occurs "when there is intellectual uncertainty whether an object is alive or not,"[61] then Andromache's doubt as to whether the figure in

---

[59]In his insightful essay, "Repetition and Ideology in the *Aeneid*" (*Materiali e discussioni per l'analasi dei testi classici* 23 [1989], 9–54), Quint interprets these false effigies and replicas of Troy in an explicitly psychoanalytic context. He views the Trojans' many abortive attempts to re-establish Troy as a kind of paradigmatic repetition compulsion of epic, specifically "an obsessive circular return to a traumatic past" (10). Because of these obsessively repeated false Troys, the repetition compulsion that informs the first half of the "Odyssean" *Aeneid* is a dramatic example of how neurosis succeeds in displacing ideology.

[60]It is perhaps because of Virgil's own fascination with the uncanny that the Andromache episode is, as Michael C. J. Putman has argued, "his most expansive addition to the legends of Aeneas's wanderings" ("The Third Book of the *Aeneid*: From Homer to Rome," *Ramus* 9:1 [1980], 7).

[61]*SE* 17:233.

Trojan armor looming before her is Hector dramatically illustrates Troy's uncanny power to survive and flourish in the human imagination. Finally, perhaps the most ambivalent symbol of Aeneas's new destiny is, as we have seen, his old father, Anchises, redolent with the promises of a new Roman future for his son, but reappearing in Book VI as still the same man who had to be carried on Aeneas's back through the flames of Troy, and who remains, throughout Aeneas's wanderings, a mental, as well as a physical burden.[62] Repeatedly, the push to Rome cannot easily cross over the *obscura limina* of a Troy that cannot be fully annihilated.

Ekphrasis and the Retroactive Trauma of Memory

Virgil's subtle yet significant link between memory and repression seems particularly evident in Book I, where a disoriented Aeneas, still enshrouded (like an uncanny Trojan shade himself) in the protective mist of his mother Venus, stops short at a series of pictures on the portals of Dido's shrine to Juno (1.441–62).

> Namque videbat uti bellantes Pergama circum
> hac fugerent Grai, premeret Troiana iuventus,
> hac Phryges, instaret curru cristaus Achilles.
> Nec procul hinc Rhesi niveis tentoria velis
> agnoscit lacrimans, primo quae prodita somno
> Tydides multa vastabat caede cruentus,
> ardentisque avertit equos in castra prius quam
> pabula gustassent Troiae Xanthumque bibissent.
> Parte alia fugiens amissis Troilus armis,
> infelix puer atque impar congressus Achilli,
> fertur equis curruque haeret resupinus inanai,
> lora tenens tamen; huic cervixque comaeque trahuntur
> per terram, et versa pulvis inscribitur hasta.
> Interea ad templum non aequae Palladis ibant
> crinibus Iliades passis peplumque ferebant
> suppliciter, tristes et tunsae pectora palmis;

---

[62]Mario Di Cesare argues that even though Anchises, through his underworld prophecy, embodies the future, his connection with a Trojan past "provides more headaches than help for Aeneas" (*The Altar and the City: A Reading of Vergil's "Aeneid"* [New York: Columbia University Press, 1974], 72). Despite the pleas of Aeneas, Ascanius, and Creusa, Anchises refuses to leave Troy for exile (II.637ff.). Following the escape from Troy, it is Anchises's misreading of the oracle that sidetracks the Trojan exiles to Crete.

diva solo fixos oculos aversa tenebat.
Ter circum Iliacos raptaverat Hectora muros
exanimumque auro corpus vendebat Achilles.
Tum vero ingentem gemitum dat pectore ab imo,
ut spolia, ut currus, utque ipsum corpus amici
tendentemque manus Priamum conspexit inermis.

(He watched the warriors circling Pergamus;
here routed Greeks were chased by Trojan fighters
and here the Phrygian troops pursued by plumed
Achilles in his chariot. Nearby,
sobbing, he recognized the snow-white canvas
tents of King Rhesus—with his men betrayed,
while still in their first sleep, and then laid waste,
with many dead, by bloody Diomedes,
who carried off their fiery war horses
before they had a chance to taste the pastures
of Troy, or drink the waters of the Xanthus.
Elsewhere young Troilus, the unhappy boy—
he is matched unequally against Achilles—
runs off, his weapons lost. He is fallen flat;
his horses drag him on as he still clings
fast to his empty chariot, clasping
the reins. His neck, his hair trail on the ground,
and his inverted spear inscribes the dust.
Meanwhile the Trojan women near the temple
of Pallas, the unkindly; hair disheveled,
sad, beating at their breasts, as suppliants,
they bear the robe of offering. The goddess
averts her face, her eyes fast to the ground.
Three times Achilles had dragged Hector round
the walls of Troy, selling his lifeless body
for gold. And then, indeed, Aeneas groans
within the great pit of his chest, deeply;
for he can see the spoils, the chariot,
the very body of his friend, and Priam
pleading for Hector with defenseless hands.)

The pictures that Aeneas views constitute an extended *ekphrasis* that uncannily unfolds vivid images of the *fata Troiana*—in short, all the fatal dooms that have made the defeated Troy such a haunting image throughout the literary history of epic. Thus Dido's temple is transformed into a crypt, an obsessive replaying of the slaughters of

the Trojan holocaust that engulfs Aeneas in a morbid memory theater of his own repressed images of Troy.[63]

As part of the *lacrimae rerum* that constitute the *fata Troiana*, Aeneas must again witness the ferocity of Diomedes, the impotence of
the Trojan soldiers chased mercilessly by their bloody pursuers,
Achilles' desecration of Hector's body while Priam begs for mercy.
The figure of Troilus, dragged by his own runaway chariot with his
spearpoint trailing in the dust, seems particularly emblematic of
how the gods abandoned Troy at its moment of defeat.[64] For that
matter, the *ekphrasis* constitutes an extraordinary intertextual moment in which not only is the fall of Troy replayed for Aeneas, but
also is the *Iliad* replayed for Virgil. Like his protagonist, then, Virgil
too must face the task of constructing Rome out of the very Trojan
ashes that serve as secondary epic's return of the repressed.

What is so remarkable about this scene is Virgil's emphasis not so
much on the *lacrimae rerum* that characterize the fall of Troy itself as
on Aeneas's moving response to the images before him. Indeed, this
scene would seem to provide us with nothing less than a glimpse of
Aeneas's unconscious.[65] From the moment of his frantic escape from
Troy, to the storm that strands him in Carthage, Aeneas has scarcely
thought of his homeland, scarcely had the opportunity to reflect on

[63]Given the violence of these scenes, seemingly lifted straight from the *Iliad*, we
can, in this context, turn to Eugene Vance in his essay "Roland and the Poetics of
Memory" (in *Textual Strategies: Perspectives in Post-Structuralist Criticism*, ed. Josué V.
Harari [Ithaca: Cornell University Press, 1979]). Vance argues that, in oral narrative,
details of violence simply made large chunks of the narrative easier to memorize:
"Thus violence may be understood as being not only the 'subject' of oral epic narrative, but also as an *aide-mémoire* or as a 'generative' force in the production of its
discourse. By extension, it is interesting to ask if the semiological prominence given to
violence in classical and post-classical culture—the sacrifices, the circumcisions, the
tortures, the beheadings, the crucifixions, the quarterings, the burnings—was not
primarily mnemonic in function" (383). Given the horror of Troy's destruction, the
violence of Virgil's *ekphrasis* is perhaps the only *aide-mémoire* available to Aeneas for
remembering Troy.

[64]For an intriguing discussion of Troilus's spear dragging in the dust as the "trace,"
a moment of "writing" as the "mimetic depiction" of history, see Françoise Meltzer's
chapter "The Spearpoint of Troilus," in *Salome and the Dance of Writing: Portraits of
Mimesis in Literature* (Chicago: University of Chicago Press, 1987), esp. 48–54.

[65]That Aeneas's viewing of the pictures of Troy's fatal dooms is an immanently
psychic moment has conventionally been emphasized by a number of critics. R. D.
Williams, for example, writes that the murals "are coming to us through the mind of
the beholder, coloured and interpreted by his own emotions" ("The Pictures on
Dido's Temple," *Classical Quarterly* 10:2 [1960], 150). Adam Parry has described Aeneas's response as a "private voice of regret" ("The Two Voices of Virgil's *Aeneid*,"
Arion 2:4 [1963], 79), while Di Cesare observes that there is something in these por-
trayals of Troy that "distills a state of mind and of feeling" (*The Altar and the City*, 1).

the circumstance of its having fallen—until he sees the tableaux of Troy's destruction on Dido's walls. Aeneas's encounter with the Trojan murals constitutes such a "disturbance of memory" that it is almost as if, like Freud standing before the Acropolis for the first time, Aeneas is thinking, "'What I see here is not real.'" In this moment of an urban derealization—of a *déjà vu* in reverse—Troy has become strange to him. Thus it is only in the city of Carthage that Troy emerges (belatedly) to convince Aeneas that it once was real.

What makes the episode at Dido's temple so moving is its disturbance and activation of Aeneas's memory, an unanticipated occasion to reflect on the possibility that there ever was a Troy after all. There is something distinctly *somatic* in Aeneas's response to Dido's pictures; indeed, his response may rank as one of the most dramatic manifestations of sheer physical affect in all of epic literary history.[66] Virgil's emphasis on his hero's physical affectivity prompts us to consider Freud's link between affect and repression in "The Unconscious": "repression results not only in withholding things from consciousness, but also in preventing the development of affect."[67] One predictable outcome of the lifting of repression can be the restoring of affect. Thus Aeneas scans the tragedy of Troy's destruction with tears (and even sobs at one point), sighs, groans, and frozen astonishment. In the midst of these affective descriptions, the reader is in the odd position of watching Aeneas watching: "Dardanio Aeneae miranda uidentur, / dum stupet obtutuque haeret defixus in uno" ("the Dardan watched these scenes in wonder, / while he was fastened in a stare, astonished" [494–95]). And for that matter, it is

---

[66]The "affective" epic prototype for Aeneas's response may have been Odysseus's lament when he hears Demodokos's song of Troy in the palace of Alkinoös in Book VIII of the *Odyssey*:

> These things the famous singer sang for them, but Odysseus,
> taking in his ponderous hands the great mantle dyed in
> sea-purple, drew it over his head and veiled his fine features,
> shamed for tears running down his face before the Phaiakians;
> and every time the divine singer would pause in his singing,
> he would take the mantle away from his head, and wipe the tears off,
> . . . but every time he began again, and the greatest
> of the Phaiakians would urge him to sing, since they joyed in his stories,
> Odysseus would cover his head again, and make lamentation.
>
> (*The Iliad of Homer*, intro and trans. Richmond Lattimore
> [Chicago: University of Chicago Press, 1951])

Like Aeneas, Odysseus too is an epic hero who remembers.

[67]*SE* 14:179.

Aeneas's audible groans that continually mediate between the reader and the hero's own experience of the murals.[68]

In this affective episode, then, Troy becomes the visual site of a mediation between psyche and history (or, more accurately, history as representation). We might wish to view the *ekphrasis* that structures this episode as readily constitutive (as perhaps a virtual allegory) of not just history, but of the process of memory itself—but only if we consider carefully what it means for Aeneas to *remember* Troy. In her magisterial study of the history of memory, Frances Yates has demonstrated that mental pictures (*imagines*) often served as the most crucial mnemonic device for Roman rhetors;[69] and she demonstrates the frequency with which ancient treatises on the *Ars memorativa*, such as the *Rhetorica ad Herennium*, emphasized sight as the faculty most intimately linked to memory. Thus, Giovanni Paolo Lomazzo, in his *A Tracte Containing the Artes of Curious Paintinge Caruinge & Buildinge* (translated by Richard Haydocke in 1598), argues that "the picture mooveth the eye, and that committeth the species and formes of the thinges seene to the memory, all which it representeth to the understanding."[70] In Lomazzo's Neoplatonic conception of visual logic, *ekphrasis* stimulates the memory which, in turn, "representeth" the beheld images to a synthesizing process of understanding.[71] Lomazzo's mnemonic scheme closely anticipates Freud's account of the process of consciousness itself, in other words, the mechanism by which the "thing-presentations" (*Sachvorstellungen*) of the unconscious are transformed into the "word-presentations" (*Wortvorstellungen*) of consciousness.

But Neoplatonic treatises on the *Ars memorativa* elide the still indeterminate connection between the "formes of things" and the mnemic processes that supposedly register them faithfully; and we must

---

[68]The reader's attention is diverted from the murals, for example, at the point at which Aeneas laments the sight of Priam, and as Page DuBois claims, it is at this point that "the audience is drawn back to the living Aeneas" (*History, Rhetorical Description and the Epic from Homer to Spenser* [Cambridge: Boydell & Brewer Ltd., 1982], 16). The "living Aeneas," I would argue, can be described further as a distinctly *affective* Aeneas.

[69]Frances Yates, *The Art of Memory* (Chicago: University of Chicago Press, 1966), 2.

[70]Quoted in Clark Hulse, "'A Piece of Skilful Painting' in Shakespeare's Lucrece," *Shakespeare Survey* 31 (1978), 19.

[71]For another kind of link between *ekphrasis* and memory, we can turn to Patrick H. Hutton, who discusses how in the *New Science*, Vico's treatise on the emergence of human consciousness, the author's "new art of memory becomes a retrospective search for the connection between our present conceptions and the lost poetic images out of which they were born" ("The Art of Memory Reconceived: From Rhetoric to Psychoanalysis," *Journal of the History of Ideas* 48:3 [1987], 378).

consider the extent to which the *ekphrasis* of Troy's destruction calls into question any static construction of memory, such as Lomazzo's. The sequential process of beholding and committing to memory, as outlined by Lomazzo's account of the visual effects of *ekphrasis*, suggests a readily recuperable chronology of events that oversimplifies and betrays the fragmentation inherent in Aeneas's mnemic experience in Dido's temple.

Throughout literary history, epic is traditionally concerned with the tracing of origins, and a recurring epic topos is the invitation to the protagonist to speak of his homeland. But there is no psychic mechanism that can re-present Aeneas's origins. His difficulties in tracing his story *a prima origine* are earlier expressed in his struggling response to the disguised Venus's urging to tell his story:

> O dea, si prima repetens ab origine pergam
> Et uacet annalis nostrorum audire laborem,
> Ante diem clauso componet Veste Olympo.
>
> (1.373–75)

> (O goddess, if I tracked my story back
> until its first beginning, were there time
> to hear the annals of our trials,
> then the evening would have shot Olympus' gates
> and gathered in the day before I ended.)

And Aeneas's difficulty in reconstructing the horror of Troy's fall is recapitulated when he later expresses his reluctance to a Dido eager for his narrative: "Infandum, regina, iubes renovare dolorem" ("O queen—too terrible for tongues the pain / you ask me to renew" [II.3]). In his commentary, R. G. Austin notes that *infandum*, or "unutterable," is a word "often used of something monstrous or unnatural . . . beyond all normal experience."[72] Troy is unnarratable, *unmemorizable*, because its horror has no precedent. Aeneas's destiny is to found Rome as the New Troy—but this quintessentially epic goal of renewal and displacement presupposes that Aeneas has come to some knowledge, some understanding, of the old Troy. Dido's murals of the narration of Troy's destruction—the disappearance, in some sense, of Troy's disappearance—fail to yield anything in the

---

[72]R. G. Austin, *P. Vergili Maronis. Aeneidos: Liber Primvs* (Oxford: Clarendon Press, 1971), 28.

nature of an unqualified revelation about the smoldering city he has
been forced to abandon. And they raise a number of questions about
the status of Troy as a knowable event in epic history: what does the
fall of Troy mean for Aeneas? How, for that matter, does it come *to*
mean anything? Despite Virgil's many allusions to Homer's Troy, we
come to realize that there *is* no Troy in the *Aeneid*, at least no Troy
that is not, in some sense, dependent on Aeneas's precarious and
emotionally charged remembrance of it. It is as though, like the unconscious itself, the existence of Troy must be inferred: it is never
knowable directly.

Virgil emphasizes Aeneas's wonder as he stands before Dido's
murals: "Animum pictura pascit inani" ("He feeds his soul on what
is nothing but a picture").[73] The image of Troy is *inani*—vain, empty,
unreal—a vivid stimulus to memory and yet the false simulacrum of
a defeated city that has been and must be forgotten in the push to
Rome. And yet Troy seemingly takes on meaning in its annihilation.
In *The Trojan Women*, another tragic representation of Troy's agony,
Euripides demonstrates that Troy enters the imagination only retroactively, after it has been destroyed. Hecuba, for one, dwells obsessively on the city as a kind of absent presence: "This is not Troy,
about, above— / Not Troy"; "Troy is a smoke, a dying flame"; "Even
thy name / Shall soon be taken from thee"; "and my City a vanished
thing!"[74] Commenting on Euripides' representation of Troy's destruction, Adrian Poole writes: "The cause and the result of the

[73]In his commentary on the *Aeneid*, Bernardus Silvestris interpreted this passage as
demonstrating the inherent falseness of Dido's images of Troy: "Aeneas 'feasts his
eyes on empty pictures.' Because the world is then new to him and he is wrapped in
a cloud (that is, in ignorance), he does not understand the nature of the world; therefore these please him, and he admires them. We understand his eyes as the senses,
some of which are true and some false. . . . We understand the pictures to be temporal goods, which are called pictures because they are not good but seem so. . . . And
thus he fills his eyes (his senses) with pictures (that is, with worldly goods)." (*Commentary on The First Six Books of Virgil's "Aeneid,"* trans. Earl G. Schreiber and Thomas
E. Maresca [Lincoln: University of Nebraska Press, 1979], 13). Thus Bernard, in no
uncertain terms, disallows the almost divine link between visual images and understanding that informs Neoplatonic theories of mnemonics. For an analysis of the "entranced gaze" before images in epic narrative, see Lee W. Patterson, "'Rapt with
Pleasaunce': Vision and Narration in the Epic," *English Literary History* 48 (1981), 455–
75. Patterson discusses how the "entranced gaze" itself "must be abrogated in order
to allow for a pedagogical discourse by which its value can be recovered at the highest
level" (459).
    Of Virgil's specific line, W. R. Johnson points out that "Animum . . . pascit" is "a
gentle catachresis, yet it is sufficient to convey much of the complexity and confusion
of Aeneas's state" (*Darkness Visible: A Study of Vergil's "Aeneid"* [Berkeley: University
of California Press, 1976], 105).
    [74]*Euripides*, intro. and trans. Richmond Lattimore (Chicago: University of Chicago
Press, 1955–59).

gods' departure is that Troy is being turned, before our eyes, into an *erēmia*. This is a word for which the English equivalents usually employed ('desolation,' 'destitution,' 'deprivation') are much too literary and abstract to convey the force of absolute blank emptiness."[75] "*Erēmia*," Poole explains, roughly translates into "where man *is not*." It is associated "with a place . . . that *was* once full, rich, substantial, informed by presence, and that is now empty, hollow, drained, inhabited only by an absence . . . felt not simply as blankness, but as an aching, vicious wound."[76]

Thus, Dido's *pictura inani* comes to signify, like the severed trunk of Priam who is now "sine nomine corpus" (II.558), the *lack* that is Troy—an *erēmia*, a gap at the core of any attempt to (re)construct a Troy that may never have been. Troy is now an *apolis*, a kind of "no city" that exists "where man *is not*" and ruled by a king who "has no name" (even as Hecuba laments that Troy's name "shall soon be taken from thee"). That is why Dido's representations of Troy, inhabiting as they do the space between forgetting and remembering, are emphasized by Virgil as *inani*, which can be translated not just as "empty," but also as "meaningless"—a hermeneutic enigma. It is as if the deep (narrative) structure not only of the *Aeneid* but also of all epic literary history were founded on Aeneas's repressed memories of the fall of Troy, a Troy that continually threatens to disappear in the gaps of "an aching, vicious wound"—like the wound of the mutilated Priam, "avulsumque umeris caput" ("his head torn from his shoulders" [II.558]).

Thus, Aeneas's poignant viewing of the tableaux of Troy's destruction is not simply an act of memory, if by "memory" we mean a conscious reconstruction of the past. Freud insisted that memory was never a conscious process, but was always implicated in the workings of the unconscious. Although it could be argued that the only "origin" of any event lies in its remembrance, memory cannot "think" its origins, particularly any memory of a city "where man *is not*." Like the faculty of memory, epic seeks to constitute its origins, but it is because of the operations of memory that epic can only begin in medias res, constructed, *nachträglich*, in the belated activations of the unconscious.[77] Throughout so much of the *Aeneid*, as we

[75]Adrian Poole, "Trojan Disaster: Euripides' *The Trojan Women*," *Arion* 3:3 (1976), 264.

[76]Ibid., 265.

[77]The ambiguity that the psychic phenomenon of *Nachträglichkeit* exerts over the "accuracy" of Virgil's own narrative (re)constructions of Aeneas's escape from Troy is demonstrated in an observation by W. F. Jackson Knight, who argues: "In the Second

have seen, Troy exists only as representations—or, more specifically, as unconscious representations of a city neither fully remembered nor forgotten. And these representations of Troy themselves enact a mimesis of representation that demonstrates why memory cannot "think" its origins—and why Dido's murals conceal as much as they reveal about Troy's past and its role in Rome's future.

For Freud, memory and repression are inextricably linked. In *The Interpretation of Dreams*, he argues: "The effortless and regular avoidance by the psychical process of the memory of anything that had once been distressing affords us the prototype and first example of *psychical repression.*"[78] But it is in his study "The Unconscious" that Freud makes his ambitious attempt to explain the "origins" of repression. In his subsection "The Topographical Point of View," Freud posits his theory of the "double inscription" as one possible model for the mechanics of repression: "When a psychical act . . . is transposed from the system *Ucs.* into the system *Cs.* (or *Pcs.*), are we to suppose that this transposition involves a fresh record—as it were, a second registration—of the idea in question, which may thus be situated as well in a fresh psychical locality, and alongside of which the original unconscious registration continues to exist?"[79] According to this theory, when an unconscious representation becomes conscious, the result is a second "inscription" (or *Niederschrift*), inscribed simultaneously in both the unconscious and preconscious levels. In this topographical hypothesis, Freud emphasizes that the first inscription has always already resided in the unconscious. The key to this particular model of the unconscious, then, is that repression occurs before the subject has ever become aware that there is a distinction between the conscious and the unconscious. Thus, for the duration of Troy's burning, Aeneas experiences his escape not as a knowable event but as a repression "held within, hidden," the primal repression, as it were, that *creates* (retroactively) an unconscious for Aeneas—an unconscious that both sets

---

Aeneid Aeneas goes from the palace of Priam to his own home under the guidance and protection of his divine mother. But elsewhere, in the First *Aeneid*, he speaks as if his mother had guided him from Troy at the start of his wanderings. This has appeared to be an unsolved difficulty, for the earlier guidance of Venus has been missed" (*Vergil's Troy: Essays on the Second Book of the Aeneid* [Oxford: Basil Blackwell, 1932], 98). The "unsolved difficulty" that Knight alludes to could be nothing less than the loss of a definitive origin inherent in Virgil's *nachträglich* "remembrance" of his own version of Troy's fall.

[78]*SE* 5:600.
[79]*SE* 14:174.

the stage for the founding of Rome, while still allowing for all of Troy's returns of the repressed. Indeed, in order for the traumatizing attraction of these Trojan images to operate on Aeneas's unconscious, Troy must always already have existed in a state of primal repression.

This again is why Aeneas's confrontation with the Trojan murals and with its psychic collage of anxiety and desire is so affecting. "Troy," the city "where man *is not*," has, in some sense, never existed for Aeneas until its belated reconstruction in the *imagines* of Dido's Trojan *Ars memorativa*—which is why Aeneas and Achates, standing dumbstruck before these unanticipated images of the *fata Troiana*, scarcely know what to make of them: "res animos incognita turbat" ("this strange happening confuses them" [515]). For Freud, the psychic economy of the unconscious consists of "thing-representations" (*Sachvorstellungen*), nonverbalized or noncathected representations that are, in Laplanche and Leclaire's conception, "elements drawn from the realm of the imaginary—notably from visual imagination."[80] The possibility of the verbalization of these images is what Freud refers to as a process of "hypercathexis." If these unspoken ghosts of memory traces fail to become hypercathected, they run the risk of inducing trauma. (As Freud explains in *Beyond the Pleasure Principle*, "In the case of quite a number of traumas, the difference between systems that are unprepared and systems that are well prepared through being hypercathected may be a decisive factor in determining the outcome.")[81] The abreactive trauma of Aeneas's beholding of the murals of Troy's destruction is the trauma of a confrontation with the aftereffects of his own primal repression. The trauma of the images of the fatal dooms of the *Troiana fortuna* is its forcing to the surface of the uncathected, "incognita" memory traces of the fall of Troy, its premature invasion of Aeneas's "visual imagination" before Troy has ever been constructed as a memorable (as a *memorizable*) event in Aeneas's conscious.

From Troy to Rome

We should now consider the relationship between the origins of Troy's repression and the future trajectory of Aeneas's epic destiny

---

[80]Jean Laplanche and Serge Leclaire, "The Unconscious: A Psychoanalytic Study," trans. Patrick Hogan, *Yale French Studies: French Freud: Structural Studies in Psychoanalysis* 48 (1975), 162.
[81]*SE* 14:174.

and, specifically, why it is so difficult for Aeneas to move on to Rome as the New Troy. A theory of history needs an origin—and the origin of the *translatio imperii* traced by the literary history of dynastic epic is, as we have seen, located in a Troy that is always already repressed. The story of the founding of Rome as the *imperium sine fine*, as the "kingdom without *end*," in effect, then, has no *beginning*—no origin in any moment more definitive than Aeneas's primal repression. Freud claims that the unconscious experiences its "founding moment" in anticathexis, an unconscious process whose only originary claim is in withholding a repressed image from consciousness—in maintaining the existence of the unconscious by means of an always already repressed image. If the push toward Rome is, in some sense, the first *conscious* (the first originary) act in epic literary history, it establishes itself as such only insofar as it is dependent on the prior inscription of a repressed Troy in Aeneas's unconscious.

What is at stake in the *Aeneid*'s epic search for an origin to Aeneas's story is, among other things, how a psychical image comes into *being*. When repressed, anticathected images are hypercathected, or made conscious, the process entails replacing a repressed representation by another representation. As a process of replacement, then, hypercathexis is a translation (or *Übersetzung*) of the originally repressed thought. As a "translation," then, the psychic process of hypercathexis reminds us of another "translation" within history, the westward translation of power known as the *translatio imperii*, seeking a final resting place for Aeneas's fragmented Trojan remnant.[82] The theory of the *translatio imperii* should be as simple as a "translation," a replacement of a Homeric for a Roman psyche. But Dido's murals pose a troublesome question: which comes first in this westward movement—Troy or Rome? Even Freud's theory of the

[82]In a December 6, 1896, letter to Fliess, Freud writes, "A failure of translation—this is what is known clinically as 'repression'" (Masson, 208). A precise link between the concept of "translation" and Virgil's version of the *translatio imperii*, which specifically entails Aeneas's "carrying over" of the precious relics saved from the flames of a burning Troy to the new empire in Latium, is enabled by Nancy Kobrin's observation that "translation," when "translated" from the Italian *traslazione*, means "the moving of things from one locus to another, referring most often and paradigmatically to bodily remains of deceased persons" ("Freud and his *Fueros*: Toward a Preliminary Semiotics of the Psychoanalytic Transference," *Stanford Literary Review* 4:2 [1987], 205). The implications of *traslazione* are that the psychic process of translation (or Freud's *Übersetzung*) is inherently necrophilic, or at the least, fetishistic. In this context of *traslazione*, one thinks, for example, of Anchises being carried by Aeneas to a new land, even as he himself is holding the *sacra . . . patriosque penates* of old Troy.

origins of the unconscious is perhaps of limited use to us in sorting out the deceptively simple chronology posed by this question. Samuel Weber has convincingly undermined Freud's positing of anticathexis as the origin of the unconscious, arguing that "the tautology of this account is unmistakable: to explain repression, Freud posits an origin in which it has already taken place." In effect, as Weber proclaims, "repression is not identical-to-itself."[83] In the movement of the *translatio imperii*, Troy cannot be "identical-to-itself" because it becomes constituted *as* Troy (as the origin of the *translatio imperii*) only retroactively in Aeneas's consciousness of Rome as his new imperial home. If repression is not "identical-to-itself," then in the *Aeneid* repression falls somewhere between a Troy that never was and a Rome that cannot be until, in Panthus's words to Aeneas, "fuit Ilium," or "Troy has been."

The first half of the *Aeneid* demonstrates that the imperial trajectory from Troy to Rome is entangled in a curious metaleptic reversal whereby the operations of the unconscious subvert any account of historical origins. Is Rome the hypercathected effect of Aeneas's primal repression of Troy, or is Rome the cause of Troy as a primal event—both in epic history and in the individual ego formation of *pius* Aeneas? Does the translation of Troy to Rome perhaps serve as less a replacement than a belated reconstruction of a Troy that may never have been, but a Troy whose primal repression is nevertheless required for translation—for the *translatio imperii*—to occur? One implication of both Freud's "topographical" hypothesis of repression and of Dido's murals would be that Troy emerges as a (repressed) concept in the unconscious not as a prior event, but only after Jupiter's prophecy of an *imperium sine fine* posits a Rome that can create a distinction between the conscious and the unconscious. It is precisely this metaleptic reversal that enables a Troy whose symbols are Roman to coexist throughout so much of the *Aeneid* with a Rome whose symbols are Trojan. And Freud's theory of the "double inscription" sheds light on why it is so difficult for Aeneas to understand what the founding of Rome *means*, why he remains so susceptible to Troy's many returns of the repressed. Is Rome as the New Troy to be perceived as an old Troy made new, or is Rome a new inscription, achieving its new status only through the repressions of the old Troy into the recesses of Aeneas's unconscious?

[83]Samuel Weber, *The Legend of Freud* (Minneapolis: University of Minnesota Press, 1982), 42, 47.

The *Translatio Imperii* as Metaphoric Repression

Freud's mechanism of hypercathexis, as, specifically, a paradigm
of "translation," an elementary form of processing psychic material,
is suggestive of linguistic processes. As such, it may at this point
justify a Lacanian "return" to Freud in the form of Lacan's conception of the unconscious as less a repository of repressed meaning
(and, hence, a possible origin if it could be recovered or deduced)
than as itself a signifying (or tropic) process. To effect such a return
is to tease out further the subtleties involved in why the search for
epic origins is always "tautological." The following discussion eluci-
dates why we can abandon any goal of pinpointing either the origin
of repression or of Troy, and why not only the *Aeneid* but all of epic
history, even as it seeks prophetic fulfillment, must struggle in vain
for an origin. This, after all, is the cue that Virgil himself may be
giving the reader when we consider that Dido's invitation to Aeneas
to tell his story *a prima origine* (1.753) may be just such a reflection of
the poet's struggles to find a linguistic expression for a "beginning"
for memory. As Austin argues, "Latin expressions for 'beginning',
'origin', are often pleonastic."[84] And as a Lacanian return to Freud
demonstrates, the pleonasm informing Dido's request may be inherent in, and indeed a symptom of, the origins of epic narrative itself.

As I discussed earlier, the westward movement from Troy to
Rome traces the origin of the theoretical structure of the *translatio
imperii*. As the "translation" (or Freudian hypercathexis) of empire,
the *translatio imperii* signals that each successive attempt at the
founding of empire throughout Western history is an act of "carrying across" (much like Aeneas's carrying of his old father Anchises
across the *obscura limina* of Troy into a new destiny). The constitutive
trope of the *translatio imperii*, therefore, is metaphor (in the Greek
sense of *metaphorein* as "carrying across" or "trans-fer").[85] But any
metaphor is always implicated in the vexed question of a lack—of
something that is missing. Aristotle defined metaphor as, simply,
"giving the thing a name that belongs to something else" (*Poetics*,
1457b). In his *De Bono*, Albertus Magnus argues that metaphors are
always inaccurate representations ("metaphorica minus repraesen-
tant rem quam propria"), claiming (with no small significance for

---

[84]Austin, *P. Vergili Maronis*, 135.
[85]For a brief reference to the "translation" of empire as "transfer," see E. R. Curtius,
European Literature and the Latin Middle Ages, trans. Willard R. Trask (Princeton: Princeton University Press, 1953), 128.

any discussion of memory and epic origins) that they can be hard to remember.[86] More recently, Derrida warns that metaphor "has to reckon with a definite absence."[87] And if, as Lacan has argued, the trope of metaphor always conceals a repression, then the metaphoric basis of the *translatio imperii* problematizes its theoretical scope as, among other things, an account of historical origins. I now turn to the process by which the literary history of epic, and its necessary reliance on what is fundamentally the psychic act of metaphor, traces the story of its own figurality.

In "The Agency of the Letter in the Unconscious or Reason Since Freud," his most sustained discussion of the signifying operations of metaphor and metonymy, Lacan argues that "the creative spark of metaphor" occurs when one signifier replaces another in the signifying chain, "the occulted signifier remaining present through its (metonymic) connexion with the rest of the chain."[88] In Lacan's conception, a metaphor functions as such only by means of this crucial "occulted signifier." In the process by which metaphor is achieved, a new signifier replaces the original signifier, which, in turn, becomes the signified for the new signifier. The structure of the *translatio imperii*, its movement from a fallen dynasty to the founding of a new *imperium sine fine*, then, necessarily involves the occulting of Troy as the originary, repressed signifier, a retroactive effacement of the very origin of metaphor. Aeneas's founding of Rome is dependent on nothing less than a repression of Troy, a forgetting of origins perhaps most vividly portrayed when Aeneas, realizing that Creusa has become lost in the city's *obscura limina* during their frantic escape, confesses to Dido, "nec prius amissam respexi animumve reflexi" ("I did not look behind for her" [II.741]). For Orpheus, the act of looking back kills; but in the *Aeneid* the repression that results from *not* looking back keeps Troy's uncanny shades alive. The *translatio imperii*, in short, becomes possible at the moment of Aeneas's anti-Orphic failure to look back, the point at which Troy becomes occulted, forgotten.

But this forgetting of Troy as the occulted signifier fails to explain the remembrances of Troy embodied in its many *returns* of the repressed—and fails to explain why it is so difficult for Aeneas to em-

---

[86]Quoted in *The Art of Memory*, 75–76.
[87]Jacques Derrida, "White Mythology: Metaphor in the Text of Philosophy," *New Literary History* 5:1 (1974), 42.
[88]*Écrits*, 157.

brace Rome.[89] In the Lacanian formula for metaphoric repression, the replaced term enacts two roles that are neither fully contradictory nor fully complementary. Because the replaced term becomes both the occulted signifier *and* the new signified, the structure of metaphor is inevitably entangled in the interplay of presence and absence. As the "occulted signifier," Troy inaugurates the signifying chain of the *translatio imperii,* pointing toward Rome as the New Troy. In the structuration of the *translatio imperii,* then, the new signifier introduced into Aeneas's symbolic universe by Jupiter's prophecy is "Rome." But Troy "falls" not only in military defeat to the Greeks, but also, in the psychic structuration of the *translatio imperii* (and of Aeneas's unconscious), "falls" from its role as original signifier to the rank of the signified. As such, Troy now inhabits a precarious mental space that "falls" somewhere between signifier and signified. As the "new signified," Troy is now paradoxically established as both the origin and the goal of Rome as the new *imperium sine fine.* One of the major lessons of Lacanian psychoanalysis is that there is no "signified" that exists in anything other than a purely hypothetical state. In the chain of signification, the new signifier does not point to something that may be "known" (or recuperable, or consolidated), but rather installs the structure of lack that insures the estrangement of the signified. Thus Rome as the New Troy is caught up in the desire of the signifying chain of the *translatio imperii*—the desire to recuperate (to re-*originate*) the *reliquias Troiae* of a city that never was.

As a kind of "once and future" city, "Troy" cannot signify itself, but perfectly exemplifies the metaleptic interplay between the signifier and signified that is inherent in Lacan's model of metaphoric repression. For that matter, the founding of the *Aeneid*'s many "False Troys" (Aeneadae, Pergamum, Buthrotum, Carthage) are also vivid demonstrations that the signifier can never signify itself. These necrophilic monuments to a Trojan past stand as the "remainder" that contaminates any process of signification. As the lack which *is* representation, these "False Troys" are scarcely any less authentic than the efforts at a Trojan *renovatio* that characterize the literary

[89]As a means of further understanding how Dido's portraits of Troy's fatal dooms serve only to exert a regressive pull on Aeneas, we can consider Françoise Meltzer's tracing of the etymology of "portrait" to the Latin *protraho,* meaning both "to bring into the open, to reveal" and "to draw out in time, to defer" (*Salome and the Dance of Writing,* 175n12). This etymology, tracing the conflicting impulses of revelation and deferral, aptly embodies the persistence of Troy as the "occulted signifier" that Aeneas tries to "forget."

history of dynastic epic; and they structure the narrative of exile that is epic history. Just as it is indeterminate whether the signified comes first or is instead a belated construction of the signifier, so also does the fall of Troy (and the abandonment of a Homeric perspective) occur somewhere between re-placement by Rome and a retroactive placement of origin, a new signified forever lost in the metonymic chain of the *translatio imperii*. Thus, the metaleptic reversal of signifier and signified that characterizes the *translatio imperii* becomes the very narrative space of exile (and desire) itself. The metaphoric repression of the *translatio imperii* both keeps the memory of Troy alive (as the return of the repressed of the literary history of epic, and as the possibility of epic narrative itself), and retroactively installs it as a dead fiction.

Back to the Future: Epic Destiny and the Compulsion to Repeat

If repression is, fundamentally, a failure of translation, then the historical "translation" of power known as the *translatio imperii* is itself dependent on a "first" repression. Weber's difficulties with the tautologies, alluded to earlier, implicit in Freud's insistence on repression as an origin in which it has already taken place, suggest a means by which we can conclude our examination of the psychic complexities of Aeneas's encounter with Dido's Trojan murals, and begin to come to an understanding of the psychic process that creates Aeneas as a *subject* for epic narrative. As both an act of remembrance and as a symptom of Aeneas's ongoing struggle with Troy's returns of the repressed—as, indeed, a remembering that Troy has been forgotten—Dido's images on the temple doors become psychically registered only in the *obscura limina* between memory and forgetting. After narrating his tale to Dido, Aeneas, of course, responding to the urging of Mercury, moves on from Carthage and forgets the images he has seen. Or, perhaps, "negates" would be a more precise term here. In "The Unconscious," Freud defines negation (*Verneinung*) as "a substitute, at a higher level, for repression."[90] Thus, for Freud, negation enacts repression at a "higher level" of psychic organization—the kind of heightened consciousness that is intimately bound up with the foundation of cul-

[90]*SE* 14:90.

ture-building—with, to return to the term with which I opened this
chapter, a kind of "failed repression." In his essay "Negation,"
Freud further articulates this failed repression as the process by
which "the content of a repressed image or idea can make its way
into consciousness, on condition that it is *negated*. Negation is a way
of taking cognizance of what is repressed; indeed it is already a lifting of the repression, though not, of course, an acceptance of what
is repressed."[91] Thus, the Trojan *ekphrasis* makes its appearance early
in Aeneas's wanderings in order to enact a psychic bargain with the
hero. It allows him a glimpse into his own repression of Troy, in
exchange for its negation, its forgetting as part of the push toward
Rome. Repression, then (at the point at which it modulates into negation), is oddly concurrent with the *lifting* of repression—much like
the mist enveloping Aeneas that lifts after he has concluded his confrontation with the (repressed) images of his past. Indeed, in Book
XII, Jupiter and Juno reach an agreement whereby the Trojans will
merge and intermarry with the Latins until Troy exists no longer:
"occidit, occideritque sinas cum nomine Troia" ("Troy now has
fallen; let her name fall, too" [828]). The psychic phenomenon of the
negation of Troy demonstrates that the development of (epic) consciousness can only be simultaneous with repression—that the poetic impulse behind "secondary" epic (as the post-Homeric *Aeneid*
and successive dynastic epics are often referred to) is precisely concurrent with *primal* repression. It is the phenomenon of negation
that in some sense underwrites the concept of *pietas*, which is so
frequently used to refer to Aeneas's grim pursuit of his epic destiny
(and yet, in the final analysis, is so difficult to translate). As a kind
of dutiful and patriotic devotion to a future Rome, Aeneas's *pietas*,
his Roman conscience, masks its origin in a negated Troy.[92]

Because Troy is remembered only through its (de)negation, the
ghosts of Troy enact the disappearance of Troy's disappearance and
guarantee the fallen city's "repetition" along the signifying chain of
empire. Thus, in some sense, we can refer to the *translatio imperii*
itself as the recapitulative repetition compulsion of the literary history of epic. The denegation of Troy originates the structure of the

[91] *SE* 19:233.
[92] In his essay "Repetition and Ideology in the *Aeneid*," Quint argues that through
the virtue of *pietas*, "Virgil thus appears to dramatize the psychological implications,
even the psychological basis of the workings of politics and of political ideology" (12).
Pietas becomes, in the *Aeneid*, a crucial site of mediation between psyche and history,
the point at which, as Quint writes, "its psychological depth may already be doing
ideological work" (13).

translatio imperii—which, in turn, becomes nothing less than the compulsion to repeat Troy as the absent presence, to keep Troy (buried) alive as it is "translated" along the metonymic chain of empire. As Freud conceives it, the psychic phenomenon of repetition, like a denegated Troy itself, also occurs somewhere between forgetting and remembering. In his essay "Remembering, Repeating and Working Through," Freud argues that the compulsion to repeat "replaces the impulsion to remember."[93] We repeat an act as an avoidance of memory because it is easier to repeat than to remember.

The link between memory and repetition is forged in Freud's insistence that memory never recalls an "event," but rather repeats a structure. "We may say," argues Freud, "that the patient does not *remember* anything of what he has forgotten and repressed, but *acts* it out."[94] The psychic basis of an unconscious "acting out" of Troy can perhaps be traced to the strange transferences that occur between Aeneas and Dido when he responds to her invitation to tell his story, an exchange that is characterized by their mutual craving to *repeat* Troy. Dido must hear again and again of Troy's woes: "multa super Priamo rogitans, super Hectore multa" ("she asked Aeneas many questions: / of Priam; Hector" [1.750]). As he narrates, Aeneas, too, experiences the need to go back and *set things right*.[95] The result of Dido and Aeneas's interplay of narration and hypnotic listening is a poignant theater of the repetition compulsion, the need to *act out* that which cannot be reenacted. Thus, in the course of their mutual transference, once again the future of Rome becomes oddly bound up with the repetition of Troy as a memory-trace.

But despite his argument that "the patient does not *remember* anything of what he has forgotten and repressed, but *acts* it out," later in the same essay Freud complicates his own definition of repetition as a kind of forgetting by arguing, "As long as the patient is in the treatment he cannot escape from this compulsion to repeat; and in the end we understand that this is his way of remembering."[96] "*In the end*," argues Freud, repetition (like the *imperium sine fine*) has no beginning. As the nonorigin of the *translatio imperii*, repetition both

---

[93]*SE* 12:151.

[94]Ibid., 150.

[95]As Ronald R. MacDonald observes, "Aeneas's account of the Fall of Troy seems shadowed by subjectives and 'If only's,' pervaded by an implicit *utinam* [a "would that . . ."], as if to express the vain wish that these terrible events really could have happened in another way" (*The Burial-Places of Memory: Epic Underworlds in Vergil, Dante, and Milton* [Amherst: University of Massachusetts Press, 1987], 24).

[96]*SE* 12:150.

establishes Troy as its origin and the carrying across (the trans-fer) of metaphor to a Rome, a New Troy that renders the idea of an old Troy enigmatic. As, in Freud's terms, a "transference of the forgotten past,"[97] repetition forgets to remember its origin.

As much as metaphor, then, transference (and its enactment of repetition) is the constitutive trope of the *translatio imperii*—which is never an "event," but rather the repetition of a structure. Implicit in the very term *"translatio imperii"* is the "translation" of *translatio[nes]* as "transference." As a privileged cornerstone of psychoanalysis, transference is a mode of displacement and revision that occurs at the moment of repression, specifically the repetition of repression. As both the displacement of empire and a "transference of the forgotten past," the *translatio imperii* traces a psychic economy of repeating that insures that the "real" subject matter of the *imperium sine fine* is the repression of Troy. By constructing the primal scene, the analyst seeks to release the analysand from the repetition of symptomatic behavior—but there is no primal scene to construct. Repression is always the transference of a forgotten past that, even if it could be remembered, is unrepresentable.

Death Wounds

In the final analysis, then, it is the dialectic between Aeneas's remembering and forgetting that has rendered the fall of Troy throughout cultural history so memorable. The *Aeneid* represents the point at which memory, as a kind of naive, affective act of unself-consciousness, modulates into epic history, an aggressive (and arbitrary) attempt at locating origins, chronologies, aetiologies, continuities—and the placement of the individual ego within that temporal panoply. "History is perpetually suspicious of memory," writes Pierre Nora, "and its true mission is to suppress and destroy it."[98] Accordingly, Aeneas's "true mission" to found Rome is ultimately dependent on a suppression of Dido's Trojan memory theater (where the unconscious is, in some sense, too free to come to terms with its own repressions) and on a subsequent annihilation of Dido herself, who, in the final analysis, is held accountable for keeping

[97]Ibid., 151.
[98]Pierre Nora, "Between Memory and History: *Les Lieux de Mémoire*," *Representations* 26 (1989), 9.

obsolete genealogies in competition with the new Julian dynasty as the chosen *pater Romanus*.[99]

If, as we have seen, the unconscious is created at the moment of primal repression, what is entailed in the state of consciousness? What does it mean, in the context of epic history, *to be* conscious? Or, most fundamentally, how does the epic hero *become* conscious? The *Aeneid* provides some intriguing answers to these questions. Negation, and its enactment of the repetition compulsion, *is* the founding moment of consciousness in the literary history of epic; and, as its own kind of failed repression, negation opens up and makes possible the narrative space for successive epics. Throughout his professional career, Freud conceived of the state of consciousness as a process of overcoming resistances—as, in its most fundamental neurological state, the breaching (*Bahnung*) of barriers within sensory neurones. The breaching of these resisting barriers gives rise to consciousness as the effect of a kind of primal transgression. Like a young Pyrrhus crashing through the portals of Priam's palace to invade the inner sanctum harboring its old and fragile king, the narrative consciousness of the *Aeneid* itself crosses a barrier, insuring that Priam's slaughter occurs not only as a culminating event in the history of the fall of Troy, but also as an event exiled in Aeneas's unconscious—a weakened barrier of resistance that Aeneas transgresses (anticathects) when he leaves Carthage and its images of Priam's death behind.

If epic consciousness requires a transgressive murder, it is significant that Dido joins Priam in violent death. And if, as Joel Fineman has argued, "Every structure must begin with . . . a murder of its diacritical source,"[100] then both Priam and Dido, as the embodiments of cities that threaten the westward movement to Rome, are doomed to fall. (We are reminded here that it is the falls of cities—and the deaths of their leaders—not their foundings, that are so often the recurring and elegiac *topoi* of the *translatio imperii*). Ironically, it is with Aeneas's sword that Dido inflicts her fatal wound: "ensem re-

[99]See Otis for a discussion of Dido as a kind of "Homeric reminiscence" (58) that must be eliminated from Virgil's Roman narrative. Similarly, Barbara J. Bono, in her *Literary Transvaluation: From Vergilian Epic to Shakespearean Tragicomedy* (Berkeley: University of California Press, 1984), places Dido "in that tragic moment of history and consciousness that succeeded the era of the Homeric epics, and that it is the task of Vergilian epic to overcome" (24).

[100]Joel Fineman, "The Structure of Allegorical Desire," in *Allegory and Representation: Selected Papers from the English Institute, 1979–80*, ed. Stephen J. Greenblatt (Baltimore: Johns Hopkins University Press, 1981), 44.

cludit Dardanium" ("She unsheathes / the Dardan sword" [IV.647]). For Dido, even to the end unreconciled to Aeneas's Roman destiny, the instrument of death must be distinctly Dardanian. As Brooks Otis so concisely puts it, "the love *wound* becomes Dido's death *wound* and Carthage's as well."[101] Aeneas's "Dardanian" sword effects the "murder of its diacritical source," and it is a weapon that will not accompany him to Rome. Although Dido's murals presented Aeneas with a (retroactive) Troy that set in motion the mechanics of a primal unconscious, it is this same repressed Troy that effects the transgressive negation that empowers Aeneas through the "murder" of Dido and a departure from Carthage. Indeed, because of the failed repression of negation, it proves to be much easier for Aeneas to leave a declining Carthage and its bleeding queen than it was to leave the "aching, vicious" wound that was Troy. Rome can only be built in the gaps of Priam's and Dido's wounds— which is why, during Aeneas's journey to the Underworld, Dido, even in her bitter silence, succeeds in making a final statement about the morality of the *translatio imperii* and of cultural memory. Refusing to speak to Aeneas, she appears, "recens a vulnere" ("with her wound still fresh" [VI.450]).

Metaphor, as the constitutive trope of the *translatio imperii*, also, in Lacan's conception, marks the subject's accession to language. But the psychic toll exacted by the translational metaphor of dynastic epic reveals one of the major differences between Homeric epic and Virgilian secondary epic. In the *Odyssey*, the mechanics of memory, Odysseus's long-delayed narration of his travels (from Books IX to XII) in the palace of Alkinoös, marks the point at which the hero can begin to return *home*. But when Aeneas narrates his escape from Troy, Aeneas becomes a "speaking" subject alienated within the Symbolic. The driving forces behind Aeneas's story are *fata*, the singular of which is *fatum*, or "that which is spoken." But, as we have seen, what Aeneas must "speak" is a Troy that is *infandum*, "unsayable" or "unutterable." The "unspeakable" story of the exile from Troy is paradoxically the moment of Aeneas's accession to subjecthood, the moment he becomes a subject "speaking" from alienation.

In the *Aeneid*, then, cultural memory always eludes the plenitude of its own ambitious narrative because of its dependence on the retroactive structures of memory to locate an origin for the *translatio imperii*. Any repetition is an attempt to repeat the origin. But the

[101] *Virgil*, 95.

effort to remember Troy merely reveals memory as the limit of representation. The exile from Troy becomes the origin of the narcissistic self in history. It is in this sense, then, that Aeneas's *diversa exilia* constitute Troy as the lost other. But the narcissistic search for the other always exiles the subject from itself. The fate of the epic subject throughout the literary history of the *translatio imperii* is the narcissism that *is* exile. If historical representations of the past are inevitably bound up with the fate of the signifier—the ghosts that haunt representation itself—then Troy as the memory-trace of epic will always elude the self-consciousness of historiography.

CHAPTER THREE

Habendi Libido:
Ariosto's Armor of Narcissism

Habendi Libido: The Subject/Object Is Armor

The Carthaginian Dido's suicide by means of a Trojan weapon at this point prompts a consideration of the relationship between weapons and epic history. Romance, as we shall see, treats (displaced) weapons very differently from Virgilian epic; and the weapons of romance, rather than carrying us further along the signifying chain of empire, double back with a vengeance on Troy as the memory-trace of epic.

In Book VIII of the *Aeneid*, Aeneas's mother Venus presents to her son the gift of a suit of armor forged by Vulcan. The shield, clearly modeled on the shield that Hephaestus makes for Achilles (*Iliad*, XVIII), is, in effect, a second Virgilian *ekphrasis*, decorated with elaborate depictions of the dynastic future of Aeneas's descendants; and it serves as Virgil's more distinctly *Roman* counterpart to the cosmogony depicted on Achilles' shield. The shield of Aeneas—with its depictions of the defeat of Antony and Cleopatra at Actium, the repulse of the Gauls from the Capitol, the nursing of Romulus and Remus by the she-wolf, the rape of the Sabines, the expansion of Rome as an empire and the triumphs of Augustus's *pax Romana*, and so on—represents the point at which cosmic allegory meets history, the point at which the autochthonous origins of Attica evolve into a new kind of *urbs*, Rome as the site of future *imperium*.

But as Philip R. Hardie has argued, there is a simpler, and perhaps more crucial, difference between Achilles' and Aeneas's shields: "In the *Iliad* Achilles stands in real need of a new set of arms after the death of Patroclus, whereas in the *Aeneid* the gift of divine armour to Aeneas does not supply a pressing lack."[1] Though military conquest will loom large in Rome's future, Aeneas's shield, at this moment more decorative than functional, is foregrounded in Book VIII more as an object to be displayed than as a necessary instrument of war. It is an ekphrastic moment, frozen in time, when the scope of Roman destiny is associated with a focus on an object *as* an object. As in the episode of Dido's *ekphrasis*, Aeneas becomes the shield's passive, and not fully comprehending, spectator:

> Talia per clipeum Volcani, dona parentis
> miratur rerumque ignarus imagine gaudet
> attollens umero famamque et fata nepotum.
>
> (729–31)

> (Aeneas marvels at his mother's gift,
> the scenes on Vulcan's shield; and he is glad
> for all these images, though he does not
> know what they mean. Upon his shoulder he
> lifts up the fame and fate of his sons' sons.)

Here, Aeneas, still in some sense not having fully achieved an epic "consciousness," is uncertain of the meaning of these representations of Rome's future. Aeneas's shouldering of the shield signals nothing less than the shouldering of a new Roman destiny. But if Homer's *telamōn*, or shield-strap, is, as Hardie points out, "allegorized in Eustathius as the axis which supports the universe,"[2] in the *Aeneid* we begin to sense a narrower focus on weapons—the weapon as fetish object for the individual ego. Thus Aeneas's shield exists somewhere between serving as a weapon in combat and a weapon to be admired for itself as an object of interpretation and spectating.

In this context, we can now move to a consideration of the *Aeneid*'s final episode. Virgil's epic ends not with the founding of Roman "civilization," but rather with the "discontents" and individual pathos of the death of Turnus. Despite the elaborate political iconography of Aeneas's shield and its promise of fulfillment of *imper-*

[1] Philip R. Hardie, *Virgil's "Aeneid": Cosmos and Imperium* (Oxford: Clarendon Press, 1986), 337.
[2] Ibid., 341.

ium, the final event in the *Aeneid* is the descent of Turnus's grudging and resentful ghost to hell. It is important to note that the ferocious rage that incites Aeneas to finish off Turnus is less a surge of Roman *pietas* than it is his sight of the ornate belt of Pallas, which Turnus had ripped from the corpse of his youthful victim in earlier combat. Aeneas is inclined toward mercy until

> infelix umero cum apparuit alto
> balteus et notis fulserunt cingula bullis
> Pallantis pueri, victum quem vulnere Turnus
> straverat atque umeris inimicum insigne gerebat.
>
> (XII.941–44)

> (high on the Latin's shoulder he made out
> the luckless belt of Pallas, of the boy
> whom Turnus had defeated, wounded, stretched
> upon the battlefield, from whom he took
> this fatal sign to wear upon his back,
> this girdle glittering with familiar studs.)

At the sight of his young friend's belt, Aeneas angrily abuses Turnus: "tune hine spoliis indute meorum / eripiare mihi?" ("How can you who wear the spoils of my / dear comrade now escape me?" [947–48]).

One could argue that what ultimately defeats Turnus is not so much Aeneas's larger motivation by the tide of a Roman destiny as it is a dispute over possession of a gaudy piece of armor.[3] None of this is to trivialize the circumstances of Aeneas's heroic slaughter of Rome's enemy Turnus, but as we move into our discussion of the *Orlando furioso*, we should be attentive to the extent to which the *translatio imperii*, as it shifts from Rome to Charlemagne's Holy Roman Empire (and, by extension, to Ariosto's Ferrara), increasingly foregrounds armor qua armor as an object of self-conscious display.

---

[3]We are reminded here too of the foolhardy Euryalus, who steals the gold-embossed armor from the slain Rhamnes, only to be captured by Volcens when the heavy armor hampers his retreat from his pursuers (IX.358ff.). And, in this context, we can also think of Virgil's warrior maiden Camilla, who, in the midst of the heat of battle (XI.768ff.), fatefully pauses to covet the shimmering purple and gold tunic and armor of the Trojan Chloreus. A precursor of Mandricardo and his fetishizing of the Trojan armor of Hector, Camilla is obsessed with Chloreus's armor. But she pays for letting down her guard to indulge her fateful obsession: she is brutally cut down by the Etruscan Arruns.

We could argue that as the *translatio imperii* becomes more exiled along the signifying chain of empire, and as the Carolingian chivalric legends become assimilated into the genre of the epic romance,[4] the armor that bears the symbols of empire also becomes fragmented, scattered, and—in the end—fetishized as something to be *possessed*.

For Landino, as for so many Florentine Neoplatonists, the defeated Troy symbolized the corruption of the senses that Aeneas must strive to leave behind. In his *Disputationes Camaldulenses* (1480), Landino argues that the regions of Troy, Thrace, and Carthage are sites of pleasure that tempt the hero into "habendi libido," the "desire to possess."[5] But Landino could scarcely have foreseen the extent to which the New Troy of Ariosto's fictive version of the Holy Roman Empire would serve as such a thorough reincarnation of the affliction of *habendi libido*, and, specifically, the desire to possess armor.

Moreover, the scattering of armor, which, as we shall see, informs so much of the narrative structure of the *Furioso*, is largely responsible for the celebrated diffuseness (not to mention violence) of its plot. In his *Arte poetica* (1563), Minturno levels the *cinquecento* literary critics' most characteristic charge against Ariosto's long epic—he assails its lack of unity in plot and structure. The *Furioso*, he complains, is "una gran massa di persone, e di cose."[6] More recently, A. Bartlett Giamatti has vividly referred to the unrestrained violence of the genre of the epic romance, in its distinctly Italian manifestation, not as a *massa*, but as a *gelatine*, or "pudding."[7] Giamatti quotes an oddly pseudocomic passage from Pulci's *Morgante* that graphically describes the "ghastly carnage" of the battle at Roncesvalles:

un tegame
dove fusse di sangue un gran mortito,

---

[4]For a discussion of Ariosto's calculated appropriation of medieval romance, see Daniella DelCorno-Branca, *L' "Orlando furioso" e il romanzo cavalleresco medievale* (Florence: Leo S. Olschki Editore, 1973).

[5]This passage from Landino is quoted by Peter V. Marinelli in his *Ariosto and Boiardo: The Origins of "Orlando Furioso"* (Columbia: University of Missouri Press, 1987), 132. Marinelli's book is, among other things, an excellent study of the Neoplatonic revival as a background for an understanding of Ariosto.

[6]Quoted in Weinberg, 2:972.

[7]"Headlong Horses, Headless Horsemen: An Essay on the Chivalric Epics of Pulci, Boiardo, and Ariosto," in *Exile and Change*, 42.

di capi e di peducci e d'altro ossame
un certo guazzabuglio ribollito. . . .
(xxvii.56)[8]

(a pan
where there was a great stew of blood,
of heads and little feet and other bones,
a kind of boiled concoction. . . .)

Pulci's *guazzabuglio* is descriptive both of the aftermath of the epic *agon* of the *Furioso* (one thinks of Rodomonte hacking the Christian army to bits) and also of a kind of entropic and terrifying dissolution that pulls and tugs at the narrative structure of the *Furioso*, where combat is violent and dismemberingly grisly, such that aggression itself becomes a dominant theme.[9] In his essay "Reflections on the Psychoanalytic Concept of Aggression," the psychoanalyst Leo Stone, sounding uncannily like a *cinquecento* critic of romance, argues that the phenomenon of aggression is "the aggregate of diverse acts, having diverse origins, and bound together, sometimes loosely, by the nature of their impact on objects rather than by a demonstrably common and unitary drive."[10] Taking a cue from Stone, I would argue that there *is* a discernible unity in the "diverse acts" and "diverse origins" of the *Furioso*'s polysemous and sprawling plot—if by "unity" we mean the way in which Ariosto's characters, driven by an instinct for mastery (and a rage of the sort that motivates Aeneas to slaughter Turnus over a belt), focus on objects (and primarily armor) as targets for their aggressivity.[11]

The very title of Ariosto's version of the *translatio imperii* brings to the fore the psychopathology of the individual epic subject. Specifically, in this chapter I argue that the aggressive search for the object

[8]Ibid., 41.
[9]For a detailed account of the topos of "the debris of battle" in Uccello's *Battle of San Romano* that provides a useful backdrop for the violent dissolution of the *Furioso*, see Randolph Starn and Loren Partridge, "Representing War in the Renaissance: The Shield of Paolo Uccello," *Representations* 5 (1984), 33–65. See also J. R. Hale, "Sixteenth-Century Explanations of War and Violence," *Past and Present* 51 (1971), 3–26.
[10]Leo Stone, "Reflections on the Psychoanalytic Concept of Aggression," *The Psychoanalytic Quarterly* 40:2 (1971), 195.
[11]On the importance of violence and the concomitant theme of madness in the *Furioso*, see Neuro Bonifazi, *Le lettere infedeli* (Rome: Officina Edizioni, 1975), 110, 119–20. On the recurring violence of dueling, see DelCorno-Branca, 57–79. See also Albert Ascoli's account of Orlando's destructive love-madness for Angelica in his *Ariosto's Bitter Harmony: Crisis and Evasion in the Italian Renaissance* (Princeton: Princeton University Press, 1987), 304–31.

becomes the principle of psychic organization for the vast economy of narcissism that constitutes Ariosto's labyrinthine narrative. Despite Orlando's fabled pursuit of the elusive Angelica, I would suggest that the *furore* of aggression is just as prominent as erotic desire in motivating the poem's "diverse acts," an aggression that consistently blurs the distinction between a quintessentially Ariostan "comic excess" (its dissonant tone of *serio ludere*) and a hostile tension that makes characters such as the Turnus-like Rodomonte and Mandricardo two of the most viscerally frightening figures in all of epic literature.[12] As we shall see, in Ariosto's epic we are presented with a demonstration as dramatic as any of how neurosis (and, specifically, narcissism) can actually deform and displace ideology. Throughout much of the narrative, Charlemagne, after all, can do little more than wait helplessly as the *furore* of his knights—the violence of their object-libido—plays itself out through narcissistic aggression. Indeed, much of the comic wit of Ariosto's epic can be traced to the extent to which the fulfillment of epic destiny within his version of the translation of power is both shaped and deformed by narcissism as the dominant neurosis of the *Furioso*. *Furore*, then, is not just the designation for Orlando's love-madness, but is also, as a primitive kind of narcissistic object-libido, the dominant psychopathology of aggressiveness and of chivalry itself gone mad in the *Furioso*.[13]

Throughout my argument, readers will immediately recognize the informing presence of René Girard's theories of mimetic desire, particularly his assertion that "the subject desires the object because the rival desires it."[14] But because Lacan has made "desire" such a problematic concept, perhaps "mimetic narcissism" might be a more exact rendering of the hostility that structures rivalry.[15] If the *Aeneid* is

---

[12]For a vivid portrayal of Rodomonte's fierceness, see Attilio Momigliano, *Saggio sull' "Orlando furioso"* (Bari: Laterza, 1946), 270–97.

[13]On the theme of irrationality in the *Furioso*, see Robert M. Durling, *The Figure of the Poet in Renaissance Epic* (Cambridge: Harvard University Press, 1965), 160–76; Mario Santoro, *Letture Ariostesche* (Naples: Liguori, 1973), 29; Ascoli, 331–61.

[14]René Girard, *Violence and the Sacred*, trans. Patrick Gregory (Baltimore: Johns Hopkins University Press, 1977), 145.

[15]In his excellent study *The Freudian Subject*, trans. Catherine Porter (Stanford: Stanford University Press, 1988), Mikkel Borch-Jacobsen seeks a more precise mediation between Girard and psychoanalysis by placing mimetic rivalry in a more properly Freudian framework of narcissism. It is Borch-Jacobsen's Freudian reworking of Girard that, later in this chapter, enables us to see mimetic rivalry as truly the obscure threshold where violence (as the aftermath of the narcissistic wound) marks the alienation of the self in the desire of the other.

fundamentally concerned with the formation of an epic consciousness that points to a imperial future as the culmination of *pietas*,
then the *Furioso*'s focus on armor as the (precarious) means to subjecthood traces the narrative of a regressive narcissism. It is this informing impulse of a regressive narcissism that, as much as anything, explains the *Furioso*'s ethical void and absence of a moral
message, which any number of critics have traditionally found so
troubling. In the *Furioso*, where cultural memory has been relegated
to the spurious "authority" of a fictive Bishop Turpin, armor situates
its wearers not in the grand spectrum of genealogical and imperial
origins, but in the origins of the individual ego in alienation and
division. If, in the end, the Christians emerge victorious, it may only
be because they have obtained more objects of narcissistic desire
than the Saracens. In the *Aeneid*, the future of the new Roman *imperium* is neatly embodied in one shield; but in the *Furioso*, where armor is scattered to the four corners of the earth, no single weapon
can claim the prestige of embodying imperial destiny. Ariosto's concern is rather the history of the individual ego and armor as the
object of its desire.

One might conclude that any story that hinges on the restoration
of "lost wits" (*senno*) must be fundamentally about ego formation;
and yet in the *selve e boscherecci labirinti* of romance narrative, we
encounter no fully developed subject. The proliferation of characters
in the *Furioso* (with its namesake being just one hero among many)
underscores Ariosto's concern not with epic consciousness but the
myriad ways in which a number of different subjects implicate
themselves in the other in order to evade a totality of self.[16] Virtually
every character (with the possible exception of the aloof, distant superego Charlemagne) seems driven simply either to look for a lost
object or to seek to identify with it. One result of this shaping of the
epic quest as a search for the object qua object is that much of the

---

See also Paul Ricoeur, who argues that "narcissism is set within a vast economics in
which not only objects but also the respective positions of subject and object are
exchanged for one another" (*Freud and Philosophy: An Essay on Interpretation* [New
Haven: Yale University Press, 1970], 125). For an intriguing account of what she al-
ludes to as "the fascinating and ambivalent circulation of desire between René and
Sigmund" (26), see Toril Moi, "The Missing Mother: The Oedipal Rivalries of René
Girard," *Diacritics* 12 (1982), 21–31, and also Sarah Kofman's chapter "An Exciting
Enigma," in *The Enigma of Woman: Woman in Freud's Writings*, trans. Catherine Porter
(Ithaca: Cornell University Press, 1985), 59–65.

[16]Ascoli has perceptively argued that "the very multiplicity of characters . . . mili-
tates against the emergence in the *Furioso* of a 'fully represented self'" (49).

Furioso's narrative is structured by a narcissistic aggression that embroils its *furiosi* in militance, rivalry, competition, bloody hostility, mutilation, and infantile rage when objects of desire become lost or unattainable. Indeed, if we turn to Freud's inquiry into narcissism, we see that narcissistic aggression is directly implicated with the nature of object-cathexis and its suspension of the subject in a limbo between self and other. Freud sees an ambiguity in the motivation of the narcissistic subject: does he want to *have* the object, or to *be* the one who possesses it?[17] As we shall see, grappling with the implications of this ambiguity may enable us to answer *why* so much of the narrative structure of the *Furioso* entangles itself in errant wandering and deferral (not to mention in endless combat among individual knights)—a wandering that is forced to follow, in particular, the labyrinthine paths of scattered armor.[18]

If we consider the culmination of Ariosto's narrative of rivalry and aggression as occurring in the loss of Orlando's *senno* and the subsequent savage dispersal of his armor—a mimetic disintegration of the integrity of the human form and, hence, a disturbingly appropriate symbol of the annihilation of the ego—then we can begin to get a sense of why armor (and anxiety over its dispersal) is what I would argue to be the privileged trope of the *Furioso*, and why armor is as dispersed throughout the narrative as the identity it seeks to consolidate in a mimesis of the human form. Occupying an obscure threshold between serving as a protective shield against the Real of physi-

---

[17]*Group Psychology and the Analysis of the Ego; SE* 18:106.

[18]For the theme of romance "error" and wandering in the *Orlando*, see Eduardo Saccone, *Il sogetto del "Furioso"* (Naples: Liguori Editore, 1974), 210–47; Eugenio Donato, "'Per Selve e Boscherecci Labirinti': Desire and Narrative Structure in Ariosto's *Orlando Furioso*," in *Literary Theory / Renaissance Texts*, ed. Patricia Parker and David Quint (Baltimore: Johns Hopkins University Press, 1986), 33–62; and Patricia Parker's chapter on Ariosto, in particular the subsection "Ariosto and the 'Errors' of Romance," 16–30, in her *Inescapable Romance: Studies in the Poetics of a Mode* (Princeton: Princeton University Press, 1979). See Daniel Javitch, "'Cantus Interruptus' in the *Orlando Furioso*," *Modern Language Notes* 95:1 (1980), 66–80, for a discussion of Ariosto's delays, deferrals, and untimely interruptions as "one of the poem's didactic aims," designed to enable the reader "to bear the unpredictable frustration of our designs and aspirations" (79). In his lengthy essay "The One and the Many: A Reading of *Orlando Furioso*," *Arion* 5:2 (1966), 195–234, and its sequel in *Arion* 3:2 (1976), 146–219, D. S. Carne-Ross also discusses the theme of thwarted expectation and deferred ending in Ariosto's narrative structure. For an account of the structure of romance as a series of intersecting quests, see Sergio Zatti, "Il *Furioso* fra epos e romanzo," *Giornale storico della letteratura italiana* 103 (1986), 481–514. Zatti also discusses how the search for the object of desire in the *Furioso* modulates into a search for knowledge in his "L'inchiesta, e alcune considerazioni sulla forma dell'*Orlando furioso*," *Modern Language Notes* 103 (1988), 1–30.

cal wounding and as a metaphor for the psychic wounds of a primitive narcissism, armor in the *Furioso* is what keeps the narrative
poised on the precarious threshold of ego formation.

Theft without Return: The Object in/of Narrative

The desired object—a helmet, a horse, a shield—is persistently in
the forefront of the narrative of the *Furioso*. But of equal prominence
is the elusiveness of ownership and possession of that object. It is
the object's elusiveness (its ineffable quality of never quite being
"there" for appropriation) that necessarily prompts a theoretical digression into the ways in which narrative in general ensures that the
object is incapable by definition of being *possessed*. Only after this
digression can we fully understand the complex relationship between narrative and narcissism that structures so much of the *Furioso*.

The privileged objects of desire in the *Furioso* both invite and resist
ownership and possession. In short, they take on lives of their own.
Thus, we may first turn to a theoretical consideration of the question: when is something no longer a *thing*? We could turn for an
answer to Lacan, who transformed that privileged Freudian "thing"
known as the phallus into a signifier. Lacan would answer that
something is no longer a thing when it finds its "proper place." In
the case of the "purloined letter," the "thing" is revealed to be not a
thing, but rather a signifier that "will be *and* not be where it is wherever it goes."[19] Or, as Derrida suggests, the "proper place" of the
purloined letter is such that "it cannot be found where it is to be
found, or else . . . can be found where it cannot be found"[20]—and
indeed, in Poe's story, the Police fail to find the Queen's stolen letter
"everywhere" in the Minister's apartment. The proper place of the
letter is the "ex-centric" place of the unconscious; and one of the
major lessons of Lacan's "Seminar on 'The Purloined Letter'" is that
the letter is not simply "lost" or "hidden"—like a thing—because it
was never possessed to begin with. Thus Lacan focuses on the moment at which a thing (a letter) is no longer a "thing" but the signifier as pure difference, the signifier that points not to some-*thing*,
but to the lack (the lack of castration) that always has its "place"
such that it always "will be *and* not be where it is, wherever it goes."

[19]"Seminar on 'The Purloined Letter,'" 54.
[20]Jacques Derrida, "The Purveyor of Truth," *Yale French Studies: Graphesis: Perspectives in Literature and Philosophy* 52 (1975), 44.

A psychoanalytic hermeneutic, then, is frequently concerned with stories about things—but, more often, with things that do not retain their status as things. Thus we are presented with stories of, for example, the cotton-reel whose loss and subsequent relocation is such a source of pleasure for Freud's infant grandson Ernst in *Beyond the Pleasure Principle*. Or, as we have seen, we have Lacan's representation of Poe's "The Purloined Letter" and its drama of the letter's "theft without return." As these two stories demonstrate, we could say that the very basis of narrative is, in some fundamental sense, not just a thing but its retroactive foregrounding in the consciousness of the ego only after the loss of the thing (which is perhaps why, as Jonathan Culler has noted, narrative is "the preferred mode of explanation for psychoanalysis"[21]). Because the existence of a thing is so closely bound up with its loss or absence (as Freud and Lacan argue, perhaps bound up with the very basis of language itself), we are left with the tendency of the thing to slip into a liminal boundary between its existence in the Real and its existence only as a (belated) representation. It then becomes possible to argue that because the grandchild's cotton-reel inhabits the boundary between the loss and regaining of the maternal presence, and because the Queen's purloined letter takes on significance only after it has been lost, the deciphering of things by psychoanalysis prefers the representational status of not-*quite*-things, of things as representations (as Freud's *Vorstellungen*).

Any narrative that focuses on the object will always, in some sense, involve the transformation of lack into a signified that inadvertently assures the object's "theft without return." The "something" does not exist, but is hypostasized as a lack "in place." And this is when the thing becomes truly lost—"stolen" by a narrative whose subject can only be inevitably constituted out of an object that has been lost.

The object in narrative "belongs" to no one and has no possessor. The *habendi libido* that drives so many of the *Furioso*'s characters, then, becomes Ariosto's demonstration of what Lacan called the "realist's imbecility," the delusion that something can be possessed. Existing only in displacement, the object inhabits the ex-centric place of the unconscious, entangling the subject in the web of its itinerary. Both narrative and narcissism are based on the theft without return, with the object in narrative being as definitionally unattainable as

[21]Jonathan Culler, *The Pursuit of Signs: Semiotics, Literature, Deconstruction* (Ithaca: Cornell University Press, 1981), 178.

the ego ideal upon which narcissism is predicated. The point at
which something is no longer a thing, then, is the precise point of
(the ex-centric place of) narcissism.

For Ariosto, purloined objects—and the entangling itinerary of
their displacements—are *the* recurring theme of interest; and there is
hardly any aspect of his narrative untouched by the theft without
return.[22] We read, for example, of Caligorante's net, made by a
jealous Vulcan to entangle Mars and Venus, but stolen by Mercury
and ending up in the possession of Caligorante (15.56). Or we can
consider Ruggiero's sword Balisarda, originally belonging to Falerina
(in the *Orlando innamorato* of Boiardo, whose own narrative was
"purloined" by Ariosto), but seized by Orlando, then stolen by Brunello, and finally ending up in the "possession" of Ruggiero. Ruggiero's horse Frontino travels an itinerary from Sacripante to Ruggiero to Ippalca to Rodomonte and back again. Rinaldo's horse
Baiardo moves from Rinaldo to Angelica to Gradasso, as does his
helmet, which we are told he had won from Mambrino. The bracelet
that, like Ruggiero's Balisarda, circulates from the *Innamorato* to the
Furioso, originally belonged to Boiardo's Morgana, but then moves
from Ziliante to his rescuer Orlando, who gives it to Angelica, who,
in turn, gives it to her shepherd host and hostess. One of Ariosto's
more fantastic creations, the hippogriff, "purloins" its inexperienced
rider Ruggiero and soars high above the narrative's epic battlefields.
Perhaps the most entangled example of the displaced signifier in the
Furioso is the magic ring that confers invisibility on its wearer. Stolen
by Agramante from Angelica in India, the ring is then given to Brunello. Bradamante seizes it from Brunello and gives it to the prophet
Melissa, who then gives the ring to Ruggiero so that he can break
Alcina's spell. Ruggiero then gives it to Angelica, who uses it to aid
her own elusive itinerary as the primary object of desire in the *Furioso*. Perhaps the character who most spectacularly embodies the
theft without return is the slippery thief Brunello. Benedetto Croce,
his imagination captivated, described Brunello as "wander[ing]
about the earth, stealing the most carefully guarded objects, with an
audacious dexterity."[23] This consummate thief, through whom pass

[22]Remarking on the importance of ownership and theft in the *Furioso*, Ascoli mentions the "poem-long series of chivalric contests revolving around possession of essentially arbitrary elements of heroic identity—a sword, a suit of armor, a horse, an
'insegna'" (217).

[23]Benedetto Croce, *Ariosto, Shakespeare and Corneille*, trans. Douglas Ainslie (New
York: Henry Holt, 1920), 109.

virtually all of the purloined objects of the *Furioso*, has a direct hand in the thefts ("originating" in the *Innamorato*) of the magic ring, Marfisa's sword, Sacripante's horse, Orlando's horse and horn, and Ruggiero's horse and sword, Frontino and Balisarda.[24] We can finally add to this list Ariosto's "lunar junkyard," with its confused heap of objects lost, vanished, or displaced: the tears and sighs of lovers, vain projects, unfulfilled desires, swollen bladders (signifying the fallen empires along the *translatio imperii*), the ruins of cities, and, most notably, lost wits as the pathogenesis of the *Furioso* itself.[25]

As much as any theme, then, the object (a helmet, a horse, a ring) and its theft without return haunt the narrative of the *Furioso*. If the purloined object occupies much of Ariosto's narrative, then I would argue that armor is the fetishized object par excellence, constituting much of the latent organization of the poem. After all, the opening line of the *Furioso*, by declaring, through Virgilian parody, the poem's subject matter as "Le donne, i cavallier, l'arme, gli amori," already implicitly links amor (or *self*-amor) and armor in a web of narcissism and bloody combat.

But it is important to understand what Ariosto is trying to accomplish by rendering combat so bloody and hostile, especially in light of the struggles of past readers to come to terms with the poem's violence. C. P. Brand worries about the discrepancy between Ariosto's chivalric ideal, which exemplifies "bravery, energy, ambition, patriotism, religious faith," and the many selfish motives of the knights, such that "the war is forgotten for long sections of the poem."[26] Moreover, D. S. Carne-Ross quotes from a letter written by Shelley in 1818, complaining simply that Ariosto was "so cruel . . . in his descriptions [of combat]."[27] But this focus on the cruelty of combat and "forgetting" of war obscures the possibility that the principal drama of the *Furioso* is the primitive drive to possess armor and weaponry (and horses) as the character's only means to "iden-

[24]Peter DeSa Wiggins points out, "It is from Brunello that Ruggiero receives his horse, his sword, and his armor, so the earliest contact of his generous and honest nature with the world implicates him in multiple theft" (*Figures in Ariosto's Tapestry: Character and Design in the "Orlando Furioso"* [Baltimore: Johns Hopkins University Press, 1986], 70). I would argue that we can easily expand on Wiggins's well-perceived observation to conclude that virtually every character in the *Furioso* is both constitutive of and victimized by "multiple theft" (without return).

[25]For an ironic reading of Ariosto's "lunar junkyard," see David Quint's essay "Astolfo's Voyage to the Moon," *Yale Italian Studies* 1 (1977), 398–408.

[26]C. P. Brand, *Ludovico Ariosto: A Preface to the "Orlando Furioso"* (Edinburgh: Edinburgh University Press, 1974), 87, 88.

[27]"The One and the Many," 174.

tity." The extent to which armor is fetishized (and, hence, why it is fought over so furiously) is demonstrated by the many names of the individual pieces of weaponry—names that confer a kind of subject-hood that renders armor as much a character throughout the *Furioso* as any of its wearers. This named armor invites ownership (and hence hostility), even as possession of these fetishized pieces of armor is only potential, never actual, because armor throughout the *Furioso* always, like the purloined letter, "will be *and* not be where it is, wherever it goes." As we shall see, time and again throughout the *Furioso* armor achieves prominence (and incites hostility and aggression) only after it has been lost or stolen. But, as Lacan reminds us, it is symptomatic of the "realist's imbecility" to think that what has been lost was once possessed. There is no possessor of armor throughout the *Furioso* other than displacement itself. Neither fully lost nor fully stolen, armor finds its "proper place" only in the ex-centric place of its wearer's unconscious.

"The armour of an alienating identity"

Before we consider how narcissism structures the narrative of Ariosto's epic romance, we must first consider the pervasiveness of the role of armor and the extent to which it is fetishized as a mimesis of (anticipated) bodily wholeness. The knight's donning of armor is in more ways than one the assumption of chivalric identity.[28] In his celebrated account of the infant's "mirror stage," which situates the subject in an indeterminate space between bodily insufficiency and anticipation of wholeness, Lacan argues that this promise of totality leads to "the assumption of the armour of an alienating identity ['l'armure . . . d'une identité aliénante'], which will mark with its rigid structure the subject's entire mental development."[29] Lacan's metaphor positions armor as both protection against bodily fragmentation and also a proleptic symbol of wholeness—in the final analysis, scarcely more than "the armour of an alienating identity," or armor as the paradoxical locus of both narcissistic identification and aggression.

Early in the narrative, we are given the following simple introduc-

---

[28]In general, one principal effect of the chivalric insignias (*insegne*) on the shields of warriors was a kind of reification of family identity, and, by extension, a validation of the bearer's own identity.

[29]"The mirror stage," *Écrits*, 4.

tion to Rinaldo: "Indosso la corazza, l'elmo in testa, / la spada al fianco, e in braccio avea lo scudo" ("With shield upon his arm, in knightly wise, / Belted and nailed, his helmet on his head" [1.11]).[30] This spare, essential description of a knight and his armor is paradigmatic of virtually all of Ariosto's characters, identifying themselves, as they do, through their weaponry. Armor plays a persistent and pervasive role throughout the *Furioso*, far beyond its obvious function to protect. It appears in contexts of savage mutilation, as when Rodomonte, wearing Nimrod's armor (another premise "purloined" from the *Innamorato*), cleaves in two the torsos of numberless Christians with his sword, leaving them immersed in pools of blood.[31] It appears in comic contexts of thwarted resolve, as in the famous episode when Ruggiero is unable to rape the naked and defenseless Angelica because he cannot remove his cumbersome armor (10.114); and in the episode where Bradamante, fearing the Ruggiero has deserted her, flings herself in despair on her bed, full dress of armor and all—only to fail in her effort at suicide (a parody of Dido?) because her sword cannot penetrate her armor (32.36–44). Armor appears in emasculating contexts, as when the three kings, unhorsed and defeated by Bradamante, throw away their swords and vow not to wear their armor for a year (33.75), and when Rodomonte, also having been defeated by Bradamante, strips himself of his armor and casts it against the rocks (35.51). It appears in Oedipal contexts, as when the mage Atlante uses his enchanted, Medusa-like shield against Ruggiero to keep his *protégé* under his protection (2.57). Finally, armor plays a role in the revelation of the gender identity of the warrior maidens Bradamante and Marfisa, whose raised helmets constitute a recurring topos, revealing their womanhood to the idolatrous awe of their onlookers. Thus, armor is implicated in any number of traumatic stages in ego formation: humiliation and castration, impotence, infantile rage, and confusion and uncertainty on the brink of the assumption of gender identity.

Most of all, however, armor becomes, throughout the *Furioso*, a fetishized object of desire, exemplified by Ullania's long journey from Iceland to Paris to offer a golden shield to the best knight in Charlemagne's camp (32.52). Significantly, Bradamante worries

---

[30]All citations of the *Orlando furioso* are taken from *Ludovico Ariosto: Orlando furioso*, ed. Lanfranco Caretti (Milan: Riccardo Ricciardi Editore, 1954). The English translation is William Stewart Rose's *Ludovico Ariosto: Orlando Furioso*, ed. Stewart A. Baker and A. Bartlett Giamatti (Indianapolis: Bobbs-Merrill, 1968).

[31]For more on Rodomonte's "Babelic" armor, see Ascoli, 254, 351, 371.

about Ullania's trophy and her commodified challenge because, perhaps better than anyone else in the *Furioso*, the heroine knows that
armor is always the locus of narcissistic aggression and competitive-
ness:

> e in somma pensa
> che questo scudo in Francia sia per porre
> discordia e rissa e nimicizia immensa
> fra paladini et altri, se vuol Carlo
> chiarir chi sia il miglior, e a colui darlo.
>
> (32.60)

> (Much evermore evolving in her thought
> Things that may chance, she finally foresees
> That through the buckler by that damsel brought,
> Will follow strife and boundless enmities,
> Amid King Charles's peerage and the rest,
> If with that shield he shall reward the best.)

No one knows better than Bradamante how the aggressive quest for
identity through armor can only become the "armour of an alienating identity."

The need to keep one's armor (and identity) intact and whole is
vividly demonstrated by the warrior maiden Marfisa, whose story
"begins" in the *Orlando innamorato*. It is worth quoting Boiardo's introductory stanza in full:

> Marfisa la donzella è nominata,
> Questa ch'io dico; e fo cotanto fiera,
> Che ben cinque anni sempre stette armata
> Da il sol nascente al tramontar di sera,
> Perché al suo dio Macon se era avotata
> Con sacramento, la person altiera,
> Mai non spogliarse sbergo, piastre e maglia,
> Sin che tre re non prenda per battaglia.
>
> (1.16.29)[32]

> (The woman I've been telling of
> Is named Marfisa, one so fierce

---

[32]All citations of the *Orlando innamorato* are taken from *Orlando innamorato*, ed. Aldo
Scaglione (Turin: UTET, 1966). The English translation is *Matteo Maria Boiardo: Orlando
Innamorato*, trans. Charles Stanley Ross (Berkeley: University of California Press,
1989).

That she remained in arms for five years
From dawn until the dark of night.
The overreaching maid had sworn
A promise to her god Macone
To wear her hauberk, plate, and mail
Till she subdued three kings in battle.)

Armed from dawn until dusk, it is as if the *guerriera* Marfisa wears the "armor of an alienating [gender] identity" because she fears a kind of dissolution if she is not "sempre armata." Her entry into Ariosto's narrative is sudden, violent, and hostile, motivated by a furious search for her stolen armor. Ariosto's transition to the backdrop for Marfisa's introduction into his narrative serves as an occasion to abandon, like one of his wayward knights, the responsibilities of epic narration. In the midst of a Christian charge against the raging Rodomonte, Ariosto suddenly interrupts his own narration:

Ma lasciano, per Dio, Signore, ormai
di parlar d'ira e di cantar di morte;
e sia per questa volta detto assai
del Saracin non men crudel che forte.
(7.17)

(But let us, sir, for love of Heaven, forgo
Of anger and of death the noisome lore;
And be it deemed that I have said enow,
For this while, of that Saracen, not more
Cruel than strong.)

What interests Ariosto at this point is not the responsibilities of a Virgilian, epic narrator of war, but rather the *ira*, or wrath, of individual narcissism. The setting is Norandino's tournament in Damascus, with the victor's prize being a set of armor mysteriously discovered by a merchant. The elusive itinerary of the theft without return haunts Norandino's tournament, for although Grifone wins the contest, his prize armor is stolen by Martano. In a second tournament a canto later, Norandino displays Grifone's stolen armor as, again, the prize. But the combat is suddenly interrupted by Marfisa's disruptive entry on horseback and sudden seizure of the armor; and, in the process of her claiming of the armour, we learn the story of the armor's dispossession and displacement: first "owned" by Marfisa, then stolen by Brunello, then ending up in the possession of the merchants, then circulating from Grifone to Martano, and back again to Marfisa.

We will return to Marfisa later in another context, but let us continue our investigation of the *Furioso*'s many thefts without return with a consideration of the strange case of Ferraù's helmet. If the theft without return is, as Lacan would have it, the privileged narrative of psychoanalysis, then we might say that the in medias res structure of Ariosto's narrative begins as the theft *with* an (inadvertent) return. While kneeling to drink at a stream—frequently the site of an entropic loss of armor so disastrous for knights—the pagan Ferraù loses his helmet when it tumbles into the water (1.14), and the helmet's sudden fall and disappearance into the depths of the water take on an illusory, dream-like quality. In the odd clumsiness of this simple loss of an object, the origin of Ariosto's massive, labyrinthine narrative is constituted; indeed, the helmet's elusive itinerary throughout the *Furioso* is worth tracing.

For Ferraù, the loss of his helmet lingers as an obsession, for although, several stanzas later, he is momentarily diverted by a futile pursuit of Angelica, the pagan eventually doubles back on the stream (in a typical gambit of Ariostan wandering) and begins to renew his search for it (long after the reader has forgotten he has ever lost it). In one of the *Furioso*'s more curious episodes of mundane, almost antichivalric detail, Ferraù is described as poised on the banks of the stream, ignominiously poking its sandy bottom with a stick in a painstaking (if not comic) effort to retrieve his helmet. Suddenly, the ghost of a resentful Argalia, whom Ferraù had slain and whose armor (all except his helmet) the pagan knight had thrown contemptuously into the stream, rises from the water to reclaim his helmet. It is at this point that we begin to question whether the lost helmet (or, for that matter, any of the dispersed armor of the *Furioso*) has any origin at all.

The loss of Ferraù's helmet—as noted earlier, a kind of theft *with* return—is significant, then, for several reasons. The sudden tumbling of his helmet into the stream becomes synonymous with "losing one's head" and thus serves as a mimetic foreshadowing of Orlando's loss of his wits and subsequent madness. Indeed, it is Orlando (or, more accurately, Orlando's head) who becomes directly implicated in Ferraù's quest for a new helmet when the pagan vows to win Orlando's helmet as his replacement. This is the very helmet, we are told, Orlando had earlier taken from Almonte (even as Orlando himself will later search for "il bel corno d'Almonte" [40.47], which will fall into Agramante's possession).[33] Orlando, reenacting in canto 12 a familiar romance topos, hangs his helmet on a tree and challenges Ferraù (whom he had encountered in Atlante's palace of illusions as they both searched for the elusive Angelica) to claim it. Angelica, invisible by means of the magic ring, snatches Orlando's helmet away, rendering the ensuing battle between the two knights meaningless. When the privileged fetish is absent, the clash between Christian and pagan is without significance. Later, while resting, Angelica hangs the helmet (by now less a piece of protective armor than a fetishized object of display) on a tree, only to have Ferraù find it and reclaim it (12.62); and we are told that he is as happy with the helmet as he would have been with Angelica. (Indeed, it is a curious fact that Ferraù exits Ariosto's sprawling narrative as of canto 35, presumably still in possession of Orlando's helmet.)

At this point, Orlando's helmet, like the purloined letter, has taken on a life of its own, eluding the concepts of possession and ownership. What should not go unnoticed in this story of two helmets, however, is the pathos of Argalia and Almonte, two characters in the *Furioso* seldom considered because their fragmented identities have been effaced in the dispersal of their armor. Argalia's regaining of his helmet seems small compensation for the loss of his armor to Ferraù, not to mention the loss of his lance (8.17) and his horse Rabicano to Astolfo. A similar dispersal is suffered by Almonte, who, though never appearing in the *Furioso*, haunts the narrative with loss—specifically, the loss of his horn to Agramante, and of both his horse Brigliadoro and, most notably, his fateful sword Durindana to Orlando.

Thus, much of the epic action of the *Furioso* is less the *agon* of Christian against Saracen than it is the individual knight's quest to gather dispersed armor (or to hold on to what is already "possessed" but threatened with loss) as an aggressive stance against mutilation and incompleteness. Like a decapitated Priam, the uncanny ghost of Argalia will not rest until his "head" is restored and he achieves wholeness through a complete dress of armor. But as Argalia and Almonte demonstrate—never fully characters, but haunting reminders of the precariousness of ownership—armor (like the purloined letter, and indeed, like the signifier itself) is not a

---

[33]In this context, it is worth noting that Lacan's description of the unconscious in his *Seminar II* is *acéphale*, or "headless," "without a head" (*Le séminaire de Jacques Lacan, livre II*, ed. Jacques-Alain Miller [Paris: Seuil, 1973], 200).

substance; it can neither confer identity on its wearer, nor can it make its wearer in any sense identical to himself. Armor in the *Furioso* can be traced only in its effects (*vestigi*) as it passes from one covetous hand to the next; and, much like the *translatio imperii* itself, armor can seem to sustain its identity only in displacement.

Mandricardo and Durindana: Armor and the Revival of Troy

Perhaps the character with the strongest and most aggressive need for narcissistic identification through armor is the fierce pagan Mandricardo. Indeed, because of his specific quest to wear the armor of Hector, he becomes the paradigmatic embodiment of the displacement of armor as a metaphor for the *translatio imperii*. Thus, once again, Troy serves as a crucial site of mediation between psyche and history. Troy (and the *Ettor troian*) again becomes the repetition of a memory-trace, serving as the absent center for Mandricardo's destructive narcissism. What Mandricardo fails to learn, however, is that Troy, like the *Furioso*'s scattered armor, can exist only in dispossession and displacement.

In Syria, we are told in canto 14 (and in the *Orlando innamorato*), Mandricardo had won Hector's armor, except for his sword and shield—the very shield, we can assume, that had served as Astyanax's bier in *The Trojan Women*. For that matter, we can best appreciate the ghoulishness of Mandricardo's quest for all of Hector's arms by turning to Euripides' play, which, like the *Aeneid* and the *Furioso*, continually evokes the absent presence of Troy's dead hero. Specifically, we can look at Hecuba's lament for Astyanax, constructed as an apostrophe to Hector's shield:

> O shield, who guarded the strong shape of Hector's arm:
> the bravest man of all, who wore you once, is dead.
> How sweet the impression of his body on your sling,
> and at the true circle of your rim the stain of sweat
> where in the grind of his many combats Hector leaned
> his chin against you, and the drops fell from his brow!
>   (1194–99)[34]

Hecuba's poignant description of Hector's shield embodies the pathos of Troy's destruction, vividly depicted by the stains of Hector's

[34]*Euripides*, trans. Richmond Lattimore (Chicago: University of Chicago Press, 1955–59).

own battle sweat on its rim. This, we can presume, is the shield that Mandricardo craves in his quest to resurrect Hector's ghost. And this is the shield that, even as it suggests the "impression" of Hector's now mutilated body, will prove to be the "armour of an alienating identity" for Mandricardo.

But despite the rich significance of Hector's bloody shield, the most unacceptable loss for Mandricardo is the absence of Hector's sword, the infamous Durindana; and Mandricardo's search for it results in two of the principal tragedies of the *Furioso*, the deaths of Zerbino and Brandimarte. Durindana perfectly embodies the way in which the uncanny ghosts of Troy continue to haunt epic history, as the spectacular itinerary of Durindana's theft without return is associated with some of the most prestigious stops along the path of exile traced by the *translatio imperii*. Boiardo reports that it had first belonged to Hector; but its initial appearance in literary history is in the *Chanson de Roland*, where, as "Durendal," it had been presented to Charlemagne by God, with the emperor promising to give it to one of his best paladins, who turns out to be Roland. Boiardo's variant narrative reports that Orlando had won the sword from the luckless Almonte in the battle of Aspromonte.[35] In Ariosto's narrative, Durindana is securely in the possession of Orlando, and Mandricardo is driven to possess it.

Obsessed with the goal of having all of Hector's possessions, Mandricardo thus becomes one of the *Furioso's* more intimidating characters. His narcissistic aggression is polarized around a hostile, object-oriented libido that fetishizes Hector's armor as much more desirable even than his lover Doralice, whom he "purloined" from Rodomonte. Conventionally, the symbolism of epic armor, like the shield of Aeneas, is proleptic, promising future glory for empire and the warriors who fight for its cause; but in the hands of Mandricardo, armor becomes a relic, a regressive monument to dead and defeated empires, retrospectively and latently couched in a narrative that manifestly concerns itself with the future of the *translatio imperii*. In Mandricardo's aggressive quest, we are again confronted with Troy as the "insistence" of the signifier throughout epic history, the point at which epic ideology is deformed by narcissism.

In one sense, Mandricardo recalls the two major fetishizers of the

---

[35]In her introduction to her translation of the *Furioso*, Barbara Reynolds identifies the link between Hector and the Carolingian matter as the thirteenth-century French poem *Aspremont*, in which Hector, a friend of Almonte, gives him his sword (*Orlando Furioso* [Harmondsworth, Middlesex: Penguin Books Ltd., 1975],1:57n2).

fragmented *Troiana fortuna* in the *Aeneid*, Dido in Carthage and An-dromache in Buthrotum, who cherish the images and scattered relics of the Trojan holocaust, seeking to keep Troy's uncanny ghosts alive. But there is one major difference: Mandricardo's search for Hector's scattered armor, his *habendi libido*, is less a form of harmless (if pathetic) necrophilic reminiscence than it is a menacing drive to-ward ego formation through imitation of Hector as his narcissistic ego ideal. It is instructive at this point to contrast the single-minded-ness of Mandricardo with the errant truancy of Ruggiero (who, iron-ically, will later slay the pagan). It is Ruggiero, not Mandricardo, whose Trojan ancestry may legitimately be traced back to Hector, serving as the foundation of a Ferrarese *imperium* and as the precur-sor of Ippolito. But throughout the *Furioso*, Ruggiero, dodging the responsibilities of epic prophecy and deferring his union with Brada-mante, squanders the empowerments of his Trojan destiny, while Mandricardo engages in an aggressive quest to bring back the ghost of Hector—in effect, to *be* Hector. Thus, Mandricardo's involvement with the *Troiana fortuna* is directly implicated with the formation of ego, specifically with a narcissistic identification with Hector—a fatal identification unvalidated by epic destiny.

Mandricardo, however, cannot attain a Hector-like surrogateship until he wins Orlando's sword Durindana, truly the obscure thresh-old for the pagan between a narcissistic insufficiency and anticipa-tion. In canto 23, Orlando, reenacting the familiar topos of object-cathexis throughout the *Furioso*, hangs Durindana on a tree, and he and Mandricardo duel, hacking at each other fiercely with broken lances, in some sense symbolizing the castrative lack of wholeness of Hector's armor.[36] But the battle (and the "completion" of Man-dricardo's identity) is deferred when, in a quintessentially Ariostan moment of arbitrary happenstance, Mandricardo's skittish horse bolts and throws him in a ditch. At this point Durindana, like so much of the scattered armor throughout the *Furioso*, is set free to take on a life of its own.

As part of the savage obliteration of his selfhood following An-gelica's running away with Medoro, Orlando throws off his armor, scattering Durindana (23.133). A canto later, Zerbino happens upon Orlando's dispersed armor, gathers up the formless arms, and

---

[36]The clash between Orlando and Mandricardo is reminiscent of the fierce encoun-ter in the *Iliad* between Ajax and Diomedes, who fight for possession of Patroclus's spear, shield, and helmet (xxiii.815ff.).

hangs them on a pine tree with the words: "Armatura d'Orlando paladino" (24.57). Unconcerned with this simple validation of ownership, Mandricardo later seizes Durindana and uses it to kill Zerbino, who tries in vain to prevent the desecration of his monument to Orlando. Ranking as one of the great tragedies of Ariosto's epic, the slaughter of Zerbino should lead us to question what he dies *for*. We could say that Zerbino dies in an effort to save Orlando from symbolic mutilation by keeping his friend's armor whole and intact (even as the paladin loses his wits—and, in his frenzy, tears the heads off shepherds). But from Mandricardo's perspective, Zerbino has to die because the Christian is attempting to desecrate Hector and to deny the pagan an "ego" in the form of a Hector-like totality; he is attempting to keep Hector torn asunder, even as he is presumably fighting to establish Charlemagne's Holy Roman Empire as the Resurrection of the New Troy. Thus Zerbino dies, we could argue, in a discontinuous seam between epic and romance, which has been created by Troy as the repetition of a memory-trace. Never fully accommodated within the superstructure of epic prophecy (not to mention unable to effect a final reunion with his lover Issabella), Zerbino is expunged from the narrative of Ferrara as a New Troy by the one knight in the epic who is unable to move beyond the ghosts of the "old" Troy.

But Mandricardo's undisputed possession of the purloined sword Durindana is further complicated by the acquisitive Gradasso, who makes it clear that, for him at least, a large part of the Saracen campaign against the Christians is based on "ownership" of Hector's coveted sword. Indeed, Gradasso is one of Ariosto's more vivid demonstrations that, in epic history, there is no effective difference between the "neurotic" subject and the "ideological" subject. At the beginning of Boiardo's *Orlando innamorato*, we are told that Gradasso intends to invade France—not to battle the Christians, but to win possession of Durindana and Rinaldo's horse Baiardo. For Gradasso's motivation by a pure object-libido, we can turn to Boiardo, since, as Ariosto concedes, "credo ch'altrove voi l'abbiate letto" ("I think you will have read the tale elsewhere" [31.91]):

> E sì come egli avviene a' gran signori
> Che pur quel voglion che non ponno avere,
> E quanto son difficultà maggiori
> La desiata cosa ad ottenere,
> Pongono il regno spesso in grandi errori,
> Né posson quel che voglion possedere;

Così bramava quel pagan gagliardo
Sol Durindana e'l bon destrier Baiardo.

(1.1.5)

(And as it happens to great lords
Who only want what they can't have,
The greater obstacles there are
To reaching what they would obtain
The more they want, they cannot gain.
Thus that bold pagan only craved
The horse Bayard and Durindan.)

Like Mandricardo, Gradasso vividly exemplifies the differences in the principles of psychic organization between the romance and epic genres. If in epic the warrior subordinates himself to the higher ethical demands of culture building and defense of empire, then romance suspends the warrior in a limbo of primitive narcissism and ethical infantilization. Gradasso envisions himself not as a cog in Agramante's Saracen campaign against Charlemagne, but rather as the aggressive pursuer of lost objects whose fragmentation is threatening his identity.

In canto 26, the *Furioso*'s principal narcissistic combatants converge for bloody combat at Merlin's fountain, with the struggle for Durindana becoming a prime focus. Malagigi had earlier interpreted the fountain for Marfisa and Ruggiero as a locus of epic destiny, decorated, much like Aeneas's shield, with prophetic representations of the Ferrarese future; as Malagigi claims, "'Non è istoria / di ch'abbia autor fin qui fatto memoria'" ("'Hitherto their glory / No author has consigned to living story'" [26.38]). But Ariosto, unlike Virgil, is less interested in the relationship between cultural memory and history than he is in responding to the narrative demands of intricately documenting the interstices of his characters' *habendi libido*. When Mandricardo and Doralice, Rodomonte, Sacripante, and later Gradasso arrive on the scene, the fountain, despite its dynastic resonances, serves as the bloody backdrop of fierce combat as the knights entangle themselves in petty feuds to win the lost objects of their desire. Ruggiero (and later Sacripante) fights Rodomonte for possession of his horse Frontino, whom the pagan stole from Ippalca in canto 23. But Mandricardo wishes to fight Rodomonte over possession of Doralice. And, more important, Mandricardo, still obsessed with the consolidation of Hector's *reliquias Troiae*, also wants to combat Ruggiero over possession of the latter's shield painted with a white eagle—for Mandricardo, not just any shield, but the shield that had once belonged to Hector. Marfisa, always armed "da il sol nascente al tramontar di sera" ("from dawn until the dark of night"), craves the slaughter of Mandricardo for his slights to her honor as a female warrior. Finally, Gradasso, entering on the scene and watching Mandricardo arm himself with Durindana, claims the long-sought-after weapon from Mandricardo, who had only just recently seized it from Zerbino. The priorities of what Eugenio Donato has referred to as this "ritualized combat"[37] are so complexly muddled that the melee is without "origin." Ignoring their (epic) pledge to fight for Agramante or Charlemagne, the warriors first indulge their narcissistic needs, competing not just for the lost object, but also for the right to claim the most immediate need for narcissistic gratification. Any summary of the ensuing abortive and confused battles, then, constitutes less a summary of the particulars of literary plot than an account of the outcome of the conflicts of object-cathexis in rivalry, competition, and aggression; and the permutations of the participants' *habendi libido* are dizzying. Ruggiero is not free to fight for Frontino because Mandricardo wants his Trojan shield. Mandricardo is not free to concentrate on possession of the shield because Marfisa wants to kill him. Rodomonte is not free to win back Doralice because he refuses to relinquish Frontino. Only the dangerous Gradasso is unencumbered in his quest for Durindana.

Furthermore, in the midst of this confusion, we must consider the *fata Troiana* and its overdetermined entanglement in this matrix of narcissism. In the heat of combat, Marfisa is compared to Penthesilea (26.81), whose bravery in combat, perhaps not coincidentally, was the last of the depictions of the fall of Troy on Dido's portals. Ariosto's reference to Marfisa as a "Pentesilea" seems ironic when we consider that, in her role as the Troy-defending Amazon, she wants to kill Mandricardo, even as he attempts to enact his own defense of Troy as the memory-trace of epic in the form of a fetishized preservation of the wholeness of Hector's armor. Ruggiero, even as he seeks epic participation in the founding of Ferrara as the New Troy, refuses to relinquish either his horse or his shield, subordinating the goals of the *translatio imperii* (as embodied in the prophecy of Merlin's fountain) to the petty demands of narcissistic rivalry. In short, the more armor is scattered and fought over, the less coherent the theory of the *translatio imperii* becomes, and the more

---

[37]"Desire and Narrative Structure," 40.

Troy emerges as the "insistence" of a ghostly signifier that makes competing claims on the participants of epic history.

Surviving the confusion of the melee at Merlin's fountain, Durindana persists as the most highly prized and deadliest piece of weaponry in the *Furioso*—as, indeed, a "character" in the drama of the *translatio imperii* itself—even until the very end of the poem. In canto 30, Mandricardo nearly kills Ruggiero with Durindana, ironically destroying Hector's coveted shield in the process: "d'uno di quei gran colpi che far sanno, / gli fu lo scudo pel mezzo diviso, / e la corazza apertagli di sotto" ("By one of those fell blows which either knight / So well could plant, his shield was cleft in twain; / Beneath, his cuirass opened to the stroke" [30.52]). The cleaving of Hector's shield (*pel mezzo diviso*), the symbolic further tearing asunder of the *fata Troiana*, also destroys Mandricardo's quest to restore an originary "wholeness" to Hector. This task can be achieved only by Ruggiero and only by means of his fulfilling the prophetic destiny of Hector's line through marriage to Bradamante—not through Mandricardo's drive to ego formation through a fetishizing of Hector's scattered armor. Indeed, Ruggiero says as much earlier in canto 26, when he warns the pagan: "tu te l'usurpi, io 'l porto giustamente" ("'Tis thou usurpest what by right is mine" [104]). Mandricardo aims Durindana at Ruggiero's helmet, but Ruggiero fatally wounds him in the armpit. Thus, Mandricardo's fatal wound both signifies the deadliness of a Troy fetish and exposes armor as a precarious protection against both the Real of physical wounding and the Imaginary "alienating identity" of narcissistic wounding. In the aftermath of Mandricardo's slaughter, moreover, Hector's sword is again without an owner

In canto 31, the struggle for possession of Durindana is renewed when Gradasso and Rinaldo challenge each other to a duel, with the winner receiving both Durindana and Baiardo. But two cantos later, the combat is (predictably) deferred when a giant black bird, perhaps conjured by Malagigi, scares Baiardo into running away. Gradasso later finds the two prizes he has been seeking but arouses the fury of Orlando, who, even as the war between the Christians and the pagans reaches its climax, defers his responsibilities until he wins Durindana from Gradasso (40.56). Durindana then becomes involved in a second major tragedy in the *Furioso* when Gradasso uses it brutally to slay Orlando's companion Brandimarte right before the paladin's eyes:

Ah Durindana, dunque esser tu puoi
al tuo signore Orlando si crudele,
che la più grata compagnia e più fida
ch'egli abbia al mondo, inanzi tu gli uccida?

(41.100)

(So cruel, Durindana, can'st thou be,
To good Orlando, to thine ancient lord,
That thou can'st slaughter, in the warrior's view
Of all his friends the dearest and most true?)

A canto later, Orlando, wielding Ruggiero's sword Balisarda, gets his bloody revenge on Gradasso, but it is small compensation for Brandimarte's death. As Orlando returns to the mangled torso of his friend, he sees Brandimarte's head and helmet split in two: "Orlando l'elmo gli lèvo dal viso, / e ritrovò che 'l capo sino al naso / fra l'uno e l'altro ciglio era diviso" ("Orlando lifts the helmet, and descries / Brandimart's head by that destructive brand / Cleft even to his nose, between the eyes" [42.13]).

In its wake, then, Durindana leaves mutilation, destruction, and death. Mutilating not only bodies but also precariously formed egos that fatally seek to use it for their own unity and consolidation, Durindana is perhaps the most fateful and dangerous of all the purloined objects of the *Furioso*, never identical to itself but experienced only through its deadly effects. The perversities that Hector's sword perpetrates against the very Christians who are fighting to establish a New Troy merely underscore its grisly irony—its uncanny resistance to attachment to any one knight, its elusiveness in any effort to be used to achieve selfhood, its deadly refusal to participate in the consolidating impulse of the *translatio imperii*. Every corpse that has known the blade of Durindana serves to signify Troy as the (deadly) memory-trace of epic history.

Narcissism and Mimesis

What makes possession of a particular piece of armor or a horse so important that a substitute cannot suffice? Why must Mandricardo have only Durindana? Why must Ferraù have only Orlando's helmet? Why must Rodomonte have only Frontino? What is at stake in this fierce libidinal investment in a particular object? The persistence and intricacy of the *Furioso's* ongoing battle for objects—such that claims for ownership cannot be settled because they interfere with prior claims of possession—get us to the very origin of ego formation. To echo Girard, Ruggiero, Rodomonte, Mandricardo—all the *furiosi* who fight so savagely throughout the narrative for possession of an object—desire the object not in and of itself, but because it is desired by someone else. The impulse behind ego formation in the *Furioso* is less to be oneself than to be (to imitate) someone else and, thus, to possess his or her chivalric accoutrements. The ontological question at stake in the *Furioso* is not "to be or not to be," but rather *to resemble*—to look like, to be like the other. Or, in a corollary of the drive toward resemblance, the need to hold on to an object, such as Ruggiero's need to keep Frontino, or Orlando's need to keep Durindana (which persists even after Ariosto restores his "lost wits"), is directly proportionate to the degree to which it is desired by others. Orlando's desire for Durindana, for example, is intensified only when Mandricardo declares his desire for it (his desire to *be* Hector). Throughout the *Furioso*, then, desire should perhaps not be viewed as a function of "lack" (except for Orlando's desire for Angelica). If, as Lacan argues, the object of desire "isn't a question of recognizing something which would be entirely given,"[38] then throughout the *Furioso*, the objects of the *furiosi's* desire—a helmet, a shield, a sword, a horse—are immediately and explicitly recognizable, such that Mandricardo knows that it is Durindana and only Durindana that he wants for his sword. This is perhaps why the *strano intricamento* (or "strange intricacy") of Atlante's palace is such an eloquent symbol for the poem as a whole. In Atlante's palace of illusions, there is "a tutti par che quella cosa sia, / che più ciascun per sé brama e desia" ("To all of them the vision, seen apart, / Seemed that which each had singly most at heart" [12.20])—in short, it is the site of object-cathexis itself.

To pose the question again, what makes the object so important in the ego formation of Ariosto's *furiosi*, such that a replacement is unacceptable (even if the result is inevitably *dis*-placement)? For Freud, narcissistic object-choice is modeled on self-love. But a problem arises because the self can only be constituted through imitation of the other—and it is in this dialectic between self and other that narcissism originates. As Lacan describes it, narcissistic identification

---

[38]"Desire, Life and Death," *The Seminar of Jacques Lacan. Book II: The Ego in Freud's Theory and in the Technique of Psychoanalysis 1954–55*, ed. Jacques-Alain Miller, trans. Sylvana Tomaselli (New York: W. W. Norton, 1988), 229.

"is identification with the other which, under normal circumstances, enables man to locate precisely his imaginary and libidinal relation to the world in general."[39] This secondary narcissism arises from the subject's paradigmatic unwillingness, as Freud argues, "to forgo the narcissistic perfection of childhood,"[40] and this infantile reluctance becomes an aggressive need to recover a primal, narcissistic perfection through the new ego ideal. In the other, or the ego ideal, we have the semblance and the promise of a mastery of a primal narcissistic perfection first achieved in the maternal breast. But for Lacan, the tragedy of an inevitable transition into a secondary narcissism is that "the human being only sees his form materialised, whole, the mirage of himself, outside of himself."[41]

It is the mechanics of secondary narcissism that makes armor such a prominent focal point of object-cathexis throughout the *Orlando*. Again, as Lacan argues, "we recognise ourselves as body in so far as these others, who are indispensable for the recognition of our desire, also have bodies, or more exactly, in so far as we have one like them [*sic*]."[42] For Mandricardo, Ferraù, Gradasso, and others, a "libidinal relaton" to the world requires not just a body, but a *body of armor* that can facilitate imitation of others. Armor is not just any object; it is nothing less than the promise of the attainment of a psychic wholeness.

But armor is also the Lacanian "armour of an alienating identity," which, even as it invites imitation, serves as a reminder that narcissistic identification can be achieved only through aggression—which is why, to echo Shelley, Ariosto's descriptions of combat are "so cruel." Now we are at the heart of why so many of Ariosto's characters embroil themselves in hostile combat not just *with* armor as a necessary protection, but also *over* armor as the fetishized object of desire and display.

In "Mourning and Melancholia," Freud argues that "identification is a preliminary stage of object-choice."[43] The desire for an object, then, is determined by the desire to imitate others. In the beginning, egotistical libido is oriented less toward sexuality than it is toward the object and its potential to allow the self to imitate the other.

[39]"The Two Narcissisms," *The Seminar of Jacques Lacan. Book I: Freud's Papers on Technique 1953–54*, ed. Jacques Alain Miller, trans. John Forrester (New York: W. W. Norton, 1988), 125.
[40]*SE* 14:94.
[41]"Ego-ideal and Ideal Ego," *Sem. I*, 140.
[42]"Zeitlich-Entwicklungsgeschichte," *Sem. I*, 147.
[43]*SE* 14149.

Desire is mimesis, and mimesis, in turn, is always the locus of hostility, rivalry, competition, and rage. "The relativity of human desire in relation to the desire of the other," argues Lacan, "is what we recognise in every reaction of rivalry, of competition, and even in the entire development of civilization."[44]

No one understood this "relativity of human desire" better than Ariosto, whose persistent linking of violence and narcissism renders a hostile mimesis one of the pervasive themes of the *Furioso*. This is why, I would argue, romance and, in particular, the romance narrative of the *Furioso*, has no *telos*, no purpose beyond an errant wandering in search of an imitative other. Despite the epic superstructure that awaits the decisive conflict between Christian and Saracen, the collective goal of the characters themselves has not advanced beyond a primitive, individualistic narcissism that desires mimesis for its own sake. Mikkel Borch-Jacobsen observes that "no desiring subject (no 'I,' no ego) precedes the mimetic identification: identification brings the desiring subject into being."[45] But the process of identification that "brings the desiring subject into being" is inevitably constituted out of rivalry such that identification (mimesis) and rivalry amount to the same thing.[46]

The collapsing of the distinctions between identification and rivalry is, then, the real subject of the seemingly endless and pointless combat that structures the narrative of the *Furioso*. Ferraù needs to imitate Orlando through possession of his helmet, Rodomonte needs to imitate the infamous legend of Nimrod, Ruggiero desires Frontino only insofar as Rodomonte desires his horse, Gradasso needs to imitate Orlando (through Durindana) and Rinaldo (through Baiardo), Mandricardo desires to imitate Orlando *and*, more resonantly, Hector. Identity is dispersed because of fragmented armor,

---

[44]"Zeitlich-Entwicklungsgeschichte," *Sem. I*, 147. Or, in Jacqueline Rose's summary, "The mirror-phase demonstrates this process whereby the subject negates itself and burdens/accuses/attacks (*charger*) the other. . ." ("The Imaginary," in *The Talking Cure: Essays in Psychoanalysis and Language*, ed. Colin MacCabe [New York: St. Martin's, 1986], 139).

[45]*The Freudian Subject*, 47.

[46]This is the point at which I would seek to emend slightly Donato's account of rivalry in the *Furioso*. Donato argues that the rivalry among the knights in the melee at Merlin's fountain arises from the individual knight's "quest for recognition through the establishment of one's superiority—that is to say, one's difference from the others" (41). But I would suggest that we can adjust Donato's interpretation slightly to argue that the rivalrous quest for superiority is a result of the knight's need to be the *same* as the others he or she confronts. It is no mere quibble to insist that rather than seeking differentiation, Ariosto's knights seek rivalrous *identifications* with their imitative combatants.

and armor is dispersed because of fragmented identity. No one in the *Furioso*—not Ferraù, Mandricardo, Ruggiero, Rinaldo, Gradasso, Almonte (or, least of all, the fragmented ghost of Hector himself)— can claim selfhood, because everyone is implicated either in his or her own or in someone else's search for identity through rivalrous imitation of the other.

Thus the bloody and hostile clashes that characterize so much of the narrative of the *Furioso* arise not so much from the epic *agon* of the internecine conflict between Christian and Saracen, but from the characters' individual hatred of each other—a hatred created by the libidinal demands of narcissistic aggression. Girard claims, "Only someone who prevents us from satisfying a desire which he himself has inspired in us is truly an object of hatred."[47] In the *Furioso* a character hates another not because he fights for Charlemagne or for Agramante, but because the other has become a desirable model for imitation—and, thereby, a threatening assault on narcissistic perfection and wholeness. Brand notes with puzzlement the curiously scrupulous fairness with which these otherwise savage battles are fought: the knights "will not strike an opponent's horse; they remove their helmet, get down from their horse, etc., if their opponent is at a disadvantage."[48] I would argue that the fairness with which Ariosto's combative knights fight is less a response to the ethical demands of the rules of chivalric combat than it is a necessary guarantee that the other remains a mimetic model worthy of imitation. Unfair treachery would put the other at such a disadvantage that he would be less a mirror image of the self, and therefore less desirable as a mimetic image of potential wholeness.

The mimetic impulse that situates the subject between identification and rivalry is why armor is such a recurring and crucial choice for object-cathexis throughout the *Furioso*—why it is never simply the subject who is the object of mimesis and identification, but rather the subject adorned with armor. Because the shape of armor mimes the human body and because, as Lacan reminds us, "the human being only sees his form materialised, whole, the mirage of himself, outside of himself," armor exists somewhere between bodily insufficiency and the anticipation of wholeness; thus it becomes the locus of both mimetic desire and of a rivalrous hatred guaranteeing that its wearer can never become whole. Though ar-

---

[47]René Girard, *Deceit, Desire, and the Novel: Self and Other in Literary Structure*, trans. Yvonne Freccero (Baltimore: Johns Hopkins University Press, 1965), 10–11.

[48]*Ludovico Ariosto*, 95.

mor absorbs the wounds of the rival's hate, it remains the trope of
the individual's narcissism; it remains, despite its mimesis of the
human form, "the armour of an alienating identity."

Armor, Androgyny, and the "Truth" of Gender

One of the principal characters of the *Furioso* scarcely mentioned
so far is Bradamante, whose androgyny serves as a vivid demonstration that throughout Ariosto's epic there is little difference between
the "ideological" subject and the "neurotic" subject. As one of the
future dynastic spouses of Ferrara, Bradamante's accession to feminine sexuality is crucial for the realization of imperial prophecy. But
as one of the most formidable warriors fighting on the Christian
side, she is also, in her characteristic way, a quintessentially "neurotic" epic subject. In her combative androgyny, Bradamante exemplifies a kind of bisexual "hysteria," caught between masculinity and
femininity. Thus, even though Bradamante is destined to marry
Ruggiero, what is left unrepresented in Ferrara's epic prophecy is
her hysterical neurosis—her need to "defer" femininity and to imitate the male as the means of securing her own narcissistic identity.
     What happens when the woman, in her hysterical bisexuality,
driven to imitate the other (a drive that dominates so much of the
narrative of the *Furioso*), strives to be like a man? The concept of
mimetic rivalry gets to the heart of the gender dynamics of the *Furioso* where the "hysterical neuroses" of not just one, but two androgynous female warriors are so prominent. The subjecthood of both
Bradamante and Marfisa can only be constituted through imitation
of the *male* other—and this dialectic marks the space of a characteristically androgynous narcissism that threatens the fulfillment of
epic prophecy. Bradamante and Marfisa can forge a "libidinal relation" to the world only through imitation of the male body—a mimesis that deforms and delays the imperial prophecy of Ferrara.
     Again, armor plays a crucial role in the narcissism of androgyny,
serving, as it does, as a reminder that narcissistic identification can
be achieved only through aggression. The androgynes Bradamante
and Marfisa serve as dramatic illustrations of Freud's contention
that, in the beginning, egotistical libido does not derive from gender—that it is oriented less toward sexuality than it is toward the
object and its potential to induce the self to imitate the other. In the
case of the androgyne, the "object" desired is the phallus that can

achieve the imitative goal of being a man, and the wholeness of armor mimes the specifically male body as the locus of both mimetic desire and of a rivalrous hatred. In his essay "Femininity," Freud argues that an original bisexuality is common to both the male and the female.[49] Thus, gender can prove to be an unstable locus for identity, and Bradamante in particular seems caught in this bisexual bind. On the one hand, because Melissa's prophecy in Merlin's cave has identified her as Ruggiero's future spouse, the ideology of Ferrarese empire has specifically gendered her "female." But because she is still caught in a primitive web of mimetic narcissism, she is gendered "male," with her armor serving to mime the male body as the locus of both imitation and rivalry. But because, as was noted earlier, egotistical libido does not derive from gender (because an early bisexuality is common to both sexes), there may be no essential maleness or femaleness among Ariosto's narcissistic *furiosi*. Through her participation in mimetic rivalry with the male, then, Bradamante may be merely reflecting her own bisexuality back to herself.

Nowhere is the collapsing of the distinctions between identification and rivalry so vividly demonstrated as in the gender confusion posed by Bradamante's aggressive androgyny. Bradamante, of course, spends much of the *Furioso* looking for her wayward dynastic lover Ruggiero, but her jealousy also insures that Ruggiero is often less an object of love than of rivalrous identification. In canto 35, Bradamante angrily challenges her dynastic spouse-to-be to a duel in which he must don his armor. The message she gives to Fiordiligi for delivery to Ruggiero makes this condition ominously explicit:

> "Un cavallier che di provar si crede,
> e fare a tutto 'l mondo manifesto
> che contra lui sei mancator di fede;
> acciò ti trovi apparecchiato e presto,
> questo destrier, perch'io tel dia, mi diede.
> Dice che trovi tua piastra e tua maglia,
> e che l'aspetti a far teco battaglia."
>
> (35.60)

> ("Say thus, from point to point, 'A cavalier
> That would in combat prove his chivalry,
> And to the world at large would fain make clear

[49]"Femininity," *New Introductory Lectures on Psycho-analysis; SE* 22:131. In this context, see also Sarah Kofman's discussion of Freud's essay in her chapter "Psychoanalysis: The Child Becomes a Woman," in *The Enigma of Woman.*

> Thy breach of faith with him, that thou may'st be
> Ready and well prepared for the career,
> Gave me this horse, that I might give it thee.
> He bids thee promptly mail and corslet dight,
> And wait him, who with thee will wage the fight.'")

For Bradamante, if Ruggiero refuses to wear his armor, then presumably he need not show for the confrontation, for only armor can render Ruggiero the imitative model that Bradamante, so to speak, loves to hate—and only armor can serve as the necessary guarantee that the (male) other remain a mimetic model worthy of imitation.

But the gender confusion that lies at the heart of Bradamante's mimetic hostility toward Ruggiero is further complicated when we must consider what happens when two androgynous women enter into combat with one another. In canto 36, the combative Marfisa, bolstered by her *gran superbia*, shows up at the duel, determined to defend Ruggiero against her female mimetic rival: "et era armata, perché in altra guisa / è raro, o notte o dì, che tu la coglia" ("And armed withal for, save in iron vest, / Her seldom would you find by day or night" [36.16]). At this point, the two warrior maidens, virtual mirror images of one another, engage in ferocious battle:

> sì l'odio e l'ira le guerriere abbaglia,
> che fan da disperate la battaglia.
>
> A mezza spada vengono di botto;
> e per la gran superbia che l'ha accese,
> van pur inanzi, e si son già sì sotto,
> ch'altro non puon che venire alle prese.
> Le spade, il cui bisogno era interrotto,
> lascian cadere, e cercan nuove offese.
> (36.48–49)

> (So blinded are the pair with spite and rage,
> That they with desperate fury battle rage.
>
> At half-sword's length engage the struggling foes;
> And—such their stubborn mood—with shortened brand
> They still approach, and now so fiercely close,
> They cannot choose but grapple, hand to hand.
> Her sword, no longer needful, each forgoes;
> And either now new means of mischief planned.)

Blind with rage, eventually pummeling one another with feet and fists, Marfisa and Bradamante are hateful to one another because, in their androgynous fury, they are so *like* one another. The question arises: Do they combat one another because the rival is another woman (and a rival for Ruggiero) or because the rival is another "man"—and thereby an opponent to be both mimed and despised? To complicate further the processes of mimetic rivalry (not to mention a version of Ariostan pornography?), when Ruggiero tries to separate the two women, Marfisa, forgetting her immediate rival, turns angrily against *him*, the very chivalric model that she had so desperately sought to emulate ten cantos earlier when she fought by his side as his companion-in-arms during the combat at Merlin's fountain: "Sol mira ella Ruggier, sol con lui parla: / altri non par che vaglia" ("She speaks but with the Child, but him descries; / None prizes, values none, 'twould seem, beside" [26.29]). Marfisa's turning against Ruggiero demonstrates not only the interplay between identification and rivalry (indeed the very paradox that is narcissism), but also the precariousness of using gender as a nexus for attempting to interpret the complexities of this narcissistic rivalry. After all, the characteristic hysterical neurosis of the androgyne demonstrates that gender is irrelevant to narcissistic libido and indeed floats freely in its pursuit of mimetic rivals.

We should be suspicious of the fact that again, as in the case of the melee at Merlin's fountain, the three-way combat among Bradamante, Ruggiero, and Marfisa is so deceptively easy to narrate; after all, this narrative constitutes not just another combat among hostile knights, but the very impasse of narcissism itself, as well as the impossibility of trying to determine (at least where androgyny is concerned) what constitutes a specifically "male" or "female" narcissism. From a distance, the three-way combat would appear to be just another clash of male knights because of the protective armor that covers the combatants' bodies. But their armor is also "covering over" the complex ways in which the blurring of gender is intimately bound up with the subtle (in)distinctions between rivalry and identification. To quote again from Girard, "Only someone who prevents us from satisfying a desire which he himself has inspired in us is truly an object of hatred." Marfisa now "hates" Ruggiero; once her imitative double, Ruggiero now becomes her rival, because she is caught in an irresolution between wanting the phallus (his phallus) and thinking she already has it. Thus the "male" armor that both Marfisa and Bradamante wear has implicated them in an uncertainty as to whether they want to imitate Ruggiero or kill him (or whether they want to kill each other as the most effective means of self-identity through imitation). Finally, the episode illustrates that armor in the *Furioso* can only be the "armour of an alienating identity," never the "truth" of gender.

The confusion inherent in this episode also lies at the heart of the improbable and complexly transvestitic episode of Ricciardetto and Fiordispina (25.27–40). Though it is not concerned with any sort of hostile rivalry, it similarly reveals the unresolvable interplay between narcissism and gender confusion; in the unfortunate ardor of her own characteristic bisexual hysteria, Fiordispina simply is never sure if she wants a man or a woman—or both. Again, in this episode Fiordispina discovers that armor hides the truth of gender difference, only for the reader to realize that there is no "truth" to be discovered there. In Ricciardetto's leisurely and titillating narrative to Ruggiero, Fiordispina happens upon an unhelmeted Bradamante asleep by a stream (again, the locus of dispersed armor). Because the female warrior's hair has been closely cropped to allow a wound to heal, Fiordispina thinks the figure she sees is a man. In a parody of his own topos of gender revelation, Ariosto presents us with an unhelmeted female warrior who nevertheless *still* appears to be male. In one of Ariosto's more bizarre tales of thwarted desire and crossdressing, Fiordispina falls in love with Bradamante, only to discover the bitter truth that the warrior is female. In a ruse to seduce her, Ricciardetto, Bradamante's identical twin brother, visits Fiordispina dressed in Bradamante's armor. The clever Ricciardetto predicts accurately that Fiordispina will fall in love only with a man who dresses like a woman who dresses like a man. Fiordispina probes Ricciardetto's body in bed and is happy "poi che tocca e vede / quel di ch'avuto avea tanto desire" ("When by touch she knew / She had obtained the object of her zeal" [25.67]). But her "discovery" is dependent on her initial responsiveness to a suit of armor that hides the truth (or lie) of gender difference. In fact, we can scarcely be sure how to summarize the uncomfortable mix of comic poignancy and perversion that characterizes this episode. Its overdetermined combination of lesbian, transvestitic, and incestuous undercurrents not only points to a comic irresolution of Fiordispina's sexual impulses, but it also forces the sexual ambiguities of Bradamante and Ricciardetto to be played out through the "armor" of their own "alienating identities."[50] If, as Barbara Johnson has claimed, "the literary maneuver as such involves a rhetorical displacement or circumvention of literal sexuality,"[51] then armor is, throughout the *Furioso*, Ariosto's privileged trope of sexual displacement, circumvention, and alienation—the "literary maneuver" that defers any resolution of gender asymmetry.

For that matter, the incestuous undertones that contaminate Fiordispina's attachment to both sister and brother provide us with a means of comparing this episode to the three-way melee involving Marfisa, Bradamante, and Ruggiero discussed earlier. It is noteworthy that both episodes escape resolution; each episode experiences a conclusion that is as arbitrary as it is unsatisfying.[52] Searching for the

[50]For more on the erotic and incestuous consequences of Ariosto's two sets of twins (Bradamante and Ricciardetto, and Marfisa and Ruggiero), see John C. McLucas, "Ariosto and the Androgyne: Symmetries of Sex in the *Orlando Furioso*," Diss. Yale University, 1983. McLucas identifies the Fiordispina episode as explicitly lesbian. But Valeria Finucci, in her book, *Subjectivity and Representation in the Italian Renaissance: Women in Castiglione and Ariosto* (forthcoming from Stanford University Press, 1992), argues that although Ariosto toys with sexual transgression in this episode, he ultimately recuperates its sexually unsettling possibilities back into a heterosexual framework.

[51]Barbara Johnson, "The Critical Difference: BartheS/BalZac," in *The Critical Difference: Essays in the Rhetoric of Reading* (Baltimore: Johns Hopkins University Press, 1980), 15.

[52]There are at least two other episodes in the *Furioso* where Ariosto must impose arbitrary conclusions in order to "resolve" the narcissistic impasses of gender confusion that his female warriors become implicated in. In canto 19, Marfisa and a group of knights are shipwrecked on the island of Laiazzo in the city of Alessandretta (itself an aftermath of the Trojan War that owes its origins to the bastard offspring of the abandoned Greek wives and their young lovers), which is ironically a kingdom of *donne omicide*, or men-hating Amazons. Marfisa learns that she and the other stranded knights can be freed only if someone in their group can accept the ludicrously rigorous challenge of defeating ten of the Alessandrettans' captive knights in combat and of then surviving a night of intercourse with ten Amazons. The grotesqueness of the challenge of the *femine omicide*, combining, as it does, prowess in hostile combat and the promise of sexual symmetry and fulfillment of identity through intercourse, is the essence of narcissism itself—and absurdly, if predictably, Marfisa insists on being chosen to accept the challenge:

> et a Marfisa non mancava il core,
> ben che mal atta alla seconda danza;
> ma dove non l'aitasse la natura,
> con la spada supplir stava sicura.
> (19.69)

> (Nor failed renowned Marphisa's valiant heart,
> Albeit for the second dance unmeet;
> Secure, where nature had her aid denied,
> The want should with the falchion be supplied.)

phallus, Fiordispina "finds" it but on a man who is acceptable only insofar as he imitates his twin sister. The melee of canto 36 is "resolved" not through any sorting out of the complex entanglements of male and female narcissism, but rather when Ruggiero, in a violent attack against Marfisa, strikes his sword against a cypress tree, releasing the voice of the mage Atlante, now in the larger service of Christian epic prophecy. Atlante informs the startled combatants that they are twins (in a recapitulation of the mimetic "doubling" and the potential playing out of the incest fantasies of Bradamante and Ricciardetto), and also Christians whose father and grandfather had been slain by Agramante's uncle. This arbitrary epic "resolution," in which the hostility of Ruggiero and Marfisa's gender rivalry is bypassed by means of a common history that renders them brother and sister, is the quintessence of epic romance—with a murderous swipe at a despised rival releasing a "prophetic moment" for future *imperium*. But this prophetic moment occurs solely in response to the demands of an hysterical narcissism. We could argue here that epic prophecy (in the form of Atlante's prophecy) emerges merely as a belated (after)effect of the neuroses of mimetic narcis-

---

Hovering between wanting and having the phallus, Marfisa's gender confusion is responsible for a lengthy, convoluted episode which is eventually "concluded" not through Marfisa's prowess either as a male or a female, but through the arbitrariness of Astolfo's horn and its power to make enemies scatter for cover. (For a fuller discussion of the implications of Marfisa's entanglements in Alessandretta, see Thomas P. Roche, Jr., "Ariosto's Marfisa: Or, Camilla Domesticated," *Modern Language Notes* 103:1 [1988], 113–33, and Deanna Shemek, "Of Women, Knights, Arms, and Love: The *Querelle des Femmes* in Ariosto's Poem," *Modern Language Notes* 104:1 [1989], 77–80.)

Another episode of extravagant sexual challenges and the ambiguity of the sexuality of the female warrior (and a narrative that captured Spenser's attention) involves Bradamante's travels with Ullania. In a parody of the gallantry between knight and lady, Bradamante and Ullania seek shelter at the Rocca di Tristano (32.69ff.), where in order to gain admittance, Bradamante, in her incarnation as a male knight, must defeat three sentinels outside the castle. Entering as a woman, Bradamante is then told by her cruel host that only the fairest woman will be allowed to spend the night. Ullania is on the verge of being thrown out of the castle, when Bradamante "reverts" to her male identity, stepping forward and demanding to be considered a male knight and thus Ullania's "proper" escort. Although a comfortable night's sleep is achieved for Ullania, the uncomfortable ambiguity of Bradamante's sexuality remains unresolved. Though she handily defeats three knights, it is only through the arbitrariness of her own speech act (her own self-declaration that she is "male") that her competition with Ullania as a female can be circumvented and "resolved." If the Alessandrettan challenge is the embodiment of a Marfisan narcissism itself, then the threshold of the Rocca di Tristano, which Bradamante crosses as a "woman" but then must leave as a "man," is an appropriate symbol of the precariousness of ego formation that haunts the *Furioso*.

sism and (as was the case with Ricciardetto and Bradamante) of the fantasies of incest. Hysterical narcissism, in short, dictates the timing and direction of imperial prophecy.

Ruggiero's attack on Marfisa, then, though a resolution for much of the romance deferral that delays Charlemagne's victory, still leaves unresolved the "cleavages" of narcissism that rend the fabric of Ariosto's narrative. The miraculous workings of epic prophecy cannot make "whole" the "hole" of a gender asymmetry that makes aggression one of the most frequent outcomes of Eros in the *Furioso*. In the final analysis, the abyss of narcissism, the unapproachable and obscure threshold that keeps Ariosto's characters poised on the brink of ego formation, may have very little to do with gender and everything to do with the "armour of an alienating identity."

Furor and Epic Ideology

Our discussion of narcissistic aggression in the *Furioso* should turn at this point to a consideration of the narrative's namesake, to the fate of Orlando himself. As a vivid counterpoint to Mandricardo's quest for bodily unity through a meticulous consolidation of Hector's dispersed armor, Orlando enacts a Pulcian *guazzabuglio* of bodily dissolution, losing his *senno* (and his identity) at the point at which he scatters his armor. Agonizing that he has lost his beloved Angelica to the foot soldier Medoro, Orlando abandons any attempt at an epic subjecthood, declaring, in one of the more memorable statements of ego *de*-formation in the literary history of epic, "Non son, non sono io quel che paio in viso" ("I am not—am not what I seem to sight" [23.128]). As a symbolic final gesture of the annihilation of self, the mad Orlando scatters his armor:

> Qui riman l'elmo, e là riman lo scudo,
> lontan gli arnesi, e piu lontan l'usbergo:
> l'arme sue tutte, in somma vi concludo,
> avean pel bosco differente albergo.
> (23.133)

> (Here was his helmet, there his shield bestowed;
> His arms far off; and, farther than the rest,
> His cuirass; through the greenwood wide was strowed.)

Orlando's fate, then, demonstrates that just as the gathering of armor throughout the *Furioso* serves as the focus of the search for identity, so also does the *sparagmos* of armor mime the ego's destruction.

When, in canto 39, Orlando regains his *senno*, retrieved by Astolfo from the "lunar junkyard" of the moon, Ariosto has the opportunity to suggest that the dispossession and displacement of armor serve as a kind of necessary prelude, or first step, to the reconsolidation of selfhood. It is worthwhile nothing that it is the gatherers of armor throughout the *Furioso*, like Zerbino and Mandricardo, who are slated for death. Zerbino's efforts to gather and monumentalize Orlando's fragmented armor are abruptly greeted by slaughter at the hands of Mandricardo, whose own effort at monumentalizing Hector's arms is eventually smashed by Ruggiero. The need to consolidate armor throughout the *Furioso* inevitably inflicts the narcissistic wound that opens the ego to itself as the other (to the other as object of mimetic desire)—the narcissistic wound that, in turn, can only lead to death.

We are told that one of the marvels of the Achillean Orlando is that, except for the soles of his feet, he is impervious to physical wounding (notwithstanding his festering love-wound for Angelica). Thus it becomes one of Ariosto's more intriguing ironies throughout his narrative that Orlando does not even need armor. We also know that the paladin (along with Astolfo) is the only character in the *Furioso* to be privileged with the restoration of his lost wits, and thus one could make a potentially interesting association between Orlando's physical invulnerability and the intactness of his newly achieved identity. But Ariosto resists the predictability of exempting Orlando from his allegory of armor as the site of an alienating identity. The poet refuses the obvious narrative move of using Orlando's willful scattering of his armor to lift him out of the narrative's cycle of narcissistic wounding by which knights embark on the deadly quest to consolidate their own identities through the armor of the other. For even after the "cure" of his love-wound, Orlando is still a *furioso* where the possession of armor is concerned.

In one of the more wildly extravagant excesses of Ariosto's serio-comic narrative, Orlando spots a beached vessel on the shores of Biserta, containing Ruggiero's suit of armor, his sword Balisarda, and his horse Frontino. In a comic moment, Ariosto can scarcely resist telling the narrative of their "purloining" all over again:

So che tutta l'istoria avete letta,
come la tolse a Falerina, al tempo
che le distrusse anco il giardin sì bello,
e come a lui poi la rubò Brunello.

(41.26)

(. . . the tale's upon record,
And ye have read it all, as well I wite;
How Falerina lost it to that lord,
When waste as well her beauteous bowers he laid;
And how from him Brunello stole the blade.)

(It is interesting to note here how armor—and the tale of its purloining—occasions what amounts to a parody of the tracing of who
"owns" the origins of narrative itself.) But it is Orlando's distribu-
tion of the armor that should command our attention here. Orlando
gives the armor to Oliviero, and Frontino to his friend Brandimarte.
But, in the absence of Durindana, the paladin keeps the ornate Balisarda for himself, which he then uses at the decisive battle of
Lipadusa.[53] The restoration of identity symbolized by Orlando's in-
halation of his lost wits is not sufficient to resist the power of object-libido throughout Ariosto's narrative. Orlando's reason for
reentering battle with the pagans is not an Aeneas-like *pietas*, but
a rapacious need for his scattered armor; and Ariosto's narration
guides us to the heart of object-cathexis itself:

Avea dai suoi compagni udito inante
che Durindana al fianco s'avea messo
il re Gradasso: onde egli per desire
di racquistarla in India volea gire,

stimando non aver Gradasso altrove,
poi ch'udì che di Francia era partito.
Or più vicin gli è offerto luogo, dove
spera che 'l suo gli fia restituito.
Il bel corno d'Almonte anco lo muove
ad accettar sì volentier lo 'nvito,
e Brigliador non men; che sapea in mano
esser venuti al figlio di Troiano.

(40.56–57)

---

[53]Wiggins has cogently noted the tragic irony implicit in Orlando's fateful distribu-
tion of arms, "when he gives Oliviero the armor that might have saved Brandimarte's
life and Brandimarte the horse that might have saved Oliviero his crushed foot" (137).

(From his companions had he heard whilere
That Durindane was in Gradasso's hold:
Hence, to retrieve that faulchion from the foe,
To India had the Count resolved to go:

Deeming he should not find that king elsewhere,
Who, so he heard, had sailed from the French shore.
A nearer place is offered now; and there
He hopes Gradasso shall his prize restore;
Moved also by Almonte's bugle rare,
To accept the challenge which the herald bore;
Nor less by Brigliardo; since he knew
In Agramant's possession were the two.)

Thus, the only Saracens the arrogant Orlando is motivated to fight
are the ones who dare to "possess" his scattered armor.[54]

Orlando's *furore* is another vivid demonstration that, within the
translations of power known as epic history, there can be no effective difference between the "neurotic" (or narcissistic) subject and
the "ideological" subject. Although superficially it would appear
that Orlando's *furore* marks the point in Ariosto's epic at which the
individual unconscious is resisting interpellation within epic prophecy, we can more properly argue that because *furore* is such a dominant psychopathology within the epic narrative, it is perhaps more a
case of the ideology of epic finally *coinciding* with neurotic *furore*. Or,

---

[54]We might note that it is Orlando's idealizing of armor that serves as the occasion
for one of the more elegiac moments in the *Furioso*. Enacting what had become, in
light of current events on the battlefield, an increasingly frequent topos in Renaissance poetry, Ariosto laments the decline of chivalry in the face of the new military
technology, specifically the invention of artillery and firearms—the very weapons
that Alfonso had used to destroy the Spanish, turning the battle of Ravenna (1512)
into such a nightmarish bloodbath: "o scelerata e brutta / invension" (11.26). In the
aftermath of the *guazzabuglio* that was Ravenna, the body count could only exceed
(narrative) imagination. Because he is driven by a desire for the fetishized fragments
of scattered armor, Orlando harbors an intense fear of the new military technology. In
canto 9, he throws Cimosco's cannon over a cliff, crying, "O maledetto, o abominoso
ordigno" (91). In his essay "Gunpowder as Transgressive Invention in Ronsard," Ull-
rich Langer quotes from a poem by Ronsard, "Les Armes," where the poet laments
that because of the invention of guns, "on ne voit plus d'Hectors . . ." (in *Literary
Theory/Renaissance Texts*, ed. Parker and Quint, 105). One sees no Hectors anymore
because the loathsome and fearful new technology mocks individual heroism and
annihilates the precious identificatory insignias of the hero's armor, smashing even its
images of physical wholeness into smithereens. As Langer observes, in the wake of
the new technology, "one no longer knows one's opponent . . ." (105). And when
one no longer knows one's opponent, then armor loses not just its physical usefulness but also its *psychic* usefulness as the site of a hostile and rivalrous narcissism.

in the specific case of the Christians, we could argue that Orlando's narcissistic aggression actually *enables* Charlemagne's campaign against the Saracens. Following the restoration of his "lost wits," Orlando seeks not Rodomonte, certainly his more properly "epic" opponent (and certainly his rival as the fiercest *furioso* in Ariosto's epic), but rather Gradasso as the possessor of his sword Durindana, and Agramante as the possessor of his horse Brigliadoro and Almonte's horn. The *furore* of Orlando's object-libido becomes the space of romance deferral, of the delay of "proper" epic combat—but this deferral actually *enables* the epic purpose of the Christians. At the point at which Orlando, afflicted with *subit'ira* ("sudden fury"), slaughters Agramante and Gradasso in rapid succession, epic prophecy finds itself realized by means of the acquisitiveness of a narcissistic object-libido.

Thus, the psychopathologies of *furore* and of narcissistic *ira* can be perceived as inhabiting a seam between the genres of epic and romance. Orlando's *furore* is spurred by an aggressive need to regain Durindana, Brigliadoro, and Almonte's horn—an acquisitiveness that marks the very narcissistic space of romance deferral. But it just so happens that this same narcissistic *furore* has the result of eliminating the pagan leader Agramante and one of his fiercest warriors, Gradasso, such that the satisfaction of (romance) object-libido becomes homologous with the responsibilities of a loftier epic *agon*. Again, it is a stroke of Ariosto's comic genius that throughout his epic there is no distinction between the "neurotic" subject of romance and the "ideological" subject of epic. Charlemagne "wins" his campaign against the Saracens because the aggressive object-libido of the Christians proves in the end to be more intense than that of the likes of Agramante, Gradasso, or Mandricardo. Thus, in the *Furioso*, the fulfillment of epic prophecy is intimately entangled with neurotic *furore*. Indeed, it is almost as if epic history, rather than interpellating the individual psyche within its translations of power, is itself engulfed by the narcissistic demands of the psyche.

Troia vittrice: Narcissism and the "Truth" of History

In light of the *Furioso's* dispersal of armor and the narcissistic rivalry it incites, what final considerations can we come to concerning the *fata Troiana* and the quest for a New Troy, which was the object of our inquiry in the previous chapter? We can conclude our discussion by speaking of a narcissism not only of individual characters in the *Furioso*, but also of a narcissism of the literary and historical concept of the *translatio imperii* itself. At the beginning of this chapter, I raised the point that, as Freud argues, there is an inherent ambiguity in object-cathexis: does the subject want to *have* the object, or to *be* the object (as if the object could be introjected)? Freud's conundrum raises a number of questions for the literary history of epic. What is entailed in the "desire" of empire such that it sets up Troy as its imitative model? What is the relationship between the *Furioso*'s narcissistic aggressivity (and its emphasis on the purloined object) and the repetition compulsion of the *translatio imperii*?

To open our investigation of these questions, we can return to the example of Mandricardo. In echo of Ronsard's "Les Armes," "on ne voit plus d'Hectors." But, as we have seen, Mandricardo clings to the remembrance of "obsolete" heroes. The narcissism of Mandricardo dictates that he wants to *be* the object, specifically a pseudo-Hector decked out in the Trojan warrior's ghostly relics. If, as Moustapha Safouan has so eloquently put it, "the subject can only signify himself on the condition of being hidden from view,"[55] then Mandricardo can achieve subjecthood only if he obliterates himself in the armor of Hector, the perfect exemplar of the Lacanian axiom that a signifier represents a subject (only) for another signifier. Less a unified subject than a collection of Trojan signifiers, Mandricardo, like Aeneas stalled in front of Dido's murals, seeks to trace the origin of his ghostly (dis)embodiment of Troy to the hideously mangled body of Hector, which, in some sense, was a unified totality only in the retrospections of memory.

If the narcissism of Mandricardo dictates that he wants to *be* a remembering of Trojan nostalgia, then the narcissism of the theoretical construct of the *translatio imperii* traces a slightly different path. The desire of the *translatio imperii*, in perhaps an even more aggressively libidinal investment than Mandricardo's, is such that it wants to *have* Troy as part of its translations of power. At the conclusion of the *Furioso*, Ariosto's version of the *translatio imperii* enacts its own object-cathexis in the form of Cassandra's pavilion, an ekphrastic backdrop for Bradamante's and Ruggiero's dynastic wedding. The pavilion, with its elaborately embroidered images of the future glory of Ippolito (and a counterpoint to the retrospective images of Troy's

[55]Moustapha Safouan, "The Dream and Psychoanalytic Treatment," in *Returning to Freud: Clinical Psychoanalysis in the School of Lacan*, ed. and trans. Stuart Schneiderman (New York: Yale University Press, 1980), 141.

doom on the walls of Dido's temple), may rank as the most spectacular purloined object in the entire literary history of the translation of empire.[56] As Ariosto tells it, its elusive itinerary began in Troy, where it was made for Hector by his sister Cassandra—an object that Mandricardo would surely have valued had he been aware of its existence. It is then purloined by Menelaus, who barters it (for the "purloined" Helen) in Egypt, where it remains with the Ptolemys until Agrippa takes it from Cleopatra to Rome. Constantine takes it to Byzantium, from which Melissa then transports it to Charlemagne's court. In short, the pavilion is perhaps the purloined signifier par excellence of the *Furioso*. Andrew Fichter argues that "the movements of the pavilion retrace the translation of *imperium* from Troy to the West"[57]—which is to argue that, as the symbolic backdrop of Bradamante and Ruggiero's marriage (and as a synecdoche for Ippolito's presumed Trojan ancestry), the pavilion validates Ferrara as the new *imperium sine fine*.

But the pavilion is also symptomatic of the narcissism of the translation of empire. Because in some sense it wants to *have* Troy, the *translatio imperii* enacts the same kind of narcissistic aggressivity as Mandricardo, but on a much grander scale and with many more ambiguous consequences for epic history. Despite the pavilion's rep-

---

[56]Cassandra's pavilion is a reminder that narratives of the displaced object or person are recurrent throughout the literary history of versions of the fall of Troy. In his *Palinode*, Stesichorus records the existence of two Helens, one true and one phantom. The "true" Helen, so his story goes, was abducted from Greece by Alexander, ending up in Proteus's custody in Egypt. Thus, the Homeric Helen of Troy was merely a simulacrum of the "real"—of the "purloined"—Helen. Also, in the *Aeneid*, Aeneas's gift to Dido (1.650–52) is a purloined veil that Leda gave to Helen, who brought it from Mycenae to Troy—only now to be presented to Dido in Carthage. Finally, there is the story of the Trojan Palladium, the statue of Minerva that protected the city but was stolen by Ulysses and Diomedes. But as R. G. Austin has demonstrated in his commentary on the *Aeneid*, the story has multiple versions, rendering the Palladium of "mysterious and debatable origin" ("Commentary," *P. Vergili Maronis. Aeneidos: Liber Secundus* [Oxford: Clarendon Press, 1964], 84): there is the version, attributed to Arctinus by Dionysius, that the Greeks unknowingly stole a fake; that the real Palladium was taken to Rome by Aeneas; that Diomedes handed over the true image to the Trojans in Italy; that, as Servius reports, the Palladium remained in Troy until discovered by Fimbria in 85 B.C. (83–85). "Real" or "fake," the Palladium, like Cassandra's pavilion, is, as these multiple versions indicate, the signifier par excellence, a proleptic anticipation of the *translatio imperii*, but known only in its effects. (For an excellent discussion of the Palladium as a representation—as both "original" and "copy"—see Françoise Meltzer's chapter "Sleight of Hand" in her book *Salome and the Dance of Writing*, 192–96.)

[57]Andrew Fichter, *Poets Historical: Dynastic Epic in the Renaissance* (New Haven: Yale University Press, 1982), 105.

resentations, like those on Aeneas's shield, of a future glory for Ferrara, the narcissism of the *translatio imperii* exerts a regressive pull on the realization of prophecy. Again, we may pose the question we considered in the previous chapter: does the translation of power to Ferrara constitute a replacement of Troy, or does Cassandra's pavilion signal its entanglement in a belated reconstruction of a "Troy" that may never have been? Though the pavilion anticipates a dynastic future for the *translatio imperii*, the elusive itinerary of its purloining may simply trace the story of the *translatio imperii*'s own difference from itself. The fate of Mandricardo illustrates the extent to which the narcissism of the *translatio imperii* must itself inhabit an ambiguous space between identification and rivalry. Just as Aeneas's founding of Rome is dependent on a repression of Troy, so also must Mandricardo's "revival" of Troy be occulted—indeed, violently expunged—from Ariosto's narrative in the form of his slaughter by Ruggiero, the only legitimate "new Hector" that the *translatio imperii* will allow in an aggressive display of narcissistic rivalry.

But despite the annihilation of Mandricardo, the pavilion makes its entrance in the final canto like an ekphrastic "return of the repressed," inhabiting the space between the future glory of Ippolito and the House of Este, and a retroactive origin in the fetishizing of Troy. Cassandra's pavilion becomes the dubious "origin" of Ferrara's celebration of itself as the new *imperium sine fine*. Almost compulsively returning us to a Troy that was defeated, the pavilion "originates" its story with Hector's death by betrayal (by *Sinon falso*). Thus, Cassandra's pavilion perfectly embodies how the movement toward the future, in the process of transference (of "translation"), is always bound up with the repetition (compulsion) of the past.[58] Enacting the disappearance of Troy's disappearance, the pavilion implies the potential futility of the *translatio imperii*'s desire to fulfill itself typologically through the dead empire of Troy (or, more specifically, the dead body of Hector). The narcissism of the *translatio imperii*, like the individual knights who fight for its *recursus*, is itself caught between rivalry and identification. Seeking to *have* Troy, the *translatio imperii* must annihilate any Mandricardan attempt at its own fetishizing of Troy. But at the same time the *translatio imperii*

[58]Ascoli elaborates on Cassandra's role as a prophet doomed never to be taken seriously: "There is nothing, and no one, in the *Furioso* that better crystallizes the position of its author, who both lies and tells the truth, who flies from both madness and reason, than the figure of Cassandra" (391).

requires Troy as its own ego ideal, its own attempt, as Freud would define it, to retrieve the image of what it once was. Thus narcissism can only lead to an identifying (and fateful) repetition—a repetition that can only be the mark of its own difference. The *translatio imperii*'s narcissistic need to have Troy situates the New Troy in an ambiguous space between insufficiency and anticipation. In short, narcissistic aggressivity always ensures that it is easier to repeat than to remember.

But, in the end, Ariosto (never one to take his subject matter too seriously)[59] may be implying that the most arrogant kind of narcissism enacted by the literary history of the *translatio imperii* is the veneration of Troy's fall as an event that *really happened* in history. Self-consciously playing the role of the epic poet, Ariosto solemnly and elegiacally depicts Sinon's treachery and the sadness of the fall of Troy by hinting darkly: "e peggiò seguito, che non è scritto" ("And direr ill was done than tales report" [46.82]). The truth of Troy's ghastly destruction, claims Ariosto, was too horrible to be captured in history's representations of the past. (This gap between event and remembrance is, of course, what Aeneas tries with such futility to bridge as he stands before Dido's representations of the past in the first book of the *Aeneid*.)

But what *is* the truth of Troy's horror as depicted on Cassandra's pavilion? Or, to repeat the simple but vexed question posed in my previous chapter: what *is* Troy? In canto 35, a skeptical St. John, Astolfo's guide to the moon, offers an alternative "truth" to the traditional versions of the Troy story. He argues, "Non sì pietoso Enea, né forte Achille / fu, come è fama, né sì fiero Ettore" ("Aeneas not so pious, nor of arm / So strong Achilles, Hector not so bold, / Was, as 'tis famed" [25]). And although Homer depicted the Greeks as victorious, St. John admonishes, "tutta al contrario l'istoria converti: / che i Greci rotti, e che Troia vittrice" ("By contraries throughout the tale explain: / That from the Trojan bands the Grecian ran" [27]). In his effort to convince Astolfo that poets (like Ariosto) often play with the truth to satisfy the narcissistic needs of their patrons (like Ippolito), St. John is stubbornly insistent: there were no heroes in the

[59]It is appropriate here to note Ariosto's frequent intrusions into his own narrative, his countless laments, boasts, apologies, confessions, requests for patience, confidences—in short, his own enactment of a poetic narcissism. For more on the (omni)presence of Ariosto's poet-narrator, see Durling, *The Figure of the Poet in Renaissance Epic*.

Trojan war; Troy should not be the subject matter for poignant legends about its destruction because it *won*; and Virgil erred in making Aeneas *pius*.[60]

St. John's argument is an intriguing and resonant moment in Ariosto's narrative, constituting a bold charge that, largely because of its narcissistic investment in Troy, dynastic epic is built on frauds perpetrated by lying poets.[61] Thus in the gap between Ariosto's contention, in canto 46, that history is merely inadequate to record Troy's fall, and St. John's charge, in canto 35, that history should take note that Troy did *not* fall, lies the "truth" of Troy's story (and of the origins of the Ferrarese House of Este). Ariosto has forced the reader either to call St. John himself a liar, or to be attentive to his charge that Troy has become implicated in the narcissism of the *translatio imperii* (a mutual narcissism of self-aggrandizing poet and patron), which requires the poignancy of a fallen Troy as the constitutive trope of its own *renovatio*. If in the *Aeneid* Virgil calls into question Aeneas's efforts to (re)construct, in Dido's memory theater, a Troy that may never have been, then in the *Furioso* St. John radically contends not that Troy eludes representation, but that it has been represented *incorrectly*, turned into a loser so that the *translatio imperii* can be endowed with a typological meaning. The object of St. John's lesson may be to show that Troy is inevitably caught up in the ambiguities of historical representation—inevitably caught up in a gap between the "truth" of epic history and the narcissism of the *translatio imperii*.

Astolfo's reentry to earth, then, is as marked by epistemological ambiguity as Aeneas's reentry through the Ivory Gate of *falsa insomnia*; but Ariosto's decadent sophistication scarcely invites any "serious" effort at resolving the crisis of a Trojan ontology throughout epic history. The poet enjoys merely posing the question of "truth," rather like a precocious schoolboy pondering questions of being and reality for the first time. The episode of St. John's skepticism consti-

---

[60]At this point, Ariosto may be thinking of the sophistic *Trojan Discourse* of Dio Chrysostom, who sought to prove that Troy was not captured by the Greeks. Attempting to cast doubt on much Homeric source material, Dio Chrysostom writes, "But as for me, desiring neither to gain your favour nor to quarrel with Homer, much less to rob him of his fame, I shall try to show all the false statements I think he has made with regard to the events which happened here, and I shall use no other means of refuting him than his own poetry" (*Dio Chrysostom*, trans. J. W. Cohoon, The Loeb Classical Library Edition [Cambridge: Harvard University Press, 1932], 1:453).

[61]For an account of St. John's depiction of the Gospel as merely the product of a patron-writer relationship, see Quint, "Astolfo's Voyage to the Moon."

tutes not a thoroughgoing investigation of truth, falsehood, uncertainty, and the role of history in their resolution, but is rather a game, a conundrum, simply one of many that the Ariostan narrator plays with his reader throughout his vast work.

But as we move to Tasso's *Gerusalemme liberata*, we discover that Tasso's Counter-Reformational reincarnation of Ferrara as the seat of the *translatio imperii* is as much a philosophical investigation of the distinction between truth and falsehood as it is an epic. And in Book III of his *Discorsi del poema eroico*, we can identify Troy as the locus of a precise contrast between Ariosto's diffidence toward the truth and the fervor with which Tasso attempts to solve these ontological problems, where Tasso converts the quintessentially Ariostan irony of the St. John episode into the humorless and dogged pursuit of historical "truth":

> Ma non dee peraventura la licenza de' pocti stendersi tanto oltre ch'ardisca dimutar l'ultimo fine de l'imprese ch'egli prendre a trattare, o pur narrare al contrario di quello che sono avvenuti alcuni ge gli avvenimenti principali e più noti che già sono ricevuti per veri ne la notizia del mondo. . . . Simile sarebbe stato l'ardire d'Omero, se fosse vero quel che falsamente sì dice, benché a proposito de la loro intenzione:
>
> > che i Greci rotti, e che Troia vittrice,
> > e che Penelopea fu meretrice.
> > (*Orlando furioso*, 35.27)[62]

> (But perhaps the poet should not stretch his licence so far that he dares to change the outcome of the enterprises he undertakes to treat, or to narrate contrary to actuality any of the main and best-known events which are accepted as true in the world's opinion. . . . Homer would have been comparably daring if what some falsely maintain in their effort to accuse him were true.
>
> > that the Greeks were defeated, or Troy victorious,
> > and . . . Penelope a whore.)

Thus Tasso implicitly ranks Ariosto alongside Dio Chrysostom and his tampering with Homer as falling outside the bounds of "la no-

---

[62]All references to Tasso's prose are taken from *Torquato Tasso: Prose*, ed. Ettore Mazzali (Milan: Riccardo Ricciardi Editore, 1959). The English translation of the *Discorsi del poema eroico* (referred to in the next chapter) is *Torquato Tasso: Discourses on the Heroic Poem*, trans. Mariella Cavalchini and Irene Samuel (Oxford: Clarendon Press, 1973). The English translation of the *Discorsi dell'arte poetica* is mine. (An excellent annotated translation of the *Discorsi dell'arte poetica* has been completed by Lawrence Rhu, forthcoming from Wayne State University Press.)

tizia del mondo." And one wonders if, of all the frivolities of the *Furioso* that Tasso found so offensive, what he may have judged to be most repugnant was St. John's presentation of an alternative *Troia vittrice* as the ultimate affront to the truth of epic history. Fundamentally concerned with the relationship among poetic truth, imitation, and invention, Tasso's epic gambit will be to underplay the metaphor of Troy as an origin for the *translatio imperii* and capitalize on the theological and imperial resonances of the "real" city of Jerusalem. But, as Tasso comes to discover, the ghost of Troy as the inevitable return of the repressed *is* the elusive "truth" of epic history.

CHAPTER FOUR

Troia Vittrice: Reviving Troy in the Woods of Jerusalem

Oscura memoria: Finding Epic Closure

In Canto VIII of Tasso's *Gerusalemme liberata*, a Danish warrior informs the Christian leader Goffredo of the death of Sweno, who was ambushed by the Arabs. He tells Goffredo that he has received supernatural orders to deliver Sweno's sword to Rinaldo, who is destined to avenge the Dane's death. In an earlier version of the *Liberata*, the episode of Sweno's sword incites far greater hostility, for Rinaldo competes with his own leader Goffredo for possession of the sword, which, in this version, assumes greater mythic proportions.[1] But in the final version, Tasso eliminated the *habendi libido* of competitive rivalry altogether. In Canto XVII, in a recapitulation of Venus's gift to her son Aeneas, the mage of Ascalon gives Rinaldo a suit of armor and a shield depicting the exploits of the House of Este, while Carlo ceremoniously presents him with the sword of Sweno; and thus the *Aeneid* is swiftly and unobtrusively subsumed under Ferrara as the new *translatio imperii*.

Sweno's (unnamed) sword, on the verge of becoming a coveted Durindana, never achieves the status of an elusive object of desire. What is remarkable about his final version is Tasso's scrupulous

---

[1]The alternate version of this episode is noted and discussed by Lawrence F. Rhu in his essay "From Aristotle to Allegory: Young Tasso's Evolving Vision of the *Gerusalemme Liberata*," *Italica* 65:2 (1988), 111–30. As Rhu observes, "The blood-spotted sword would lose its stain of gore when gripped by the hand of its rightful inheritor" (125).

avoidance of the hostile narcissism of the *Furioso*, where armor is "purloined" and fought over as the privileged site of ego formation. Considering, but then refusing, the surrender of Sweno's sword to the elusive itinerary of the theft without return, Tasso rejects the entangled narrative of object-libido. If, in the *Furioso*, a helmet is as important as a woman (or victory in battle), then the *Liberata* refuses to fetishize the concepts of ownership and possession.[2] In Canto xvi, Carlo and Ubaldo hold up their magic shield, the *lucido scudo* of epic prophecy, to Rinaldo, and the insidious spells of Armida's narcissism are instantaneously disenchanted. A canto later, the mage presents Rinaldo not with the "armour of an alienating identity," but the armor of epic consolidation, embodying nothing less than the fulfillment of the *translatio imperii* itself. Thus imitative rivalry is bypassed for the grander scheme of epic destiny.

Or, rather, we should say that the imitative rivalry of individuals is rejected in favor of Tasso's theorizing of the larger question of how the poet should represent history and historical "truth" in epic. At the heart of Tasso's epic aesthetics, as meticulously outlined in his *Discorsi dell'arte poetica* (1587), is history—or, more accurately, the representation of a history that cannot be *remembered*. Thus, once again, as we saw in the case of the *Aeneid*, the faculty of memory gains significance within the literary history of epic. For Tasso, the subject matter of epic must not be libidinal (like Ariosto's), but historical—not, however, the contemporary history *de' nostri tempi* (the immediacy of whose current events resist poetic representation), but rather the history of *tempi remotissimi*. The history of more distant eras naturally lends itself to representation (affords the most poetic freedom) because, simply, memory cannot recall it: "però che, essendo quelle cose in guisa sepolte nel seno dell'antichità ch'a pena alcuna debole ed oscura memoria ce ne rimane, può il poeta a sua voglia mutarle e rimutarle." ("Because those things are so buried in

---

[2]Tasso's only narrative of a theft without return occurs in Canto ii. In an episode undoubtedly owing its narrative origins to the story of the Trojan Palladium, Aladino and Ismeno steal an icon, or *imago*, of the Virgin Mary from a Christian church, only then to have it stolen from the mosque. Sofronia, sacrificing herself for the Christian cause, announces to Aladino that she stole the icon. When we bear in mind that the icon is wrapped in a veil, the episode can be seen as a kind of enactment of the Lacanian axiom that the signifier always does its work veiled. In effect, Sofronia volunteers herself as a "signified," standing in place of the icon as the purloined signifier. Sofronia and her lover Olindo are eventually saved from a burning death by Clorinda, but what this odd episode never resolves is the mystery of this *furto* (ii.21), or theft without return. We never learn who really stole the statue or who "owns" it by the end of Tasso's narrative.

the depths of antiquity that scarcely any feeble and dim memory of them remains, the poet can choose to change and rechange them."). That which cannot be remembered by a "debole ed oscura memoria" constitutes, as we saw earlier in the chapter on Virgil, what Freud refers to as a "successful repression," which is crucial for the foundations of culture. Thus, we may say that for Tasso, the proper subject matter of epic is based on a kind of Freudian "successful repression" as the (highly representational) history of *tempi remotissimi*.

Because he never thought in terms of the workings of a narrative "unconscious," Tasso could scarcely have foreseen the psychic consequences of any epic exploitation of a "debole ed oscura memoria."[3] To be sure, a dim memory of past history effectively opens up the aesthetic space for the conscious poetic exercise of what he refers to throughout the *Discorsi* as a "gran commodità di fingere," or the freedom to invent. What such a reliance on the screening effects of memory cannot predict, however, is, as we shall see, the return of the epic author's repressed in any narrative of the *translatio imperii*.

The attempt to locate a narrative unconscious in the *Liberata* must begin with the question: what for Tasso is the precise relationship between history and "truth"? Tasso privileges history as the proper subject matter for epic because history is *true*. And, as we saw at the conclusion of the previous chapter, Tasso uses Troy and the Homeric "truth" value of its fall as a paradigmatic kind of historic assumption for epic. In both the *Discorsi dell'arte poetica* and in the more expanded *Discorsi del poema eroico* (1594), Tasso isolates the historical truth of the fall of Troy as the kind of bedrock historical event where poetic representation, the "gran commodità di fingere," must not be so freely exercised as to do something so outrageous as to portray a *Troia vittrice*.

What is ironic about Tasso's conscious calling attention to Troy as a paradigmatic epic truth in his *Discorsi* is his (seemingly) conscious underplaying of the metaphor of Troy as an origin for the *translatio imperii* throughout the *Liberata*. The elusiveness of Troy to representation, which had so thoroughly engaged the poetic imaginations of Virgil and Ariosto, is of little interest to Tasso, who is more con-

---

[3]Tasso's suppression of the unconscious is demonstrated early in his *Discorsi dell'arte poetica*, where he refers to "la compassione d'Edippo che per semplice ignoranza uccise il padre" ("the pity of Oedipus who, through simple ignorance, killed his father"). Tasso's dismissal of the psychic resonances of the son's ambivalence toward the father as mere "semplice ignoranza" is not only hasty, but also ironic in view of his own Oedipal struggles with his father Bernardo.

cerned with establishing the generic integrity of the epic romance. Thus, even as he narrates his version of past epic history as a kind of "successful repression," Tasso could scarcely have predicted the extent to which Troy would make its return as epic history's most psychically resonant "failed repression." More than ever in epic history, Troy, as the "city not seen" of dynastic epic, will persist as a focal point for the elusive intersection between psyche and history. Tasso's manifest epic subject is, of course, the historical matter of the Crusades and the Christians' recovery of Jerusalem under the leadership of Goffredo. Embodying a complex convergence of Moslem, Jewish, and Christian influences (not to mention its fall to Pompey and Rome in 63 B.C.), the "purloined" city of Jerusalem is a vastly overdetermined locus for Tasso's treatment of epic history. And when we focus on Jerusalem's specific status in the *Liberata* as a "besieged city" in imminent danger of attack from outside its walls, we can begin to perceive the repressed return of Troy, even more than Jerusalem itself, as determining the deep structure of Tasso's epic.

As a backlash against the *soverchia lunghezza* (or "excessive length") of Ariosto, Tasso sought to write a perfectly unified epic, and his *Liberata* underwent years of revision and scrutiny as mediated through Aristotelian literary theory. Put simply, Tasso's plan for the *Liberata* was to write a tightly compressed narrative about the defeat of a city. In his *Discorsi dell'arte poetica*, Tasso warns: "Ciascuno in somma, che materia troppo ampia si propone, è costretto d'allungare il poema oltre il convennol termine" ("In sum, he who proposes for himself subject matter that is too diffuse is forced to stretch the poem beyond a suitable limit"). For Tasso, then, knowing the point at which to put closure on a narrative (recognizing its *convennol termine*) is one of the greatest challenges for the epic poet.

Commenting on the concept of in medias res as the prototypical narrative gambit for epic, James Nohrnberg has noted that "epic must begin late in the total action if it is to limit its possible expansion."[4] Having warred against the Saracens for six years in Asia, Tasso's Crusaders (after years of poetic revision) are, at the very outset of the epic narrative, preparing for an assault on Jerusalem, leaving little room for (narrative) maneuver. But even the tight compressions of this narrative cannot stem the tide of romance *lunghezza*. The woods surrounding Jerusalem not only serve as the

[4] *The Analogy of "The Faerie Queene,"* 7.

threshold of the culmination of epic narrative (occurring, as they do, "late in the total action"), but they also mark the starting point of Troy as Tasso's return of the repressed.

The Epic Sublime

Under the pressure imposed on him by Aristotle's *Poetics*, a Latin translation of which had been published in 1536 by Alessandro de' Pazzi, Tasso was driven to transform Ariosto's errant fantasies and write a perfectly unified epic.[5] And, as was suggested earlier, it is as if Tasso were primarily concerned not so much with the evolution of the *translatio imperii* throughout epic literary history, as with the evolution of *cinquecento* epic literary theory and its emphasis on unity over multiplicity. Much more than Ariosto, one of whose dominant pseudocomic effects in the *Furioso* is the erosion of the distinction between the "neurotic" and the "ideological" subject, Tasso was determined to investigate the way in which the individual libido is situated (indeed castrated) within culture, the way in which the origin of the individual must be located within the group. It is, therefore, no mere coincidence that in the opening canto of the *Liberata* Tasso refers to Goffredo's superior presence of mind as a leader as "senno," the same word that Ariosto had used to describe the "lost wits" of the frenzied Orlando.

Thus, unlike Charlemagne, of whom the reader is often scarcely aware throughout most of the *Furioso*, Tasso's epic leader Goffredo is consistently foregrounded as the locus of authority and discipline in the *Liberata*; indeed one of the major developments of the opening book is the ceremony of Goffredo's election as supreme commander of the Crusaders. For that matter, the plot of Tasso's epic abounds with the sheer presence of leaders, Saracen and Christian alike, who persistently focus on the grim responsibilities of epic *agon*.[6] Whereas the *Furioso* begins in medias res with the strange dispersals of Ariosto's *erranti*, the epic action of the *Liberata* is framed around such overtly authoritative acts of leadership as the speeches of Goffredo

[5] For the authoritative survey of the literary critical background of the Ariosto–Tasso debate, see Weinberg, *A History of Literary Criticism in the Italian Renaissance*, 2:954–1073.

[6] As Judith Kates writes, "In contrast to the Ariostan array of 'donne, cavalieri, amori, arme, cortesie, audaci imprese,' Tasso's invocation claims as the poem's subject the classically restrained 'arme pietose e 'l Capitano'" (*Tasso and Milton: The Problem of Christian Epic* [Lewisburg, PA: Bucknell University Press, 1987], 66).

and Piero l'Eremita to the Crusaders (I); Goffredo's, Aladino's, and
the Egyptian Caliph's formal reviews of their troops (I, III, XVII);
attempts at negotiation with the Christians by the pagans Argante
and Alete, followed by Goffredo's and Argante's formal declaration
of war (II); Goffredo's inspirational speeches to his troops in the
wake of famine (V), his leading of his army to the Mount of Olives to
receive the sacrament (X), and his quelling of mutiny in the Christian
camp (VIII); Goffredo's and Raimondo's prayers to the Almighty
(VII, VIII, XIII); Solimano's providing of reinforcements for the pagans (IX); and so on.

Tasso's insistence on a conspicuously martial, and indeed Iliadic,
framework—on these acts of negotiation, strategy, troop review, decision, and divine intercession—reveals a machinery of epic *agon*
that is, of course, entirely in accordance with his accompanying
commentary, the "Allegoria del poema." Here Tasso chooses as his
central (and essentially Platonic) metaphor for his epic the body poli-
tic and its harmonious functioning when controlled by the mind as
the seat of understanding. Thus, in Tasso's allegorical conception,
Goffredo is to be interpreted as the narrative's dominant superego,
the ultimate hero of civic action and *pietà*, who consolidates the way-
wardness of his less disciplined soldiers. As Piero l'Eremita orders
the Christians: "fate un corpo sol di membri amici; / Fate un capo,
che gli altri indrizzi e frene" ("Make but one head that may direct
and restrain the others" [1.31]).[7] And as Raimondo reminds Goffredo: "Duce sei tu, non semplice guerriero" ("You are a leader, not
a mere soldier" [VII.62]).[8]

If, as Baxter Hathaway argues, it is with Tasso's conception of
Goffredo that "the idea of the perfect exemplar reached its culmination" in epic poetry,[9] then it is important to consider the effects of
his obsession with "perfect" leadership on his poetic project. Why is
the concept of the leader—"l'idea d'un perfetto cavaliere," as he
calls it in his *Discorsi del poema eroico*—so important to Tasso, and

[7]All references to the *Gerusalemme liberata* are taken from the *Gerusalemme liberata*,
preface by Lanfranco Caretti (Turin: Giulio Einaudi, 1971). The English prose translation is Ralph Nash, *Torquato Tasso: Jerusalem Delivered* (Detroit: Wayne State University
Press, 1987).

[8]Goffredo, like Aeneas, must be reminded repeatedly throughout the *Liberata* that
he is not an individual, but an epic *institution*. (I am grateful to David Quint for
pointing this out to me.) Even as Goffredo is reminded that he is no "semplice guerriero," in contrast, the fierce warrior Argante, on the pagan side, refers to himself as a
"privato cavalier" (VI.13)—not an epic institution, but the locus of individual libido.

[9]Baxter Hathaway, "Tasso's Perfect Exemplars," in *The Age of Criticism: The Late
Renaissance in Italy* (Ithaca: Cornell University Press, 1962), 151.

how does it contribute to the narcissism inherent in epic romance? Tasso's attempt at creating a "perfetto cavaliere," an embodiment of *sapientia* who wields power and dominance over wayward subordinates, is not unlike Freud's analysis of "group psychology" and the leader of the "primal horde" in the prehistory of man and the formation of community. Of the leader, Freud argues that "his ego had few libidinal ties; he loved no one but himself"; the leader is, in Freud's conception, "absolutely narcissistic."[10] And we can note that Goffredo is the only knight in the Christian camp unmoved by the tempting presence of the beautiful Armida, unwilling to "forfeit," in Freud's terms, even a small part of his narcissism for her.

Goffredo can be seen as Tasso's "corrective" for Ariosto's Charlemagne, who remains too distant to control the narcissism of his wayward knights. Tasso's structure for the *Liberata* is designed to consolidate narcissism into a kind of collective energy that can convert individual repressions into greater Christian glory.[11] For Tasso, the problem of epic romance becomes, then, the problem of how narcissism can be converted into sublimation. Tasso's plan for his epic is, in effect, to close the gap between the "neurotic" and the "ideological" subject—not comically, like Ariosto (whose presentation of *furore* results in the *coinciding* of neurosis and ideology), but rather punitively, by a *subordination* of neurosis to ideology. Any soldier not properly sublimated will not be permitted participation in

[10]*Group Psychology and the Analysis of the Ego; SE* 18:123, 124.

[11]As Freud writes in *Totem and Taboo*, "It appears that where a powerful impetus has been given to group formation neuroses may diminish, and at all events temporarily disappear" (*SE* 13:142). Sergio Zatti has also analyzed the tension between the individual psyche and a larger epic ideology that informs the *Liberata*. Zatti interprets Tasso's epic as an ongoing struggle between "il corpo collettivo dell'unità cristiana" ("the collective body of the Christian unit") and the "fenomenologie multiformi del pagano" ("the multiform phenomenologies of the pagan") (*L'uniforme cristiano e il multiforme pagano: Saggio sulla "Gerusalemme liberata"* [Milan: il Saggiatore, 1983], 155, 152); he frequently poses this tension in explicitly Freudian terms. Zatti perceives romance as a kind of "return of the ideological repressed," a "desiderio molteplice" ("multiple desire") (145) that continually works to erode "repressione cristiana" (148). Zatti also sees this tension at work within the Christian camp itself, where the "represso ideologico" of Goffredo must combat the "represso sessuale" (169) of his own errant warriors. For Zatti, Tasso consistently posits Goffredo's unitary ideology of singular leadership in tension with the centrifugal, wandering multiplicity ("la spinta centrifuga" [175]) of the Christian knights pursuing their private quests. My concern in this chapter is less with the *agon* between ideology and repression than with the extent to which Tasso fails to control the slippages between an Ideological sublimation and a repressive narcissism, such that, as we shall see, the operations of ideology and repression begin to look the *same*. I mainly emphasize how Tasso's narrative itself has an unconscious; the result is a psychic discontinuity that overdetermines the meeting ground between the unconscious and history (ideology).

epic history. Accordingly, unlike Ariosto's epic, whose title reflects the psychopathology of the individual, Tasso's epic is named after a city as the locus of cultural sublimation.

But Tasso's "Allegoria" demonstrates that the *Liberata* is, in effect, structured by a bargain. Goffredo serves as a sort of idealized father, a military ego ideal that has been established as such by the narcissism of his more infantilized soldiers, in exchange for their total acceptance of his consolidating power as a moral conscience (or what Tasso refers to in his "Allegoria" as "l'intelletto"). But, as Goffredo discovers, the bargain is a precarious one. Because the mimetic identifications that are inherent in the act of establishing the ego ideal as such are, as Freud has argued, inherently narcissistic, the bargain is enabled only through the very narcissistic impulses that the ego ideal seeks to castrate and destroy. Goffredo comes to discover that the transferences that allow for military consolidation never fully relinquish the narcissism from which they are initially constituted.

Tasso's effort to establish the *Liberata* as perhaps the first genuinely sublimatory epic of the *translatio imperii* prompts at this point a broader, more theoretical investigation of the psychic operations of sublimation and Freud's largely unsuccessful attempt to show how sublimation bypasses the mechanics of repression. Freud's theoretical troubles can, perhaps, shed more light on why Tasso's emphasis on sublimation as the ideological "solution" to the errancies of romance cannot prevent the return of the repressed in the *Liberata*.

For Freud, sublimation was the great link between psychoanalysis and a philosophy of culture. Sublimation occurs when the sexual instinct is converted into civilized activity. In the economy of sublimation, energy is displaced from the instinct to a higher cultural aim without any loss of intensity—and, as Freud strives to make clear, without repression. But to what extent can sublimation also be perceived as a cultural neurosis? This is one of the central questions posed by the narrative structure of Tasso's sublimatory epic. Even as it strives to hierarchize the "ideological" and the "neurotic" subject, the *Liberata* also demonstrates that sublimation is never very far from repression. Specifically, as we shall see, Tassoan sublimation is never very far from narcissism. And, as we know already, a repressed Troy is never very far from the narcissism of epic narrative.

What is the possibility that, in psychoanalytic theory, sublimation and narcissism end up as inevitably interrelated? Narcissism is the path to the other that reflects the ego as its own object of interest. Specifically, narcissism displaces itself onto an ideal ego, which, according to Freud, "finds itself possessed of every perfection that is of value." But the direct dependence on a libidinal relation with an ideal ego that constitutes primary narcissism is, for Freud, "the conditioning factor of repression."[12] The subject's narcissism has been displaced from autoerotism to an ideal ego as the new "target" of self-love. And in this operation of displacement lies the essence of neurotic repression; the setting up of the ideal ego both "defends against" autoerotism and also represents that same act of repression.

The high cultural aims of sublimation seem far removed from the darker operations of narcissistic repression. But Freud foresaw a slippage between narcissism and sublimation, a perception which could, perhaps, be viewed as one of the principal factors explaining why, as Laplanche and Pontalis have maintained, "the lack of a coherent theory of sublimation remains one of the lacunae in psychoanalytic thought."[13] After all, with its emphasis on the often ethically superior demands of the ego ideal, narcissism too is motivated by a concentration on a "higher" aim. Specifically, in his essay "On Narcissism," Freud was concerned that the formation of an ego ideal would be confused with the sublimation of instinct: "It is true that the ego ideal demands such sublimation but it cannot enforce it; sublimation remains a special process which may be prompted by the ideal but the execution of which is entirely independent of any such prompting."[14] A successful sublimation, then, depends on the "enforcing" capabilities of the ego ideal. But the relative strength of this "enforcement" determines the potential slippage between narcissism and sublimation. Narcissism, Freud insists, is not a kind of successful sublimation: "As we have learnt, the formation of an ideal heightens the demands of the ego and is the most powerful factor favoring repression; sublimation is a way out, a way by which those demands can be met *without* involving repression."[15]

And yet, Freud's distinction notwithstanding, we are left with the lingering sense that the diversionary operations of sublimation and narcissism contaminate one another. Narcissism, we could say, is sublimatory insofar as its autoerotism is submerged and displaced onto a higher ego ideal. But sublimation is narcissistic in that the demands of a higher activity are often inescapably "the most power-

[12]*SE* 14:94.
[13]J. Laplanche and J.-B. Pontalis, *The Language of Psycho-Analysis*, trans. Donald Nicholson-Smith (New York: W. W. Norton, 1973), 433.
[14]*SE* 14:94–95.
[15]Ibid., 95.

ful factor favouring repression." Sublimation is always "prompted by the ideal," and despite Freud's warnings, it is impossible to see how the diversions of the sexual instinct that constitute sublimation can bypass the repressive displacements of narcissism.[16] A crucial question here is, to what extent is displaceable energy to be viewed as sublimatory or narcissistic? Even if sublimation does represent the fulfillment of idealistic demands *"without,"* as Freud insisted, "involving repression," the origin of sublimation still resides in a kind of narcissistic libido. The very displacement of energy that, in sublimation, is supposed to liberate the subject from repression traces the same diversionary path that, in narcissism, is the very essence of the neurotic symptom. In the final analysis, sublimation may be inherently "neurotic."

As we return to the *Liberata*, it is not surprising to discover that it is the ongoing ambivalence of epic history's relationship with Troy that finds itself most entangled in this obscure threshold between sublimation and narcissism. As we have seen, the translation of power that constitutes the *translatio imperii* is itself a sublimation whose higher cultural aim is to replace Troy as the new *imperium sine fine*. But as we have also seen, throughout the literary history of epic this same sublimatory replacement of Troy becomes in fact a narcissistic *displacement* onto Troy, the city not seen, as the ego ideal of epic; and thus the exile from Troy (as the other constituted by an ego ideal) becomes the "origin" of narcissism in epic history.

In determining the extent to which Tasso succeeds in his project to shape the *Liberata* as a truly sublimatory epic, let us turn to some of the psychic consequences of Tasso's conscious underplaying of the metaphor of Troy as an origin for the *translatio imperii*. The relics of a Trojan *sparagmos* are almost conspicuously absent from the *Liberata*. There are no murals obsessively replaying Troy's doom. There are no would-be Hectors fetishizing Trojan armor. Even the "armi novelle" (XVII.58) depicting the deeds of Rinaldo's ancestors, an epic topos where a recalling of Troy would seem almost formulaic, make no mention of the Estes' putative Trojan descent. Unlike the *Aeneid*, where the faculty of memory is consistently and intimately linked

---

[16]Leo Bersani has also noted some of the slippages between narcissism and sublimation, arguing that "the most mysteriously dysfunctional aspect of human development may be the ego's repudiation of its own erotic worth and its willed subjection to an antierotic ideal" (*The Culture of Redemption* [Cambridge: Harvard University Press, 1990], 41). For more on the "repressive" nature of sublimation, see Jean Laplanche, "To Situate Sublimation," *October* 25 (1984), esp. 21–26.

with Troy, the *Liberata* erases the significance of Troy from its cultural memory.

In rejecting Troy as a crucial metaphor for his narrative, Tasso attempts, in effect, to relieve epic history of its narcissistic investment with Troy, looking instead to a Christianized Jerusalem as the sublimatory "beyond" of Troy, the apotheosis of a Freudian "higher social or ethical valuation" that can lift the *translatio imperii*, epic history's own (failed) attempt at a sublimatory philosophy of culture, out of the neurosis of the *Troiana fortuna*. Early in his epic, Tasso resists the latent, repressive seductions of the city not seen by allowing Goffredo's soldiers an emotional glimpse of Jerusalem:

> Ali ha ciascuno al core ed ali al piede,
> nè del suo ratto andar però s'accorge:
> ma quando il sol gli aridi campi fiede
> con raggi assai ferventi e in alto sorge,
> ecco apparir Gierusalem si vede,
> ecco additar Gierusalem si scorge,
> ecco da mille voci unitamente
> Gierusalemme salutar si sente.
>
> . . . .
>
> Al gran piacer che quella prima vista
> dolcemente spirò ne l'altrui petto,
> alta contrizion successe, mista
> di timoroso e riverente affetto.
>
> (III.3,5.1–4)

(Each man has wings in his heart and wings on his feet, nor yet is aware how quickly he is marching; but when the sun beats down on the dusty fields with stronger rays and rises high—lo there Jerusalem coming into view, lo there Jerusalem being pointed out, lo there Jerusalem greeted by the voices of thousands in unison.

. . . .

To the great pleasure breathed gently into each man's breast by that first glimpse, succeeded a deep contrition, mingled with fearful and reverent emotion.)

As they indulge themselves in "rotti singulti e flebili sospiri" ("broken sobs and tearful sighs"), the weeping Crusaders experience a comprehensive catharsis for their emotions through their vision of Jerusalem as perhaps epic's first "city seen." Unlike Aeneas, for whom both the tragic past of Troy and the proleptic destiny of Rome are embodied in a city not seen, Goffredo's Crusaders are granted not simply a visionary representation of their destiny, but the real city itself—a real presence that seemingly thwarts any potential for Jerusalem to become the unconscious other of epic desire.[17] By means of their vision of Jerusalem, the Crusaders can see, in effect, precisely where the epic psyche will intersect with history.

The sublimatory ideal of the Christians is, of course, the liberation of Jerusalem from Aladino's pagans. How is it, then, that Troy comes to serve as the inadvertent ego ideal for the *Liberata*? The answer lies in Goffredo's decision to *delay* his troops' storming of Jerusalem in favor of his preferred military strategy of building siege-towers.[18] Ironically, Troy becomes Tasso's return of the repressed when the poet decides, early in his epic, to curb the forces of the psyche, specifically the *terribile ardimento*, or the "formidable fear-lessness," of Rinaldo as the *Liberata*'s paradigmatic *furioso*. If the *Orlando furioso* can be characterized as the great narrative of psychological madness run amuck in epic history, then the *Liberata* can be read as the attempt to control the unchecked furor so typical of Ariostan romance and so distasteful to the Counter-Reformational critical sensibility as a whole. In Canto III, the fierce pagan Argante slays Dudone, the head of the *avventurieri* who are aiding the Crusader cause. Afflicted with "aspra vendetta", or "harsh vengeance" (50.2), Rinaldo craves instant retribution; and when he suspects that no immediate action is forthcoming, he demands: "Or qual indugio è questo?" ("Now what delay is this?" [50.4]). The precise reason for the suspected *indugio* is Goffredo's decision to storm Jerusalem not by unleashing the immediate and uncontrolled furor of his soldiers, but rather by patiently constructing siege-towers. Goffredo's imposed *indugio*, then, amounts to a decision to take Jerusalem in a distinctly epic (a distinctly Pharsalian) way. Rather than give Rinaldo free rein to assault Jerusalem (like a Rodomonte turned loose to wreak havoc on Paris), Goffredo initiates the more properly epic strategy of the patient building of siege-towers. Goffredo responds to Rinaldo's anger at the delay in avenging Dudone's death simply by surveying the topography around Jerusalem and issuing the order for the felling of trees. The only damage Goffredo's men will

[17]Tasso's description of the Crusaders' viewing of Jerusalem echoes Virgil's passage in the *Aeneid*, early in Book VII, when Aeneas's men first spot the shores of Italy after their long journey. But Rome, of course, will remain the "city not seen" for Aeneas.

[18]In his use of the chopping down of trees to build siege-towers as the central military action of his epic, Tasso was undoubtedly influenced by Lucan's *Pharsalia*, III, 373ff., where Caesar, stalled outside the fortified walls of Marseilles and in need of revetments to support his assault towers, orders his men into the forest to fell trees.

inflict is "inusitati oltraggi" ("unwonted outrages") (75.2) on the surrounding forest.

The trees of Jerusalem and their potential to serve as siege-towers become the synecdochic embodiment of Tasso's effort to shape the *Liberata* as a truly sublimatory epic. If, as we have seen, sublimation displaces energy from a lower instinct to a higher cultural aim, then the trees serve as the focal point of Tasso's displacement of Rinaldo's uncontrolled furor onto the construction of siege-towers as the more properly "epic" (the more properly sublimatory) way to capture Jerusalem. Moreover, it should be emphasized here that in the process of displacing furor from an immediate assault on Jerusalem itself to its *trees* instead, Tasso has realized one of the more ambitious goals established for the epic poet in his *Discorsi*, which is to make epic and romance generically identical: "Imita il romanzo e l'epopeia le medesima azioni; imita co 'l medesimo modo; imita con gli stessi instrumenti: sono dunque della medesima spezie" ("Romance and epic imitate the very same actions; they imitate in the very same way; and they imitate with the same means; they are, therefore, the same genre"). By making romance generically identical to epic, Tasso can thereby curtail the dilations of romance as the psychic other of epic. By making romance and epic one and the same, Tasso can strive to eliminate the generically discontinuous seams of epic romance, and thereby create, for perhaps the first time in epic history, a clear distinction between the "neurotic" and "ideological" subject. The ravages of the psychological madness run amuck that defers so much of Ariosto's romance can now be displaced from the psyche of Goffredo's *furiosi* to Jerusalem's trees, Tasso's privileged synecdoche for epic purposiveness.

But the epic *indugio* (and its sublimatory displacement onto trees) results in more than Goffredo bargained for. One major (psychic) consequence of the delay is that it has the narrative effect of recapitulating the deep structure of Homer's *Iliad*, specifically by (over)determining Jerusalem as Troy, the paradigmatic "besieged city" of epic. Goffredo wants Jerusalem to fall in a way appropriate to epic— but the more Goffredo's *indugio* postpones a Christian storming of Jerusalem, the more the proposed siege of Jerusalem begins to retell Troy's epic origin in the *Iliad*.[19]

---

[19]None of this is to deny that the *Liberata*, of course, incorporates numerous conscious echoes of the *Iliad*. One thinks, for example, of Helen's identifying of the Greek warriors for Priam as the immediate source for Erminia's identifying of the

Thus, Goffredo's careful determination of the way in which Jerusalem must fall becomes in more ways than one the recapitulative repetition compulsion of the *Liberata*. Through the *Liberata*'s (inadvertent) recalling of Troy as the besieged city, Troy finds itself falling *again* in epic history—or, to couch the consequences of this fall in more psychic terms, somewhere in his goal to eliminate the discontinuous seams of epic romance, Tasso has somehow felt the need to *kill Troy again*. We are now in a position to appreciate the enormous irony of this development in view of Tasso's calling attention to the fall of Troy in his *Discorsi* as paradigmatic of a kind of epic and historical truth that, *pace* Ariosto's St. John, must not be tampered with poetically. For Tasso, the defeat of Troy constitutes an essential "truth" in epic history. For the reader, however, the possibility that Tasso has unconsciously constructed his epic in such a way as to kill Troy again is of far-reaching psychic significance. Not only is Jerusalem the paradigmatically overdetermined city for the history of the Middle East, but its participation in epic history also proves to be overdetermined by its reincarnation as a (repressed) Troy. It is in this sense, then, that Troy, dynastic epic's city not seen, uncannily succeeds in becoming the other for an epic designed, in effect, to deny its psychic resonance.

The Jerusalem forest as the new epic locus of the *Liberata*'s romance furor constitutes a sublimatory act that successfully accomplishes Tasso's goal of collapsing an undisciplined romance madness back into epic purposiveness. But this same act of sublimation is achieved only by means of an *indugio*—and it is within this typically romance space of delay and deferral that the narrative begins its portrayal of Jerusalem as a besieged Troy (and of Troy, in effect, as the other of Jerusalem). Tasso's narrative gambit for preserving the generic integrity of his version of the *translatio imperii* is to convert the dilatory space of *indugio* into epic purposiveness; but the delay that such sublimation requires begins to transform itself into the narrative space of narcissism. At the point at which Jerusalem-as-Troy becomes the besieged city of the *Liberata*, Goffredo's willed *indugio* begins to recapitulate the story of narcissism throughout the literary history of epic, specifically the narcissistic tendency in epic to establish Troy as its ego ideal—as the origin of its narrative—even as Troy is repressed.

Christian soldiers for Aladino in Canto III. But the point I wish to emphasize here is that Tasso's epic, even as it in many ways becomes a kind of second *Iliad*, persists in repressing the city of Troy itself as the defeated city of epic.

In a way that Tasso could not have predicted, the Crusaders' goal of liberating Jerusalem from the pagans becomes the merely manifest content of the *Liberata*, while the "real" story of Tasso's epic becomes the latency of a repressed Troy. In other words, before the Christians can realize their sublimatory ideal, Jerusalem simply must fall like Troy—and Jerusalem must fall like Troy because of Troy's uncanny persistence as the ego ideal for epic. Here we are at the heart of why the *Liberata*, despite its emphasis on the "truth" of history, is an inherently "neurotic" epic. The structure of neurosis is, for Freud, twofold: there is a repressed impulse, and a conscious act that both defends against and also represents this repressed impulse. In short, neurosis is a representation of the processes of repression. Thus, even as Tasso seeks to "defend against" the narrative unconscious of romance by means of Goffredo's (distinctly offensive) siege-towers, these same siege-towers become a synecdochic representation of a repressed need not only to seek Troy as an origin, but also to kill Troy again.

Moreover, it is because of Troy's latent influence as a repressed metaphor that the narrative of the *Liberata* is not just "neurotic," but is, more specifically, inherently narcissistic. As we have seen, narcissism is constituted by a displacement of energy onto an ideal ego—a displacement that inevitably becomes "the conditioning factor of repression." And, as we have also seen, one of the uncannier consequences of Tasso's sublimatory displacement onto the epic forest of Jerusalem is an inadvertent setting up of Troy as the ideal ego of a new narrative of *indugio*—a new displacement that becomes the very "conditioning factor of repression" for the *Liberata*. Jerusalem, as the first city seen of epic history, must be assaulted in order for Tasso's Crusaders to realize their sublimatory goal. But the manner in which this assault is consciously delayed so that Jerusalem can be defeated "properly" also becomes the (unconscious) "conditioning factor of repression" for the epic narrative. Tasso has put the sublimatory impulse of his epic in the odd position of being identical to a repressive narcissism itself: the sublimatory impulse of proper epic assault transforms itself into a representation of a repressed Troy as the ego ideal of the *translatio imperii*.

Genera ne la selva

Above all, what we may conclude from the foregoing discussion is that the woods of Jerusalem may very well be the most overdetermined locus in the literary history of epic. They serve as a representation of epic purposiveness, even as they inherit the narrative space of romance deferral. And they are the privileged locus of Tasso's efforts at shaping the *Liberata* as a truly sublimatory epic, even as their arboreal spirits, as will be discussed later, reflect the narcissism of Goffredo's individual *erranti*. A number of questions, then, present themselves at this point. How is it that the woods of Jerusalem come to *be* so overdetermined? If we are justified, as I believe, in arguing that a narrative unconscious is embedded in the deep structure of the *Liberata*, then how does the simple (and single) act of the cutting down of trees become the narrative's merely arbitrary solution to its overdetermined contradictions? How is it that a single narrative site can become so overdetermined that Tasso's self-consciously constructed narrative cannot safely declare itself "out of the woods" even after its trees are destroyed? How is it somehow inevitable that a repressed Troy would emerge from these trees? To what extent is Rinaldo's ultimate cutting down of the trees the arbitrarily epic solution to what Tasso may have discovered to be the unresolvable repressions of romance—and, in particular, the unresolvable problem of Troy as the return of the repressed within the literary history of epic?

The answers to at least some of these questions may originate in the *Discorsi*, where Tasso goes to great lengths to eliminate any psychic force of the other by means of his emphasis on the *verisimile*. Tasso argues that the truth of the *materia nuda* of history must be shaped and refined into the *verisimile*, or "la sembianza della verità" (the "appearance of truth"), a key, yet curiously unstable, concept in Tasso's epic history because it must inhabit an obscure threshold between "l'autorità dell'istoria" (the "authority of history") and "la licenza del fingere" ("the freedom to create"). Although the *verisimile* in epic poetry is "propria ed intrinseca dell'essenza sua" ("proper and intrinsic to its essence"), one of the greatest challenges for the epic poet, as Tasso sees it, is to achieve a harmonious joining of the *verisimile* with the delights of the *maraviglioso*, a difficult poetic task never achieved by the likes of Ariosto, whose fantastic hippogriff is, in Tasso's estimation, emblematic of the failure to accommodate the wondrous into epic. For Tasso, the *verisimile* and the *maraviglioso*, though "diversissime" ("very different"), must, like epic and romance, be joined together in "un'azione medesima" ("one and the same action"). But as the largely ineffable juncture between poetry and history—as the gap where representation inevitably renders history an "absent cause"—the *verisimile* becomes difficult to achieve. The narrative must record the "truths" of epic history, even as it must accommodate the poetic pleasures of the *maraviglioso* as part of its representation of history. If Tasso is aware of the *maraviglioso* as serving as a kind of poetic "other" for his concept of the *verisimile* (they are, after all, "diverssisime"), then he is also aware of the need to collapse the *maraviglioso* into the *verisimile* as a guarantee that his narrative cannot be subverted by the potentially psychic play of fantasy.

Tasso seeks to confine many of his marvels, like Ismeno's arboreal enchantments, to the woods of Jerusalem; and thus, the woods serve not only as the locus of his attempt to collapse the distinction between epic and romance, but also as the locus of his attempt to join the *verisimile* and the *maraviglioso* in "un'azione medesima." But the result for Tasso's epic is that the *maraviglioso* will also find itself transformed into the complex intersections of psyche (as the "origin" of fantasy) and epic history. We might at this point turn to Freud's "Two Principles of Mental Functioning" for an intriguing summary of the psychic origin of fantasy: "With the introduction of the reality principle one mode of thought-activity was split off: it was kept free from reality-testing and remained subordinated to the pleasure principle alone. This is the act of *phantasy-making* [*das Phantasieren*], which begins already with the game of children, and later, continued as *day-dreaming*, abandons its dependence on real objects."[20] Herbert Marcuse expands on Freud's characterization of fantasy as a "game of children," claiming that the stubborn persistence of the pleasure principle means that "the forbidden images and impulses of childhood begin to tell the truth that reason denies."[21] Marcuse's claim is worth repeating: the fantasies of childhood *begin to tell the truth* that reason will not allow.

What are the possibilities that a poetic "truth" can reside not simply in the historical past of an epic *verisimile*, but also, more significantly, in the forbidden images—in the *meraviglie*—of an infantile "return of the repressed"? This is a question that Tasso's epic theory does not fully confront. Despite its heavy reliance on Aristotelian authority, the *Discorsi del poema eroico* is not always confident in its declaration of what constitutes integrity in the use of the poetic image. Consciously echoing Aristotle, Tasso nevertheless seems

[20]*SE* 12:222.
[21]Marcuse, *Eros and Civilization*, 21.

vaguely petulant and ill-tempered in his effort to separate the verisimilar from mere phantasm:

> Perché se i poeti sono imitatori, conviene che siano imitatori del vero,
> perché il falso non è; e quel che non è, non si può imitare: però quelli
> che scrivono cose in tutto false, se non sono imitatori, non sono poeti,
> ed i suoi componimenti non sono poesie, ma finzioni più tosto. (P. 522)

> (If poets are imitators, it is fitting that they imitate truth, since the false
> does not exist, and what does not exist cannot be imitated. Those who
> write what is wholly false, then, not being imitators, are not poets, and
> their compositions are not poems but rather fictions; hence they either
> do not deserve, or deserve far less, the name of poet.)

It is in passages such as these, of course, that Tasso is seeking to
defend himself against readers who crave fantastic marvels like Ariostan hippogriffs. In the *Liberata*, Tasso attempts to confine these
absurd fantasies to Plutone's hell:

> Qui mille immonde Arpie vedresti, e mille
> Centauri, e Sfingi, e pallide Gorgoni;
> Molte e molte latrar voraci scille,
> E fischiar Idre, e sibilar Pitoni,
> E vomitar Chimere atre faville;
> E Polifemi orrendi, e Gerïoni;
> Diversi aspetti in un confusi e misti.
>
> (IV.5)

> (Here might you see a thousand filthy Harpies and a thousand Cen-
> taurs and Sphinxes and pale Gorgons; a myriad ravenous Scyllas howl-
> ing and Hydras hooting and Pythons hissing and Chimaeras belching
> forth black flames; and horrible Polyphemuses and Geryons; and in
> strange monstrosities, not elsewhere known or seen, diverse appear-
> ances confused and blended into one.)

In Edward Fairfax's 1600 translation of the *Liberata*, the unnatural
creatures that inhabit hell are, simply, "unlike themselves, and like
naught else";[22] and his translation comes very close to Tasso's claim
in the *Discorsi* that "il falso non è."

---

[22]*Torquato Tasso: Jerusalem Delivered*, trans. Edward Fairfax, intro. John Charles
Nelson (New York: Capricorn Books, 1963).

Thus, with his concept of the *maraviglioso*, Tasso, like so many contributors to *cinquecento* literary criticism, concerns himself with the vexed question of the origin of images and their link between signifier and signified.[23] Like Mazzoni, who sought to make a careful distinction between the icastic imagination, whose images are veri-similar, and the phantastic imagination, that concocts mere products of a hyperinventive fantasy,[24] Tasso attempted to be scrupulous about eliminating from his poetry any traces of an image whose sig-nifier could not hook up clearly to a signified that imitated truth—to a signified that did not threaten, in Sidney's words in his *Apology for Poetry*, to "infect the fancy with unworthy objects." Just as Goffredo seeks to impose order on his troops through the "reality principle" of his disciplinary authority, so also does Tasso demand a signified that can anchor the signifier in poetic truth—a signified that can render the signifier, to paraphrase Fairfax, "like itself." In the *Liberata*, any image that did not ultimately meet these requirements was consigned to the realms of the false imagists and artificers, like Is-meno, or the magus Idraorte and his niece, the deceptive and beau-tiful enchantress Armida, whose "fictions" of orphaned distress—her "finto dolor" (IV.77)—eventually scatter Goffredo's knights in her service.

But despite his efforts to limit false images and phantasms to the special hell of "imitatori" (which included, presumably, his prede-cessor Ariosto), Tasso seems persistently engaged with the wedge between signifier and signified that inevitably attenuates the process of representation. His "Allegoria" dwells less on how to insure po-etic truth than it does on descriptions of the free and unrestrained play of false images. He speaks of "il fuoco, il turbine, le tenebre, i mostri e l'altre sì fatte apparenze" ("the fire, the whirlwind, the darkness, the monsters, and other feigned semblances")—that al-ways signal the "imagine di male." We are warned of the many "in-gannevoli argomenti" ("deceiving allurements") that haunt his long poem; and we are told explicitly of the perverse magic of the pagan enchanter Ismeno—of his "incanti . . . ne la selva che ingannano con delusioni" ("the enchantments in the woods, deceiving with il-

[23]For an account of Renaissance critical controversies concerning the integrity of imaginative poetry, see John Guillory's chapter "The Genealogy of Imagination," in his *Poetic Authority: Spenser, Milton, and Literary History* (New York: Columbia Univer-sity Press, 1983).

[24]Mazzoni himself was, of course, influenced by Plato's distinction in the *Sophist* (236a–d) between "eikastic" and "phantastic" imagination.

lusions") and of how they signify only "la falsità de la ragioni e de le persuasioni, la qual si genera ne la selva" ("the falsity of the reasons and persuasions, which are generated in the woods").

In short, because of Tasso's epic theory, we always know that false images can be "found" in the woods. But what are we really to make of the phantasms inhabiting the *Liberata*'s overdetermined woods? How misguided and deluded *are* the Christian soldiers when they swear that the woods surrounding Jerusalem are inhabited by spirits, when one in particular reports to Goffredo that "Ch'io credo (e il giurerei) che in quelle piante / Abbia la reggia sua Pluton traslata" ("I believe [and I would swear to it] that Pluto has transferred his palace into those trees" [XIII.23]).[25] Despite the commonplace metaphor of the sinister evils of the Wandering Wood that structures so much of epic romance (and so much of the *Furioso*, in particular), Tasso nevertheless seemed ambivalent toward the woods as the locus of poetic endeavor—a tendency almost certainly owing more to the genre of pastoral than of romance. Is a susceptibility to the spirits of the tenebrous woods a definitive sign of moral weakness, or does it render the wanderer in the forest a type of Orphic hierophant with special access to sylvan inspiration? In the estimation of Goffredo, who needs the wood from the surrounding forest to build siege-towers to storm the walls of Jerusalem,[26] his wayward knights, convinced that they sense the immanence of Ismeno's sylvan enchantments, are truants to the cause of empire. But for *erranti* such as Tancredi, these sylvan secrets, "i miracoli del bosco," unfold imaginative truths that cannot so easily be violated

---

[25]In the *Pharsalia*, after Caesar sends his men to cut down the trees outside of Marseilles, Lucan writes: "Lucas erat longo numquam violatus ab aevo, / Obscurum cingens connexis aera ramis, / Et gelidas alte submotis solibus umbras" (III.399–401) ("The axe-men came on an ancient and sacred grove. Its interlacing branches enclosed a cool central space into which the sun never shone, but where an abundance of water sprouted from dark springs)." Like Goffredo's wayward knights, the axe-men are terror-stricken: "Sed fortes tremuere manus, motique verenda / Maiestate loci, si robora sacra ferirent, / In sua credebant redituras membra secures" (429–31) ("Yet the loneliness and solemnity of the grove awed his very toughest soldiers; they shrank from their task, convinced that if they struck at the sacred trees the axes would rebound, turn in the air, and chop off their legs"). (My citation of the *Pharsalia* is from *M. Annaei Lvcani: Belli Civilis*, ed. A. E. Housman [Oxford: Basil Blackwell, 1926]. The English translation is Robert Graves's *Lucan: Pharsalia* [Baltimore: Penguin Books, 1957].)
[26]As Thomas P. Roche, Jr., phrases it in his essay "Tasso's Enchanted Woods," Goffredo requires the "literalization of the metaphor" of the trees (in *Literary Uses of Typology from the Late Middle Ages to the Present*, ed. Earl Miner [Princeton: Princeton University Press, 1977], 621).

with the swing of an axe—or with the arbitrary poetic shift from the metaphorical to the literal.

The burden of literary history, in short, makes it difficult for Tasso to dispel the spirits in the woods. Certainly we find within Neoplatonic theory a rich precedent for Tasso's choice of the Jerusalem woods and its strange phantasms as a kind of originary locus of poetic inspiration. Ficino explicitly interpreted Plato's *Phaedrus*, which he took to be the philosopher's first dialogue, as a pastoral eclogue where indwelling, local deities preside in a hushed, numinous setting of potential inspiration.[27] As Adam Parry observes of the *Phaedrus*, "The ambiance is one to suggest and reinforce that vision of natural truth with which Socrates wishes to counter Lysian rhetoric. Here the gods still live, who have no place in the sophistic milieu of the town."[28] In such a scheme, the forest of Jerusalem becomes the *silva*, glossed in Servius's commentary on the *Aeneid* as "prime matter," the material substrate of chaotic elements that nevertheless holds the potential, if properly animated, for achieving the realm of the Intelligible. It is this sylvan prime matter (the *hyle* of Aristotle's *Metaphysics*, 1032a), with its tendency toward decay, that both opposes the harmony of the One and invites "translation" into the higher forms of the supramundane.[29] For Ficino the pastoral setting, the seat of prime matter, is both the "vision of natural truth" and the necessary prelude to poetic inspiration, a hymnic setting whose local inhabitants testify to divine presences. Thus when Phaedrus, walking barefoot with Socrates along the bank of the Ilissus, is counseled to remain silent during the divine chirping of the cicadas, it is a sure sign that the sylvan prime matter of the woods is teeming with the deities of an Orphic, poetic rapture.

Taken in a Phaedran context, it is no mere coincidence that in the *Aeneid*, just prior to the visionary moment of Venus's epiphany, dressed as one of Diana's huntress-nymphs, before her son, Virgil makes it a point of describing the mysterious and hushed presence

[27]For a fuller discussion of Ficino's emphasis on the *Phaedrus* as the archetypal pastoral, see Michael J. B. Allen, *The Platonism of Marsilio Ficino: A Study of his "Phaedrus" Commentary, Its Sources and Genesis* (Berkeley: University of California Press, 1984), 114.

[28]Adam Parry, "Landscape in Greek Poetry," *Yale Classical Studies* 15 (1957), 15.

[29]William Nelson observes that by the time of the Renaissance, Servius's definition of *silva* "enters the dictionaries, and Cooper defines the word not only as 'wood' but also as a 'store of matter digested together'" (*The Poetry of Edmund Spenser: A Study* [New York: Columbia University Press, 1963], 159). Nelson stresses its potential for animation into higher forms when he describes the *silva* as "the material stuff upon which the divine ideas are impressed" (159).

of the Carthaginian forest: "tum silvis scaena coruscis / Desuper, horrentique atrum nemus imminet umbra" ("the backdrop—glistening / forests and, beetling from above, a black / grove, thick with bristling shadows" [1.164–65])—the locus of mystery itself. And, significantly, Tasso's own pastoral drama the *Aminta* (subtitled *Favola boschereccia*) resounds with Orphic allusions to the responsiveness of nature to the human imagination. At one point, Aminta claims, "Ho visto a 'l pianto mio / Risponder per pietate i sassi e l'onde, / E sospirar le fronde" ("I have seen rocks and waves in pity answer my complaint, / and the leaves sigh" [1.ii.246–48]).[30] Moreover, Dafne testifies,

> Amano ancora
> Gli arbori. Veder puoi con quanto affetto
> E con quanti iterati abbracciamenti
> La vite s'avviticchia a 'l suo marito.
>   (1.i.150–53)

> (Even the trees are in love.
> You can see how dearly and how often
> the vine entrails herself with the one to whom
> she is wedded.)

One suspects that the Phaedran topos of the *silva* as the locus of inspiration and epiphany (and its personified descriptions of sighing leaves, sensuous vines, and amorous trees) never quite relinquished its hold on Tasso's poetic imagination, even as he abandoned pastoral to "progress" to epic.[31] And, not surprisingly, the generic battle internal to the narrative structure of the *Liberata* seems less the tension between epic and romance than the struggle of epic to overcome the lures of pastoral. What else are we to make of Erminia's pastoral escape to a shepherd's cottage on the banks of the Jordan, "infra l'ombrose piante" ("among the shady trees" [VII.1]), an episode otherwise entirely unrelated to Tasso's epic superstructure?[32]

---

[30]All references to the *Aminta* are taken from *Torquato Tasso: Aminta*, intro. A. Tortoreto (Milan: Antonio Vallardi, 1946). The English translation is *Aminta: A Pastoral Drama*, ed. and trans. Ernest Grillo (London: Dent, 1924).

[31]For a full discussion of pathetic fallacy in Tasso's pastoral, see Richard Cody, *The Landscape of the Mind: Pastoralism and Platonic Theory in Tasso's "Aminta" and Shakespeare's Early Comedies* (Oxford: Oxford University Press, 1969), 44–56.

[32]During her pastoral interlude, the love-struck Erminia carves Tancredi's name "in

How do we explain the fact that the epic triumph of Goffredo's Cru-saders is contingent less on successful combat with the pagans on the battlegrounds of religious conflict than on the simple vanquish-ing of trees? And how do we come to terms with Greene's aesthetic claim that "in the finest of his magical fantasies, the enchanted wood, Tasso is very great indeed"[33]—the very wood that Tasso's own poetry must also castrate and destroy? (In the final analysis, how significant is it that the poet's own name, "Torquato Tasso," meaning literally a "twisted yew tree," echoes the "tassi" that fall to the axes of Goffredo's men in III.76?)

In his "Allegoria" that accompanies the *Liberata*, Tasso seems to renounce the free play of the pastoral imagination, arguing: "I fiori, i fonti, i ruscelli, gl' instrumenti musici, le ninfe [on Armida's isle] sono i fallaci sillogismi" ("The flowers, the fountains, the rivers, the musical instruments, the nymphs, are false syllogisms")? (We will return later to the significance of this intriguing metaphor.) But even as in his *Discorsi* Tasso abandons pastoral to accept the challenge of formulating his own epic theory, and even as he favors the *verisimile* as "propria ed intrinseca" to epic poetry, he continues his fascina-tion with and association of (pastoral) trees and poetic image. In the second book of the *Discorsi del poema eroico*, he observes that "niuna selva fu già mai ripiena di tanta varietà d'alberi di quanta diversità di soggetti è la poesia" ("no forest was ever so full of such a variety of trees as poetry is of a variety of subjects" [pp. 514–15]). Given Tasso's own emphasis in the *Liberata* on the forest as the locus of the poetic image itself, his Orphic analogy between literary *copia* and trees strikes the reader as more than mere coincidence. Also in the second book of his treatise, Tasso suggests to the reader that "la materia [of poetry] è simile ad una selva oscura, tenebrosa e priva d'ogni luce" ("the material [of poetry] is like a dark forest, murky and without a ray of light" [p. 514]). Here, Tasso may be implying an elemental play on words between *materia* as the fictive inventive-ness of poetry, and the *hyle* as the substrate of prime (sylvan) matter

---

mille piante" ("on a thousand trees" [VII.19]). In an extensive footnote, Murrin argues convincingly that in the *Liberata* there is only one grove of trees outside Jerusalem (*The Allegorical Epic*, 238n49). Thus, we are presented with the extraordinary poetic pros-pect that the very trees inscribed with Tancredi's name are also the trees that eventu-ally become Goffredo's siege-towers. (For a reading of Erminia's pastoral interlude as "the point at which the potential fulfillment of desire and desire's negation cross paths," see Marilyn Migiel, "Tasso's Erminia: Telling an Alternate Story," *Italica* 64:1 [1987], esp. 65–68.)

[33]*The Descent from Heaven*, 207.

itself. Although the *selva oscura* contain incredible images that must
be subordinated to the gravity of *imperium* (and of epic unity), their
tenebrous and unreal shades will not relinquish their hold on
Tasso's own imagination—almost as if he suspects, in spite of himself, that an essential poetic truth resides there.

In this context, we are reminded of Freud's "act of *phantasy-making*," which he claims begins with children's games—or with what
Marcuse refers to as "the forbidden images and impulses of childhood [that] begin to tell the truth that reason denies." In his "Allegoria," as we have seen, Tasso attacks his own creation Ismeno and
the mage's phantasms, which signify only "la falsità de la ragioni
("the falsehood of reason"). But Tasso can never quite rid himself of
the notion of a (childlike) poetic truth that achieves its own cred-
ibility in the forests of the imagination. In Book II of his *De rerum
natura*, Lucretius writes: "As children in blank darkness tremble and
start at everything, so we in broad daylight are oppressed at times
by fears as baseless as those horrors which children imagine coming
upon them in the dark." In quoting this passage, Murrin notes that
Tasso, in his own edition of Lucretius, had underlined this passage.[34]
But why? Certainly Tasso's interest in these lines is ambiguous. Did
he underline them to reinforce his suspicion of "baseless" images?
Or did he underline them as part of his ongoing fascination with the
murky (but poetically fertile) interplay of dark places, fear, and
imaginative horrors, which, again to echo Marcuse, "begin to tell the
truth that reason denies"? Thus, even as Tasso clings stubbornly to
the poet's obligation to be credible, he persistently acknowledges
the power of child-like inventiveness.

Despite the aesthetic self-consciousness of the *Liberata*—its scrupulous privileging of the "broad daylight" of the epic versimilar over
the "blank darkness" of the false images of the *maraviglioso*—the
woods of Jerusalem serve as the locus of an unconscious play of
fantasy. To echo Theseus in *A Midsummer Night's Dream* (v.i), the
woods of Jerusalem are the "local habitation" for Tasso's "forms of
things unknown." And even though the forest is doomed to the
hacking castration of epic purposiveness, we are nevertheless permitted a lengthy sojourn in its dark recesses. In Book III, Tasso's
description of the Christians' initial assault on the forest for the construction of their siege-towers suggests an underlying ambivalence
concerning the cruelty of their project:

[34]*The Allegorical Epic*, 233n1.

L'un l'altro esorta che le piante atterri,
E faccia al bosco inusitati oltraggi.
Caggion recise da' taglienti ferri
Le sacre palme, e i frassini selvaggi.
(III.75)[35]

(One man spurs on another to cut down the trees, and to do unwonted outrages to the wood. The sacred palms fall, cut by the cleaving steel, and the woodland ashes.)

Here Tasso would seem to be demonstrating that Goffredo's epic strategy is, simply, leading to murder in the forest. The "inusitati oltraggi" of epic purposiveness is also the destroyer of invisible arboreal spirits (invisible because the woodsmen are not Orphically inspired?), of "le fère e gli augei" exiled from their shady bowers.[36] As Clorinda's spirit will insist later in Canto XIII, "Son di sensi animati i rami e i tronchi" ("Branches and trunks are animate with sense" [43]). The "inusitati oltraggi" of Goffredo's soldiers against the *meraviglie* of the trees establish the Jerusalem forest as the *Liberata*'s problematic intersection of psyche and history—the point at which epic *oltraggi* meet their other in the invisible spirits of the *maraviglioso*.

Androgyny and Narcissism Revisited: Love-as-Death

The *Liberata*'s most memorable (and most "marvelous") arboreal spirit is, of course, the phantasm of Tancredi's beloved Clorinda, whom he nightmarishly confronts as a bleeding branch in Canto

---

[35]Tasso's passage seems indebted to Virgil's description of the felling of the trees by Aeneas and his men to make an altar for Misenus's tomb. On the threshold of the Sibyl's uncanny cave, "Procumbunt picae, sonat icta securibus ilex, / Fraxineaque trabes cuneis et fissile robur / Scinditur, advolvunt ingentis montibus ornos" (VI.180–83) ("The pitch pines fall; / the ilex rings beneath ax strokes; their wedges / now cleave the trunks of ash and splintering oaks. / They roll the giant rowans down the mountain)."

[36]Theodore Ziolkowski writes, "Mme du Deffand, when asked if she believed in ghosts, replied: 'Non, mais j'en ai peur [No, but I'm afraid of them].' I have long felt a deep and spontaneous sympathy with that wise and witty woman of the Enlightenment, whose respect for reason did not preclude a reverence for those aspects of life, inaccessible to pure rationalizing, that are sometimes uncritically called supernatural" (*Disenchanted Images: A Literary Iconology* [Princeton: Princeton University Press, 1977], vii). Like Mme du Deffand, Tasso may not believe in ghosts, but he does seem persistently afraid of them.

XIII. In the next two sections of this chapter, I discuss the extent to which Tasso establishes Clorinda as the paradigmatic "marvel" of the *Liberata*, the vanquishing of whose arboreal spirit is part of his epic strategy to collapse the *maraviglioso* back into the *verisimile* in "un'azione medesima." Through the destruction of Clorinda, Tasso seeks to reinstate the Jerusalem woods as the locus of sublimation for his epic, the point at which Tancredi's narcissistic investment with *meraviglie* can be converted into the sublimatory vanquishing of trees. As perhaps Aladino's fiercest and most skilled defender of Jerusalem, Clorinda must inevitably be marked for death; but this is only a partial explanation of why she must be so brutally eliminated from the narrative. The real "truth" of why the Amazon Clorinda must be destroyed is that she embodies an uncanniness that lingers as its own kind of poetic "truth." The *inusitati oltraggi* must eventually be unleashed not only against the Jerusalem trees, but also against Clorinda, whose androgyny is the site both of narcissistic aggressivity and of Tancredi's futile quest for identity through an attempt to embrace sexual difference and division.

Tancredi's love for the "vergine gloriosa" Clorinda, Tasso's version of the female warrior, is, of course, a major subplot in the *Liberata*. But to what extent is it really a "love" story? What damage are we doing to Tasso's story of Tancredi and Clorinda by reading it as a narrative of love? And to what extent do we set ourselves up for disappointment when we read it as such? In a letter to Francesco Rinuccini, Galileo complains "Che l'amor di Tancredi verso Clorinda ovvero tra esse . . . sia sterilissima cosuccia in proportione tra l'amore di Ruggiero, e Bradamante, adornato di tutti i grandi avvenimenti, che tra due nobili Amanti sogliono"[37] ("that the love of Tancredi for Clorinda, or between them . . . is a most sterile thing in relation to the love of Ruggiero and Bradamante, embellished with all the fine episodes that are wont to occur between two noble lovers").

But Galileo may have been too hasty in his reading. Indeed, what could potentially be more "sterile" than the love of Bradamante and Ruggiero, ordained in the cave of the aged Merlin and sealed by a destiny that cannot fail? Surely there is more intrinsic interest in Tasso's narrative of love, involving, as it does, the death—no, the *murder*—of one of the lovers. Unlike Ariosto's warrior maidens Bra-

[37]This letter is quoted and translated in Margaret Tomalin, *The Fortunes of the Warrior Heroine in Italian Literature: An Index of Emancipation* (Ravenna: Longo Editore, 1982), 182–83.

damante and Marfisa, who are happily accommodated into the dynastic future of Ferrara, Clorinda is violently murdered by the one who adores her. To understand fully this ambivalent mix of love and death in Tasso's narrative, we must consider the literary history of the Amazon as the complex background of the Tancredi–Clorinda subplot. Only then will we be able to appreciate their deadly encounter as no mere love story, but as the ravages of a mutual narcissism that resists the imposing of the epic verisimilar.

First, we must review the case of Ariosto, who (unlike Virgil and Tasso) resisted the impulse to "kill off" his Amazons. Specifically, a return to Marfisa and the relationship between the fierce intensity of her narcissism and her status as an androgynous warrior will, perhaps, shed some light on the differences in Tasso's portrayal of the Amazon. It is not merely coincidence that, throughout the *Furioso*, Marfisa is both Ariosto's most arbitrarily pugnacious figure and virtually the only principal character who is not defined by another's object that she aggressively seeks to possess. Her object-libido is focused not on the purloined object but on her own ego.[38] It is not the fragment of another knight's weaponry that she desires, but her own armor as most constitutive of her own identity: "però che già sue furo, e l'ebbe care / quanto si suol le cose ottime e rare" ("Once hers, and dear to her; as matters are / Esteemed by us as excellent and rare" [18.108]). Marfisa, "armata sempre" throughout Ariosto's narrative, looks for knights to unhorse and defeat, but her many imitative rivalries are merely a manifestation of her own ego-libido. Her aggressive quest for herself in the other is simply her most effective means of expressing a drive to *resemble herself*, taking, in effect, her own body as her love-object, and, in the process, tracing a regressive narcissism that is both more infantile and more violent than perhaps even Mandricardo's search for self through Hector's armor. Marfisa's primitive narcissism inhabits an obscure threshold between object-love and autoerotism, marking the point at which object-libido doubles back on the ego itself.

In this sense, then, Marfisa is an anomaly within the tradition of the Amazon in romance epic: unlike, for example, Bradamante or Spenser's Britomart, her femininity inspires no love or adoration anywhere in Ariosto's narrative. Scarcely an ego at all, undifferentiated from herself by means of her own ego-libido, Marfisa angrily

[38]"We see also," observes Freud, "an antithesis between ego-libido and object-libido. The more of the one is employed, the more the other becomes depleted" ("On Narcissism;" *SE* 14:76).

declares to Mandricardo, "nè d'altri son che mia: / dunque me tolga a me chi mi desia" ("Nor theirs am I, nor other's, but my own, / Who wins me, wins me from myself alone" [26.79])—a stark contrast to the confession of the love-struck and nearly insane Orlando: "Non son, non sono io quel che paio in viso" (23.128). More traditionally (and certainly this is the case in Tasso's epic), the androgyny of the female warrior both inspires adoration and becomes the locus of a destructive division that destroys her and her admirers. Neither fully male nor fully female, the androgynous female warrior is arrested on the very threshold of ego formation. "Consciousness of self," argues Borch-Jacobsen, "begins by splitting in two and warring with itself. It appears to itself as (the) other, and this means that the experience of consciousness (phenomenology) is inaugurated in internal violence, in a duel unto death."[39] As we shall see later, the price of achieving an epic subjecthood will be, for Tasso's Clorinda, a "war" with herself that can only result in death.

The prototype for the female warrior can be found, of course, in Plato's androgyne, the union of male and female, whose story of being torn asunder by an angry Zeus (and the subsequent "fall" into sexual difference) is narrated by Aristophanes in the *Symposium*. The story of the Platonic androgyne searching for its other half has traditionally been viewed as a kind of primal myth of wholeness achieved through gender symmetry—as, indeed, the very principle of Eros itself. In *The Ego and the Id*, Freud defines Eros as a force of unification (*Vereinigung*) that preserves all life, an impulse that seeks to combine things in ever greater wholes.[40] Thus, the Platonic androgyne is quite literally *erotic*, an organic life-principle that promises a consolidation into sexual wholeness.[41] But in *Beyond the Pleasure Principle*, Freud also points to the regressiveness inherent in Eros—its tendencies, like the death drive, to "*restore an earlier state of things.*"[42] Freud explicitly links this regression to an originary state to a kind of primitive narcissistic unity and completeness; but it is the narcissism of a "return" to death.

[39]*The Freudian Subject*, 90.
[40]*SE* 19:64.
[41]For a discussion of Renaissance depictions of the two halves of the hermaphrodite as reflecting an androcentric narcissism, an image of "erotic sameness" linked to a "bond between men" that necessarily effaces the woman, see Carla Freccero's essay "The Other and the Same: The Image of the Hermaphrodite in Rabelais," in *Rewriting the Renaissance: The Discourses of Sexual Difference in Early Modern Europe*, ed. Margaret W. Ferguson, Maureen Quilligan, and Nancy J. Vickers (Chicago: University of Chicago Press, 1986), 152–53.
[42]*SE* 18:36; italics Freud's.

Freud's link between Eros and narcissism is the key to understanding why the androgyne is such a precarious site of ego formation. The androgynous Amazons of epic romance, in particular, exist somewhere between an anticipation of bodily symmetry and unity, and a narcissism that can potentially render the androgyne as the site of violence, the site of a "duel unto death." The particular complexity of the ego-libido of the androgynous warrior lies in its impossible goal of playing off sexual symmetry to attain an intact self-sufficiency; aggressively seeking a rivalrous imitation of the (male) other in order to shore up the (female) self, the androgynous warrior is not only doomed to fail, but is also the locus of danger for any male (like Tancredi) who becomes the target of her rivalrous identification.

The source of the androgynous warrior's destructive division lies in a confused and ill-defined narcissism that places her on an obscure threshold between wanting to *have* the phallus and wanting to *be* the phallus. In her essay on Barthes' *S/Z*, Barbara Johnson argues the impossibility of any attempt to use the other as a means to sexual symmetry: "a structure that is supposed to involve the creation of a complementary union between two separate terms—man and woman . . .—becomes, rather, a structure in which the initial separability of the two terms cannot be taken for granted, while at the same time the unity of each individual term consists of its infinite capacity for division."[43] The androgynous warrior becomes, then, a dramatic illustration of Johnson's axiom that the subject cannot "embrace the other's division"[44]—which is precisely, as we shall see later, what Tancredi attempts to do with Clorinda. Because the female warrior must struggle, to echo Borch-Jacobsen, with her own "internal violence," any male warrior who chooses her as the object of his own narcissistic quest is doomed to a crushing duel unto death.

The seemingly self-sufficient intactness of the androgynous warrior, her extraordinary combination of physical prowess, beauty, and *gran superbia*, insures her attractiveness to the male warrior, whose own narcissistic self-love becomes dependent on her arrogance. In his essay "On Narcissism," Freud argues that a person who loves has, in effect, "forfeited part of his narcissism,"[45] resulting in the standard Petrarchan narrative of the lover's loss of self-esteem when his haughty object of desire refuses to return his love. But we

---

[43]"The Critical Difference: BartheS/BalZac," in *The Critical Difference*, 18.
[44]Ibid., 19.
[45]*SE* 14:98.

must not hastily dismiss this dynamic as an example of mere "unre-quited love." Here Borch-Jacobsen's analysis of the mutual interplay between love and narcissism is useful:

> the ego, in the last analysis, is by no means lost in erotic ecstasy. On the contrary, one might even say that woman is all the more apt to represent the ego (and thus to satisfy her narcissism), in that she is more inaccessible to object love—that is to say, *more narcissistic*. That is why Freud also remarks that those men "who have renounced part of their own narcissism," far from choosing women who will love them (as men), are attracted to those women who reflect back to them the image of an intact narcissism.[46]

What the narcissism of the male warrior is seeking is an aloof (and, indeed, aggressive) rejection of his love (which, in Freud's terms, is simply the forfeiture of a portion of his own narcissism). He is impressed not with "womanly" submission, but with aloof self-sufficiency (and indeed, Clorinda is at one point described as a "sol fuggitiva," a "solitary fugitive" [1.48]), a combative and aggres-sive haughtiness that is capable of reflecting back to him "the image of [his own] intact narcissism." "Love does not adapt itself to the two sexes," continues Borch-Jacobsen. "On the contrary, it neutral-izes the sexual opposition on the basis of a fundamental homosex-uality. 'Men' and 'women'—men *as* women—love themselves as homosexuals."[47] Borch-Jacobsen's conflation of "men *as* women" il-lustrates the inadequacy of summarizing the romance epic topos of the combat between male knight and female warrior as simply a "battle between the sexes." There can be no battle *between* the sexes, but only a battle *within* men *as* women and women *as* men, as both genders struggle to strengthen their own ego-libido through the other.[48] The female warrior seeks combat with the male as part of her

---

[46]*The Freudian Subject*, 108.

[47]Ibid., 112.

[48]Rossini's operatic portrayal of Tancredi's love for Clorinda and the consequences of their eventual death-duel are the subjects of Hélène Cixous's essay "Tancrède Con-tinue" (in her *Entre l'écriture* [Paris: Des Femmes, 1986], 141–68). Referring to the Tancredi–Clorinda subplot as "l'autre histoire" (141) of the story of the conquering of Jerusalem, Cixous deconstructs the "mystère de 'femme' et 'homme'" (146), which she sees at the heart of Tancredi's mistaking Clorinda for a man just prior to their death-duel. Cixous's densely deconstructive essay celebrates a "jouissance à l'autre qui ne dit pas son sexe" (142); and the play of gender that she perceives as charac-terizing their encounters is reflected in the *jouissance* of Cixous's own confusingly gendered pronouns. Thus, both Tancredi and Clorinda are described as "un elle et

need to *be* the phallus through a wielding of the phallus (her phallic lance), and the male knight responds with even greater intensity to her hostile self-sufficiency as part of his narcissistic need to have his own ego-libido reflected back to him. This mutual combativeness, this futile attempt to "embrace the other's division," can only lead to violence and often, in particular for the woman, death, which is why Tasso designates Clorinda's death-duel with Tancredi as her "ora fatale" ("fatal hour") (XII.64).[49]

If the narrative of the *Liberata*, unlike that of the *Furioso*, does not preoccupy itself with the effects of object-libido—the quest for identity through purloined armor—Tasso nevertheless offers us another narrative of narcissistic aggressivity: the quest for identity through the futile attempt to embrace sexual difference and division. Suspended on the threshold of gender identity, the Tassoan ego that we see exemplified in Tancredi and Clorinda seeks not consummation through gender symmetry (not, in effect, through the higher organizational impulses of Eros), but rather a "consummation" of his/her own ego-libido through hostile or fateful engagements with the narcissism of the other. Tancredi and Clorinda are suspended on the threshold of ego formation, unable to avoid the consequences of their mutually destructive narcissism. We are perhaps well reminded at this point that Ovid's Narcissus died without ever knowing himself, without ever resolving the question of whether he was the lover or the beloved. Tancredi and Clorinda not only fall short, like the characters of the *Furioso*, of becoming fully formed "selves," but also, despite the seeming battle between the sexes that characterizes their encounters, remain suspended in a regressive phase prior to the assumption of gender identity and sexual differentiation.

With this theoretical framework in mind, we are now in a position to examine how the androgyne's "internal violence" plays itself out

---

une il et une ellil et une ilelle" (147). When Cixous writes that their story is "l'histoire d'un Tancrède qui aime un héros qui est une femme qui est en réalité un héros qui est une femme et s'il l'aime c'est parce que c'est une femme" (166), what she deliberately obfuscates in this vertiginous display of linguistic *jouissance* is the gender of the direct object in the "l'aime." But what is overlooked in Cixous's creative play of gender is the violence of Tancredi's and Clorinda's "duel unto death"—the aggressivity inherent in seeking a rivalrous imitation of the other, and the deadliness of attempting to "embrace the other's division." (Later in this chapter, I argue that it is not "Tancrède Continue" but rather Cixous's essay "Fiction and Its Phantoms," where there is no mention of Tancredi or Clorinda, that ironically serves as a more comprehensive gloss on their strange encounters.)

[49]Later in the same canto, Argante refers to Clorinda's "fatal morte" (103).

in the centuries prior to Renaissance epic. Ancient Greece had a vested interest in marginalizing the Amazon as an exile, a barbarian (living, in some accounts, as far away as northern Anatolia), and a threat to the integrity of the Greek polis;[50] and, as a consequence, throughout epic literary history the Amazon is associated with violence and death. The "wounded Amazon," for example, is a recurring theme in ancient Greek sculpture. Moreover, Guy Cadogan Rothery calls attention to the remains of friezes from the Temple of Aesculapius, housed in the Central Museum in Athens, which depict fierce Amazonomachies and various graphic stages of dying in battle: an Amazon, wounded in the throat, slipping from her horse; a mutilated Amazon barely staying astride a rearing horse; a wounded Amazon being pulled off her horse by a Greek warrior.[51] Dietrich von Bothmer has meticulously collected scores of Attic amphoras and vases, depicting Amazonomachies in which lances are explicitly poised on the verge of mutilating the genitalia of both male and female combatants.[52] Abby Wettan Kleinbaum has studied numerous Roman sarcophagi of the second century A.D. depicting similar scenes of mutilation; she quotes Carl Robert's amazement: " 'nowhere does one see so many slaughtered horses, so many Amazons pulled down by the hair, or by the helmet, as on these reliefs.' "[53] In these examples and many others, Amazons are associated with uncontrollable passions (embodied in their runaway horses), with wounding, and with violent death. As objects of both fascination and revulsion, the Amazon—and the ineffable paradox of her androgyny—could meet her fate only in erotic mutilation and death at the hands of the warrior who, in Rothery's words, "dreads but does not fully comprehend" the victim of his hostility.[54]

The Amazon's destructive union of Eros and Thanatos (glossed over in Shakespeare's *Midsummer Night's Dream* by the witty charm of Theseus's reminder to Hippolyta, "I woo'd thee with my sword") inevitably led to violent combat. As Kleinbaum speculates:

---

[50]For an account of the Amazons' threat to the Greeks, see Page du Bois, *Centaurs and Amazons: Women and the Pre-History of the Great Chain of Being* (Ann Arbor: University of Michigan Press, 1982), 30ff.

[51]Guy Cadogan Rothery, *The Amazons in Antiquity and Modern Times* (London: Francis Griffiths, 1910), 17–18.

[52]Dietrich von Bothmer, *Amazons in Greek Art* (Oxford: Clarendon Press, 1957).

[53]Abby Wettan Kleinbaum, *The War against the Amazons* (New York: McGraw-Hill, 1983), 34.

[54]*The Amazons in Antiquity and Modern Times*, 1.

She is therefore a suitable opponent for the most virile of heroes, and a man who has never envisioned harming a woman can freely indulge in fantasies of murdering an Amazon. The conquest of an Amazon is an act of transcendence, a rejection of the ordinary, of death, of mediocrity—and a reach for immortality. If the Amazon excels in military prowess, then the skill of the hero who defeats her is even more extraordinary.[55]

Thus, from the outset the Amazon became a favored target for the narcissistic aggression of the male warrior, with her death offering more libidinal and narcissistic satisfaction than the vanquishing of the male imitative rival.

The theme of the prestige earned by killing a female warrior has, perhaps, its literary origins in Achilles' slaughter of Penthesilea, the Amazon who comes to the aid of Troy after Priam's death. (We are reminded here that although Virgil later honors Penthesilea by featuring her bravery on Dido's murals [1.491–93]), he also predicts her death as a "bellatrix, audetque uiris concurrere uirgo" ["a warrior who dares to fight with men"].) Rothery cites the example of the *Aethiopia*, a long continuation of the *Iliad* written by Arctinus of Miletus in 770. In Arctinus's version of the slaughter of the Amazon, Achilles brutally (but no less erotically) kills Penthesilea by piercing her left breast.[56] But what makes Arctinus's version of this slaughter so disturbing is Achilles' bizarrely sympathetic reaction, following his sadism, to his victim, for as he attempts to strip Penthesilea of her armor he is seized by her beauty (strangely released by her bodily mutilation) and is stricken with remorse.[57] In a similar vein, Margaret Scherer discusses a fourth-century B.C. Apulian krater that depicts Achilles tenderly catching Penthesilea as she slumps from her horse.[58] And Kleinbaum cites the example of a second-century Roman sarcophagus depicting Achilles lovingly holding Penthesilea's lifeless body.[59] This topos of "Achillean remorse," as Roth-

[55] *The War against the Amazons*, 1.
[56] The breast, of course, serves as the symbol of both the physical prowess and the eroticism of the Amazon. Sarah B. Pomeroy writes, "One explanation of their [the Amazons'] name is that it is derived from *a* (without) *mazos* (breast). According to this fanciful etymology, they cut off their right breasts in order to draw their bows more easily" (*Goddesses, Whores, Wives, and Slaves: Women in Classical Antiquity* [New York: Schocken Books, 1975], 24).
[57] *The Amazons in Antiquity and Modern Times*, 12.
[58] Margaret Scherer, *The Legends of Troy in Art and Literature* (New York: Phaidon Press, 1963), 96.
[59] *The War against the Amazons*, 35.

ery calls it, points to the strange mixture of sadism and masochistic adoration that characterizes the male warrior's response to the Amazon. Love is activated only by the sight/site of the mangled corpse of the Amazon; aggressively seeking Penthesilea's armor as a means of annihilating her identity, Achilles ends up "forfeiting" a portion of his own narcissism by means of this remorse.[60]

Moreover, the topos of Achillean remorse would seem to mark the literary origins of the oscillation between hostile revulsion and adoration that characterizes the male warrior's response to the Amazon throughout the dynastic epic of the Renaissance.[61] Giamatti discusses the topos of the knight being struck with wonder when the female warrior reveals her gender, arguing that the raised helmet of the female warrior (and its Petrarchan exposure of her flowing, golden hair) reveals a kind of divinity, a mysterious and visionary moment that results in "opposites reconciled, here a masculine might and a feminine beauty contained and displayed in [a] single figure."[62] But Giamatti's argument, dependent as it is on the *discordia*

---

[60]As this example demonstrates, the literary history of the Amazon is often implicated in a kind of Ariostan object-libido that aggressively seeks self-validation through another's armor. The female warrior Camilla, appearing in Book XI of Virgil's *Aeneid*, is a dramatic illustration of an Ariostan association between armor and narcissistic wounding. With the prowess of Turnus, on whose side she fights against the Trojans and Etruscans, she smashes warriors and leaves their bodies strewn on the battlefield. She is as frenzied (*furens*) as Turnus, but is unmistakably female, with the characteristic "unum exserta latus," or bared breast (649), of the Amazon. In the midst of the heat of battle, however, Camilla fatefully pauses to covet the armor of the Trojan Chloreus and is brutally cut down by Arruns, an Etruscan who, in the familiar topos of combat with the Amazon, stabs her in her exposed breast.

(By way of digression, it is worth noting here that Tasso undoubtedly borrowed from Virgil's Camilla for the depiction of his virago Clorinda. One indication that Camilla and Clorinda are both slated for exile from epic history [and for brutal slaughter] is the bizarre circumstance of their nurturings as infants. Both are saved from death in infancy by men—Camilla, by her father Metabus, while fleeing from the Volscians, and Clorinda, by Arsetes, her future eunuch, who saves her from the Christian Senapus. The infant Camilla sucks at the udders of wild mares, while Clorinda is nursed by a lioness. The implication is that these two "salvage" Amazons are barely civilized, unable to be accommodated to the epic constraints of the founding of culture. In this context, we can also think of Ariosto's Marfisa, who, like Clorinda, was suckled by a lioness after being "purloined" by Arabs.)

[61]Centuries later, the death-duel between Achilles and Penthesilea was to become the subject of Heinrich von Kleist's drama *Penthesilea*. In this grotesque tragedy, however, the erotic sadism is reversed such that it is Penthesilea who wavers between loving Achilles and longing to conquer him in battle.

[62]"Spenser: From Magic to Miracle," in *Exile and Change*, 78.

concors of the hybrid "Venus armata" so favored in Renaissance Neo-platonism,[63] overlooks the androgyne's "internal violence," which undermines any embodiment of "opposites reconciled." In the literary history of epic, the female warrior's destructive "difference within" incites sadism as often as it inspires adoration.

Giamatti's essay associates armor (specifically, the female warrior's raised helmet) and its exposure of feminine beauty with the mysterious moment of the reconciliation of opposites. But in earlier treatments of the Amazon, armor is seldom linked with moments of vision and revelation, but rather serves as the locus of a mutually destructive narcissism that cannot resolve sexual division. As we have seen, Achilles "forfeits" a part of his narcissism and falls prey to the beauty of Penthesilea only when the armor he so aggressively seeks to possess covers a corpse, not a living vision of opposites reconciled. Indeed, in the many medieval versions of the fall of Troy, and of the slaughter of Penthesilea in particular, the topos of Achillean remorse is displaced by savagery through armor (of the sort that Ariosto no doubt exploited), a duel unto death that leads not to opposites reconciled, but to the slaughter of both combatants.

In *The Destruction of Troy*, for example, an alliterative and loose translation of Guido's *Historia troiana* dating from the twelfth century, the narrator characteristically revels in the brutal detail of Penthesilea's slaughter. Having been severely wounded by Penthesilea, Pyrrhus (the son of Achilles and, ever since Dio Chrysostom's *Trojan Discourses*, the "heir" as murderer of Penthesilea) unleashes his fury against the Amazon:

> Than Pirrus with payne, in his pal angur,
> ffor all the trunchyn of þe tre, þat tenit hym sore,
> Noght hedit his harme, ne his hurt meuyt,
> And meuyt with malis to þe myld quene.
> Sho was bare of hir breast to þe bright mayll,
> Hade no helme on hir hede fro harmys to weire . . .
> But Pirrus hym paynet with all hys pure strenght,
> And flang at hir felly with a fyne swerd;
> Share of þe sheld at a shyre corner;

---

[63]For an account of Venus as a hybrid goddess embodying a paradigmatic *discordia concors* for Renaissance Neoplatonism, see Edgar Wind, *Pagan Mysteries in the Renaissance* (New Haven: Yale University Press, 1958), 73ff.

> Vnioynet the Jawmbe of þe just arme,
> þat hit light on þe laund lythet full euyn.
>
> (xxvii.11103–15)[64]

Interestingly, in this account, Penthesilea is without protective armor, "unarmed" and, subsequently, "*dis*-armed" in the ensuing combat.

In the *Laud Troy Book* (ca. 1500), however, Penthesilea is fully armed, with her weaponry becoming the focal point of her brutal slaughter. In this version, Pyrrhus also dismembers her arm, but not before a troop of Greek warriors charges her, smashes her armor, and wounds her in the head:

> Many a Grewe & Gregais tho
> 3ede aboute that dou3ti quene
> And did hir mochel wo & tene,
> Thei brak hir helm & hir hauberk
> And made al blod hir white scherk,
> Thei brast on-sonder many a mayle,
> The stalworthe lace of hir ventayle,
> Sicurly In-to her hare
> Thei maken hir hed naked & bare.
>
> (17114–22)[65]

Pyrrhus then follows up his savage slaughter by hacking her body into pieces:

> And Pirrus In his greuance
> Toke on hir a foule vengaunce,
> For he lefft not of hir a spot.
> That he ne hit hewe as flesch to pot.
>
> (17135–38)

Pyrrhus's ferocious desecration of Penthesilea's body, in some sense an attempt to annihilate the unacceptable paradox of androgyny itself, is followed by his own death from the wound earlier inflicted by her. Thus the narrative version of the *Laud Troy Book* is as grisly a demonstration as any of how androgyny—and the consequences of its narcissistic wounding—inevitably incites a duel unto death.

---

[64]*The Destruction of Troy*, ed. George O. Panton and David Donaldson (London: Early English Text Society Series, 1879).

[65]*The Laud Troy Book*, ed. J. Ernst Wülfing (London: Early English Text Society Series, 1902).

Murder in the Woods

This foray into the literary history of the Amazon suggests that Tasso could not possibly have foreseen the psychic consequences of using the destruction of an androgyne to force the marvels of his forest to speak the "truth" of the epic verisimilar. Tasso's narrative gambit of allowing narcissism to flourish unchecked, only to emphasize even more the power and authority of sublimation when it does reassert itself, seems workable enough within his epic theory. But in actual poetic practice, as we shall see in this section, narcissism lingers as its own kind of poetic "truth."

As we examine the death-duel of Tancredi and Clorinda, we gain a sense that Tasso, unlike Ariosto, could foresee no possibilities for accommodating his version of the female warrior into epic history. In the *Riposto della 'Infarinato*, which records a dialogue between Tasso and Infarinato on the subject of love, Tasso contends,

> E senza dubbio sarà più convenevole al maschio quella dell'amante, ed alla donna quella dell'amata perché l'eccellenza delle donne consiste nella bellezza, la quale muove ad amare; siccome quella degli uomini è nel valore, che si dimostra nelle operazioni fatte per amore.[66]

> (And without doubt it will be more suitable [the role] to the male that of the lover and to the woman that of the loved, because the excellence of women consists in their beauty which moves [man] to love; just as that of men lies in valour which is demonstrated in deeds done for love.)

But if, to repeat Borch-Jacobsen, the narcissism of men and women dictates that they "love themselves as homosexuals," then Tasso's neatly symmetrical assessment of the love between a man and a woman demonstrates no insight into the "internal violence" that inevitably renders love the mutual interplay of an unresolved narcissism. Nor can this vision of love come close to accommodating the androgyny of his own creation Clorinda.

Not surprisingly, it is in the mysterious woods—where the clashes of epic combat meet the phantasms of the unconscious—that Tancredi first espies the virago Clorinda, surely one of the stranger of the *Liberata*'s many *miracoli del bosco* (miracles of the woods). (In Canto II.38, in fact, Clorinda is described as wearing "abito straniero" ["foreign clothes"].) Her sudden appearance is all the

---

[66]Quoted in Tomalin, 182n29.

stranger when we consider that, despite her importance in the narrative, Tasso, in a remarkable example of literary "repression," never mentions her in his prefatory "Allegoria." Unlike any number of Tasso's historical Crusaders, most notably Goffredo, Clorinda is an invented character, a *meraviglia* whose existence is almost totally dependent on Tancredi's imagination. And, as we shall see, all of Tancredi's successive encounters with Clorinda follow the pattern of emphasizing his dumbstruck responses to her—his tendency to view her not as a real woman, but as a phantasm.

Tancredi's initial encounter with Clorinda in Canto I is marked by the fateful need to rest after battle near "un fonte vivo" ("a fresh spring" [1.46])—always the site of danger for the unwary knight errant of romance (such as Ferraù, for example, in the opening canto of the *Furioso*). Not surprisingly, then, it is in this mysterious locus of cynosure that Tancredi, like Aeneas suddenly glimpsing his huntress-mother, spies Clorinda clad in full armor, but with her long hair unbound—a common topos, and yet the very paradox that marks the androgyny of the female warrior, as well as the fateful moment of "forfeiture" of the knight's own narcissism. Tasso, emphasizing the intensity of Tancredi's love at first sight, underscores the importance of the visual in his Petrarchan adoration for her: "Egli mirolla, ed ammirò la bella / sembianza" ("He saw her and marvelled at her lovely countenance"); and, not coincidentally, he apostrophizes Clorinda as "Oh meraviglia!" (47), thus already implicating her alien androgyny as, perhaps, one of Ismeno's phantasms—part human and part visionary essence—a conclusion facilitated by the poet's later apostrophe to the spirit in the tree that Tancredi attempts to cut down as "Oh meraviglia!" (XIII.41).

But, to return full circle to the terms of our discussion at the beginning of the previous section, we must not say that Tancredi's encounter with Clorinda constitutes love, but rather the mutual interplay of a destructive narcissism. Clorinda's "dangerous division" within herself seeks the narcissistic destruction of the male other (embodying both an imitative model and wearing the "armour of an alienating identity"), while Tancredi "forfeits" his narcissism to Clorinda so that she will reflect back to him the image of an intact narcissism. Tancredi's love for Clorinda can only anticipate a duel unto death as it is "nato fra l'arme amor di breve vista" ("a love born amid arms, from a fleeting glimpse" [45]). Although Clorinda flees from her admirer almost as quickly as she appeared—like a Diana before the dismembering gaze of Actaeon has done its voyeuristic damage—this *meraviglia* leaves in her wake an image that, in Tancredi's imagination, takes on a life of its own:

> Ma l'imagine sua bella e guerriera
> Tale ei serbò nel cor, qual essa è viva;
> E sempre ha nel pensiero e l'atto e 'l loco
> In che la vide, esca continua al foco.
>
> (1.48)

(but her lovely and war-like image he so preserved in his heart that it is alive; and always he has in his memory both the gesture and the place in which he saw her, a constant fuel to his flame.)

As we will see, Tancredi's persistence throughout the *Liberata* in treating her as an image calls into question the existence of the "real" Clorinda, rendering her prone to a duplication and doubling that make her, like Plutone's daemonic phantasms, "unlike herself."

Their second encounter occurs in Canto III, when Clorinda, fiercely and single-mindedly devoted to the pagan cause, attacks Tancredi with her spear. The ensuing battle is characterized by a furious clash of armor reminiscent of the destructive and narcissistic combats between Penthesilea and Pyrrhus in the *Laud Troy Book*:

> Clorinda intanto ad incontrar l'assalto
> Va di Tancredi, e pon la lancia in resta.
> Ferírsi a le visiere, e i tronchi in alto
> Volaro e parte nuda ella ne resta;
> Ché, rotti i lacci a l'elmo suo, d'un salto
> (mirabil colpo!) ei le balzò di testa.
>
> (III.21)

(Meanwhile Clorinda moves to meet Tancredi's assault, and puts her lance in rest. They struck one another on the visor and the shafts flew high, and she remains partly denuded by it: for her helmet, its laces broken, he struck bouncing from her head [a marvelous blow!])

But Tancredi, suddenly smitten with her beauty, is frozen in the midst of battle, and, as in his initial encounter with Clorinda, he can only helplessly stop to gaze:

> Ei, ch'al cimiero ed al dipinto scudo
> Non badò prima, or lei veggendo impètra:

> Ella, quanto può meglio, il capo ignudo
> Si ricopre, e l'assale; ed ei s'arretra.
>
> (III.23)

(He who never before paid heed to crest or painted shield now, seeing her, is turned to stone; she covers her naked head as best she can, and attacks him, and he retreats.)

It is worthwhile noting here that Tasso's allegory of narcissistic wounding is further complicated when one of Goffredo's Crusaders, an "uomo inumano" ("inhuman man"), treacherously wounds Clorinda from behind, much like the Greeks who ambush Penthesilea:

> Pur non gì tutto invano, e ne' confini
> Del bianco collo il bel capo ferille.
> Fu levissima piaga; e i biondi crini
> Rosseggiaron così d'alquante stille,
> Come rosseggia l'or che di rubini
> Per man d'illustre artefice sfaville.
>
> (III.30)

(Yet it fell not all in vain, and wounded that lovely head, where it joins her fair neck. The wound was very light; and the blonde hair reddened with a few drops, as reddens the gold that sparkles with rubies by the hand of a famous artisan.)

Tasso's description, reveling as it does in the painful aesthetics of the mingling of Clorinda's blood with her amber hair, is at once both gruesome and erotic, and a reminder that, as with the topos of the "wounded Amazon" in ancient Greek sculpture, the androgynous warrior incites an ambivalent interplay of adoration and sadism. This strange encounter ends when an angry Tancredi pursues the "uomo inumano," while the aloof Clorinda, indifferent to the obsessions of her protector, wanders off, wound and all, to continue her own brutal slaughters of other Christian knights. But in this encounter lingers the possibility that Tancredi is arrested not simply by her uncanniness, but by an uncanniness that characterizes the precarious and ill-defined threshold of ego formation itself.

Their third encounter occurs in Canto VI when Tancredi, on his way to fight Argante in single combat, is granted another one of his privileged and sudden glimpses of Clorinda. Again, as in the case of their previous encounters, the episode is noteworthy for his excessive reaction to her unexpected appearance:

Poscia immobil si ferma, e pare un sasso;
Gelido tutto fuor, ma dentro bolle:
Sol di mirar s'appaga, e di battaglia
Sembiante fa che poco or più gli caglia.

(VI.27)

(Then he stops motionless, and seems a stone; outside all frozen, but
within he boils. He is content merely to gaze, and he shows that little
he cares for battle any more.)

Clorinda is not just a beauty, but a representational scandal—the
scandal of an irreconcilable internal violence that defies gender symmetry and paralyzes her onlookers. Transformed to virtual stone by
the sight of Clorinda (and distracted from his crucial battle with Argante), Tancredi reacts as if he were glimpsing Medusa's head itself;
and now we are at the heart of why Tancredi's encounters with
Clorinda are so dependent on the visual. As Freud argues, "The
terror of Medusa is thus a terror of castration that is linked to the
sight of something."[67] Although Tancredi adores the *sembianza* who
appears before him, the androgynous Clorinda, as the site of an internal violence, is thus also the "sight of something"—of, specifically, the fear of castration; and thus we could argue that, in an
uncanny way, their encounters are as much a site of anxiety as they
are of adoration for the warrior who, to echo Rothery, "dreads but
does not fully comprehend" the object of his gaze. Freud maintained
that the characteristic stiffening response to the (never fully determi-
nate) absence of the phallus is both a reaction of fear and terror, and
a compensatory erection, a consolation to the spectator that "he is
still in possession of a penis."[68] Thus, because the *heimlich* means, as
Freud tells us, on the one hand, "what is familiar and agreeable, and
on the other, what is concealed and kept out of sight,"[69] the phenomenon of the uncanny often involves the fear of castration—the
anxiety that the phallus is being "kept out of sight." In the case of
Clorinda, whose narcissism dictates that she wants both to *have* and
to *be* the phallus, her status as an androgyne renders her a particularly unsettling sight/site of the mutual interplay between narcissism and castration. One aspect of the internal violence that characterizes the androgyne is the uncanniness of the spectator's attempt
to determine whether she has a phallus or whether it is being "kept

[67]"Medusa's Head," *SE* 18:273.
[68]Ibid.
[69]"The Uncanny," *SE* 17:224–25.

out of sight." We must remember that it is her intactness—her haughty aloofness—that insures her attractiveness to the male warrior, whose own narcissistic self-love becomes dependent on her arrogance. But if we consider that some portion of her arrogance is, in turn, a consequence of her own compensatory anxiety that she lacks the phallus, then the androgyne is the sight/site of the mutual interplay between narcissism and castration anxiety for both male and female. Any encounter between the two can only be an uncanny moment in which they both meet their imitative rival—but an identificatory rival who is the site not only of imitation, but also of castration.

Tancredi's confused mix of Achillean remorse and castration anxiety is a circumstance that inevitably leads to a duel unto death. In Canto xii, Clorinda, wearing black amor as if in preparation for dying—"(infausto annunzio!) ruginose e nere" ("[unlucky omen!] rusty and black" [18])—slips out of Jerusalem at nightfall and, under cover of darkness, sets fire to Goffredo's strategic siege-towers. Accidentally locked out of the gates of the city and pursued by the Christians, she fatefully (and fatally) ends up in single combat with Tancredi, who cannot recognize his adored *sembianza* in the darkness. But the fact that it is nightfall and that Clorinda is wearing a different set of armor is not sufficient to allay the aura of inevitability about their deadly encounter. It is commonplace for critics to interpret Tancredi's killing of Clorinda as "unwitting"—but the episode amounts, simply, to murder. It is as though Tancredi, craving "guerra e morte" (52), "recognizes" his unknown combatant enough to know that her internal violence is a castrating danger that the male warrior must violently annihilate. The clash of the "armor of their alienated identities" resounds through the woods: "Cozzan con gli elmi insieme e con gli scudi" ("they dash together their helmets and their shields" [56]). Tasso's account of their prolonged battle underscores the bloodshed, wounding, and blind rage that result when the internal violence of gender asymmetry, castration anxiety, and narcissistic aggression collide in one narrative moment:

> Torna l'ira ne'cori, e li trasporta,
> Benchè debili, in guerra. Oh fera pugna!
> U' l'arte in bando, u'già la forza è morta,
> Ove in vece d' entrambi il furor pugna.
> Oh, che sanguigna e spazïosa porta
> Fa l'una e l'altra spada, ovunque guigna,

Nell'arme e nelle carni! e se la vita
Non esce, sdegno tienla al petto unita.

(XII.62)[70]

(Wrath returns to their hearts and hurries them on, though weak, to battle. Ah savage struggle! where skill is banished, where strength is dead, where in their place the madness of each is waging the fight! Oh what a wide and bloody breach in armor and in flesh the one sword and the other makes, wherever it lights! and if life does not depart, wrath it is that holds it bonded to the breast.)

Like Penthesilea's death at the hands of Pyrrhus, Clorinda's slaughter is, not surprisingly, both savage and erotic at the moment when Tancredi finally stabs her between her breasts, inflicting a fatal wound. Moreover, the topos of Achillean remorse comes into play when, upon removing his unknown victim's helmet, Tancredi "recognizes" his beloved ("ahi conoscenza!" ["alas the recognition!"])—as if, in the recesses of his unconscious, he had not already. The horror of his realization that his beloved is now a mutilated corpse (but a "bel corpo," nonetheless)—that, in effect, the threat of castration has itself suffered castration—both recapitulates and parodies the horror of castration anxiety, so often, in Freud's words, "linked to the sight of something." Alive, the destructive division of the androgynous Clorinda threatens castration; dead, she activates the internal violence within Tancredi himself. Thus Tasso's own topos of errant *distrazione* as embodied in Tancredi becomes an ambivalent combination of Achillean remorse and castration anxiety.

Tancredi's affliction with Achillean remorse is so severe that for the remainder of the *Liberata* he fails to purge himself of the memory of Clorinda's murder—a lingering memory that guarantees his later inability to confront the *selvaggio orrore*, or "wild horror," of the Jerusalem wood. Complying with her dying wish, he baptizes her, and at her funeral, in a recapitulation of Zerbino's memorial fetishizing of the "dead" Orlando's armor, "le sui armi, a un nudo pin sospese" ("he had her armor displayed above, hung from a leafless pine" [95]). But even though Clorinda's baptism would signal her accommodation within the happy scheme of Christian salvation, Tancredi

---

[70]Durling also quotes this passage, noting that Tasso's embedded exclamations in his own description of the battle ("Ah fera pugna!"; "il furor pugna!," and so on) reveal "a mixture of admiration and horror" (*The Figure of the Poet*, 191). Thus Tasso, like Tancredi, may be experiencing his own Achillean remorse of admiration and sadism toward Clorinda as he narrates the intensity of the combatants' hostility.

Translations of Power

remains obsessed with her image, as the topos of Achillean remorse (Tancredi's peculiar mixture of both mourning *and* melancholia) assumes a gruesome and morbid life of its own. Because of her sudden appearances and disappearances, Clorinda, even when she was alive, seemed phantasmic and unreal. As a consequence, throughout the first half of the *Liberata*, Tasso depicts her as prone to duplication and ambiguous representation. In Canto VI Erminia, herself consumed with her unrequited love for Tancredi, "purloins" Clorinda's armor (91–92) and becomes a simulacrum that Tancredi desperately pursues. In Canto VII, during fierce combat between Raimondo and Argante, Satan conjures up an image of Clorinda to incite Oradino to shoot Raimondo, who is beginning to triumph over Argante, with an arrow. Tasso himself savors the uncanny likeness of the devil's image:

> E la sembianza di Clorinda altera
> Gli finse, e l'armi ricche e luminose:
> Dièglì il parlare, e senza mente il noto
> Suon della voce, e il portamento e il moto.
> (VII.99)

([He] counterfeited for it the face of the proud Clorinda, and her rich and luminous armor; he gave it speech and [without her mind] the well-known sound of her voice, and her manner and bearing.)

Thus Clorinda's susceptibility to duplicity renders her vulnerable to co-opting as one of Ismeno's enchantments, and it is inevitable that her murdered spirit become a denizen of Jerusalem's tenebrous woods.

Given her susceptibility to phantasm and duplication, it is not surprising that Clorinda, following her death, should reappear twice to Tancredi to exacerbate his remorse and mourning—once in a dream, to attempt to absolve him of his guilt (XII.91), and again as one of Ismeno's arboreal enchantments, a *misero tronco* (or "wretched tree-trunk") that torments Tancredi for his cruelty as he seeks to cut down the tree she inhabits. But, as we shall see, Clorinda's animistic reappearance in the woods is noteworthy in that it is enabled not so much through Ismeno's magic as through Tancredi's own narcissism, specifically in the form of his excessive grief over his dead beloved.

Having slaughtered the castrating threat to his own ego formation, Tancredi must now contend with the torments of the memory of her *empia ferita* ("pitiless wound") that lingers within him: "Già simile all'estinto il vivo langue / Al colore, al silenzio, agli atti, al sangue" ("The living man lies languishing like to the dead, in color, in silence, in attitude and in blood" [xii.70]). His obsessional self-reproach for her death calls to mind Freud's analysis in "Mourning and Melancholia" of the narcissism involved in the ego's melancholic identification with the lost object.[71] We can turn to Paul Ricoeur for a summary of Freud's analysis that is uncannily relevant to Tancredi's fear of Clorinda's reappearance in the woods: "instead of being displaced onto another object, the libido was withdrawn into the ego and employed in establishing an identification of the ego with the abandoned object. Thus the ego receives the blows intended for the object. In this way an object-loss becomes an ego-loss and the ego is mistreated."[72] Thus, melancholia is inevitably an effect of narcissism, whereby the libido implodes into and punishes the ego by identifying with the lost object. Ricoeur's summary also enables us to understand more clearly how Tancredi's encounter with the murdered spirit of Clorinda in the woods becomes the point at which the familiar (and figuratively "familiar") topos of the bleeding branch throughout epic literary history meets the uncanny,[73]

[71]In a passage with no small significance for Tancredi's torment, Freud writes, "The complex of melancholia behaves like an *open wound*, drawing to itself cathectic energy . . . from all directions, and emptying the ego until it is totally impoverished" (*SE* 4:252). It is almost as if Tancredi, as part of his melancholia, has introjected the painful laceration of Clorinda's *empia ferita* into his own ego. For a discussion of Tancredi as the paradigmatic figure of melancholia in Tasso's corpus, see Giorgio Petrocchi, *I fantasmi di Tancredi: Saggi sul Tasso e sul Rinascimento* (Rome: Salvatore Sciascia, 1972). In her essay, "Mo(u)rning and Melancholia: Tasso and the Dawn of Psychoanalysis" (*Quaderni d'italianistica* 11:1 [1990], 13–27), Juliana Schiesari provides a fascinating analysis of Tasso's dialogue *Il messagiero* as a treatise on the poet's melancholy written during his incarceration at Sant'Anna. And in the process of exploring the analogies between Tasso's and Tancredi's melancholia, Schiesari also points out the interplay of melancholia and castration anxiety that afflicts Tancredi. For a fuller discussion of how Tasso endlessly shapes melancholic loss into his own narcissistic gain, see Schiesari's chapter on Tasso in her book, *The Gendering of Melancholia: Feminism, Psychoanalysis and the Symbolics of Loss in Renaissance Literature*, forthcoming from Cornell University Press, 1992.

[72]*Freud and Philosophy*, 131.

[73]The mythological and literary history of the topos of the bleeeding branch has been explored by Charles Speroni, "The Motif of the Bleeding and Speaking Trees of Dante's Suicides," *Italian Quarterly* 33 (1965), 44–55, and by Leo Spitzer, "Speech and Language in *Inferno* xiii," in *Dante: A Collection of Critical Essays*, ed. John Freccero (Englewood Cliffs, NJ: Prentice-Hall, Inc., 1965), 78–101. The bleeding branch topos within the more specific context of comparative epic has been discussed in a comprehensive series of articles by William J. Kennedy ("The Problem of Allegory in Tasso's *Gerusalemme Liberata*," *Italian Quarterly*, 15–16 [1972], 27–51; "Irony, Allegoresis, and Allegory in Vir-

to create a moment that oscillates between the grief of an inward narcissism and the terror of an ontological uncertainty. For Goffredo, who has no patience for his fearful knights, the cutting down of the Jerusalem trees is *literally* the "moment of truth" for the epic cause of the Crusaders. But for Tancredi, at once grieving and terrified, the cutting of the tree, the cutting of Clorinda's *misero tronco*, is a moment of *doubt*—or, more accurately, a moment when the "truth" can be nothing but uncanny:

> Pur tragge alfin la spada, e con gran forza
> Percote l'alta pianta. Oh meraviglia!
> Manda fuor sangue la recisa scorza,
> E fa la terra intorno a sè vermiglia.
> Tutto si raccapriccia, e pur rinforza
> Il colpo, e le fin vederne ei si consiglia.
> Allor, quasi di tomba, uscir ne sente
> Un indistinto gemito dolente.
>
> (XIII.41)

(Yet in the end he draws his sword and with his mighty strength he smites the towering tree. Oh marvellous! the split bark issues blood and stains the earth about it crimson. He is completely horrified, and yet redoubles the blow and tells himself to see it through to the end. Then he hears issue forth, as from the tomb, a muffled sorrowing groan.)

When the wounded spirit of Clorinda screams, "Ahi! troppo, disse, / M'hai tu, Tancredi, offeso" ("Alas too much have you wronged me, Tancred; now let this much suffice" [42]), Tancredi drops his weapon in terror, afraid to damage the tree further. The knight, already undermined by grief and guilt, cannot, unlike Rinaldo after he is freed from Armida's enchantments, finish the task of hacking down trees for siege-towers because, in the end, to echo Ricoeur, the narcissistic ego *"receives the blows intended for the object"*—something that Goffredo cannot comprehend when he hears of Tancredi's inability, in effect, to inflict violence on the trees. The tree that Clorinda inhabits must be spared, in exchange for the "inflicting of blows" onto Tancredi's own ego.

Tancredi's melancholia *requires* that there be the spirit of Clorinda

---

gil, Ovid, and Dante," *Arcadia* 7 [1972], 114–34; "Ariosto's Ironic Allegory," *Modern Language Notes* 88 [1973], 44–67); "Rhetoric, Allegory, and Dramatic Modality in Spenser's Fradubio Episode," *English Literary Renaissance* 3 [1973], 351–68.

in the tree so that he can "mistreat" his own ego. In the woods of Jerusalem, then—Tasso's locus of the primary narcissism of a regressive childhood—the fearful imagination and the narcissistic needs of the ego refuse to let go. In another of his characteristic associations between dark forests and childish inventiveness, Tasso, early in Canto XIII, describes the fear of Goffredo's sylvan workmen:

> Qual semplice bambin mirar non osa
> Dove insolite larve abbia presenti;
> O come pave nella notte ombrosa,
> Immaginando pur mostri e portenti.
> (XIII.18)

(As an innocent child has not the courage to look where he has a foreboding of strange spirits, or as in shadowy night he is afraid, imagining monsters and prodigies still; so did they fear.)

And yet, despite their infantile regression to a *semplice bambin*, the workmen, unlike Goffredo, know that, in Marcuse's words, "the forbidden images and impulses of childhood begin to tell the truth that reason denies." Ismeno's enchantments present their own "truth"—which is why any effort by Tancredi (or Goffredo, or the reader) to probe their limits further is to miss the point of the Jerusalem woods. For Ariosto's Orlando, the psychopathology of *furore* constitutes an excessive mourning for Angelica that eventually gets converted into epic purposiveness. But Tancredi's mourning for Clorinda simply remains excessive.

If, for Freud, the *Aeneid* was the privileged expression in epic literary history of the return of the repressed, then Tancredi's encounter with Clorinda in the woods, as he describes it in his *Beyond the Pleasure Principle*, was for him one of the great demonstrations in all of literature of the repetition compulsion, the point at which Tancredi "wounds his beloved again."[74] But I would argue that it is another of Freud's essays, "The Uncanny" (published a year earlier than *Beyond the Pleasure Principle*), that provides the most subtle and far-reaching gloss on the complex "sylvan hermeneutic" of the Jerusalem woods. And, for that matter, the similarities between Tasso's narrative of his magical woods and Freud's essay on the origins of terror are them-

---

[74]*SE* 18:22. See Margaret W. Ferguson's noting of Freud's allusion to Tasso in her *Trials of Desire: Renaissance Defenses of Poetry* (New Haven: Yale University Press, 1983), 126. I comment further on Freud's allusion in the final section of this chapter.

selves uncanny. If one of the primary epistemological crises occurs, as Freud argues, "when there is intellectual uncertainty whether an object is alive or not,"[75] then Tancredi's terror at Clorinda's arboreal simulacrum gets us to the very heart of the uncanny; and thus by so dramatically extending the boundaries of the bleeding branch topos into the "sensi occulti" (XIII.40) of the unconscious, Tasso has carved out one of the more ontologically elusive (and narcissistic) narrative spaces in all of epic literary history.

Because she is both her own simulacrum (and yet "unlike herself") and reflects back to Tancredi the image of his own intact narcissism, Clorinda exists throughout so much of the *Liberata* as the phenomenon of the "double" itself; his creation of a phantasmic double for Clorinda (and, in his melancholia, a phantasmic double for himself as well) *is* the narrative space of the uncanny—the point at which the *heimlich* shades into the *unheimlich* to produce a spirit that is neither dead nor alive. For Freud, the double, created within the unconscious recesses of a primary, infantile narcissism, also can become "a thing of terror," like a Medusa's head.[76] Neither fully alien nor fully familiar, the Clorinda that Tancredi fears he is "wounding again" is an uncanny daemon that mocks the boundaries between imagination and reality whose integrity Tasso is so obsessed with preserving in his *Discorsi*. Her spirit is both the "real" Clorinda and, to echo Hélène Cixous in her richly insightful commentary on "The Uncanny," a "cleavage, substitution, redoubling of the self"[77]—a dramatic demonstration that, in the realm of the unconscious, the return of the repressed (or the repetition compulsion) is also, more accurately, the return of the double. As a product of what Freud calls "the subject's narcissistic overvaluation of his own mental processes," the double is both "an insurance against the destruction of the ego"—conjured by an infantile primary narcissism— and "a thing of terror,"[78] or, in Cixous's words, "the hiding-place of castration."[79] Seemingly playing off Tasso's own characteristic topos of uncanny trees, Cixous alludes to the enigmas of the *unheimlich* as "branches" that trace an entangled network of "cleavage . . . and, finally, the recurrent return of what is similar."[80] In the realm of the

[75]"The Uncanny;" *SE* 17:233.
[76]Ibid., 236.
[77]Hélène Cixous, "Fiction and Its Phantoms: A Reading of Freud's *Das Unheimliche*," trans. Robert Dennomé, *New Literary History* 7:3 (1976), 539.
[78]*SE* 17:240, 235.
[79]"Fiction and Its Phantoms," 538.
[80]Ibid., 539.

uncanny then, the return of the repressed, as explored by Tasso, is always, more specifically, the return of the *similar* as the "hiding-place of castration."

Cixous's commentary on "The Uncanny" also allows us to gain a better understanding of why Tasso keeps so much of his narrative nocturnal, dark, forbidden, phantasmic, entangled in a sylvan locus of "luce incerta" (XIII.2).[81] Of "The Uncanny," Cixous argues that Freud "keeps his text in these indistinct and libidinous regions where the light of law does not yet cast its logic."[82] Likewise, Tasso, despite his overt preference for the *verisimile*, cannot resist the pull of images "where the light of law does not yet cast its logic" over "i fallaci sillogismi" ("Allegoria") of the pastoral imagination.

Freud's concept of the "pleasure principle" inherent in the repetition compulsion, then, is not adequate to explain the complex (and often contradictory) interplay between infantile narcissism and anxiety that constitutes the impulse to repeat. For Tasso, the repetition compulsion is not just the return of the repressed, but the return of the (repressed) similar that torments the subject with doubt, uncertainty, and, in the final analysis, fear of death. The repetition compulsion alone is insufficient to explain either Tancredi's terror at the "familiar" reappearance of his beloved or his desire to mutilate her again. Tancredi must kill off these "things of terror" that originate from within the recesses of his own primary narcissism. As Cixous argues, "resemblance does not inspire fright if such resemblance does not proceed from itself in spite of itself. Thus, the double becomes exteriorized not only as anguish but as a *return* of anguish. Narcissus is accoutred in anguish."[83] The repetitive return is not a thing of terror unless it emanates from narcissistic anguish. Not just simply repetition, the uncanny *is* the implosive impasse of narcissistic anguish—the anguish that comes, for Tancredi, with the realization that the double destroys the ego, and, for Tasso, with the realization that poetic "truth" can never be completely alien (like Ismeno's images) or completely familiar. *Heimlich* within *unheimlich*, woman within man, life within death—these "divisions within" are why

---

[81]David Quint has noted, "Indeed, perhaps more than any other epic, the *Liberata* is a nocturnal poem" (*Origin and Originality in Renaissance Literature: Versions of the Source* [New Haven: Yale University Press, 1983], 108). And certainly Tasso's epic recapitulates many of the *Aeneid*'s errors in sensory perception and nocturnal uncertainty.

[82]"Fiction and Its Phantoms," 538.

[83]Ibid., 542.

Clorinda is fated to be the source of anguish for any warrior who seeks her as the reflection of his own narcissism.

Thus, we can see that there is much more involved in Tancredi's melancholia for Clorinda than simply a poignant grieving for a lost beloved. J.-B. Pontalis has argued that melancholia (at the point at which it begins to modulate into a more conscious kind of mourning) is "a complex process . . . whose teleological purpose has been said to be to 'kill the dead.'"[84] One suspects that what is ultimately at stake in Tancredi's encounter with Clorinda in the woods is his own fear of death—perhaps the first (and only?) great psychological expression of the fear of death in all of epic literary history. "Primitive narcissism," argues Otto Rank, "feels itself primarily threatened by the ineluctable destruction of the self." Thus "thanatobia," as Rank calls it, often involves "the impulse toward murder against the double."[85] Tancredi's strange mix of mourning for and hostility against the double Clorinda, falling as it does in the gap between (melancholic) self-punishment and the (mournful) impulse to, echoing Pontalis, "kill the dead," enacts not the typical *distrazione* of the wayward knights of romance epic, but an unconscious response to "real" fears that threats to the destruction of the self are immanent in the trees. Tancredi's thanatobia (not to be confused with cowardice) is as much a fear of himself as it is of arboreal spirits—which is why his experience of primitive narcissism will always find its "moment of truth" in the uncanny trees of Jerusalem.

In the end, what can we make of the dead androgyne Clorinda? Despite the narrative patness of Clorinda's eleventh-hour baptism, Tasso cannot dispel the scandal of her androgyny. If, as Freud argued, Eros carries with it an inherently regressive tendency to "restore an earlier state of things," then Clorinda's nocturnal suicide-mission against the Christians (her seeming need, in a sense, to seek out Tancredi as her killer) enacts her own narcissism—the narcissism of the death drive that seeks a "prior return" to a state before the struggle with the "internal violence" of androgyny. Clorinda may be the uncanny limits of a narrative crisis for Tasso. Because she is at once both intolerable for the male narcissist (knight and

---

[84] J.-B. Pontalis, "On Death-Work in Freud, in the Self, in Culture," in *Psychoanalysis, Creativity, and Literature: A French-American Inquiry*, ed. Alan Roland (New York: Columbia University Press, 1978), 85.

[85] Otto Rank, *The Double: A Psychoanalytic Study*, trans. and ed. Harry Tucker, Jr. (New York: New American Library, 1979), 83, 76.

poet) and incapable of annihilation (because she is a double), she may be the limit of fiction itself.

Freud introduces his essay "The Uncanny" by confessing that he felt "impelled to investigate the subject of aesthetics."[86] Freud's insistence on the uncanny as a distinctly *aesthetic* concept is adumbrated by Tasso's fascination with "i fallaci sillogismi" in his own prose treatises. As we have seen, Tasso's *Discorsi* are, among other things, theories of aesthetics that attempt to probe the limits of the familiar and the alien. And Tasso's goal of collapsing the distinctions between the *maraviglioso* and the *verisimile* both signals his (unwitting) intention to open up the aesthetic space of the uncanny for his own epic narrative, and suggests an implicit anxiety that a singular (and usually miraculous) action may not be capable of eliminating its mysteries. Like Tancredi's attempt to annihilate Clorinda with the blows of his axe, Tasso seeks in one narrative "blow" to annihilate and collapse the distinctions between the *maraviglioso* and the *verisimile*. But the final "truth" of Clorinda is that the uncanny can refer only to itself. As Cixous writes,

> So, of the *Unheimliche* (and its double, fiction) we can only say that it never completely disappears . . . that it "re-presents" that which in solitude, silence, and darkness will (never) be presented to you. Neither real nor fictitious, "fiction" is a secretion of death, an anticipation of nonrepresentation, . . . a hybrid body composed of language and silence that . . . invents doubles, and death.[87]

The "truth" of Tasso's uncanny narrative, then, is that the hybrid body of Clorinda will always dwell in the woods of Jerusalem—as the "anticipation of nonrepresentation" by the narcissism of the male other.

Troy and the Second Murder

Pontalis's characterization of melancholia as a tautological impulse to " 'kill the dead' " echoes, in its own uncanny way, the warning on the tall *cipresso* in the woods: " 'non dée guerra co' morti aver chi vive' " (" 'the living ought not wage war with the dead' " [xiii.39]). In

---

[86]*SE* 17:219.
[87]"Fiction and Its Phantoms," 548.

Pontalis's conception, the narcissism of melancholia must always lead to the defiance of the interdiction that the living must not disturb the dead. What we must consider at this point, however, is the significance of Tancredi's compulsion not just to kill the dead, but the doubly tautological impulse—when he "pur rinforza / il corpo" ("yet redoubles the blow" [41])—to kill the dead *again*. The Freudian repetition compulsion that characterizes this episode reveals that much more is at stake in the woods of Jerusalem than simply Tancredi's love-melancholia. As we shall see, what finally ensures that the woods of Jerusalem become the *Liberata*'s overdetermined intersection between psyche and history is the phenomenon of the "second" murder as the narrative's failure to repress Troy as the memory-trace of epic.

In her *Trials of Desire*, Margaret Ferguson has isolated and analyzed the Tassoan impulse to kill the dead again as its own kind of recurring topos throughout the poet's career. She quotes the following passage from the *Apologia in difesa "Gerusalemme liberata"* (1585), in which Tasso defends his dead father, Bernardo (again, the lingering influence of the dead father in the literary history of epic), against the many critical attacks on his epic, *L'Amadigi di Gaula* (1560): "Perché mio padre, il quale è morto nel sepolcro, si può dir vivo nel poema, chi cerca d'offender la sua poesia, procura dargli morte un'altra volta" ("Because my father, who is dead in his sepulchre, may be said to live in his poem, anyone who seeks to offend his poetry, attempts to give him death a second time" [59].)[88] In defense of his father, Tasso here deplores the (Oedipal) impulse to attack a dead author. But in the *Liberata*, Tasso's deploring of what amounts to his father's "second" death gets displaced onto the trees of Jerusalem, where Tancredi inflicts a "morte un'altra volta" on the arboreal spirit of Clorinda—for Freud, as vivid a demonstration as any in literature of the compulsion to repeat that which has been repressed.

Ferguson interprets the repetition compulsion that informs this

[88]*Trials of Desire*, 59. Ferguson's ground-breaking chapter "Torquato Tasso: The Trial of Conscience," in *Trials of Desire*, constitutes an explicit engagement between psychoanalysis and Renaissance epic, particularly in her discussion of Tasso's composing of his *Gerusalemme conquistata*. Ferguson especially stresses Tasso's Oedipal conflicts with his poet-father Bernardo and with his predecessor Ariosto, and his identification with his own protagonist Goffredo as a "paternal authority." For more on Tasso's Oedipal ambivalence toward his father, see Zatti, *L'uniforme cristiano*, 107–14. Zatti argues that Tasso, needing punishment from the father, collaborates with paternity as a persecuting authority.

episode as Tasso's "profound allegorical meditation on the relation between the writer, who is also a reader, and his precursors," most notably Virgil's, Dante's, and Ariosto's episodes of the bleeding tree.[89] In Ferguson's conception, Tancredi's second assault on Clorinda becomes, in effect, an act of the "wounding of past texts" that constitutes a dynamic reworking of his epic precursors. His attacks on his father Bernardo's critics notwithstanding, Tasso comes to learn that the poet who does not "wage war" with the authoritative texts of the past "would himself be dead as an author."[90]

The *selvaggio orrore* of the Jerusalem wood can perhaps be viewed not just as the inevitable meeting place of the narcissism of Tancredi and Clorinda, but also as perhaps the inevitable meeting place of critics of the *Liberata* and their interpretive will-to-power. Thus, the impulse to analyze the *Liberata* will inevitably become an overdetermined *compulsion* to return to the trees as the central enigma of Tasso's epic. The aim of my own critical compulsion to return to the trees is, in the final analysis, to examine Tancredi's second "murder" of Clorinda as symptomatic of Tasso's own repression of Troy as the recapitulative repetition compulsion of the *translatio imperii*. The intertextual (and largely conscious) act of what Ferguson refers to as Tasso's "wounding of past texts" that characterizes this uncanny episode must also take into account Tasso's far more unconscious compulsion to kill Troy *again* in the woods of Jerusalem; and it is now time to induce the *segni ignoti* (the "unknown symbols") of the trees to answer the question of why Tasso inadvertently kills the origin of epic again. One question raised by Ferguson's intertextual analysis of this episode is, how far back in the intertextual past does a poet have to go before it is no longer necessary to experience the compulsion to "wound" a source? I would argue that the intertextual "origin" of Tasso's uncanny episode in the woods is perhaps not so much the bleeding man-bush of Virgil's Polydorus (himself an exiled Trojan) as it is Homer's burning Troy, the city not seen of dynastic epic.

The more one returns to the enigmatic trees of Jerusalem, the more one begins to suspect that the uncanny androgyne Clorinda, "repressed" as a character in Tasso's "Allegoria" and "killed again" by the narcissism of the *micidial* ("murderous") Tancredi, has much in common with Troy, also repressed by Tasso as the origin of the

[89]Ibid., 127.
[90]Ibid.

translatio imperii and killed again by the unconscious of his epic narrative. As a means of exploring this comparison further, let us first review the many overdetermined reasons why Clorinda must die. Despite Tancredi's beatific vision of Clorinda following her baptism, her animistic reappearance in the tall *cipresso* assures her status as a *meraviglia* who resists accommodation into the epic *verisimile*. The destruction of the androgyne is supposed to make the woods of Jerusalem speak the "truth" of an epic verisimilar. But if we remember that, for Tasso, the *maraviglioso* and the *verisimile* must be joined in "un'azione medesima," then Tancredi's compulsive act of killing Clorinda again reveals the futility of any such attempt to eliminate her "marvelous" qualities in one murderous blow. The blow, after all, can only be struck again and *again*.

For Freud, the compulsion to repeat occurs because something has been repressed. We have seen that Clorinda must be killed again by Tancredi because she presents an intolerable affront to his narcissism. But why must she also, in effect, be killed again by her own creator Tasso? In Canto XII, as we have seen, Clorinda departs on a nocturnal mission to set fire to Goffredo's siege-towers, the very synecdoche of Tasso's effort to shape the *Liberata* as a truly sublimatory epic. Clorinda's aggression against these siege-towers reveals them as standing in an unresolvably contradictory relationship to Troy as the return of the repressed in epic literary history. As discussed at the beginning of this chapter, because they are symbolic of Goffredo's effort to defeat Jerusalem in an appropriately epic manner, these same manifestly epic siege-towers find themselves transformed into a narrative unconscious for the *Liberata* as they also serve as the means by which Troy (as Jerusalem) must fall again in epic history. As Aladino, Argante, Solimano, and the other pagans find themselves transformed into Trojans defending their city against the Greeks-as-Crusaders, Clorinda's burning of the siege-towers has the effect of seeking to rescue Jerusalem from its gradual recapitulation of Troy as the paradigmatic besieged city of epic. In short, the very character who will herself suffer a "morte un'altra volta" seeks to deliver Troy from its fate of being killed again.[91]

----

[91]Jerusalem never seems more like the besieged Troy than when the city hears the news of Clorinda's death:

> Confusamente si bisbiglia intanto
> del caso reo ne la rinchiusa terra.
> Poi s'accerta e divulga, e in ogni canto

The trees of Jerusalem, then, become the inevitable graveyard for those doomed to be killed again. As one of Aladino's fiercest defenders of Jerusalem, Clorinda must be slated for death by Tasso's narrative. But what Tasso's narrative (as well as Tancredi's melancholia) does not fully factor in is the extent to which she will have to be killed again. Clorinda is the *Liberata*'s paradigmatic defender of a city; and defenders of cities in epic history have their ways of returning as repressed revenants, as Hector returns to Aeneas. And, for that matter, Clorinda herself, as we have seen, is the return of Penthesilea as the Amazonian defender of Troy, "killed" into life as one of the images on Dido's murals.[92] Clorinda's nocturnal, deadly clash with Tancredi results not only in her own death, but also in yet another murder of Penthesilea in epic history. In theory, the compulsion to repeat occurs because there is something that does not want to be remembered. Thus, even as Tasso refuses to "remember" Troy as the memory-trace of epic, it persists in making its repressed return through Clorinda.

Indeed, it is because of a repressed and forgotten Troy that Tasso's narrative finds itself entangled in an impossible double bind, with Clorinda as its paradoxical center. Troy (as Jerusalem) does eventually fall, an event that, in its own unconscious way, is consistent with Tasso's epic theory identifying a *Troia vittrice* as the most outrageous affront to the "truth" of epic history. But the cost of assuring that Troy is defeated is a recurring (and, as Pontalis might argue, a melancholic) compulsion to repeat its fall. Hence, although Clorinda is slated for annihilation on the battlefield, as the narrative unconscious for the *Liberata*, the "return" of Clorinda's spirit in the woods enacts the repetition compulsion that *is* Troy itself throughout the literary history of epic.

> de la città smarrita il romor erra
> misto di gridi e di femineo pianto;
> non altramente che se presa in guerra
> tutta ruini, el 'l foco e i nemici empi
> volino per le case e per li tèmpi.
>
> (XII.100)

(Meanwhile in the city under siege the sad event is whispered about confusedly. Then it is verified and becomes common, and the news spreads through every district of the disheartened city, mingled with cries and women's wailing: not otherwise than if taken in battle the whole city were falling, and flames and wicked enemies sweeping through its houses and its shrines.)

[92]We could argue that Clorinda, as the return of Penthesilea, also represents the return of the medieval sagas of the "matter" of Troy, long repressed in Italian epic romance by the preferred "matter" of Charlemagne.

In her own way, Clorinda survives, then, because she is a reminder that, *pace* Tasso's epic theory, the city not seen of Troy itself
survives as a kind of *Troia vittrice* in epic history. The very successful
repressions of an *oscura memoria* that enable the historical representation of *tempi remotissimi* now haunt the narrative in the form of Troy
as epic's paradigmatic failed repression. The second death of
Clorinda becomes the synecdoche for the repetition compulsion that
is Troy; and she survives as a revenant because she serves as a reminder that Troy itself persists throughout the literary history of
epic as the forgotten origin of the *translatio imperii*. From the outset,
Tasso's plan for his epic was to "forget" any overt narration of Troy
as a means of eliminating the narcissistic investment of the *translatio
imperii* in it. But what he did not foresee was how Troy would have
to be killed again (and again) because his narrative, at least up to
this point, had been so successful in repressing it. In effect, when
the trees warn, "'non dée guerra co' morti aver chi vive,'" they are
warning Tasso that the time has come to "remember" Troy as the
repressed origin of epic narrative.

It is commonplace for critics to view Tasso's episode in the woods
of Jerusalem as a generic clash between epic and romance where, at
the point at which Rinaldo succeeds in cutting down the animistic
trees in Canto xviii, epic itself succeeds in vanquishing the errors
and phantasms of romance. But if we merely posit the *Liberata* as a
battleground between a sublimatory history waging a generic, literary war against a fictional narcissism, then we risk overlooking
the psychic resonance of the discontinuities between epic and romance—discontinuities that demarcate the space of the narrative
unconscious of Tasso's epic, despite his attempts, ultimately, to
make the genres identical. In a psychoanalytic reading, there is
much more at stake in the episode if we argue that Tasso could not
foresee the psychic consequences of placing his clash between fiction and history in the *selvaggio orrore* of the Jerusalem wood, a locus
so treacherously overdetermined as the meeting ground between
psyche and history that we are no longer left with the clearly demar-
cated boundaries of epic and romance.

Let us take a final look at Clorinda's participation in this generic
discontinuity. On the one hand, it is Tancredi's narcissism that enables Clorinda's reappearance in the woods. As we have seen, his
melancholia requires that there be a spirit of Clorinda in the tree so
that he can mistreat his own ego. We can grant that it is part of
Tasso's plan for his sublimatory epic to foreground the individual

subjectivity of Tancredi (his narcissistic melancholia) the more pow-
erfully to demonstrate why it cannot be interpellated into Goffredo's
larger epic design. But what Tasso could not anticipate is the repressed reason why Tancredi's narcissism never gets accommodated
into epic. Tancredi's narcissistic melancholia resists sublimation because his ego ideal is Clorinda (Clorinda as "Trojan" defender of the
city)—and Clorinda represents the unconscious at work in epic history; specifically, she represents the repressed possibility that Troy
(as Jerusalem) can never be defeated.

   The woods, then, serve as the locus of a dual repression of narcissism's reliance on the ego ideal—a repression that can be successfully sustained only by means of a second murder. Even as
Tasso seeks to repress Troy as the ego ideal of epic history, so also
does Tancredi seek to kill Clorinda as the ego ideal of his narcissistic
melancholia. Thus, even though Clorinda is brutally eliminated from
the narrative by her own lover (even though, we could say, she
remains successfully unrepresented in the manifest narrative of Jerusalem's "liberation" by the Christians, not to mention in the "Allegoria"), her "molto un'altra volta" insures her survival as a "lack"
within Tasso's epic narrative. Despite Tasso's efforts to collapse epic
and romance in one and the same action, Clorinda's "second" murder becomes the generic edge along which the (after)effects of a repressed Troy leave their traces.

   As the ego ideals of narcissism, as the victims of a "second" murder that leaves them unrepresented in the manifest narrative, both
the twice murdered Clorinda and the twice defeated Troy constitute
(retroactively) the narrative unconscious of the *Liberata*. This is why,
despite Tasso's efforts to transform the uncanny trees of Jerusalem
into the purposeful siege-towers of epic, the woods persist as the
overdetermined locus of the generic discontinuities of epic romance.
In the end, both Clorinda and Troy, as the "anticipation of nonrepresentation," demonstrate that to indulge the impulse to kill
again is to admit that something in the past has not been laid to
rest.[93] As the overdetermined mediation between (poetic) psyche

[93]Tasso's characteristic repetition compulsion, his repetitive need to kill Troy again,
is continued (repeated again) in his heavily revised *Gerusalemme conquistata* (1593).
Many significant revisions of the *Liberata* occur near the end of the poem, which
explicitly imitates the *Iliad*. For example, a new character, Ruperto, is killed, Pa-
troclus-like, spurring the Achillean Riccardo to revenge, while Argante, like Hector,
has a wife and son. The return to the primal scene of a Trojan siege is so complete
that, as Quint writes, "the reader of the *Conquistata* senses the sacrifice of Tasso's

and history, the trees (and any attempt to cut them down) will always be inherently "neurotic"—and will always result in Troy being "killed" into life as the memory-trace of epic history. The phenomenon of the "molta un'altra volta" will always result in a *Troia vittrice.*

---

poetic personality as he subordinates his own inventions to the Homeric model" (*Origin and Originality,* 117). Tasso's *Lettere poetiche* document the poet's increasing defensiveness in the face of criticism of the *Liberata,* a defensiveness more and more inclined to give in to authority. Thus, one of Tasso's major responses to the many critics of the excesses of his *Liberata* was to write what was, in effect, a new poem, drastically revised from the earlier one—but a new poem that, at the point at which it doubles back on the "old" *Iliad,* ensures that Troy is killed a "third" time.

CHAPTER FIVE

The Alienating Structure
of Prophecy in "Faerie Lond"

The *Vel* of Faerie

This study of dynastic epic began with a consideration of the significance of the city not seen, key cities of antiquity that have served as crucial sites of mediation between psyche and history. If the historical and narrative space of the *Aeneid* traces a path between Troy and Rome as the cities not seen by Aeneas, and if Tasso inadvertently "remembers" an unseen Troy, even as he celebrates Jerusalem as a city finally seen and recaptured by the Crusaders, then Spenser's *Faerie Queene* succeeds in providing a vision of the heavenly city itself. In perhaps the most expansively visionary moment of Spenser's epic (and in a calculated attempt at "overgoing" Tasso), the seer-prophet Contemplation offers Redcrosse a glimpse not just of the earthly Jerusalem, but of the "new Hierusalem, that God has built" (1.10.57.2).[1] But the "new Hierusalem" is also quickly revealed as unattainable for mortals. As Contemplation tells Redcrosse, enraptured by his vision of "this great Citie," he must "backe returne" to "Faerie lond" to rescue Una in fulfillment of the quest that Gloriana has assigned him.

The privileged intersection, then, between psyche and history in *The Faerie Queene*, the fulfillment of Tudor epic destiny in Protestant

---

[1]One should note, though, that Goffredo is also granted a vision of the celestial Jerusalem in Canto xx of Tasso's *Gerusalemme conquistata*. (All references to *The Faerie Queene* are taken from *Edmund Spenser, The Faerie Queene*, ed. A. C. Hamilton [London: Longman, 1977].)

world empire, is "Troynouant." Or is it rather Cleopolis, which is, according to Redcrosse, "The fairest Citie . . . that might be seene" (1.10.59.3)—(or *not* seen)? Built by the fairy Elfinan, descendant of Tros, founder of old Troy itself, Cleopolis is ambitiously posited by Spenser as an ideal Troy—the "polis of Clio"—the city where the *translatio imperii* becomes realized as Fame itself.[2] Whereas Ariosto exiles fame to the moon, Spenser restores it to the imperial city. Spenser's enigmatic Faerie lond, then, is conceived as a land of fame—from Petrarch's *Trionfi* to Chaucer's *House of Fame*, the ultimate "narcissistic" search for glory (and for Gloriana as the ultimate "glori"-fication of Elizabeth).

And yet, throughout *The Faerie Queene*, we come to realize that Cleopolis is also the apotheosis of the city not seen of epic. Guyon's reading of the *Antiquitie of Faery lond* in Eumnestes' chamber of memory in Book 2, for example, fails, despite its providential and narrative orderliness, to culminate in any vision of the elusive Cleopolis or of Panthea, its beautiful "towre of glas" (1.10.58). And Arthur, thinking he can locate Gloriana in the "famous" city where she resides, dissipates his dynastic potential in an endless and vain search for it. Instead of unveiling Cleopolis, Spenser often broods about cities of *de*-famation: the wicked infamy of Nineveh and Babylon, of "fatall" Thebes, of a Rome (like Du Bellay's) fallen from pride, and— most resonantly—to "sad Ilion" itself (1.5.47ff.; 4.1.22ff.). In Lucifera's "dongeon deepe," Redcrosse's dwarf is granted his own parodic vision of the imperial city—a grim reduction of Rome's ancient glory to "carkases of beasts in butchers stall" (1.5.49.2):

> Great Romulus the Grandsyre of them all,
> Proud Tarquin, and too lordly Lentulus,
> Stout Scipio, and stubborne Hanniball,
> Ambitious Sylla, and sterne Marius,
> High Caesar, great Pompey, and fierce Antonius.
>   (49.5–9)

In short, all that remains of the dynastic legacy of the *Aeneid* is "the antique ruines of the Romaines fall" (49.4).[3] And even as Cleopolis

---

[2]For what remains one of the best and most thorough discussions of the historical background of Spenser's concept of "Faerie"—and specifically of Cleopolis as the embodiment of Fame—see Isabel E. Rathborne, *The Meaning of Spenser's Fairyland* (New York: Columbia University Press, 1937).

[3]Like Du Bellay, Spenser was fascinated with the decline of Rome as empire's city

continually recedes throughout *The Faerie Queene* as the ultimate de-realized city not seen of epic, by Book 6 Troynouant itself is threatened by the Blatant Beast, in whose "vile tongue and venomous intent" (6.1.8) we witness the lapsing of heroic "Fame" into mere *fama*, or "rumor," as perhaps the mightiest destroyer of empire.

The receding of Cleopolis as an imperial city is just one of the many strange consequences of Spenser's Faerie lond as the setting for his epic. Even though Faerie lond is, as Thomas P. Roche, Jr., has called it, "the major metaphor of the poem,"[4] it remains largely unrepresentable (despite Spenser's coy suggestion that the reader might be able to find "that happy land of Faery" by being attentive to "certaine signes" [2.Proem]).[5] Its topography defies spatial conception, and, despite the potential transferences adumbrated between Cleopolis and Troynouant as the "cities not seen" of Tudor epic destiny, Spenser offers no precise ontological distinctions between the designations "faerie" and "Briton."[6] To add to the strange-

---

no *longer* seen. In his translation of Du Bellay's *Antiquitez*, "Ruines of Rome," an almost obsessive meditation on Rome's "deepe ruines," Spenser laments that the beholder of the city's fragments "nought of Rome in Rome perceiu'st at all" (III.2). As Andrew Fichter argues, Spenser's "ambivalence toward the classical past remains unresolved throughout the thirty-three sonnets of the poem. He is simultaneously fascinated and repelled by the imagined spectacle of ancient power and glory that he glimpses through a landscape of stone and ashes" ("'And nought of *Rome* in *Rome* perceiu'st at all': Spenser's *Ruines of Rome*," *Spenser Studies: A Renaissance Poetry Annual*, 2, ed. Patrick Cullen and Thomas P. Roche, Jr. [Pittsburgh: University of Pittsburgh Press, 1981], 183–92). Spenser's fascination with the city of antiquity that can never quite be identical to itself reappears in his melancholic lament "The Ruines of Time," which focuses on Verulam, a decaying relic from the old Roman Britain. As a city "[o]f which there now remaines no memorie, / Nor anie little moniment to see" (4–5), the effaced Verulam suffers a fate even worse than Rome. (For a valuable discussion of Spenser's borrowings from Du Bellay, see Anne Lake Prescott, *French Poets and the English Renaissance: Studies in Fame and Transformation* [New Haven: Yale University Press, 1978], 39–52. For a comprehensive account of Spenser's Orphic preoccupations with the city as the site of both "cultural longevity" and of "corruptible mortality," see Lawrence Manley, "Spenser and the City: The Minor Poems," *Modern Language Quarterly* 43 [1982], 203–27.)

[4]Thomas P. Roche, Jr., *The Kindly Flame: A Study of the Third and Fourth Books of Spenser's Faerie Queene* (Princeton: Princeton University Press, 1964), 32.

[5]In his essay on Spenser, Coleridge referred to Faerie not as a geographical location, but as a kind of "mental space" (*Coleridge's Miscellaneous Criticism*, ed. T. M. Raysor [Cambridge: Harvard University Press, 1936], 36). For a discussion of the implications of Coleridge's depiction, see Roche, *The Kindly Flame*, 33, and Isabel G. MacCaffrey, *Spenser's Allegory: The Anatomy of Imagination* (Princeton: Princeton University Press, 1976), 58–59, 71–72.

[6]The lack of distinction has prompted James Nohrnberg to observe that Spenser's epic often seems concerned to show "the way in which the faerie is an allegorical Englishman, and the Englishman an honorary faerie" (*Analogy*, 780). For a further

ness, a practical joke recurring in *The Faerie Queene* is the changeling theme, that is, the abduction by fairies of an unweaned Briton infant into Faerie lond, where the displaced child, "chaunged by Faeries theft," must struggle to discover its "name and nation." It is these recurring Faerie thefts (without return) that render Spenser's epic, as much as anything else, a story of the aetiology of infantile trauma.

Redcrosse, we learn from Contemplation, is not a faerie knight at all, but is a Saxon "sprong out from English race" (10.60.1).[7] As Contemplation narrates, although Redcrosse was born in England,

> From thence a Faerie thee vnweeting reft,
> There as thou slepst in tender swadling band,
> And her base Elfin brood there for thee left,
> Such men do Chaungelings call, so chaunged by Faeries theft.
>
> (10.65.6–9)

Two books later, Merlin tells Britomart that although her future dynastic spouse Arthegall sojourns in Faerie, he

> Yet is no Fary borne, ne sib at all
> To Elfes, but sprong of seed terrestriall,
> And whilome by false Faeries stolne away,
> Whiles yet in infant cradle he did crall.
>
> (3.26.4–7)

And Britomart herself, though destined to become one of Tudor England's dynastic spouses, confesses to Redcrosse that she tra verses Faerie "withouten compasse," wandering far "fro my natiue soyle, that is by name / The greater Britaine . . ." (3.2.7). Most notably, Arthur, the paradigmatic avatar of Tudor prophecy, is in-

---

discussion of how Spenser's allegory continually invites us to read "Faerie" and "Briton" against one another, see my "Vocative and the Vocational: The Unreadability of Elizabeth in *The Faerie Queene*," *English Literary History* 54:1 (1987), 1–30.

[7]This unexpected disclosure of Redcrosse's ancestry raises a number of problematic questions for Spenser's narrative of Tudor destiny. What are we to make of the fact that Redcrosse is identified specifically as a "Saxon"? As a Saxon, what will Redcrosse's role be in the decades of internecine warfare between Briton and Saxon as recorded in Merlin's later prophecy to Britomart in Book 3? Does his Saxon heritage point to a future consolidation of Briton and Saxon lines prior to a Tudor *renovatio*? Or does it indicate an ill-defined fragmentation of Saxon and Briton lines and, by implication, an undermining of the efficacy of Arthur's role in England's destiny as the "Briton Prince"?

structed by Timon and Merlin in Britain—although, following his dream of Gloriana, he immediately leaves the land of his historical destiny to "seeke her forth in Faerye land" ("Letter to Raleigh").

So much of the narrative of *The Faerie Queene*, then, is structured by the disorientation of these knights of English destiny, dislocated within the labyrinths of Faerie and scarcely cognizant of "name and nation," such that the enigmatic and obscure thresholds between Briton and Faerie can only result in an alienation of the subject and deferral of empire. The structure of epic prophecy in *The Faerie Queene* seems more distantly theoretical than in the other epics we have studied—held forth more as a putative and hypothetical possibility than a realizable trajectory—and yet, oddly, exerting more pressure for completion.[8] Prophecy in *The Faerie Queene* is more a rupturing force that is the cause of anxiety. Thus, characters such as Arthur, Britomart, Arthegall, and Redcrosse are obsessed with learning their "name and nation"; and the trajectory of Tudor destiny continually struggles to interpellate its Briton subjects into imperial ideology, even as these same knights suffer a *méconnaissance*, misrecognizing their own destiny as they wander aimlessly through Faerie.[9] The concept of "Faerie," then, becomes less a locus for epic *agon* than a kind of psychic edge of discontinuity, which prevents the Briton subject from ever quite recognizing itself as a self. It is as if the unity and wholeness embodied in the figure of Una are continually undermined by the field of (not *one* but) the other, where the coordinates of Faerie must be mapped.

With its many avatars of duplicity—Archimago, Duessa, Proteus,

---

[8]The institution of marriage as an imminent destiny, for example, is continually foregrounded in *The Faerie Queene*, specifically the putative marriages of Arthur and Gloriana, Britomart and Arthegall, Redcrosse and Una, and the scarcely married Scudamour and Amoret. But within the bounds of Spenser's narrative itself, only the nondynastic Florimell and Marinell and the English rivers the Thames and the Medway succeed in actually getting married. It was the unmarried chastity of Elizabeth herself that no doubt generated much of the anxiety that informs the prophetic structure of *The Faerie Queene*. For more on Elizabeth as a source of male anxiety, see Pamela Joseph Benson, "Rule, Virginia: Protestant Theories of Female Regiment in *The Faerie Queene*," *English Literary Renaissance* 15:3 (1985), 277–92, and Louis Montrose, "*A Midsummer Night's Dream* and the Shaping Fantasies of Elizabethan Culture: Gender, Power, Form," in *Rewriting the Renaissance*, ed. Ferguson et al., 65–87.

[9]Epic prophecy traditionally posits a simple temporal scheme of proleptic fulfillment in the future, but Spenser has structured Tudor destiny as temporally alienating. Thus, among other things, the allegory of the dynastic spouses Britomart and Arthegall refracts them through the dual temporal scheme of the chronicle time of Merlin (and of Uther Pendragon's war with the Saxons) and the contemporary time of Elizabeth.

the False Florimell, and so on—much of the narrative of *The Faerie Queene* unfolds precariously in the other. It is as if its figures of duplicity (not to mention its many veiled idols and simulacra) wage a symbolic assault not just on Una (as the "whole" Truth), but also on the illusion of a unified subject for epic. Because Spenser's Briton knights seek their name and nation in Faerie lond, it seems as if there is something in Faerie that is going *unrepresented* in Britain—an alienating consequence that demarcates the space of the narrative unconscious of *The Faerie Queene*. Spenser's Faerie lond, then, can perhaps be defined as where the subject can only first appear in the other; it is the conceptual edge that defers the (Briton) subject in a temporal lag such that it is always belated in discovering *where it was*. Just as knights like Redcrosse circulate from Britain into Faerie lond to serve Gloriana and then, presumably, "returne backe againe," so also do they trace a circular path with the other—none of which is to say that the subject's encounter with the other is ever reciprocal. We can think, in this context, of Lacan's elusive concept of the *vel*, a point of alienation—a "neither one, nor the other"— that occurs at the intersection between the subject and the other.[10] In *The Faerie Queene*, accession to subjecthood (that is, "interpellation" into Tudor epic history) inevitably occurs somewhere in the obscure threshold of the *vel*, the point at which the Briton subject leaves England and re-emerges in Faerie as the field of the other. Thus, even as Arthur, Britomart, and Arthegall retain their dynastic ontology as "Briton," there is something in the ("Faerie") other that forces a kind of imperial *aphanisis*, a "fading" of the Briton subject into what Lacan would call a shady area of "non-meaning." The problem is not, however, as simple as saying that "Briton" is history, while "Faerie" is imaginative fiction; nor should we pose simple analogies that interpret "Briton" as consciousness and "Faerie" as the unconscious. Faerie lond seemingly exists to make the (Briton) subject "disappear" into a *vel* of "non-meaning"; it is this *vel* that itself constitutes the unconscious for *The Faerie Queene's* "fading," receding subjects.

This chapter focuses on two of the principal dynastic characters in *The Faerie Queene*, Britomart and Arthur, and their attempts to become epic subjects within the *vel* of Faerie. I show how Britomart and Arthur, as the paradigmatic (and traumatized) "infants" of *The*

---

[10]For a fuller discussion of the *vel*, see Lacan, "The Subject and the Other: Alienation," *Four Fundamental Concepts*, 209–14.

Faerie Queene, are to be viewed less as epic subjects than as sites of alienation that, almost by definition, impede the completion of Tudor prophecy. The alienation experienced by Britomart and Arthur demonstrates how the lineaments of the Spenserian epic subject emerge (retroactively) as structured by a seam between neruosis and ideology. Specifically, by focusing on wombs and mirrors (Britomart), and dreams and caesuras (Arthur), I show how the Spenserian subject has become so psychically overdetermined that it becomes impossible for the narrative of *The Faerie Queene* to achieve dynastic closure. Like Arthur's dream of Gloriana, which constitutes its prophetic premise, the structure of *The Faerie Queene* is massively overdetermined. As a fragment, Spenser's epic literally invites an "analysis interminable"; like a dream, it is seemingly always subject to further interpretation. Britomart and Arthur, the paradigmatic "royall Infants" of the narrative, are the two characters who most eloquently tell the story of overdetermination (the story of how neurosis always displaces epic ideology) that *is* Spenser's *The Faerie Queene*. Finally we will see that Spenser's Troy(nouant), as the city not seen of his version of dynastic epic, is less a city than a function of desire—not a city, but a traumatizing split in the subject, a theoretical principle of structuration that is the sustaining of epic narrative (of its theoretical endlessness) itself.

Britomart: Dynastic Anxieties

In the *Orlando furioso*, where dynastic epic fully establishes itself as the genre of genealogical continuity, the prophetess Melissa, disguised as Atlante, lectures the wayward Ruggiero about the necessary course of epic destiny:

> Se non ti muovon le tue proprie laudi,
> e l'opre escelse a chi t' ha il cielo eletto,
> la tua succession perché defraudi
> del ben che mille volte io t' ho predetto?
> Deh, perché il ventre eternamente claudi,
> dove il ciel vuol che sia per te concetto
> la gloriosa e suprumana prole
> ch'esser de' al mondo più chiara che 'l sole?
>
> (7.60)

(If thine own single honour move not thee,
And the high deeds which thou art called to do,

Wherefore defraud thy fair posterity
Of what, was oft predicted, should ensue?
Alas! why seal the womb God willed should be
Pregnant by thee with an illustrious crew,
That far-renowned, and more than human line,
Destined the sun in glory to outshine?)

Melissa's vivid imagery of Ruggiero's denial of seed to Bradamante's womb makes explicit that the founding of empire and its genealogical continuities are directly dependent on the act of impregnating the female. Melissa foregrounds *il ventre* as the space where maternal fecundity and the Name-of-the-Father converge as the ideological guarantor of the place in history of their dynastic offspring. What Melissa seeks to teach Ruggiero is that the dynastic womb is the origin of the subject for epic history—the place where mere physical reproduction cedes place to social production in the service of empire.

Yet throughout so much of *The Faerie Queene*, written as it was for a queen who was not realizing her reproductive and, hence, dynastic potential, the phallocentric impulse toward genealogical continuity is often expressed as an anxiety about the nature of sexuality and gendered subjects. The implicit pun of Book 3, even more than the "perfect (w)hole" of the wound, may be the "mis-conception" that genealogical continuity is securely situated on a bedrock of sexual difference, and that consummation necessarily entails penetration of just such a perfect (w)hole. By focusing on the dynastic progenitors Britomart and Arthegall, Book 3 struggles, against the backdrop of Elizabeth's virginity, to position sexual difference and physical penetration as the guarantors of dynastic continuity. The kind of sexual terror that Amoret experienced on her wedding night with her aggressive husband Scudamour is unacceptable within a framework of imperial and social production.[11] In short, the Sabines must be raped so that empire can be founded. Chastity, "that fairest vertue, farre aboue the rest" (1.Proem), must be sustained only until one's "proper" sexual partner has been found (even if, as in the case of Arthegall, one's partner represents *saluagesse sans finesse*)—after which wombs must be penetrated and inseminated to alleviate the

---

[11]For a treatment of Amoret's sexual fears in marriage, see A. Kent Hieatt, "Scudamour's Practice of *Maistry* upon Amoret," *PMLA* 77 (1962), 509–10, and Roche, *The Kindly Flame*, 72–88. Amoret's sadistic wounding, "entrenched deepe with a knife accursed keene" (3.12.20.6), by Busyrane is, among other things, the painful trauma she must suffer because she will not allow her womb to be penetrated by Scudamour.

anxieties latent in imperial phallocentrism. Otherwise, chastity threatens to become nothing less than the neurotic displacement of imperial ideology. "The hymen," writes Gayatri Spivak, "is the always folded . . . space in which the pen writes its dissemination."[12] Spenser's very act of writing the imperial history of Tudor empire, then, becomes dependent on a symbolic breaking of the hymen, the spilling of virginal blood (Elizabeth's, Britomart's) that can color the blank page of history—virginal blood that identifies painful wounding with male (and imperial) authority, female blood that must be shed within an overdetermined interplay of menstruation, defloration, and birth in the name of dynastic continuity.[13]

But Book 3 is profoundly ambivalent about the very chastity (and sexual difference) it is seemingly structured by. Recurrent throughout its narrative are fears of "unnatural" acts of copulation, "bad" reproduction, monstrous diversions of sexual energy that seek to annihilate cultural interdictions of sexual difference. Glauce, in particular, confesses to Britomart her anxieties about an endogamous and sodomitic sexuality that mocks the bounds of social production. She alludes darkly to "th' Arabian Myrrhe" (2.41.1), who tricked her father into committing incest with her; to Biblis, who lusted after her brother, loving "natiue flesh against all kind" (41.3); to Pasiphaë, who "lou'd a bull" (41.6); and, most resonantly for the epic uncon-

[12]"Translator's Preface" to Jacques Derrida, *Of Grammatology*, trans. Gayatri Chakravorty Spivak (Baltimore: Johns Hopkins University Press, 1976), lxvi.

[13]The wound, of course, is a recurring trope throughout *The Faerie Queene*; much of the epic would appear to be Spenser's investigation of a metapsychology of the trauma and the extent to which it serves as the beginning of consciousness itself. Significant episodes throughout the narrative are particularly devoted to a virtual epistemology of the wound and its relationship to a narcissistic subjectivity. Guyon, Redcrosse, Britomart, Timias, Amoret, Marinell, Malecasta, and Adonis are among the many characters in Book 3 alone who suffer vividly depicted wounds. The wounds are variously "deepe," "sory," and "cruell"; they "engore" and "deform," opening up huge, gaping orifices. In its painful hydraulics, blood trickles, flows, gushes, coagulates, soaks, purples, stains, steams—it is even wallowed in, in sacrificial abjection. As Jonathan Goldberg summarizes it in his chapter "Others, Desire, and the Self," a study of the trope of wounding in Book 4, "repeatedly, lovers find that instead of a self they have a wound" (*Endlesse Worke: Spenser and the Structures of Discourse* [Baltimore: Johns Hopkins University Press, 1981], 86). If, in Kerrigan's summary, the wound is "the master trope of subjectivity" ("Introduction" to *Interpreting Lacan*, ed. Smith and Kerrigan, ix), then throughout *The Faerie Queene* subjects are, as it were, troped into being through the painful trauma of the narcissistic wound. Spenser's preoccupation with the penetration of the female womb, I would add, is another variant on this painful trauma. (For an excellent discussion of the deforming nature of Cupid's wounds in Book 3, see A. Leigh DeNeef's chapter "From Amor to Amoret" in his *Spenser and the Motives of Metaphor* [Durham: Duke University Press, 1982].)

scious, to Narcissus, outrageously "both loue and louer" (45.3)—as if, for Glauce, love could be anything other than "narcissistic."

Moreover, entry into the imperial symbolic and its demands for exogamous union are mitigated throughout Book 3 by the specter of incestuous impulses that take their cues from the unnaturalness of Myrrhe and Biblis. Thetis-like devouring and groveling mothers, like Cymoent and Venus, retain incestuous control over their charges.[14] In a maternal display of erotic necrophilia as depicted on Malecasta's tapestry, Venus lovingly cleanses the wound of her Adonis, transforming him finally into "a dainty flowre."[15] Likewise, Marinell's mother Cymoent is a particularly vivid embodiment of maternal narcissism, seeing reflected in her son the "deare image of my selfe" (4.36.1). After Marinell's wounding by Britomart, Cymoent almost erotically wipes "the gelly blood / From th' orifice" (4.440.6–7), less a tender image of maternal healing than an elaborate realization of male castration anxiety. For that matter, the adolescent Marinell would appear to be the paradigmatic psychotic of *The Faerie Queene*. The young knight represents, perhaps, the epic's greatest threat to genealogical continuity, rejecting, as he does, the split from the (m)other; he refuses to accede to castration but rather fades away in an *aphanisis* (a loss of sexual desire) that signals a kind of lack of lack, withdrawing libidinal cathexis from anything in the world

[14]For more on the maternal presence in Book 3, see Jonathan Goldberg, "The Mothers in Book III of *The Faerie Queene*," *Texas Studies in Literature and Language* 17:1 (1975), 5–26. Despite Spenser's foregrounding of the role of mothers in Book 3, where "in this maternal world," as Goldberg writes, "fathers are, at best, shadowy" (5), I argue later in this chapter that fathers are more omnipresent in the narrative than is initially apparent.

[15]The Spenserian forest of Book 3, much like Tasso's animistic woods, is "alive" with flowers, traditional Ovidian monuments to the narcissistic wounding of love and sexuality. Spenser's paradigmatic "flower" of Book 3 is, of course, Florimell, who, like that innocent gatherer of flowers, Proserpina, is always vulnerable to "de-floration." As an erotic symbol, the flower is richly overdetermined. As well as a substitute for the phallus, the brilliant color of the blossoming flower can also be associated with the erotically inflamed pudendum of the female genitalia, evoking the breaking of the hymen and the staining of the virginal bed.

But because it is overdetermined, the flower also signifies the pain of castration. While Adonis bathes, the Venus depicted on Malecasta's tapestry "secretly would search each daintie lim, / And throw into the well sweet Rosemaryes, / And fragrant violets, and Pances trime" (1.36.6–8), as if flowers could compensate for her maternal emasculation of her young lover. After Adonis is savagely gored (castrated?) by the boar, Venus "Transmews" him to a "dainty flowre," again as if the flower's "stem" could serve as a substitute for his phallus. The beautiful bursts of floral color call to mind the stains of wounding—part gorgeous, part symbolic of the pain of the castrating wounds of narcissism—which is why the wounded lover must always, like Adonis, end up being "transmewed" to a flower.

other than his fetishistic devotion to his "rich array / Of pearles and pretious stones of great assay" (4.18.4–5), a glittering substitute for Cymoent's maternal (oceanic) phallus. And finally, the Squire of Dames narrates to Satyrane the story of the "Geauntesse" Argante, daughter of Typhoeus, who raped "mother Earth" herself (perhaps the ultimate enactment of a fantasy of maternal incest). The strange tale takes an even more bizarre turn when we learn that, while still in their mother's womb, Argante and her twin Ollyphant "in fleshly lust were mingled both yfere" (7.48.8).

This overdetermined fantasy (this "thing far passing thought" [48.5]), of rape, intrauterine enclosure, and incest within the womb (truly *incestus* as the most outrageous extreme of unchastity) exposes many of Book 3's central anxieties about sexuality.[16] When is it permissible to "unseal" and impregnate the womb? How can the dynastic progenitor avoid reenactments of fantasies of maternal incest when the womb is penetrated? What, in the final analysis, separates the dynastic Arthegall from the monstrous Typhoeus? What are the precise symbolic boundaries between endogamy and exogamy—given that they are so dangerously blurred within the overdeterminations of the imaginary?

Pervasive in Book 3 are the enigmatic spaces of feminine enclosure, what Alice Jardine has referred to as "the incestuous nondifference of the maternal space" (233).[17] The receptive hollows of female chasms, archaic reminders of a primordial intrauterine bliss and wholeness, are recurrent even in the most widely disparate episodes. Merlin's cave is "low vnderneath the ground, / In a deepe delue, farre from the vew of day" (3.7.6–7); Marinell is raised by Cymoent in a "rocky caue" (4.20.3); Proteus's bower is "an hollow caue" carved out "in the bottome of the maine" (8.37.1–5); the boar

---

[16]For a provocative account of how "patriarchy appropriates fertility through an upward displacement of the womb" (254) in Book 3, see David Lee Miller's chapter "The Wide Womb of the World" in his *The Poem's Two Bodies: The Poetics of the 1590 Faerie Queene* (Princeton: Princeton University Press, 1988). Of Chrysogonee's birth "withouten pain," Miller argues that it does not "introduce an allegory of radically feminine creativity . . . for the 'mother' from which Belphoebe and Amoret allegorically proceed is the male poet's female brain" (240). Miller claims that for Spenser, "maternity re-presents the paternal origin or degenerates toward chaos" (221).

[17]For an excellent discussion of "boundaries and spaces" that connote the female, see Alice A. Jardine, *Gynesis: Configurations of Women and Modernity* (Ithaca: Cornell University Press, 1985). For a discussion of the feminine and its resistance to the narrative of the mapping of sexual difference, see Teresa de Lauretis's chapter "Desire in Narrative" in *Alice Doesn't: Feminism, Semiotics, Cinema* (Bloomington: Indiana University Press, 1984).

that gored Adonis is kept by Venus in a "rocky Caue" (6.48); the witch conjures the False Florimell in a "secret mew" (8.4.3); most resonantly, the cyclical generation of the Garden of Adonis is described as the "wide wombe of the world" (6.36.6). These fecundating hollows of *(un)heimlichkeit* are both nostalgic and castrating—the promise of a return to infantile bliss, and yet the threat of the dissolution of the phallus in "fleshly slime" (3.6.3.5). These cavernous and watery "wombs" seemingly fight against the negation of the mother, attempting to restore generative power to the *mater* as "matter." But they also demonstrate the phallocentric anxiety that paternity is difficult to signify—that, in the midst of these swollen and "wide wombs," paternity requires social (and imperial) validation.

In this context it bears noting that throughout Book 3 the act of copulation or the precise moment of sexual penetration is curiously occulted. The sexual act happens suddenly, mysteriously, furtively. Merlin, we are told, was "wondrously begotten, and begonne / By false illusion of a guileful Spright, / On a faire Ladie Nonne . . ." (3.13.3–5). Marinell's father Dumarin, espying Cymoent "a sleepe in secret wheare," simply "by her closely lay" (4.19.7–9). When Appollo sleeps with Liagore, one of the wounded Marinell's attending nymphs, we are told that "he loued, and at last her wombe did fill / With heauenly seed . . ." (4.41.5–6). As Chrysogonee, mother of Belphoebe and Amoret, is resting "farre from all mens vew," bright sunbeams, enacting nature's fantasy of an Immaculate Conception, "pierst into her wombe" (6.6–7). (One thinks here of Jove's seduction [rape?] of Danaë, falling into her lap as a shower of gold, as if rape were to be "conceived" as a gift of the gods.)[18]

But there is something left unrepresented in these curious episodes of insemination, something elided in these circumlocutionary descriptions, inhabiting, as they do, an obscure threshold between seduction and rape. In these elegant metaphors of impregnation, what becomes of the sheer physicality of sex?[19] If the act of copulation "embodies" sexual difference (the phallic penetration of a

---

[18]On the lavish "Tapets" of Busyrane's palace are elaborate and lengthy depictions of the "straunge disguize[s]" assumed by Jove during his many rapes of mortal women (11.30–35).

[19]In this context, we can anticipate the Isis Church episode of Book 5, in which, in an allegory of dynastic impregnation, Britomart dreams that she tames the angry crocodile at Isis's feet, after which "of his game she soone enwombed grew" (7.16.5). As Kenneth Gross writes, "The whole sequence is given a truly oneiric rapidity, with the moment of conception strangely elided . . ." (*Spenserian Poetics: Idolatry, Iconoclasm, and Magic* [Ithaca: Cornell University Press, 1985], 177). (For more on the erotic nature of Britomart's dream, see Angus Fletcher, *The Prophetic Moment: An Essay on Spenser* [Chicago: University of Chicago Press, 1971], 259–76.)

feminine "perfect [w]hole"), then at what point during penetration is this sexual difference most realized through representation? At the point at which rape and seduction are transformed into elaborate literary tropes, are we to suppose that these episodes are constructed to depict some sort of primordial or mysterious power of the womb? Or do they demonstrate anxieties about the phallus and its always ambivalent return to the womb? Chrysogonee's strange, and indeed miraculous, impregnation by sunbeams (not to mention her later childbirth "withouten paine" [6.27.2]), more than just a circumlocution of the often painful penetrations of copulation (such as those later feared by her daughter Amoret), would appear to be a move toward rendering sexuality a metaphor—a denotational compromise brought about by the unrepresentability of the phallus.

One of the central questions of Book 3, ever mindful of its virgin queen, then, becomes, How *does* one signify the phallus and its act of penetration and insemination? Barbara Johnson argues that "if human beings were not divided into two biological sexes, there would probably be no need for literature"[20]—which is perhaps why Spenser retracted his 1590 ending to Book 3, in which Scudamour and Amoret are entwined hermaphroditically "in long embracement" (12.45.9).[21] Without sexual division and its disastrous attempts to embrace the other's "division within," there can be no narrative. But Johnson also questions the ability of literature "to say the truth of sexuality."[22] Certainly Book 3, with its emphasis on chastity, sexuality, and sexual difference as the origin of imperial history, pushes tentatively against the limits of fiction and of representation itself. Moreover, as if to complicate even further its representational task, Spenser's epic chooses androgyny and its threats to the phallus as its central vehicle for chastity and the social construction of gender.

Thus, when Britomart makes her initial appearance in Book 3, she does so as a kind of return of the repressed within the literary history of epic and its recurring obsession with female androgyny. Specifically, she seems to be a return of the kind of deadly internal violence that rendered Clorinda such an uncanny source of castration anxiety for Tancredi in the *Liberata*. Fiercely protecting her chastity

[20]*The Critical Difference,* 13.
[21]For more on Spenser's original ending, see Donald Cheney, "Spenser's hermaphrodite and the 1590 *Faerie Queene, PMLA* 87 (1972), 192–200.
[22]*The Critical Difference,* 13. Similarly, Shoshana Felman writes that sexuality can never be "the 'text's meaning': it is rather that through which meaning in the text *does not come off,* that which in the text . . . *fails to mean"* ("Turning the Screw of Interpretation," in *Literature and Psychoanalysis,* ed. Felman, 112).

by means of her "enchaunted speare," Britomart circumvents the representation of gender; and because (like Ariosto's Marfisa) she "would not disarmed be" (3.1.42), Britomart and her androgynous aggressivity seemingly represent her noncomplicity with the laws of gender signification. Spenser's account of Guyon's assault on Britomart early in the book vividly illustrates this noncomplicity: "They bene ymet, and both their points arriued" (1.6.1). Here Britomart is, for the moment at least, established as a representational (and reproductive) scandal, refusing to yield to or absorb phallic penetration, but rather repelling it by means of her own phallic counteraggression. When the unfortunate ardor of the lustful Malecasta (or "bad chastity"), a character reminiscent of Fiordispina in the *Orlando furioso*, moves her to seduce Britomart in the Castle Ioyeous, Spenser describes Malecasta as "all ignoraunt of her [Britomart's] contrary sex" (1.47.2). And as Malecasta discovers, because Britomart herself is "all ignoraunt of her contrary sex," Spenser's female warrior threatens to become the subversion of meaning itself—which is the dangerous lesson that Malecasta learns when, lying next to Britomart, she "softly felt, if any member mooued" (1.60.7). Unveiling the castrative horror of the theme of Balzac's *Sarrasine*, Roland Barthes writes, "It is fatal . . . to remove the dividing line, the paradigmatic slash mark which permits meaning to function."[23] Not surprisingly, then, Britomart "lept out of her filed bed, / And to her weapon ran, in minde to gride / The loathed leachour"—in effect, an aggressive attempt at the restoration of "meaning."

Thus, if Tasso's Clorinda, despite her murder by Tancredi, is, in some sense, incapable of annihilation, if she is the uncanny limit of fiction itself (as the "anticipation of nonrepresentation" by the narcissism of the male other), Britomart never quite accedes to that (deadly) edge that subverts the functioning of meaning. Perhaps because of Book 3's overt and pervasive anxieties about the nature of sexuality, gender, and reproduction (perhaps, in short, because of anxieties about the libidinal economy of Elizabeth herself), the internal violence of Britomart's androgyny is itself eventually castrated and inscribed by the phallus before it can subvert the structure of imperial narrative. As we shall see, Merlin's mirror of epic destiny will serve to contain Britomart's unrepresentable threshold of anatomical difference, and will secure the limits of the imperial text

[23]Roland Barthes, *S/Z: An Essay*, trans. Richard Miller (New York: Hill and Wang, 1974), 215.

such that the androgyne is no longer a subversion of the phallus, but is rather made to serve as the inscription of sexual difference that *is* the phallus. If, in the *Liberata*, androgyny poses the continual threat of male castration, in Merlin's mirror androgyny can exist only in *relation* to castration. Thus, the mirror becomes the site/sight of imperial phallocentrism's dependence on the castrated androgyne for dynastic continuity—the solution, in effect, for "dynastic anxieties."

Britomart: Gender as Trauma

It is in the depths of her father's closet, less a closet than one of Book 3's many hidden, womb-like enclosures where thresholds are approached but never quite transgressed, that Britomart views her reflection in a mirror devised by Merlin's "deepe science" (2.18.7). In an epic persistently unsettled by avatars of duplicity and "subtile sophismes"—Archimago, Duessa, Proteus, and even Merlin himself—the mirror is identified as the locus of perfect representation:

> It vertue had, to shew in perfect sight,
>   What euer thing was in the world contaynd,
>   Betwixt the lowest earth and heauens hight,
>   So that it to the looker appertaynd.
>
>   (2.18.7)

The "perfect sight" reflected by the mirror would seem to be an almost miraculous closure of the gap between signifier and signified. The mirror, "like to the world it selfe" (19.9), proffers its mimetic reflections without anxiety that the image will somehow require further interpretation.

And yet, because the mirror is gazed into only insofar as "so that it to the looker appertaynd," we are confronted, despite its reflection of "perfect sight," with an interpretive gap. The images in the mirror acquire meaning only through the tropological, "appertayn[ing]" perceptions of the viewer; and the mirror's surface does not "contayn" meaning so much as it invites meaning only to conceal deeper lacunae of repressed meanings, undermining any straightforward notion of "the world it selfe." Between the poet's rhyming of "contaynd" and "appertaynd" exists the gap inhabited by representation. The mirror's images, in short, can never "reflect" anything other than the viewing subject not quite seeing itself as it really is. And within the mirror's powerful exegetical force lies the precise edge between the "neurotic" subject and the "ideological" subject, as well as the provenance of Britomart's desire.

It seems appropriate that the adolescent Britomart, on the threshold of sexual maturity, should seek her image in a mirror. In his *De amore*, Ficino writes that according to Aristotle, in his *De insomniis*, "women, when the menstrual blood flows down, often soil a mirror with bloody drops by their own gaze."[24] Initially, however, the "menstrual" Britomart sees nothing of interest in the mirror: "Her selfe a while therein she vewd in vaine" (22.6). This is a curious line, eliciting an anxiety of interpretation for which we must pause. "In vaine" she scans the surface of the mirror and its "perfect sight" *for something to view*. She views "her selfe" but is struck with no particular thoughts about this "selfe"—perhaps the precise moment of primary narcissism itself. As she earlier narrates to Redcrosse, Britomart, like Arthur, in her infancy "taken was from nourses tender pap" to be "trained vp in warlike stowre" (2.6.3). Thus, Spenser, as he will again in the case of Arthur, rather remarkably calls attention to a neonatal infancy (and to the psychic vicissitudes of an "early childhood development").

We must not allow Spenser's brief allusion to his heroine's infancy (and its relationship to an epic subjectivity) to pass unexamined. Prior to her abrupt removal from that privileged *objet a* the "tender pap," we are invited to imagine the neonatal Britomart as experiencing the psychic history of every infant, enjoying a perfect homeostasis with the (m)other. In this pre-Oedipal phase, we can imagine her seeking and finding identificatory validation in the presence of her (m)other—a process of introjective merging, during which the narcissistic infant Britomart would have no sense of alienation or of differentiation. Put another way, the affective logic of her cathexis with the (m)other would exclude any sense of "self," a realization that by definition can occur only through the psychic trauma of differentiation—the fall into "selfhood," as it were. Thus, when we are told that Britomart seeks her mirror reflection "in vaine," she is, in effect, reenacting the stage of primary narcissism when fusion with the (m)other entails a perfect merging with the images that the infant assimilates (the mirror, in other words, as "perfect sight").

But Britomart is soon to discover that the self is never immediately

---

[24]Marsilio Ficino, *Commentary on Plato's Symposium on Love*, trans. Sears Jayne (Dallas: Spring, 1985), 160.

present to itself. This reflective stage of a primary narcissism lasts only an instant before Britomart is moved to an "appertayn[ing]" of the representation in the mirror. The differentiating trauma of self-consciousness imposed by the mirror ruptures Britomart's unwary fusion with herself such that "she gan againe / Her to bethinke of, that mote to her selfe pertaine" (22.9). What appears to be Spenser's harmless tautology is nothing less than the traumatic dialectical structuration of otherness that rend(er)s the sense of "self."[25] In this second phase of her glance in the mirror, we are told that she is no longer "vew[ing]" but rather "auising" or *remembering* "her selfe." The reflection in the mirror has now wedged a *temporal* gap such that Britomart's image of herself is no longer an abject fusion but rather an external image that is subject to re-membering—an image not of coherence but a triggering of the mnemic traces of an earlier neonatal wholeness.

Thus, in her brief encounter with Ryence's mirror (with the encounter serving, in its own way, as an Aeneas-like enactment of epic "memory"), Britomart experiences nothing less than the obscure threshold of (self-)consciousness itself. The repetitive similarity of lines 22.5 and 22.9 is only apparent; in fact, Britomart can never be the same as when she first entered her father's closet. The key word here is "againe" (22.8): she "gan *againe*" to "auise" herself. This second assessment of "self" is an act of repetition, and here we must pause to consider what is entailed in this repetition. To do even something so elementary as to acknowledge cognitively that a repetition has occurred, we must presuppose an originary moment of homeostasis during which, simply put, *nothing happens*. Thus, the concept of repetition carries us back again to Britomart's infancy.

Almost like the circular figure of organic wholeness in Plato's *Timaeus*, the neonate enjoys a fulfillment that is always immanent. But throughout the pre-mirror phase, the infant receives intimations of fragmentation and alienation—specular anticipations of future separations from "nourses tender pap" that lay the foundation for the trauma of repetition. The absence of the (m)other—of the source of identification—means that something *has happened*, a disturbance of stasis whose trauma is eventually registered by the infant as repeatable. When Britomart "gan againe" to consider herself in the mirror,

---

[25]In his *Spenserian Poetics*, Kenneth Gross suggests that Britomart's glance in Ryence's mirror is Spenser's version of a Lacanian *stade du miroir*, especially, as Gross writes, "the notion that the outward, erotic drives of the ego originate in the displacement of an original narcissism onto an external or alienated image . . ." (148).

her act of repetition recapitulates earlier *fort/da* playings out of absence and presence, with the repetition serving as a metaphor for
her own loss of homeostatic "self" to differentiation and the loss of
wholeness that always occurs retroactively in any act of repetition.
Britomart's act of "auising againe" *is* originary loss, with the mirror
serving as the inevitable trope of the self who is not quite "her
selfe."

The mirror episode is a moment of traumatic excitement for Britomart. Her originary act of viewing her "selfe" in the mirror is not
cognitively registered and elicits no recognition. But it is the repetition of the glimpse that elicits the trauma retrospectively. Britomart's
glance in the mirror strives to be a quest for totality, a specular anticipation of wholeness, a drive toward full presence and self-posses-
sion, but it yields instead fragmentation and self-division. Thus Merlin's "deepe science" exposes Britomart's recognition of her "selfe"
as, in fact, a *mis*recognition of the self that is not quite the self—of
the self that always lags behind its own origin.

After her act of specular *méconnaissance*, Britomart espies the image of the "salvage" Arthegall, clad in the "armour of an alienating
identity," and the fictional alienation of her "selfe" is soon to be
complete: "Eftsoones there was presented to her eye / A comely
knight, all arm'd in complete wize" (24.1–2)—Arthegall as the very
embodiment of the ego ideal. The Freudian ego ideal absorbs the
narcissistic ambitions of "what one would like to be"—an outer projection of what one seeks to imitate. As a mimetic projection, the
ego ideal then becomes a *Vorbild* (literally, a "picture-in-front") that
is in the extraordinary position of watching the subject watch itself.
Arthegall then serves, in some sense, as Tudor imperial prophecy's
assurance that Britomart *is seen seeing herself in front of her own image.*
Though Arthegall is, as the (phallic) ego ideal, what the androgynous and combative Britomart "would like to be," he steals away her
subjectivity through his own objectifying gaze.[26] The *Vorbild* becomes the ego's breathless attempt to close the gap between where
the ego was and where the ego should be. In a remarkable literary
moment, then, the "deep science" of Merlin's mirror has devised a
(Freudian) *Vorbild* that witnesses the (Lacanian) *méconnaissance* of the
epic subject, a *méconnaissance* that assaults the barriers of primary

---

[26]On the alienating function of the gaze, Lacan writes, "It is not only that I see the
other, I see him [her] seeing me, which implicates the third term, namely that he
knows that I see him [her]" ("The object relation and the intersubjective relation,"
Sem. I, 218).

narcissism and forms the discontinuous edge between neurosis and ideology.

Initially, as was the case with her own first viewing of her image, Britomart takes little note of this "salvage" figure before her: she "liked well, ne further fastned not, / But went her way" (26.2–3). But she is soon stricken (belatedly) with unexplained grief and anxiety: "She wist not, silly Mayd, what she did aile, / Yet wist, she was not well at ease perdy, / Yet thought it was not loue, but some melancholy" (27.7–9). Britomart's "melancholy" is, as we shall see, not only the pain of a secondary narcissism—not only a longing to close the gap between her and the *Vorbild*—but also nothing less than the pain and psychic trauma of the very process of becoming gendered.

After her alienating encounter with the mirror, Britomart suffers "her first engraffed paine" (17.5), the pain not of mere "love" (whatever, as Spenser suggests throughout his epic, that could possibly be), but of the castrating trauma of gender determination. Indeed, Merlin's mirror itself is (en)gendered in such a way that it could only be Britomart, not Arthegall, who is destined to be inscribed by the gaze of the other and suffer a subsequent "engraffed paine." If, as Lacan maintains, there can be no *rapport sexuel*, then the mirror demonstrates how gender is created solely as an effect of the process of symbolization.

The circumference of Merlin's "glassie globe" (21.1) is described as "round and hollow shaped" (19.8)—in effect, a simulacrum of vaginal or intrauterine enclosures. Merlin's mirror, then, becomes an uncanny anticipation of Luce Irigaray's privileged trope of the speculum which, among other things, serves as the surgical instrument gynecologists use for the inspection of bodily cavities. In Irigaray's conception, the speculum "makes a *hole*—sets itself up pompously as an authority in order to give shape to the imaginary orb of a 'subject.'"[27] The speculum is deceptive, for although its concave shape conforms to uterine enclosures, it penetrates these spaces and determines their representation. As sure as the concave configuration of the surgeon's speculum penetrates female bodily cavities, so also does the signifying space of Merlin's "hollow shaped" speculum "penetrate" Britomart's unconscious, representing her divided "selfe" to herself. Viewed in this light, Merlin's later prophecy to Britomart that her "name and nation" will come "from the sacred

---

[27]Luce Irigaray, *Speculum of the Other Woman*, trans. Gillian C. Gill (Ithaca: Cornell University Press, 1985), 144.

mould / Of her immortal wombe" (4.11.8–9)—more than simply a topos of epic destiny—takes on added significance. The mirror is both the means by which Arthegall is represented to Britomart—a process of symbolization occurring in the metaphorical womb of the "hollow" mirror—and a simulacrum of the site of penetration, of the "sacred mould" wherein pregnancy inevitably becomes the "embodiment" of nature and culture.

From this point on in the narrative, Britomart is fated to be inscribed by the alien discourse of the "salvage" Arthegall. As the newly prophesied dynastic progenitor for Troynouant (as Britomart's "Imperious [and "Imperi-all"] Loue" (2.23.2), Arthegall embodies all the patriarchal and cultural laws of the epic founding of civilization imposed by the symbolic; for that matter, he is perhaps *The Faerie Queene*'s most powerful reminder that empire is dependent on genealogical continuity. But despite Merlin's prophecy and its presumption of dynastic symmetry (the formation of empire through the destined union of man and woman), we should note that Arthegall represents not harmonious, exogamous union (not, we may say, *rapport sexuel*), but rather a site of alienation that will from this point on inscribe a lack in Britomart, who can now experience herself only in relation to the gaze of the other in the mirror. It is, in this sense, perhaps less accurate to represent Arthegall as the object of Britomart's love than it is to view him as a function of desire, the "phallic signifier" who creates Britomart as a desiring subject at the point of repression of childhood experience. In short, the character "Arthegall" is the point at which epic prophecy realizes itself as the alienating gaze of the other.

Spenser's mirror episode demonstrates that sexuality—a specifically "ideological" or dynastic sexuality—can only be constituted through trauma. Before she is subjected to Arthegall's gaze in the mirror—before he was "presented to her eye"—Britomart, much like the "psychotic" Marinell, had foreclosed on the concept of gender difference. But the phallic and imperial interdiction of Arthegall proclaims the Oedipal laws of knowledge of gender. Plainly, there can be no reciprocity between the viewing subject and its image. Where there is loss, there is representation; this is why Arthegall is "presented to her eye" at the precise moment of Britomart's (mis)recognition of herself as the external image of the other, which will always mediate her sense of self. In Merlin's imperial mirror it is now encoded that Britomart must accept her castration and displace her "lack" onto Arthegall—not just the "royall seed" of "the antique

Troian blood" (3.42.8), but also the representational agent of a traumatizing sexual difference.

Despite Book 3's recurring "wombs," and despite its focus on what we might be tempted (wrongly) to call the female subjectivity of the "royall Maid" Britomart, it is the absent phallus that dictates the symbolic structuration of the "destined descents" of Merlin's prophecy. In his invocation, prior to Merlin's prophecy to Clio, the Muse of History, Spenser celebrates, in explicitly parturitional terms, his two dynastic spouses, "From whose two loynes thou afterward did rayse / Most famous fruits of matrimoniall bowre" (3.3.6–7). The act of physical penetration of the womb, the very act that Book 3 so often struggles to represent, has served as the origin of empire within dynastic epic history ever since Aeneas's marriage to Lavinia. But what Book 3 demonstrates is that the phallus always functions as the abstract, *veiled* (or, in Spenser's case, "imaged") signifier—all the more powerful in its absence, an absence illustrating the Lacanian axiom that sexual difference is merely symbolic of the symbolic itself. In Spenser's version of imperial prophecy, the phallus does not have to be present to signify, to dictate the position of women (and, especially, androgynous women) within exogamous exchange.[28] In *The Faerie Queene*, the difference of the sexes, as the

---

[28]That the absent phallus does not readily signify itself is demonstrated in Britomart's complaints to Redcrosse and to Glauce. Searching in vain for her dynastic spouse, she demands of Redcrosse: "Tell me some markes, by whiche he may appeare . . . / What shape, what shield, what armes, what steed, what sted" (2.16.3.6). And to Glauce she confesses her fears that in Arthegall, she is searching for a "bodie farre exild" (2.44.9).

The "exild," absent phallus in Book 3 may be "embodied" by the figure of Adonis. Having once been "transmewed" by Venus to a "dainty flowre," Adonis is a presiding life-principle for his Garden, "eterne in mutabilitie . . . that liuing giues to all" (6.47.5–9). But his savage goring by the boar indicates that he is also the castrative wound on which the entire third book is structured. Nohrnberg writes that because Adonis is wounded in the thigh, he is "the phallus by synecdoche" (*Analogy*, 566). Gross refers to him as "the wounded source" (*Spenserian Poetics*, 196), and Miller writes that Adonis "seems half like a penis sheathed in an anamorphic vagina and half like a corpse laid out for burial" (*The Poem's Two Bodies*, 276). At this precise midpoint of the 1590 edition of Book 3, we come across Adonis hidden in "the thickest couert" of the *mons veneris*, where "there yet, some say, in secret he does ly, / Lapped in flowres . . ." (6.46.4–5)—the site/sight of a perfect (w)hole. If Arthegall goes largely unconceptualized as the unsignifiable principle of dynastic procreation, Adonis, like Balzac's La Zambinella, is represented as what Barthes calls a "structural artifice" (*S/Z*, 164), which sustains narrative by means of division and castration. The fate of Adonis points to archetypal fears of castration lurking within Spenser's narrative of dynastic succession—the point at which dynastic epic meets the gesture of castration. Not just, as Barthes would call it, "hermeneutic truth," the castration of

crucial structural principle that insures dynastic continuity, rests not on anatomical distinctions, but on the absent phallus as the symbolic principle of structuration that assures the place and function of the (imperial) father.

Ryence's mirror, passed from the prophet-mage to the father, serves as Spenser's privileged symbolization of the phallus—all the more representationally elegant because the phallus makes its evanescent appearance as nothing more than a mirror image. The fact that we never see Ryence (only his mirror) is symbolic of the fact that imperial paternity does not base itself on genetic reproduction, but is the ideological position of exogamy, serving to initiate the operations of social exchange wherein Britomart is passed from the father to the future husband as the structure of her alienation in the other. "If the phallus is a signifier," writes Lacan, "then it is in the place of the Other that the subject gains access to it."[29] Ryence's mirror is the object whereby epic destiny constitutes itself out of the *méconnaissance* of the androgyne, a *méconnaissance* that alienates (and domesticates) through the power of the absent phallus. If epic history is dependent on the ideological position of the absent phallus, if the lesson of Ryence's mirror is that anatomy *is* (epic) destiny, then the woman within epic history must be made to stand in for (anatomical) difference and loss.

Despite her combative androgyny, then, there is little in the internal violence of Britomart that would indicate that Spenser is exploring a new kind of female subjectivity.[30] If Tasso's Clorinda challenged the very limits of representation within the framework of epic history, Spenser's dynastic narrative portrays a Britomart who is immanently "representable" through Merlin's mirror. It is almost as if, in Britomart, Spenser has chosen to close off an impulse within the literary history of epic that had long been fascinated with the ontogeny of female bisexuality and its inhabiting of the margins of

---

Adonis is the point at which the narrative *tells itself* of the truth of the absent phallus/penis.

[29]*Feminine Sexuality*, 83.

[30]For an excellent reading of Britomart as motivated by female perspectives, see Maureen Quilligan, *Milton's Spenser: The Politics of Reading* (Ithaca: Cornell University Press, 1983), 185–91. For more recent efforts at defining a female subjectivity for Britomart, see Susanne Lindgren Wofford, "Britomart's Petrarchan Lament: Allegory and Narrative in *The Faerie Queene* III, iv," *Comparative Literature* 39:1 (1988), 1–21. Sympathetic as I am to their efforts to shape a distinctly "female" subjecthood for Britomart, I contend that Spenser's narrative of male anxieties (dynastic and phallic) in Book 3 do not permit it.

imperial history. Mindful of a Virgin Queen uninscribed by the (real) phallus, Spenser "domesticates" his androgyne to the point that, in her establishing of the *Vorbild* Arthegall as her ego ideal, Britomart at times does little more than serve as an anticipation of the classic Freudian portrayal of the emergence of womanhood as structured on penis envy. Throughout Book 3, Britomart's pugnacious defenses of her chastity, "that fairest vertue, farre aboue the rest," seem little more than a symptom of female hysteria, wherein the woman is uncertain whether she is male (refusing to accept the fact of castration) or female. Insofar as Spenser's chastity can be interpreted to mean "chaste" love within marriage, it can only mean acceptance of castration following the "transgression" of penis envy.

For Freud, both the male and female infant are inherently bisexual, such that there would be nothing inherently unusual about a female androgyne.[31] In a Freudian narrative, then, early bisexuality is, for the woman, the norm—not the exception. Penis envy (like Britomart's experience with Ryence's mirror) becomes every girl's discovery of her own castration. Even (or especially) at the point at which Britomart assumes the armor of Angelica, the Saxon queen defeated by the Britons, whose armor was hung in a church by Ryence and eventually passed on to Britomart (4.39), her relation to castration remains unchanged within a phallic order.

Arthur: Just-Missed Encounters with Epic Destiny

For Lacan, a "good" story would be one that misrecognizes its own narrative, one that evades the totality it anticipates. All "good" stories are narratives of desire, structured around a quest for an elusive object. But the object of the quest for Lacan is not merely elusive, for mere elusiveness would render the *méconnaissance* of the narrative "unrecognizable." The Lacanian object of desire "isn't a question of recognizing something which would be entirely given."[32] The evanescent object of desire is not *entirely given*; in other words, it is not something (like Britomart's viewing of her "selfe" in Ryence's mirror) that would already have been there in the beginning—or it might have been there, but only belatedly, constructed

---

[31]As Sarah Kofman writes, in Freud, "one is not born a woman, one becomes a woman" (*The Enigma of Woman*, 122).

[32]"Desire, Life and Death," *Sem. II*, 229.

through those cherished fictions by which we deceive ourselves into thinking we have achieved totality, such as narration and memory.

What Lacan would have "recognized" in Spenser's Arthur is how epic destiny has appropriated the calculus of Arthurian narrative (the anticipatory trajectory of the *rex quondam rexque futurus,* or "once and future king") only to unravel its peculiar temporal logic as a narrative of deferral seeking an object that may not already have been there. Shoshana Felman defines a riddle as a narrative delay structured on the promise that "in time you'll learn."[33] But if Oedipus learns the horror of his riddle "in time" (though not *just* "in time"), Arthur's "iust terme" (1.9.5.9)—the precarious mythic space that Merlin offers as the completion of "self" in epic destiny—unfolds not disclosure but a belatedness that insists on Arthur's structuration in terms of an object that has never been entirely given (Gloriana), rather than of a totality he anticipates. "In time" Arthur does not "learn" the mystery of his "loues and lignage"—for that matter, the answer is "hidden yit" (1.9.3.4)—but rather continues to evade his own narrative, to misrecognize his own history. We might say that Spenser's Arthur supplants the symbolic myth of a castrated Oedipus with the prior imaginary myth of the impossibility of being oneself. What we finally learn from Arthur is that, as François Roustang has put it, "one doesn't so easily become 'the subject of one's own story.' "[34]

As we have seen, epic is traditionally concerned with the tracing of origins, with first causes, and yet its in medias res structure implies that there is a certain sense in which epic wants to be read retroactively. All of which brings us to Arthur's dream of Gloriana, the "Faerie Queene" who represents the fulfillment of the hero's epic destiny as the head of a Tudor *renovatio.* Arthur's dream fantasy precariously situates the narrative premise of Spenser's epic in the imaginary—in epic history as infolded within the psyche. Because fantasy is quintessentially "neurotic," then, in *The Faerie Queene* the epic quest for origins is no longer simply genealogical in nature, but also profoundly psychoanalytic—an intimate interplay of history and psyche.

But Arthur's dream makes discerning the bedrock of narrative within it especially problematic; the temporal complexities of a primal scene for Tudor epic beginnings is not readily forthcoming. For

---

[33]Shoshana Felman, *Jacques Lacan and the Adventure of Insight: Psychoanalysis in Contemporary Culture* (Cambridge: Harvard University Press, 1987), 150.
[34]François Roustang, "Uncertainty," *October* 28 (1984), 92.

Spenser, dream visions as the source of epic origins would have had a venerable epic literary history, starting with Anchises' revelation to Aeneas of a Roman *imperium* in Book VI of the *Aeneid*, that rich primal scene for all dynastic epic. Yet, as Servius worries in his commentary, because Aeneas passes a giant elm which is the "home of empty Dreams" (VI.283) to enter Hell, and because the hero exits by the Ivory Gate of false dreams, the somnambular frame to Anchises' prophecy "indicates that all this is feigned, since both the entrance and the exit are counterfeit and false."[35] The origin of epic destiny, suggests Virgil, may be no more substantial than a dream.

If, in Virgil, we participate in and experience Aeneas's dream directly as its readers, Spenser's Arthur narrates his dream to Una through a secondary elaboration, a narration within a narration, that constitutes an even more insubstantial counterfeit than Aeneas's vision. And we might pause at precisely this point to consider the implication of this dream as *narrated* and the extent to which this narration detracts from the "meaning" of the dream itself. Again, we must keep in mind that "one doesn't so easily become 'the subject of one's own story'"—not even in our dreams.

The most conspicuous moment of the text's ready offering of its own interpretation—when, paradoxically, we are closest to the unconscious organization, to one of the darker of Spenser's many "darke conceits" in *The Faerie Queene*—is the moment of Arthur's consciously proclaimed intention to become the subject of his own story through the narration of his dream. André Green refers to such freely offered interpretations as an "Ariadne's thread": "Such a thread stretches the text toward its goal, has the last word, represents the end point of its ostensible meaning."[36] If easy passage out of the labyrinth of textual interpretations is what we are seeking, then we will readily accept these Ariadne's threads. But perhaps we should "listen" to Arthur's narration more carefully.

The response of generations of readers of *The Faerie Queene* to Arthur's deceptively simple dream illustrates how willingly we accept its Ariadne's thread, how unhesitatingly we work with the manifest content of his dream in order to construct its (and the entire poem's) meaning, rather than move backward (taking our cue from epic's desire to be read retroactively) to the oneiric structure of the dream's latent content—in effect, how readily we accommodate Arthur's

---

[35]This passage from Servius is quoted in Michael Murrin, *The Allegorical Epic*, 40.
[36]André Green, "The Unbinding Process," trans. Lionel Duisit, *New Literary History* 21:1 (1980), 17.

tenuous *parole* into a systemic *langue* of mythic genealogy. It is as if generations of readers have been reluctant to confront the possibility that the fulfillment of Tudor imperial history may be dependent on nothing more substantial than Arthur's dream. Arthur's (manifest) narration of his dream of Gloriana results in the premise of *The Faerie Queene*'s detaching itself from the (latent) text of the dream and plunging us prematurely into hermeneutics. We merely beg the question of Spenser's fragile premise if we assume an unproblematic and inherent narrative structure in Arthur and Gloriana's putative millennial marriage.

Like every mythic hero, Arthur struggles to know the meaning of his history, hence his eagerness to respond to Una's invitation to speak of his "name and nation." It is a quintessentially epic moment, reminiscent of Dido's desire to hear Aeneas's story *a prima origine*. But the problem is that dream language is unassimilable as conscious language; a dream, in short, cannot speak for itself. For that matter, we cannot even be certain what it means for Arthur to proclaim that he has *had* a dream. As Freud warned, dreams have no semantic content, but are a structure of dislocations (*Entstellungen*) whose connections can never be fully traced. Arthur's narration of his dream, surely *The Faerie Queene*'s most obscure threshold between the dual ontologies of Briton and Faerie, becomes also a characteristically Lacanian moment, not because of its content, but because of what it says about Arthur's desire to speak, to communicate. What Spenser is foregrounding here is not the quest to find Gloriana and marry her, but rather the quest itself and Arthur's need to speak his loss. (Indeed, he speaks *because* he has experienced loss.) Despite Arthur's anxiety (like Servius's) as to "whether dreames delude, or true it were" (1.9.14.5), we search in vain for either truth or falsehood in his dream. Thus the reader who accepts too literally Arthur's secondary elaboration of his dream runs the risk of becoming alienated in the entanglements of Arthur's being spoken by the discourse of the other. The dream, as we shall see, functions so that Arthur can name his desire (retroactively) as Gloriana; and his (just-missed) encounter with the Faerie Queene constitutes not the origin of Tudor imperial destiny, but an act of *méconnaissance* as the only way Tudor prophecy can realize itself.

Infantilized throughout so much of *The Faerie Queene* as the "Briton Prince," Arthur suffers his own kind of infantile neurosis as he seeks (retroactively) to achieve his proleptic name as the "Arthur" of imperial destiny. Like Freud's Wolf Man, the most celebrated case in psychoanalysis of an infantile neurotic, Arthur strug-

gles to construct a history for himself (and to negotiate possible forgotten traumas) through memories and narration. Through Arthur's
fantasy, then, we have come full circle back to the memory that
structures the first half of the *Aeneid*. At its core, fantasy is its own
act of "remembering"—the scene of seduction that lies on an obscure threshold between real event and fantasy. Arthur's dream
demonstrates that the memory of seduction is always more powerful
than the seduction itself. For Freud, the subject knows its origin
only in fantasy; typically, the origin of the subject takes shape as a
myth of the origin of sexuality. Thus, one of the crucial structuring
questions of psychoanalysis is a "timely" one: when does sexuality
begin?

But as the case of the Wolf Man so dramatically demonstrates, the
going is treacherous when one has to trace origins in a dream. "I
have no reason to doubt the correctness of this memory," writes the
Wolf Man in a letter to Freud in June 1926, "verifying" his infamous
dream of the wolves perched in the tree.[37] The Wolf Man writes the
letter to protect Freud against Otto Rank's apostasy as to what "really" constitutes a primal scene. But the protective gesture is ironic
because Freud's unwitting breakthrough in his analysis of the Wolf
Man is the recurrent possibility that the "correctness" of the patient's recall is perhaps the least reliable indicator of what "really"
happened in the past. Like the story of the Wolf Man, the story of
Arthur is a mnemonic myth that must struggle to build a chronology
out of the retroactive structure of a dream that seeks in vain to represent an originary event.

Epic consciousness has to create for itself a past, which can then
be imbued with meaning. Unlike Britomart and Arthegall, Arthur is
the only dynastic avatar in *The Faerie Queene* who is given no prophetic validation of his imperial destiny, and, as we have seen, his
assurance of dynastic participation in a Tudor *renovatio* is achieved
only through a dream. Yet even at this tenuous point we must push,
if we can, for further clarification. Arthur narrates his dream to Una
thus:

> Most goodly glee and louely blandishment
> She to me made, and bad me loue her deare,
> For dearely sure her loue was to me bent,

---

[37]Quoted by Maria Torok, "What Is Occult in Occultism? Between Sigmund Freud
and Sergei Pankeiev Wolf Man," in Nicolas Abraham and Maria Torok, *The Wolf
Man's Magic Word: A Cryptonymy*, trans. Nicholas Rand (Minneapolis: University of
Minnesota Press, 1986), 93.

As when iust time expired should appeare.
But whether dreames delude, or true it were,
Was neuer hart so rauisht with delight,
Ne liuing man like words did euer heare,
As she to me deliuered all that night;
And at her parting said, She Queene of Faeries hight.

(1.9.14)

What can we state unequivocally about this dream that would grant it the humble status of an event, much less a founding "prophetic moment" for Tudor dynasty? Arthur's erotic encounter with Gloriana is ontologically unsettled—neither fully a dream nor fully the occurrence of a "real" event. The possibility that Gloriana's "louely blandishment" with the Briton prince might have actually taken place is perhaps empirically demonstrated by the "nought but pressed gras" (15.2) she leaves behind—but the (re)"pressed gras" is also nature's signification of her absent presence, the interpretive gap of her "place deuoyd" (15.1), which inscribes both the grass and Arthur with loss.

What happened during (before?) this odd interlude? A dream, writes Samuel Weber, "cannot be comprehended in the present tense";[38] and the mechanics of repression always trace a complex temporal sequence. Arthur, afflicted with "inward bale," knows that the "royall Mayd" who appeared before him in the dream is Gloriana, but *how*? Is she a dream wish that antedated the dream? In his *Project for a Scientific Psychology*, Freud writes: "We invariably find that memory is repressed which has only become a trauma by *deferred action*."[39] Thus any event is, in some sense, *nachträglich*, taking shape only later in deferral. When, we might ask, was Arthur first afflicted with the trauma of his "inward bale"? Did Gloriana ever appear before Arthur—the dream seems to suggest that she did—or does this supposed (or wished for) real event only take form as a belated reactivation in his dream? The cognitive processes of *Nachträglichkeit* are as hard to explicate as Arthur's recondite dream, for its trajectories of psychic causality are not to be confused with memory, which recalls a real event. The curious temporal logic of *Nachträglichkeit* problematizes (which is to say by no means that it eliminates) the status of the real event, demonstrating that the evasive event is constituted as such only in belated activations such as

[38]*The Legend of Freud*, 67.
[39]*SE* 1:356.

dreams—the reconstitution of meaning through deferral. Because a dream can take on meaning only retrospectively, it is only through dream deferral that Arthur's perceived encounter with Gloriana can even be said to have occurred. What might on the surface appear to be a chronological link between a supposed real event and Arthur's dream must instead be perceived as a belated temporality that stands as his representation of a (pre)supposed encounter.

Arthur's dream revision, then, a privileged trope for *Nachträglichkeit*, enacts a dialectic between forgetting and a latency that can only be inferred from the repression that makes us suspect its presence in the first place. The *Entstellung* of Arthur's not-quite-dream makes us suspect that the "real" encounter (and the "real" Faerie Queene) is beyond representation, an impossibility that Arthur's overly semanticized narration to Una further obscures. Because Arthur's encounter with Gloriana is always belated, his quest for her throughout *The Faerie Queene* is attenuated by the possibility that his signification of her—both in his dream and on the stone "shapt like a Ladies head" (1.7.30.3), which he wears on his baldric as the mute hieroglyphic of her presence—will never correspond to Gloriana herself. As the signified in Arthur's dream, Gloriana is both the forgotten event and the fact of the signified's belatedness. Thus—and now we are at the heart of the psychoanalytic matter—the narrative deferral that impedes Arthur's search for her is caused not simply by his desire, but by a desire that is a dialectically structured product of psychic belatedness; the temporal delay of the narrative and of Arthur's desire enacts a *Nachträglichkeit* that assures that Gloriana will of necessity never be found. The founding moment of *The Faerie Queene* (and of a Tudor *renovatio*) is not a beginning point for narrative at all, but rather an indeterminate temporal dialectic between past and future. The temporal complexity of Arthur's dream reveals, as we have seen, that desire does not always recognize something that would have been already there.

Gloriana, herself, then, is less a "character" than a temporal lag opening up the space of representation for Arthur—which is why, as Arthur laments to Guyon, he "yet no where can her find" (2.9.7.8). One of the signifiers most damaging to Arthur's quest to become the subject of his own story is Guyon's shield, "Whereon the Faery Queenes pourtract was writ" (2.8.43.3). Indeed, the shield's image, engendering "whole desire" (9.7.3) in Arthur, proves to be almost fatal. In his fight with the raging Pyrochles, who has stolen the shield from Guyon, Arthur is scarcely able to defend him-

self because "his deare hart the picture gan adore" (8.43). The deadliness of the shield is oddly observed by Arthur when, admiring its
"pourtract" of Gloriana, he remarks to Guyon, "Full liuely is the
semblaunt, though the substance dead" (9.2.9). Much like Lacan's
own *semblant*, the result of the subject's narcissistic identification
with the object that "does not endure indefinitely,"[40] the "semblaunt" of Gloriana's image that is the object of Arthur's narcissistic
fixation is, quite simply, "substance dead," unrecuperable within Arthur's trajectory of questing. But if Gloriana is "dead," then where
does this leave Arthur—and us, as the readers of his imperial quest?

If we are to understand more fully Gloriana's role in *The Faerie
Queene*, we must cease to view her merely as an "object" of Arthur's
desire. To give up this conception of Gloriana is to begin to appreciate Spenser's poetic subtlety in creating a character so crucial to his
narrative structure that it could not be sustained without her continued absence. The literary history of epic has finally culminated, in
The Faerie Queene, in a narrative so dependent on desire that it has
taken on a life of its own—independent of "desired" characters.

In the character of the fugitive Angelica, Gloriana's epic prede-
cessor as the elusive woman of desire in the *Orlando furioso*, Ariosto
brilliantly deploys the endlessly deferred structure of romance to
create an object of desire who keeps the longings of her many pursuers aroused through encounters that are just missed. One thinks
of Atlante's Palace where Angelica intensifies the erotic frustrations
of Orlando by being heard wherever he is not: "(e s'egli è da una
parte, suona altronde), / che chiegga aiuto; e non sa trovar donde"
("if here / The restless warrior stand, it sounds from there, / And
calls for help he knows not whence nor where" [12.16]). No storyteller knew better than Ariosto that desire is released retroactively
through these just-missed encounters. But one important way in
which Spenser has "overgone" his epic predecessor is in his deploy-
ment of Gloriana as not merely elusive, but as the absent source of
desire in *The Faerie Queene*. Gloriana is less a character than a narrative elegance—the belated remainder that is the aftereffect of the
beginnings of representation in a primal *Nachträglichkeit*. In all of
epic romance there may be no more hauntingly beautiful image than
the "pressed gras," nature's trace that Gloriana leaves behind in the
wake of Arthur's dream. The image haunts us because as a mimesis
of the originary *objet a* of infantile experience, the "pressed gras" is a

---

[40]"The Dream of Irma's Injection," *Sem. II*, 269.

void to be filled, the site where lack is rendered visible—the emptiness that structures the *méconnaissance* of Arthur's history.

Unlike Angelica, Gloriana, then, is less an object of desire than the void (the "place deuoyd") that constructs desire around a lack that is perceived only belatedly—which is why Arthur will always be too early or too late to see her.[41] In Book 3, when Arthur pursues the elusive Florimell (perhaps the only true Angelica-like object of desire in *The Faerie Queene*), it may be less accurate to say he is being disloyal to Gloriana than that Gloriana's belated ontology as the narrative's structural inadequacy *guarantees* that he will slide along the signifying chain of desire to yearn for others like Florimell.

If desire is a temporal phenomenon, then throughout any narrative of desire, timing is crucial; and the timing of Arthur, struggling as he does to fulfill his prophecy "in iust terme," should be the particular object of the reader's scrutiny. Let us consider, then, why Arthur awakens from his dream when he does. Perhaps what he ultimately seeks in his dream is (like Britomart) the just-missed encounter, aborted "all so soone as life did me admit" (1.9.3), with the *objet a* of the mother. Substituting for this lost merger is instead a second just-missed encounter with Gloriana, the missed encounter of desire that occurred somewhere in the belated temporal lag between the dream and his awakening.[42] If, as Freud argues, a dream is always a wish fulfillment, then, in a strange way, maybe Arthur gains as much as he loses from his moment of awakening. It is as if Arthur desires not Gloriana, but rather a *missed encounter* with Gloriana as the (retroactive) verification of his identity. This space of awakening, then, becomes Spenser's elegant condensation of Atlante's Palace, Ariosto's theater of just-missed encounters of desire. The content of the dream is perhaps less important to Arthur than the nature of his encounter with Gloriana as just missed; for it is in this just-missed "place deuoyd" that Arthur can emerge as the speaking, desiring protagonist of *The Faerie Queene*.

[41]The *nachträglich* dialectic between being too early and too late is the very essence of desire. Laplanche and Pontalis write that the temporal characteristics of human sexuality make it a privileged battlefield between "what is too much or too little, too early (birth) and too late (puberty)" ("Fantasy and the Origins of Sexuality," *The International Journal of Psycho-Analysis* 49 [1968], 1–18)

[42]In *The Four Fundamental Concepts*, Lacan sets forth his concept of the *tuché* as "the encounter with the real"—the encounter "in so far as it may be missed, in so far as it is essentially the missed encounter" ("Tuché and Automaton," 55) of the trauma. More specifically, Lacan conceives of the *tuché* as the "missed encounter" that is lost between the dream and the awakening.

Despite the surface simplicity of Arthur's dream, at the point at which Arthur awakens to his just-missed encounter with Gloriana, we have reached (if only retroactively) the "navel" of his dream. "Even in the best interpreted dreams," writes Freud, "there is often a place that must be left in the dark, because in the process of interpreting one notices a tangle of dream-thoughts arising which resists unravelling."[43] This "place" that must be left uninterpreted Freud calls the "navel," the knot or tangle that yields no further meaning. A Lacanian return to Freud's account of the navel might choose to rephrase it as the movement in a dream of the signified (long-since repressed) above the bar of signification. In Arthur's dream, the real "place deuoyd"—Freud's "place that must be left in the dark"— might be the moment of Arthur's awakening, the uninterpretable moment when the signified of the other attempts to cross the bar. Insisting on representation, the signified of the other must be re-repressed by Arthur's act of awakening.

Samuel Weber interprets Freud's navel of the dream not as a locatable object or moment of interpretation, but as a movement that entangles: "Or rather, the tangle (*Knäuel*) of dream-thoughts does not stay in place, it begins to invade the thoughts that constitute the light of day."[44] The movement of the signified exists somewhere in the obscure threshold between Freud's "place that must be left in the dark" and Weber's "thoughts that constitute the light of day"— in short, the moment of awakening from a dream at just the point of its insistence on signification. As the navel of the dream (and as the restless signified of the other), Gloriana does not "stay in place," but leaves behind a mimesis of the void, the hole in Arthur that constitutes literally the navel of the infant.

But the restless movement of the dream's navel, which leaves in its wake a "place deuoyd," also points Arthur to "the light of day" of his awakening. The navel (as the dream's refusal of interpretation that culminates in the awakening), then, might be the impossibility of the merger with the *objet a* of the maternal body. As Arthur narrates to Una,

> For all so soone as life did me admit
> Into this world, and shewed heauens light,
> From mothers pap I taken was vnfit:
> And streight deliuered to a Faery knight.
> (1.9.3)

[43]*SE* 5:530.
[44]*The Legend of Freud*, 76–77.

If the signified tries to cross the bar, as it does in Arthur's dream, then the split subject (like the newborn infant) must move into the light of day. From a dream that tries to remember the infant's originary "heauens light," Arthur awakens "just in time." To dream on would mean to re-"join" with the other (mother), which would mean that desire, the beginning of the narrative of *The Faerie Queene*, the founding of a Tudor *renovatio*, would never be "born." Attempting to become the subject of Spenser's epic, Arthur awakens from his dream because it is time to respond to the call of the many myths and ideologies of *The Faerie Queene* that are seeking to structure its hero as the *rex quondam rexque futurus*.

After his just-missed encounter with the signified of his dream, the changeling Arthur is forced to construct his identity from a sliding chain of signifiers, unreliable building blocks for one seeking to become the subject of his own story. In his futile quest for Gloriana, Arthur flamboyantly traverses Fairie Lond wearing "bauldrick braue," "iuory sheath," hilts of "burnisht gold" and "mother pearle," "haughtie helmet" plumed with "loftie crest," and shield of "Diamond perfect pure" (1.7.29–33).[45] But despite these trappings of questing splendor—these relics whose lavish descriptions partake of a rich tradition of the fetishizing of armor throughout epic literary history—Arthur demonstrates the difficulty of situating himself as the subject of one's own story. If Arthur is overdetermined, it is because the signifiers of his subjecthood, surrounding the loss of Gloriana, can never equal the sum of their parts.

Arthur: The Untimeliest Cut of All

Arthur's just-missed encounter with Gloriana establishes Spenser's hero as a desiring (and alienated) subject within the realm of Faerie. What remains to be seen is the extent to which he will also be alienated within the peculiar temporal logic of Tudor epic prophecy. Arthur's alienation within the trajectory of his own epic destiny returns us to the point where we began this study of dynastic epic—back to memory and its problematic relationship to epic origins. Because it occurs retroactively, fantasy (like Arthur's dream) is always a kind of memory; but memory is, in turn, always a kind of temporal trauma. If Arthur is fated by the narrative structure of *The Faerie*

---

[45]For more on the overdeterminations of Arthur's shield in particular, see Gross, *Spenserian Poetics*, 128–44.

Queene to be a dreaming hero, he is also established as a *remembering* hero. Thus, in his tour of Alma's turret in Book 2, Arthur quickly bypasses the "idle fantasies" of Phantastes' fly-infested chamber and enters Eumnestes' chamber of memory. But, as we shall see, epic memory as prophetic meaning in *The Faerie Queene* can be revealed only in the retroactive space of a *méconnaissance* that always occurs too early or too late to be anything more than "neurotic."

Arthur's reading of the *Briton moniments* in Eumnestes' chamber (2.10) constitutes a distinctly textual moment, not only because British history, "from Brute to Vthers rayne," is here presented in written form, but also because, as a kind of primal act of cognition, memory is, in some sense, made possible through writing.[46] If, in the *Aeneid*, Aeneas's memory is activated through mural images, in Eumnestes' chamber memory is a text that stimulates remembrance through its distinctly written forms. It is as if the written text of memory has been proffered to its reader Arthur so that he may call forth from within himself that which has long been denied from collective memory. As the locus of memory, Eumnestes' chamber can be viewed as an allegory of epic endeavor itself. It is the repository of Mnemosyne's "scryne" and her powers to consolidate both past and future in a providential vision that can accommodate the epic subject into transhistorical prophecy.[47] Thus it is Mnemosyne (and Eumnestes' chamber) who becomes the ultimate tool of *imperium*, giving history meaning as the epic subject moves toward the future founding of dynasty. Just as significantly, Mnemosyne, as the mother of the Muses, is also the mother of the source of poetic authority itself and thus the point of origination to be invoked in any epic recording the founding of the *imperium sine fine*; she is the pow-

[46]The episode seems designed almost as a redemption of the *Phaedrus*, where writing is condemned as a hindrance to memory. In response to Theuth, the Egyptian inventor of writing, Thamus argues: "if men learn this, it will implant forgetfulness in their souls; they will cease to exercise memory because they rely on that which is written, calling things to remembrance no longer from within themselves" (257a).

[47]If we consider Book 1 with this temporal scope in mind, we can see that the hyperopic power of memory to trace the point of convergence between past and future informs much of that book's heavily typological structure. During the great prophetic moment of the first book, Spenser describes the mount where the prophet Contemplation unfolds his vision of the New Jerusalem to Redcrosse as a syncretic, analogical conflation of Mt. Sinai, the Mount of Olives, and Parnassus. The mount's retroactive reincarnation as the Mount of Olives stimulates an "endlesse memory" (10.54.3) of Christ, who typologically subsumes both (past) Old Testament law and (future) New Testament revelation. In turn, this "endlesse memory" is inscribed and eternized by "famous Poets verse" (10.54.7) on Parnassus, where remembrance and poetry are primordially united.

erful agent whereby the gap could be closed between imperial poetry and a timeless source of meaning.

For that matter, it is in Eumnestes' chamber that we are shown
the very roots of human cognition itself; and we can now begin to
sense just how crucial is Arthur's sojourn in Eumnestes' chamber to
the development of an epic subjecthood. Eumnestes' chamber is
slated to become nothing less than a rite of passage in Arthur's
quest to recollect his origins and to know himself. His reading of the
Briton moniments would suggest that the hero is about to experience
an archetypal act of filiation as he searches for his ancestral origins.
Indeed, Britain's future is directly dependent on Arthur's self-
knowledge (on his becoming an epic subject); and the *Briton moniments*, which trace Arthur's origins and genealogy, presumably represent Spenser's convergence of the recollection of origins and the
fulfillment of epic prophecy.

But because they are presented as historiographical chronicles, the
Briton moniments, comprising a lengthy and frankly tedious recording of the random contingencies of early British history, fall consid-
erably short of a mnemonic sublime.[48] Whereas in Book 1 Contemplation offered Redcrosse the happy prospect of Christian prophecy
sweeping beyond the failures of the old pagan, Roman prophecy,
the *Briton moniments* force us to backtrack, offering only a disap-
pointing reiteration of history and unrealized prophecy with no apparent move toward conclusiveness. In fact, it seems scarcely possible to commit the Brutus succession to memory, given that when the
last of Brutus's "sacred progenie" died out, "in the end was left no
moniment / Of Brutus, nor of Britons glory auncient" (10.36.8–9).
Thus we are presented with a virtual parody of the "dew heritage"
(10.45.9) of the dynastic continuum of empire. In the *Moniments*,
leadership is continually "disthronized," "reseized," "repulsed,"
and "vsurped," while at other times kings simply die "without issue" (10.54.1)—perhaps a not-so-veiled warning to Elizabeth on the
dangers of ignoring "dew heritage." In the end, there seems little
difference between the "saluage wildernesse" (10.13.6) that Brutus
sets out to tame and the presumed "imperiall state" (10.13.6) he
seeks to leave to future generations of Britons.

---

[48]One of the most detailed treatments of what he calls the "uninterrupted mayhem"
of the *Briton moniments* and the reader's difficulties in attempting to order and interpret the chaos of centuries of civil disobedience, usurping, murdering, pillage, and
carnage can be found in Harry Berger, *The Allegorical Temper: Vision and Reality in Book
II of Spenser's "Faerie Queene"* (New Haven: Yale University Press, 1957), 90ff.

It is impossible to detect any meaningful subtext to the chronicle's randomly shifting alliances between Britain and Rome or to its richly promising, but never fully realized, allusions to Joseph of Arimathea, Constantine, and, for that matter, Arthur himself. (To Arthur's reading of *himself* as subject we return later.) It is impossible to discern any structuring of the complex convergence of Roman *imperium*, British destiny, epic historiography, and Christian typology deployed in Eumnestes' chronicle. The sack of Rome by Donwallo's sons is endowed with no dynastic resonance, but is mentioned only incidentally alongside the "ransacking" of Greece, France, and Germany (10.40). Lud's "raedifye[ing]" of the "ruin'd wals" (10.46.4) of Troynouant, an act of culture-building that is presumably the very foundation of epic endeavor, is immediately overshadowed by the Romans' defeat of Lud's successor Cassibalane. The narrative pauses not at all at the account of Arthur's defeat of "ambitious Rome" (10.49), but moves on to devote equal space to the unremarkable reign of Tenantius. At these junctures, the narrative plays out the interactive impulses of aggression, submission, and subversion while in the process defying totalization and epic causality.

Thus, Eumnestes, "this man of infinite remembrance," seer of "things foregone" (2.9.56), dissipates rather than shapes an epic teleology. Arthur and Guyon (who, even as Arthur reads the *Briton moniments*, will later read the more harmonious Elfin chronicle, *Antiquitie of Faerie lond*, in yet another strange intersection between Briton and Faerie) see the old man seated in a chair with his histories and chronicles scattered before him, "tossing and turning them withouten end" (58.2). The epic poet, as Spenser tells us in his "Letter to Raleigh," must "deuine of thinges to come," but in Eumnestes' chamber, where present events accrue instantaneously as past records through "endlesse exercise" (59.2), the future tense of epic fulfillment can never be considered.

Such are the pitfalls of chronicle memory. If, in the *Aeneid*, memory seems intimately associated with repression (and the return of the repressed, and the repetition compulsion)—in short, with all the "neurotic" ambivalences between memory and forgetting that implicate Virgil's narrative in the mnemic labyrinths of the unconscious—then Eumnestes' chamber of memory, residing in the (re)cognitive space of Alma's turret, seemingly reifies memory, draining the faculty of memory of its psychic resonances. In Eumnestes' chamber of dusty chronicles, "all worme-eaten, and full of canker holes" (57.9), the cognitive process of memory itself seems old, archaic. As Arthur's confrontation with his "name and nation," the *Briton moniments* present their reader not with the richly ambivalent matrix of memory, repression, and forgetting that intersects Virgil's Trojan *ekphrasis*, but rather with a self-consciously "antique history."[49] As a representation of Britain's origins "from Brute to Vthers rayne," Eumnestes' "auncient booke" is, in the final analysis, proffered not as the ongoing process of remembrance itself, but as received history, a static moment in the narrative of *The Faerie Queene*, a conspicuous allusion to history as "history." The psychic collage of anxiety and desire that constitutes Virgil's *ekphrasis*—its entangling of Aeneas's unconscious in its subtle enactment of the disappearance of Troy's disappearance—has ceded place to Eumnestes' epitaphic foregrounding of the past as *passed*. Most significantly, Alma's turret is distanced from Troy itself and its affective powers. As Arthur and Guyon approach the turret's cognitive chambers of imagination, judgment, and memory, the reader is told that the collective wisdom and good counsel of these three men surpass that of aged Nestor, "by whose aduise old Priams cittie fell" (9.48.6). We are told that Eumnestes himself remembers the wars of "old Assaracus" (56.9), a haunting standard by which to measure the scope of his memory. The frame of Alma's turret is itself described as stronger than "that proud towre of Troy . . . / From which young Hectors bloud by cruell Greekes was spilt" (45.8–9). But in Eumnestes' chamber, Troy, the privileged memory-trace of the *translatio imperii*, seems archaized, even obsolescent, distantly reduced to a necromantic fetish, no longer the city not seen of an epic Imaginary, but merely "old Priams cittie."

To understand fully the way in which the self-consciousness of the presentation of memory in the *Briton moniments* impedes the formation of their principal reader, Arthur, as a subject of epic prophecy, we must first consider an important distinction between Aeneas and Arthur not just as epic protagonists, but as distinctly *remembering* protagonists. Both Aeneas's and Arthur's encounters with memory yield a quintessentially uncanny moment when they confront *themselves* in the very representations of a history they are presumably outside of. Aeneas's unexpected confrontation with the uncanny occurs while he is absorbed in Virgil's *ekphrasis* of the fatal dooms of

---

[49]For an extended discussion of Spenser's use of "antique" and "antiquity" throughout his epic, see Judith H. Anderson, "The Antiquities of Fairyland and Ireland," *JEGP* 86:2 (1987), 199–214.

Troy: "Se quoque princibus permixtum agnovit Achivis" ("He also recognized himself in combat with the Achaean chiefs" [1.488]). As R. G. Austin notes in his commentary, "What is remarkable is the quiet way in which Aeneas is slipped into the description, with no emotional content."[50] The very brevity of this description of Aeneas, inserted so unobtrusively and unassumingly within the other *imagines* of Troy's woes and revealing a warrior in action so radically different from the exile now standing as a passive observer before the murals, underscores the uncanniness of this (not-fully-confronted) self-confrontation.

Occurring as it does in Dido's memory theater of Troy, Aeneas's self-recognition is also an act of remembrance. At the point at which he departs from Carthage, Aeneas demonstrates that the Trojan images (including his own), the burden of the past, will no longer interfere with his understanding of an epic future. But a confrontation with one's image often constitutes less a moment of self-recognition than an act of *méconnaissance*. As we have seen, for Lacan the "specimen story" of psychoanalysis is one that misrecognizes its own narrative, tracing a *méconnaissance* that evades the totality it anticipates. As, among other things, a kind of self-remembrance, the psychic operation of *méconnaissance* is always associated with (belated) acts of memory. And it is not surprising that Arthur too should be confronted with his own *unheimlich* image in the *Ars memorativa* that is the *Briton moniments*. Thus, as simply and unobtrusively as Aeneas is met with his own image, Arthur reads how Britain languishes under Roman rule, "till Arthur all that reckoning defrayd" (10.49.8).[51]

---

[50]"Commentary," *P. Vergili Maronis. Aeneidos: Liber Primvs*, 164.

[51]In *Le morte d'Arthur* (v.10), Malory suggests that Arthur's defeat of Rome is a crucial moment within the *translatio imperii*. In the aftermath of Arthur's defeat of the Roman emperor Lucius, Gawain confronts Priamus, a heathen knight whose name recalls Troy's fallen king. Priamus boastfully declares his descent from the "ryght line" of Hector. After an exchange with Gawain, however, Priamus announces his intention to become a Christian, a typical illustration of the instantaneous conversion topos of Christian epic. In this brief but significant episode, Malory's Arthur both defeats the pagan forces of a misguided Rome and presides over the conversion of one of Troy's scattered survivors, subsuming two ruined dynasties within the framework of a Christian Britain.

A. Kent Hieatt refers to Arthur's "defray[ing]" of "that reckoning" in the *Briton moniments* in his piecing together of what Arthur's role in *The Faerie Queene* would have been had Spenser completed an entire twenty-four book epic, whose plan the poet originally posits in the "Letter to Raleigh" ("The Passing of Arthur in Malory, Spenser, and Shakespeare: The Avoidance of Closure," in *The Passing of Arthur: New Essays in Arthurian Tradition* [New York: Garland, 1988], 181–84).

But Arthur's self-recognition, unlike Aeneas's, is unsettled by the
hero's "recollection" of himself not in the past but in a brief and
evanescent vision of his future. Thus (even though the event is recorded as occurring in the past), the question becomes: what "self"
is Arthur reading at this point? What happens, not just when the
mind represents its own activity to itself, but also when the self
must see itself as refracted on an obscure threshold between past
and future? The Arthur who reads the *Briton moniments* (and the
Arthur who must realize the dynastic ambitions of Troynouant) fails
to respond to the Arthur who defeats "ambitious Rome," offering no
affective indication that self-recognition has occurred—that the trajectory of memory traced by the *Briton moniments* has yielded anything other than a literal moment of misrecognition. Arthur's *méconnaissance*, his *mis*-"reading" of himself, is at the crux of the complex
temporal framework that structures the *méconnaissance* of the narrative of *The Faerie Queene* itself. As the *rex quondam rexque futurus*,
Arthur anticipates a Tudor *renovatio*. But here a temporally vertiginous question must be posed: can a self, who must still seek,
typologically, to fulfill his epic destiny, read (can he *memorize*) that
same self as always already having performed a future act recorded
as a *historical* act in an "auncient booke" of memory that is itself
always already old and belated? When Arthur reads himself as enacting a future event that is already recorded as past, the result is a
dizzying temporal logic that situates the "Briton Prince" somewhere
in an obscure threshold between a Lacanian *méconnaissance* and a
historical obsolescence. Because he is the *rex quondam rexque futurus*
of Tudor destiny, we can only conclude that when Arthur "reads"
himself, he has already become everything that he will have been,
and he can seek to become (retroactively) only what he already was.

   To paraphrase Lacan, it is as if Arthur (unlike Britomart when she
sees herself in Merlin's mirror) is "not looking at the very place from
which he sees himself."[52] Literally un-*affect*ed by what he reads, Arthur alienates his own self-alienation, refusing to concede that he
has been dispossessed of his own look (of his own "reading")—refusing to concede that he has, in effect, *lost* some portion of himself.
As in the case of his dream of Gloriana, Arthur has simply come to
Eumnestes' chamber too early (or too late) to "read" himself, almost
as if he can be represented in the *Briton moniments* only under the
condition that he fails to "read" himself. In the obscure temporal

---

[52]"The Line and Light," *The Four Fundamental Concepts*, 103.

threshold between a Troy that might, in some sense, never have
been, and a Rome that, in some sense, cannot be until Troy "has
been" (*fuit Ilium*), Aeneas, as we have seen, develops a retroactive
unconscious that establishes him as a subject for the narrative of
epic destiny. But the act of Arthur having to remember himself as
past (as already epitaphic, already one of the "Briton moniments" of
Eumnestes' dusty chronicle)—of having to (mis)recognize himself as
an historical artifact before he has advanced beyond his (infantile)
stage as "Briton Prince"—results in no such formation of historical
unconscious. If the constitutive ground of subjecthood is *loss*, the
fall, as it were, into memory, we have difficulty in viewing Arthur as
a subject for epic history.

    In his hero's reading of the *Briton moniments*, Spenser presents us
with the extraordinary development of Arthur as both implicit participant in and reader of the chronicles of his ancestry. At the point
at which the chronicle reaches the reign of "Vther," Arthur's father,
the text breaks off: "After him [Aurelius] Vther, which Pendragon
hight, / Succeeding There abruptly it did end, / Without full point,
or other Cesure right" (10.68.2–3).[53] Following the rules of classical
prosody, a "Cesure right" would presumably come at the end of a
metrical foot, at the very least maintaining a prosodic equilibrium.
But the chronicle's "Cesure wrong" fragments the pentameter in
mid-iamb. The rending "Cesure wrong" that "abruptly" terminates
Arthur's reading and fragments the *Briton moniments* ("as if the rest
some wicked hand did rend" [68.2]) at the point of Vther's reign, is,
in some sense, the synecdochic fragmentation of epic telos itself; it
would seem to mark the end of the document's Briton *Ars memorativa* and the beginning of Arthur's own entry into the narrative
text of British history.[54] Ever since the *Aeneid*, representations of his-

---

[53]In his *Art of Rhetorique*, Thomas Wilson defines narrative as a "plain and manifest
pointing of the matter and an evident setting-forth of all things . . ." (in *The Renaissance in England: Non-Dramatic Prose and Verse of the Sixteenth Century*, ed. Hyder E.
Rollins and Herschel Baker [Lexington, MA: D. C. Heath, 1954], 593). Thus the
"point" missing in the *Briton moniments* is more than a mere concluding mark of punc-
tuation. It is, as Wilson argues, the very shaping impulse of narrative—the "setting-forth" that endows narrative with a purposeful form. The "full point" needed to
bring the *Briton moniments* to conclusion is nothing less than the kind of totalizing
narrative that only imperial closure can provide.

[54]In her essay "Spenser's Caesuras" (*English Literary Renaissance* 11 [1981], 261–80),
Debra Fried offers an excellent analysis of this often overlooked cesura, arguing that,
because "repeatedly in *The Faerie Queene*, to stop or to breathe or rest is to become
vulnerable to being cut off or seized" (273), the cesura marks the point at which the
chronicle is subject to seizure by others. Fried asks, "Is Arthur reading an abandoned

tory in the epic have traditionally been constituted through ancestral lines of descent from father to son, initiating archetypal acts of filiation as epic sons search for their origins. The rending "Cesure wrong" could thus be seen as constituting the mnemic traces of a nascent Arthurian unconscious—the point at which the higher psychical organization of cultural memory cedes place to the origin of Arthur as the subject of his own narrative, as, indeed, the epic "son" of a "father." "The unconscious," observes Lacan, "is that chapter of my history which is marked by a blank . . . .: it is the censored chapter."[55] With the onset of the terminating "blank" of the *Briton moniments*—with, in effect, an unconscious—perhaps it would be now that Arthur can truly begin to *remember* his ancestral origins. But, as he has all along throughout his reading of the *Briton moniments*, Arthur misrecognizes his own narrative, and hence "forgets" to remember.

The formation of subjecthood necessarily involves the birth of an unconscious—in Freud's scheme, a process that involves, like the narrative of epic history itself, a transference and a belated reconstitution of origins. That Arthur is distinctly a not-*yet*-ego is revealed not only in his (belated) lament to Una that his name and nation are "hidden yit," but also, perhaps more significantly, in the denial by the "Cesure" of his entry into the narrative at a point prior to the moment of his birth.[56] Effaced in the gap that terminates Eumnestes' "text withouten end," Arthur's "origin" must "begin" (like epic it-

---

chronicle or a censored one?" (262). I would argue, however, that the *Briton moniments* are censored less by repressive political forces from without than by their own self-censorings from within.

[55]"Function and Field of Speech," *Écrits*, 50.

[56]Further evidence of Arthur's birth as "marked by a blank" is found in the dubious circumstances of his conception. Geoffrey of Monmouth's *Historia regum britanniae* narrates how Merlin transformed Uther into a likeness of Gorlois, the husband of Igerna (unnamed in Eumnestes' chronicle, but curiously and meticulously identified as "Lady Igrayne" in his "Letter to Raleigh"), to trick her into seduction. Thus Arthur is conceived in the unreal conceptual space of daemonic deception and false imagery. Arthur's origins, his birth as a *subject*, may be traced only to a kind of displacement from the maternal womb onto Uther as paternal metaphor.

Spenser's attention to the curious circumstances of Arthur's elided conception and birth may perhaps have been influenced by John Leyland's chronicle, *A Learned and True Assertion of the Original, Life, Actes, and Death of the most Noble, Valiant, and Renoumed Prince Arthure, King of great Brittaine* (1554), where, at the beginning of his history, Leyland announces: "I will now attempt somewhat more, circumspectly to finde out Prince Arthures Originall, euen from the very egge" (trans. Richard Robinson, in Christopher Middleton, *The Famous Historie of Chinon of England*, ed. William Edward Mead [London: Early English Text Society, No. 165, 1925], 18). Spenser, too, seems inclined to push his account of Arthur's origins "euen from the very egge."

self) with a belated narration to Una—back in Book 1—of a postnatal exile (perhaps the most traumatic story of exile for an epic protagonist since Aeneas's frantic escape from the flames of the burning Troy), specifically his being rudely torn "from mothers pap" (1.9.3.7) and "streight deliuered" into Faerie lond. But at the conclusion of the *Briton moniments* (of, in effect, another kind of remembering), Arthur's infancy "begins" not with his mother's originating womb, but with his father Vther—literally, the Name-of-the-Father. And the presence of Vther as a paternal signifier (just prior to the castrating "cut" of the rending "Cesure") makes us suspect that what may be at stake in Spenser's presentation of memory throughout this episode in Eumnestes' chamber is the very possibility that there cannot be such a thing as the totality of an Arthurian ego.

The ego does not exist, writes Freud in *The Ego and the Id*, until "the individual's first and most important identifications, his identifications with the father in his own personal prehistory."[57] In the Arthurian "prehistory" constituted by the gap in Britain's history, the infant Arthur, as we have seen, has left behind a first phase of maternal engulfment in the "mothers pap" that fulfills all desire (much like the son Aeneas's enshrouding in the protective mist of his mother Venus) to enter a second phase of Vther as paternal metaphor. Thus, like the westward movement of the *translatio imperii*, the formation of the ego, structured as it is on an originary replacement of the (m)other, also traces a metaphor. The paternal signifier in effect raises the child's desire to a higher degree; and it is precisely in this metaphoric transference of desire to a higher degree that a primal memory can "originate." As a higher psychic organization of desire, the paternal metaphor renders the homeostatic bliss of unity with the (m)other a distant "memory," retroactively replacing it with merely the memory-trace of a satisfaction.

The formation of an Arthurian subject for Tudor epic narrative, then, like the formation of the New Troys that constitute the signifying chain of the *translatio imperii*, can occur only retroactively. In the *Briton moniments*, the Arthurian subject cannot, in some sense, "know" his origins (with "origins" here no longer serving as a casual metaphor for the beginnings of name and nation, but rather for the rite of passage of, perhaps, birth itself) because the primal narcissism always already sustained in the (m)other is constituted as such only through the paternal metaphor that denies the origin as any-

[57]*SE* 19:31.

thing other than a memory. Arthur cannot recollect his "birth" because the formation of the ego is dependent on the foreclosure of a recollection of its own origin. The Freudian axiom that memory cannot "think" its origins predictably results in the installing of the repetition compulsion and all its ambivalent waverings between remembering and forgetting, inhabiting the space between, in Freud's terms, "a repetition of the forgotten past," and, in its own curious fashion, "a way of remembering"—in the case of the formation of the ego, a repetition compulsion that "forgets" to remember its originary unity with the (m)other.

But let us continue not with Vther as the Name-of-the Father, but rather with a return to/of the (repressed) "Cesure." We can scarcely be certain what this "Cesure," which neither fully remembers nor fully forgets, might mean for the formation of an Arthurian subject. All we can say for certain is that in Spenser's vastly overdetermined epic, the "Cesure" is its most overdetermined moment—perhaps the most psychically overdetermined moment in all of epic history. We could argue that the gap in the text, the metaphorical "cut"—the privileged Lacanian trope for the castrating lack that *is* subjecthood—signifies (by, in some sense, failing to signify) that Arthur has negotiated a transference of desire to a second degree, and a subsequent metaphoric construction of his ego (of ego-as-metaphor). Arthur's negotiation of the "Cesure" (his acceptance that there is nothing to *read* beyond the gap) could signal his identification with another, even more castrating, metaphor: the paternal metaphor of Vther as, in effect, not only the formation of an Arthurian unconscious through primary repression, but also (and more significantly for its appearance as the terminus of the *Briton moniments*) the achieving of the transference that installs memory as the retroactive mark of castration. Put simply, a gap always invites a transfer (or a *translatio imperii*) across it.

But it is by no means certain that this overdetermined gap in the text marks the formation of an Arthurian unconscious. We could also argue that the gap is not only the lack that is castration, but also (much more literally) the *deferral* of transference—specifically, of the narrative of the translation of empire that delays Arthur indefinitely as the (Infant) Briton Prince, as the not-yet-("hidden yit")-ego of Tudor history. At the point of the threatening "gap" of castration embodied in Vther's paternal metaphor, Arthur, as the *rex quondam rexque futurus*, enacts the evasion of his own totality and, in effect, denies his castration (as if he is recognizing that his birth has come both too early *and* too late). The *Briton moniments* terminate because Arthur refuses (or forgets) to remember his lack. All that remains of the filial drama of the terminus of the *Briton moniments* is the "Cesure," marked as an "vntimely breach" (68.6) and unassimilated in Arthur's memory.[58] Denying the second degree of desire as the origination of memory inherent in the paternal metaphor, the Infant Prince—almost literally the *infans* ("the one who does not speak")—repudiates memory and refuses to "speak" a loss into epic subjecthood. Denying both filial and imperial transference, Arthur (unlike Aeneas) is neither father nor son, and (unlike Oedipus) refuses to be "born" into the life of his history.

The only memory Arthur carries with him into the "romance middle" of *The Faerie Queene* is not the void of the paternal signifier (as the signifier of an impossible identity), but the "place deuoyd," the "pressed gras" of Gloriana. Even within the context of the explicit historical and political pressures of Book 5, it becomes extremely problematic to talk about a euhemeristic "Arthur" at all as the hero of the *The Faerie Queene*. The formation of the unconscious means the receiving of a name—in effect, becoming a representation of itself. But the Infant Prince *has* no name—none, that is, other than the name of "Arthur," a name inferred only retroactively by *our* memory of the legends of British history. Thus Arthur traces another narrative of the just-missed encounter. On this crucial *méconnu* threshold of subjecthood, Arthur is, as Lacan so inimitably puts it,

---

[58]Despite its interruption of the *Briton moniments*, the "vntimely breach" that brings the narrative of memory to a halt, may, in fact, have placed us at the obscure neurological threshold of memory itself. In his physiognomy of the brain, as outlined in his *Project for a Scientific Psychology*, Freud identified the origin of memory as "breaching" (*Bahnung*), a key neurological function that occurs when the neurones in the brain open up a path that resists, then retains the print or trace of an impression. Somewhere between the neuronal interplay of resistance and retention, then, lie the "origins" of memory, an origin that is neither fully forgetting (resisting) or remembering (retaining). Falling somewhere between the discharges of these resisting and retaining neurones, breaching is both a representation of memory and a denial of the memory of origins. Breaching, then, as the neurological enactment of the belatedness of memory, provided for Freud a physiological account of why memory cannot "think" its origins. Perhaps even more significantly, the "vntimely breach" of the *Briton moniments* is *literally* "vntimely"—un-tense-like—opposed to the chronological advance of time itself. Its neurological processes enact a belatedness that is the retroactive mechanism of memory itself. (For an extended reading of Freud's *Project* and its problematizing of the concept of "origins," see Derrida's essay "Freud and the Scene of Writing," in *Writing and Difference*, trans. Alan Bass (Chicago: University of Chicago Press, 1978), 196–231.

"missing the right meeting just at the right moment."[59] The "Ce-sure," marking Arthur's just-missed encounter with his own epic subjecthood, also shows that memory (and birth, and trauma) always comes not in "iust time," but too early or too late.

[59]"Analysis and Truth or the Closure of the Unconscious," *The Four Fundamental Concepts*, 145.

CHAPTER SIX

Obsessional Time:
Waiting for Death in Epic

Festina lente

As the *rex quondam rexque futurus* whose moment of self-recognition within Tudor prophetic destiny is cut short by an "vntimely breach," Arthur underscores the highly ambivalent relationship between epic history and time—an ambivalence that necessarily situates every dynastic epic on the obscure threshold not only between history and psyche, but also between time and psyche. After all, the practice of psychoanalysis itself is intimately and ambivalently bound up with temporality. We can consider, for example, Lacan's controversial "variable length" encounters during which he often chose to conclude the "fifty-minute" session prematurely and arbitrarily as a means of disrupting the analysand's control over his own narrative. Moreover, even before the analysand ever reaches the analyst's couch, the waiting room can become a drama of uncertainty and anticipation, a tug-of-war between therapist and patient as to who will be (too) early or (too) late for their future encounter. There is also the crucial matter of when the analyst finally decides to present the analysand with a diagnosis or an interpretation. In *The Question of Lay Analysis*, Freud cautions, "You must wait for the right moment at which you can communicate your interpretation to the patient with some prospect of success."[1]

[1]*SE* 20:220. For a rich and valuable discussion of the importance of time as a structuring principle for psychoanalysis, see John Forrester, *The Seductions of Psychoanalysis* (Cambridge: Cambridge University Press, 1990), 168–218.

But how does one know the "right moment" to interpret? Arbitrary suspensions of time, waiting, delay, the prospects of being too early or too late—all constitute the temporal power play that is interpretation. The reader, like the analyst, must bide time and play an ill-defined waiting game for the purposes of deciding when an interpretation can be sprung on a text. Such a waiting game is of signal importance when interpreting epic romance, whose typical narrative gambits of deferral, wandering, dilation, and aimlessness serve to disguise such crucial "right moments" of interpretation. Like the relationship between analyst and analysand, the intersubjective exchange between the deferrals of the text of epic romance and of a reader anxious to apply interpretive closure (like Pyrochles seeking Occasio in Book 2 of *The Faerie Queene*) foregrounds time as a precious (and often misunderstood) commodity for both psychoanalysis and the narrative of epic history.

In his fascinating account of the obscure threshold that constitutes "psychoanalytic time," John Forrester defines the obsessional neurotic as the notorious procrastinator of psychoanalytic dialogue. Deploying strategies of hesitation and delay, the obsessional neurotic always enacts a "seduction" of the analyst—presenting an interpretive challenge for the analyst because of "the ability to make nothing happen either very quickly or very slowly." Always discontinuous with time, the obsessional "will work so as to produce nothing—to fill up the time of waiting with acts that are not acts,"[2] much like Arthur's tediously prolonged reading of the *Briton moniments*. Thus the obsessional and the analyst—and the subject and reader of epic romance—often find themselves playing a paraodoxical game of *festina lente*, glossed by Erasmus in his *Adagia* as, "hasten your flight . . . in such a way that you do not anticipate the appointed time."[3] In this temporal struggle between obsessional neurotic and analyst, the crucial question becomes: how does one end the seemingly endless period of waiting? The process of intersubjective "working through" that characterizes psychoanalysis is, like the structure of epic romance, theoretically endless—unless someone, the analyst or the poet, intervenes to call the bluff and *punctuate* the dialogue.

In his subtle account of the intersubjectivity between analyst and analysand, Forrester exposes the complex psychic subtext of interruption as a temporal phenomenon. When the analyst interrupts,

---

[2]Ibid., 170, 171.
[3]Quoted by Nohrnberg, in *The Analogy of "The Faerie Queene,"* 324, from Margaret Mann Phillips, trans., *Erasmus on His Times* (Cambridge, 1967).

the patient is, in effect, being told: "What you are saying is so significant—because it is so unimportant and sterile—that we must hear
of it, far more than you, reckoning by the clock, thought we would
have of it, far more than you, reckoning by the clock, thought we
would have to hear."[4] Arthur's delay, his interminable reading of
the "sterile" *Briton moniments*, then, is parodied by the "Cesure" that
punctures the hero's "obsessional" time. Again, as Forrester writes,
the interrupting analyst "shows the subject that the 'and then?' of
narrative time is mirrored by the 'oh, nothing' of obsessional time,
and can be parodied to everyone's advantage and satisfaction."[5] The
"Cesure" parodies Arthur's own delays, concealing its own "oh,
nothing" of deferral, which effectively cuts Arthur out of the dynastic narrative, inserting Britomart and Arthegall (and Merlin's own
problematic prophecy) in his place. The caesura terminates Arthur's
dynastic delay, initiating its own temporality of a "time between" in
which Arthur is free to indulge his fantasy for Gloriana—and to prolong his own obsessional waiting even further.

Like the obsessional neurotic, the narrative of *The Faerie Queene*,
the "end" point of the literary history of dynastic epic, is alienated
within a series of just-missed encounters with the proper timing of
epic history. In this context, we can identify the rending "Cesure,"
the "vntimely breach" of the *Briton moniments*, as a (premature) signifier of the tendency toward deferral that haunts all of epic romance. The caesura is the mark par excellence of a disjunctive temporality—a nondiscursive disturbance in the text that thwarts the
anticipations of the *Moniments'* historical syntax.[6] Calling attention to
another kind of time outside of the text, the "Cesure" represents an
extraordinary moment in the literary history of epic. It represents
the text, not as hermeneutic meaning, but as pure temporal act.

As we have seen, Arthur, like the obsessional neurotic, exists on
an obscure threshold between anticipation and nonhappening. The

[4]*The Seductions of Psychoanalysis*, 172.
[5]Ibid., 173.
[6]In "The Agency of the Letter in the Unconscious," Lacan writes, "For the signifier,
by its very nature, always anticipates meaning by unfolding its dimension before it.
As is seen at the level of the sentence when it is interrupted before the significant
term: 'I shall never . . .', 'All the same it is . . .', 'And yet there may be . . .'. Such
sentences are not without meaning, a meaning all the more oppressive in that it is
content to make us wait for it" (*Écrits*, 153). To these meaningful interruptions that
make us wait, one could add the terminating sentence of Merlin's prophecy, "But yet
the end is not" (3.3.50).

rending "Cesure," as a prosodic mark of intervention, is just such a psychoanalytic act of punctuating (paradoxically, "without full point"); it calls Arthur's bluff of delay, cutting short the narrative dialogue (the intersubjective exchange between the reader of *The Faerie Queene* and Arthur as reader of the *Briton moniments*) with its own temporal act of delay. The trajectory of Tudor prophetic destiny (not to mention of Elizabeth as both reader of *The Faerie Queene* and proleptic head of Tudor *imperium*) waits interminably for Arthur to finish Eumnestes' text "withouten end." We could say that the *Briton moniments* prolong Arthur's experience of reading, even as Arthur's reading prolongs his own anticipation as the *rex quondam rexque futurus*. Or should we say that *The Faerie Queene* itself acts as its own textual intervention at the point in Book 3 at which epic prophecy yields to Merlin?

Alone among the epics we have examined, the overdetermined "endlesse worke" of *The Faerie Queene* is frustrating to interpret because it has no ending; for that matter, Spenser's epic is highly self-conscious of its unfinished status. In no other epic we have studied has the concept of time been so persistently foregrounded as a source of preoccupation, and even anxiety;[7] indeed, in his prefatory "Letter to Raleigh," Spenser has to admit to a potential temporal confusion posited by his epic's putative twelve-book structure: "The beginning therefore of my history, if it were to be told by an Historiographer should be the twelfth booke, which is the last." Because, as Spenser also admits in his "Letter," the beginning of his epic "depend[s] vpon other antecedents" that are almost impossible to consolidate, *The Faerie Queene* traces a complex network of retrogressions, interruptions, and reiterations. Repeatedly, it finds itself stalling in the temporal lassitude of being positioned "in the middest" or, even more ambiguously, on the deferred threshold of "a-while." Even as the (retroactive) "endlesse memory" of Merlin's prophecy (as Spenser's continuation of the abortive *Briton moniments*) anticipates the moment "when the terme [of Tudor epic destiny] is full accomplished" (3.3.48), the prophecy lapses into its own "long protense" of obsessional time; and the prophecy's dynastic avatar Britomart is told she will have to suffer the temporal trauma of a "hard begin" that is destined to "end" with Merlin's obsessional

---

[7] For an analysis of Spenser's concept of temperance as "good timing," see *The Analogy of "The Faerie Queene,"* 305–26.

delay: "But yet the end is not." Repeatedly throughout *The Faerie Queene*, Spenser's characters trace a "returne backe againe" to "former course," mocking Merlin's visionary "streight course of heauenly destiny." Not surprisingly, the figure of "Tyme" itself makes its appearance in the "Mutabilitie" cantos (with Mutabilitie herself embodying a characteristically Spenserian preoccupation with time), depicted as "an hory / Old aged sire, with hower-glasse in hand" (7.6.8).

Increasingly throughout *The Faerie Queene*, it is almost as if Spenser seeks to escape from the ambiguous "long protense" of his own epic of deferral, becoming preoccupied with retrograde and nostalgic glimpses of "the record of antique times" and "the image of the antique world."[8] Although in his "Letter to Raleigh" Spenser depicts the "poet historicall" as unproblematically "recoursing to the thinges forepaste, and diuining of things to come," Spenser's own "euerlasting scryne" of epic history cannot, as we saw at the beginning of the previous chapter, resist morbidly retrospective, *de casibus* reviews of the falls of empires as one of his characteristic epic topoi.

Thus, one suspects that the continual impulse toward retrospection and "endlesse" preoccupations with time always signals a larger preoccupation with death. With this in mind, our final consideration of epic history will focus on the (transhistorical) locus of Spenser's Garden of Adonis, whose temporal cycles reveal that epic history has, all along, been masking its most obsessional impulse of all—the wait for death.

---

[8]Berger writes that "Spenser's frequent references to the antiquity of his story serve to locate it in the qualitatively 'early' or archaic world. Antiquity is not merely 'a long time ago' . . . but also a particular primitive phase of psychocultural experience" ("'The Faerie Queene,' Book III," in *Revisionary Play: Studies in the Spenserian Dynamics* [Berkeley: University of California Press, 1988], 93). The nostalgic impulse is so preoccupying that Spenser implies a wish to abandon his own epic project so that (much like Arthur) he can go back and read of prior epic feats:

> For all too long I burne with enuy sore,
> To heare the warlike feates, which Homere spake
> Of bold Penthesilee, which made a lake
> Of Greekish bloud so oft in Troian plaine.
>
> (4.2.3–6)

Here, Spenser's nostalgic impulse puts us squarely back not only in the Iliadic world of Homer, but also in Carthage in front of Dido's murals (whose final image, we remember, is that of Penthesilea)—the traumatic origin of dynastic epic as the memory-trace of Troy.

The "Matter" of Life and Death in Epic

Spenser's Garden of Adonis (3.6) is perhaps the most enigmatic *locus amoenus* in all of epic literature—and thus, though "farre renowmd by fame" (29.9), the one most resistant to interpretation and not easily placed within a dynastic framework. Unlike Spenser's other privileged loci of transcendence, such as, for example, Mount Acidale, where Calidore freely spies on Colin piping to his "troupe of Ladies dauncing" (6.10.10.7), or on Arlo Hill, where Faunus feasts his eyes on the bathing Diana (7.7.45–46), the invaginated enclosure of the Garden of Adonis, where there is neither subject nor object (where there is no privileged point of orientation), disables the acquisitive gaze of the voyeur and defies our powers of conceptualization. It is hidden, private, latent. The Garden, then, poses a number of recondite problems. What are its precise boundaries?[9] Does one wall or do two concentric walls surround it? What is the function of the "double nature[d]" Genius? And, most problematically, how are we to interpret the presence of Time itself?

As we have seen, the prophetic structure of dynastic epic is traditionally structured on a principle of paternal ideology far removed from the operations of actual genetic reproduction. But the Garden of Adonis, as Spenser's account of natural generation, as a transcendent center of organic vitality that underwrites the germinal principles of procreation—as, indeed, "the first seminarie / Of all things" (30.4)—is Spenserian mythopoesis at its most elemental, a simple (yet no less elusive) myth of how, in the "wide wombe of the world," the fertile, primal fluids of menses and semen commingle mysteriously to create animate matter. As such, Spenser's embryogenetic Garden reminds us of another immanently mythopoetic document about "first things"—Freud's controversial *Beyond the Pleasure Principle*, a work that was never fully accepted by his imme-

---

[9]Berger has emphasized "the very difficulty of visualizing this garden with any precision" ("Spenser's Gardens of Adonis," in *Revisionary Play*, 142); and Donald Cheney, who also prefers to conceive of this strange locus in the plural as "gardens," writes that "the very discontinuity of the topography . . . suggests that the passage is dialectical rather than descriptive in its structure" (*Spenser's Image of Nature: Wild Man and Shepherd in "The Faerie Queene"* [New Haven: Yale University Press, 1966], 132). More recently, Gross has remarked that "within the description of the Garden itself, surfaces, persons, and structures continually recede and give way to others, each explaining and failing to explain the one preceding" (*Spenserian Poetics*, 186). Miller writes, "We seem to slide laterally into the Garden by a process of association; the transitions are metonymic in their appearance of arbitrariness . . ." (*The Poem's Two Bodies*, 224).

diate circle of followers.[10] Much as Spenser's Garden of Adonis has
puzzled generations of Spenserians, *Beyond the Pleasure Principle*, and
its positing of the often misunderstood "death drive" (or *Todestrieb*),
confounded the psychoanalytic community; it is at once Freud's
most speculative work and the one most difficult to interpret. One
cannot help feeling that the source of these works' shared interpretive difficulty is their concern not so much with questions of metaphysics as with the fundamental principles of biology (or even *meta-
biology*) and of the genesis of life itself. Freud, who throughout his
career perhaps never fully abandoned the possibility that psychoanalysis could eventually be accommodated into neurophysiology,
himself confesses at the end of his work that "it should be made
quite clear that the uncertainty of our speculation has been greatly
increased by the necessity for borrowing from the science of biology.
Biology is truly a land of unlimited possibilities."[11] So also, we could
say, may the Garden of Adonis be viewed as a land of unlimited
possibilities where, as Berger remarks, "Life as *bios* has triumphed
over the forms of thought and culture."[12] As we shall see, perhaps
what is at stake in the biological emphasis of both works is a presentation of the profound but elusive links between the laws of biology
and the formation of consciousness itself. As Spenser's *Beyond the
Pleasure Principle*, the episode of the Garden of Adonis is a privileged
myth of psychogenesis, lying far outside the bounds of genealogy
and the paternal metaphor of dynastic continuity.[13]

We can perhaps attempt to conceptualize (if not actually visualize)
the Garden of Adonis through a series of analogies. Like the dizzying torques of a möbius strip, the Garden is simultaneously center
and circumference of its own generational processes.[14] It is perhaps
more fruitful, then, to conceptualize its obscure lineaments not topo-

[10]As Laplanche has remarked, "Never had Freud shown himself to be as profoundly *free* and as audacious as in that vast . . . metabiological fresco" (*Life and Death*,
106).

[11]*SE* 18:60.

[12]"Spenser's Gardens of Adonis," in *Revisionary Play*, 144.

[13]As Nohrnberg notes, the name "Adonis" is derived from Eden. But even more
noteworthy in this context, Nohrnberg also quotes from an anonymous note ap-
pended to Comes's *Mythologiae*, where the author writes that the "Greek word *hedonai*, which signifies pleasure, seems to derive from the Hebrew Eden" (*Analogy*,
517). Viewed in this light, then, Spenser's Garden of *hedonai* would indeed appear to
be the poet's own exploration of a "pleasure principle."

[14]Terry Comito has noted that "when we speak of the forms of a garden, we are
talking about ways of organizing space" (*The Idea of the Garden in the Renaissance* [New
Brunswick: Rutgers University Press, 1978], 25). But, as Roche writes, Spenser's Garden "is everywhere and nowhere *in particular*" (*The Kindly Flame*, 120).

graphically or spatially, but rather as an unspecified system of organic energy, where the tensions of its ineffable copulatory rhythms strive to achieve a kind of systemic homeostasis: "Yet is the stocke [physical matter] not lessened, nor spent, / But still remaines in euerlasting store, / As it at first created was of yore" (36.3–5). And like Freud's hypothetical "undifferentiated vesicle" in *Beyond the Pleasure Principle* and its vulnerable cortex that must resist or filter stimuli, Spenser's quasi-Platonized "formes" that replenish the world enact a dialectics of economy that alternates between an active tendency to bind energy into higher principles of biological organization ("All things from thence doe their first being fetch, / And borrow matter, whereof they are made" [37.1–2]) and a conservative tendency to discharge energy—almost, as Freud might say, in an evacuative effort to reduce tension. Thus the "formes" of this immortal, composted "seminarie" inevitably "returne backe by the hinder gate" (32.9) and seek a stasis as they "first created [were] of yore" (36.4). It is as if the Garden's "formes" aim for a principle of constancy, "seeking," as Freud writes of his struggling "vesicle," "to reach an ancient goal by paths alike old and new."[15] Though Spenser's "formes" are thrust aggressively into the world to "inuade / The state of life" (37.4–5), they also seemingly yearn for a quiescence that would release them from the endless cycle of being "sent into the chaungefull world againe" (33.7); it is almost as if they yearn to bury themselves, once and for all, in the Garden's "fruitfull soyle of old" (31.1).

The Garden of Adonis, then, is a world of origination and regeneration, where the hidden seeds, the *logoi spermatakoi*, of its immortal "formes" replenish the world in a "continuall spring" (42.1). But despite the Garden's celebration of the potential for life, we must also consider the symbolic resonance of "Old Genius," whose uncanny "double nature" results from his inhabiting the obscure threshold of the dual gates of life and death. Because the "formes" of Spenser's "seminarie" are (merely) "borne to liue and die" (30.5), we are presented not only with the impulses of life and the "potentialities" of its fertile seeds, but also with an allegory of the *soma* passing on its way to death. Through the obscure processes by which its potential "formes" continually "borrow matter," the Garden is, in this sense, literally "erotic," in so far as it is the binding of energy into higher life forms that constitutes Eros as an ancient bio-

[15]*SE* 18:38.

logical principle; and the systemic energy of the Garden enacts the
embryological rhythms whereby ontogeny is continually recapitulating phylogeny. But in order for these vast rhythms of life to pulsate
unimpeded—in order for the evolutionary successes (and succes-
sions) of perpetual generation to occur—the shock of innumerable
traumas must be suffered by isolated organisms. Freud's mythopoetic "beyond" to the pleasure principle invites us to imagine the un-
told story of *natura naturans* as the darker, conflictual rhythms of
stressed organisms seeking to resist unwanted invasions, excitations, perturbations—of unceasing efforts by embattled cellular pro-
tozoa to conserve energy, to resist traumas that attempt to breach
fragile cortical layers, to develop preparatory anxiety mechanisms
for the anticipation of such traumas. One can imagine that to be
"borne to liue and die" in Spenser's garden implies these invasive
traumas.

The heart of the "beyond" of the pleasure principle is reached
when Freud announces, "*It seems, then, that an instinct is an urge inherent in organic life to restore an earlier state of things* which the living
entity has been obliged to abandon under the pressure of external
disturbing forces."[16] Organic life, argues Freud, is inherently inertial,
inherently protective of its precious initial state of quiescence—in
short, inherently unerotic. The organism is literally conservative,
endlessly filtering and neutralizing stimuli not solely for the purposes of binding energy (or, in Spenser's terms, "borrow[ing] matter"), but in an often frantically regressive effort to maintain homeostasis—to seek endlessly (and nostalgically) "to restore an earlier
state of things," to "returne, where first [it] grew." The excitatory
activity of cellular consolidation into higher life forms is, in a word,
traumatic. The phylogenetic processes of organic life that are readily
seen as natural, according to what Laplanche has termed an "ideology of progress" within evolution,[17] may also be viewed as protective responses to traumatic stimuli. As much as procreation, the
"natural" state of things may be to return to an inorganic state—to a
zero-degree sum of energy. "We shall be compelled," Freud argues,
"to say that '*the aim of all life is death*' . . ."; and the function of the
instincts of self-preservation is, when all is said and done, "to assure
that the organism shall follow its own path to death."[18] Freud proposes a simple biological narrative: "For a long time, perhaps, living

[16]Ibid., 36; italics Freud's.
[17]*Life and Death*, 108.
[18]*SE* 18:38, 39; italics Freud's.

substance was thus being constantly created afresh and easily dying, till decisive external influences altered in such a way as to oblige the still surviving substance to diverge ever more widely from its original course of life and to make ever more complicated *détours* before reaching its aim of death."[19] The vast rhythms of perpetual generation, then, may be little more that unanticipated divergences resulting from "decisive external influences"—divergences that constitute "ever more complicated *détours*" from the desired quiescence of an originary inanimation. It is possible for us to imagine that Spenser's "formes" may be tired of responding to the evolutionary telos of the Garden's cycles of generation and their traumatizing excitations, which disturb inertial quiescence into life—tired of participating in the hard labor of immortality, by which their *rationes seminales* must continually struggle to transmit the distinguishing features of species from one generation to the next. Just as Freud's originary vesicles must be submitted to being "created afresh" only to die off quickly, so also may the Garden's "formes" be weary of being "grow[n] afresh" (33.3), only to have the scythe of wicked Time "mow the flowring herbes . . . / Where they doe wither, and are fowly mard" (39.4–6).

But it is not merely a case of the organic yearning to be inorganic. As Freud emphasizes, life "shall follow its own path to death." Derrida glosses the Thanatopic enigma of Freud's "death drive" thus: "Such would be the function of these component drives: . . . to die one's own death, to help . . . in death's being a return to the most proper, to the closest to oneself, as if to one's origin, according to a genealogical circle: to send oneself [*s'envoyer*] . . . to avoid a death which would not amount to itself."[20] The genealogical circle traced by the perpetual generations of the Garden of Adonis may also be the genealogical circle whereby life seeks, once and for all, to "againe returne" to its originary inanimation, to its own death, to its own *proper path* to death, wherein, as expressed by Spenser, "the substance is not chaunged, nor altered" (38.1). This is the truth of the Garden that "Old Genius" and "wicked Time" alike may know.

The ultimate allegory of the Garden of Adonis, then, may be a kind of *reverse* psychogenesis, the striving of the organism to de-evolve to a primal state before not simply life, but consciousness itself. As part of his mythopoetic impulse in *Beyond the Pleasure Prin-*

---

[19]Ibid., 38–39.
[20]Jacques Derrida, *The Post-Card: From Socrates to Freud and Beyond*, trans. Alan Bass (Chicago: University of Chicago Press, 1987), 355–56.

ciple, Freud contemplates nothing less than the genesis of consciousness itself, arguing that consciousness also originates in the excitatory processes by which the organism receives stimuli: ". . . an excitation has to overcome a resistance, and . . . the diminutions of
resistance thus effected is what lays down a permanent trace of the
excitation, that is, a facilitation."[21] Consciousness occurs, then, as an
invasive breaching of protective layers, the residue, or permanent
trace, of excitations that the organism could not successfully ward
off. Where there is breaching, there is internal energy. As perceived
by Laplanche, consciousness is a "specific formation within the
mnemic systems, an internal object cathected by the energy of the
apparatus."[22] Consciousness, then, actually grows in response to increased excitations and calls for ever-more-complex bindings of energy.

The process of representation itself occurs when the organism
seeks to defend itself against an overabundance of undischarged
stimuli. One result of the higher consolidation of consciousness,
then, is the binding energies of Eros as a cathexis of representations,
which occur because psychic energy is seeking to bind and discharge itself.[23] And what would this Eros cathect onto? We are now
free to speculate that the first "*ur*-binding" of a primal consciousness
may have been a not-fully-developed ego (or nascent self-consciousness) seeking to organize or consolidate itself through a process of
self-representation—a representation of the ego to/for itself—all of
which constitutes the process of narcissism itself. Narcissism, much
more than repression, is the first psychic experience, a libidinal investment of the self *for* itself. Narcissism, then, is literally "erotic"
(literally Eros-like) in that it seeks ever higher forms of unity by
binding its energies into a consolidation of self.

In this sense, then, all literary narrative is inherently narcissistic.
But the narrative of narcissism is also inherently deadly. "All narrative," argues Peter Brooks, "is obituary."[24] For that reason, epic romance and its psychic economy of deferral, its meandering ara-
besques that double back on themselves, seem "safest" for its heroes

[21]*SE* 18:26.
[22]*Life and Death*, 66.
[23]In his discussion of the complex relationship between narcissism and the repetition compulsion, Weber observes that "if psychic energy distinguishes itself from
other forms of energy by its quality of being bound (or bindable), what it is bound *to*
is a representation" (*The Legend of Freud*, 126).
[24]"Freud's Masterplot," in *Literature and Psychoanalysis: The Question of Reading: Otherwise*, ed. Felman, 284.

when the "obsessional time" of its narrative is designed to stall the cathexes of imperial narcissism. For in epic, the formation of consciousness (the narcissistic accession to subjecthood) means inevitable death; and in epic, where subjects must continually seek (Eros-like) to represent for themselves their place in history, the narrative of narcissism seems especially deadly because death does not follow its "proper path."

A possible epic prototype for the Garden of Adonis and its cyclical rhythms of life and death occurs in Virgil's Elysium (not surprisingly, on the verge of epic prophecy), where Aeneas, spotting mysterious shades drinking from the waters of Lethe (the river not of epic memory but of forgetting), asks Anchises who they are. The old father explains:

> Quisque suos patimur manis, exinde per amplum
> mittimur Elysium et pauci laeta arva tenemus;
> donec longa dies perfecto temporis orbe
> concretam exemit labem, purumque relinquit
> aetherium sensum atque aurai simplicis ignem.
> has omnis, ubi mille rotam volvere per annos,
> Lethaeum ad fluvium deus evocat agmine magno,
> scilicet immemores supera ut convexa revisant
> rursus et incipiant in corpora velle reverti.
>
> (VI.743–51)

> (First each of us must suffer his own Shade;
> then we are sent through wide Elysium—
> a few of us will gain the Fields of Gladness—
> until the finished cycle of the ages,
> with lapse of days, annuls the ancient stain
> and leaves the power of ether pure in us,
> the fire of spirit simple and unsoiled.
> But all the rest, when they have passed time's circle
> for a millennium, are summoned by
> the god to Lethe in a great assembly
> that, free of memory, they may return
> beneath the curve of the upper world, that they
> may once again begin to wish for bodies.)

But Anchises' explanation "explains" very little, such that Aeneas's initial confusion still seems justified: "O pater, anne aliquas ad caelam hinc ire putandum est / sublimis animas iterumque ad tarda reverti / corpora? Quae lucis miseris tam dira cupido?" ("But, Father, can it be that any souls / would ever leave their dwelling here to go / beneath the sky of earth, and once again / take on their sluggish bodies? Are they madmen?" [719–21]). Given his own struggles with the *iter durum* of epic destiny, Aeneas, as if in anticipation of the tragedies of Rome's founding that lie ahead, is astonished that souls would ever give up their quiescence to return to earthly travail. The *Aeneid* never fully dispels this enigma.

In the *Orlando furioso*, in the depths of Merlin's cave, Ariosto explicitly links the accession to epic subjecthood with death. Melissa's prophecy to Bradamante foretells the future doom of Ruggiero, who will be brutally murdered by the Pontieri of the Maganza clan (3.24). The sorcerer Atlante, himself eventually entombed in a funereal *cipresso* (for Tasso's Clorinda, also, the tree of death), is all too aware that the plot of the movement of the *translatio imperii* to Ferrara will write his ward's obituary; and he seeks to keep Ruggiero sequestered in his notorious palace, which, though inimical to the fulfillment of epic destiny, is a safe haven where Atlante can defer Ruggiero's cathexis onto the "narcissism" of Ferrarese empire.[25] One of Spenser's more explicit borrowings from Ariosto occurs, then, in his own version of Merlin's prophecy, where the mage hints darkly of Arthegall's "last fate" (3.3.28) in which he will be "too rathe cut off by practise criminall / Of secret foes." (Again, we see how a death that has not followed its proper path, like birth, always comes "too rathe," or too early.)

For that matter, the very vehicle of epic prophecy, Merlin himself (like Atlante entombed in the *cipresso*), already inhabits an obscure threshold between life and death. In the *Furioso*, Melissa points out to Bradamante:

> Col corpo morto il vivo spirto alberga,
> sin ch'oda il suon de l'angelica tromba
> che dal ciel lo bandisca o ve l'erga,
> secondo che sarà corvo o colomba.
> Viva la voce; e come chiara emerga,
> udir potrai da la marmorea tomba,

[25]For a discussion of Atlante's actions as a "stay of execution" for the doomed Ruggiero, see David Quint, "The Figure of Atlante: Ariosto and Boiardo's Poem," *Modern Language Notes* 94:1 (1979), 77–91; see also Albert Ascoli, *Ariosto's Bitter Harmony*, 361–76, who points out that in the penultimate canto of the *Furioso*, which describes the furious final battle between Ruggiero and Rodomonte, the final words of the last three lines are "errore," "differire," and "morire," Ariosto's explicit linking of romance error, deferral, and death (364).

che le passate e le future cose
a chi gli domandò, sempre rispose.

(3.11)

(This is the ancient memorable cave
Which Merlin, that enchanter sage, did make:
Thou may'st have heard how that magician brave
Was cheated by the Lady of the Lake.
Below, beneath the cavern, is the grave
Which holds his bones; where, for that lady's sake,
His limbs (for such her will) the wizard spread.
Living he laid him there, and lies there dead.)

As Britomart and Glauce discover, Spenser's Merlin too suffers a living death "buried under beare" (3.3.11). And even though Spenser never refers to it, the reader knows that Arthur himself will be killed by Mordred. In Book 1 Spenser tells the reader that Arthur was given a suit of armor by Merlin as a "young Prince, when first to armes he fell" (7.36.7). But, in an oddly misplaced elegiac moment, the poet adds, almost parenthetically, "But when he dyde, the Faerie Queene it brought / To Faerie lond, where yet it may be seene, if sought" (36.8–9). Thus we are presented with a brief and evanescent foreshadowing of the deadly termination of Arthur's "prophetic moment"—a moment reduced to a memorial fetish through his enervate armor. In the midst of these references to prophecies of deferral and "epic death," we can also ponder the resonance of the prophecy of Ovid's old Tiresias (himself embodying a kind of "living death"). In the *Metamorphoses*, Tiresias tells the mother of Narcissus that her son will live to a ripe old age, "si se non noverit" ("Only / If never he comes to know himself" [III.348]). Here, the prophetic narrative of narcissism almost literally writes its own obituary.

Waiting for Troy

Seeking a return to Troy, epic romance always seems to "follow its own path to death." To turn the screw of interpretation in the literary history of epic, then, is to understand the nature of epic's encounter with Troy as always just missed. As we have seen in the case of Arthur, the just-missed encounter is, perhaps, the paradigmatic psychic symptom of the quest for Troy. "For what we have in the discovery of psycho-analysis," writes Lacan, "is an encounter, an essential encounter—an appointment to which we are always called with a real that eludes us."[26] Its own intertextual aggressions (its need to compete with its predecessors in literary history) mean that epic narrative is always in a state of repetition; it is always narcissistically seeking to "repeat" Troy as the just-missed memory-trace of epic origins.

Perhaps this is the truth that Spenser's faerie knight Paridell knows when, sitting with Satyrane and Britomart at Malbecco's banquet table, and endeavoring with "gracious speech, and skill his words to frame" (3.9.32), he weaves a glib and pseudosophisticated redaction to the *Troiana fortuna*, focusing outrageously on the genealogy of his ancestor Paris as, in Paridell's estimation, that "most famous Worthy of the World" (34).[27] In an obvious parody of epic's fetishizing of its Trojan origins, the knight recites how Parius, son of Paris and Oenone, like a would-be Aeneas "gathred the Troian reliques sau'd from flame" (36.8) and escaped to the Isle of Paros, Paridell's "natiue soile" (37.8). Meanwhile Britomart, seemingly unconcerned with the ease in which Troy can serve as the origin of pseudogenealogies, recapitulates Aeneas's affective response to Dido's murals. Spenser describes her as "empassiond" (38.4) at the very mention of Troy, "sighing soft awhile" (39.1) before begging Paridell for more.

Knowing that Troy can only ever be a just-missed encounter with destiny, Paridell, parodying Aeneas's own tale of Troy at Dido's banquet table, opens his narrative of the *Troiana fortuna* with a self-consciously nostalgic, du Bellayan apostrophe:

> Troy, that art now naught, but an idle name,
> And in thine ashes, buried low does lie . . .
> What boots it boast thy glorious descent,
> And fetch from heaven thy great Genealogie,
> Sith all thy worthy prayses being blent,
> Their of-spring hath embaste, and later glory shent.
>
> (3.9.33)[28]

---

[26]"Tuché and Automaton," *The Four Fundamental Concepts*, 53.

[27]Roche discusses the absurdity of Paridell's veneration of his ancestor Paris, observing, "The history that Paridell relates is at times distorted by his own selfish interests. His forgetfulness and omissions reveal to the reader his essential lack of understanding of his lineage" (*The Kindly Flame*, 66).

[28]Paridell's apostrophe to the "idle name" of Troy recalls a passage in Lucan's *Pharsalia* where Caesar, in pursuit of Pompey following the battle at Pharsalia, happens upon the plain of a barely recognizable Troy (IX.964–99). Caesar sees the nearly

Uncannily aware that Troy is the paradigmatic "neurotic" city of epic history, Paridell plays cynically with the eager Britomart's repetition compulsion—her need, like Dido, to hear of old Troy again. In Paridell's view, it is futile for epic history to continue its appeal to Troy's deracinated "of-spring" as the foundation of a "great Genealogie" that could transform the Trojan holocaust into a new *imperium sine fine*.[29] For Paridell, the ashes of Troy symbolize not the hope for an imperial *renovatio*, but merely "direfull destinie" (33.5) and "balefull ruine" (34.4), resistant to epic consolidation.

Not satisfied with Paridell's necromantic vision of "Xanthus sandy bankes with bloud all overflowne" (35), Britomart craves a happy reconstruction of Aeneas's "Troian reliques sau'd from flame" (even as she defers Arthegall's and her triumphant view of Troynouant, the city not seen of Tudor destiny) by entreating him "back agayne / To turne your course" to narrate the outcome of Aeneas's adventures following the destruction of Troy. But Paridell continues his assault on Britomart's "auncient Troian blood" by offering an account of Aeneas that portrays him not as a dynastic founder compelled by imperial destiny, but rather as a romance wanderer, passively subject to the workings of fate. He narrates Aeneas's escape from the flames of Troy to the sea,

> Where he through fatall errour long was led
> Full many yeares, and weetlesse wandered
> From shore to shore, emongst the Lybicke sands,
> Ere rest he found. Much there he suffered.
>
> (41.4–7)

---

dried-up Xanthus, the overgrown grave of Hector, the ruined palace of Assaracus nearly obliterated by "silvae steriles et putres robere trunci" ("barren woods and rotting tree trunks" [966]). Although he notes that "nullum est sine nomine Saxum" ("a legend clings to every stone" [973]), Caesar's sojourn as a Trojan "tourist" is, in the final analysis, viewed by him as little more than a delay in his pursuit of Pompey—an indifference to Troy's venerable history that is consistent with Lucan's cynical tone throughout his epic.

[29]In effect, Paridell's contempt for Troy's "great Genealogie" also calls into question Spenser's own efforts to use his poem to celebrate "my glorious Soueraines goodly auncestrie" (3.4.6), in other words, to celebrate Elizabeth as the most glorious descendant of the Trojan line. In this context, we can also consider the wicked enchantress Alcina's slander of Charlemagne's Frankish Empire in Ariosto's *Cinque canti*. She refers to Charlemagne's ancestors as "una vil gente che fuggì da Troia / sin all'alte paludi de la Tana" ("a despicable nation that fled from Troy all the way to the deep swamps of the Don" [1.45–46]). (The edition cited is *Cinque canti*, ed. Lanfranco Caretti [Turin: Einaudi, 1977]).

The venerable resonances of the *fata Troiana* are diminished not only by Paridell's emphasis on Aeneas's "fatall errour," but also by his contention that Aeneas "hardly praised his wedlock [to Lavinia] good" (41.9), reducing Aeneas's imperial marriage to the bathos of domestic discord.[30]

Britomart renews the discursive battle of Trojan genealogies when, in a courteous but firm attempt to counter Paridell's slanted narrative, she exalts the founding of Britain's Troynouant, imperial history's latest (unseen) attempt at a Trojan *renovatio*: "But a third kingdome yet is to arise, / Out of the Troians scattered of-spring" (44.7). In particular, Britomart seeks to glorify the conquering of Albion by "The Troian Brute" (46.1), eponymous founder of Britain and of Troynouant's ancestral line. In response, Paridell, with treacherously deceptive graciousness,[31] offers an account of Brutus that he claims he has heard from old Mnemosyne, patron of Eumnestes' chamber of memory. Shaping, in effect, a second version of the *Briton moniments*, Paridell uses his narrative to undermine the Brutus line in England, culling from Geoffrey of Monmouth's *Historia regum Britanniae* a fact with no particular resonance in Geoffrey, but crucial to his own redaction. Focusing on the motive for Brutus's setting sail for Albion in the first place, Paridell narrates:

> For that same Brute, whom much he did aduaunce
> In all his speach, was Syluius his sonne,
> Whom hauing slaine, through luckles arrowes glaunce
> He fled for feare of that he had misdonne,
> Or else for shame, so fowle reproch to shonne.
>
> (48.1–5)

Thus Albion derives its ignominious origin from the fugitive flight of a Brutus calumniated by the accidental slaying of his father Silvius.

---

[30]The outrageous compression of the *Aeneid* that characterizes Paridell's narrative may have as its source Ovid's irreverent, anti-Augustan account of Aeneas's journey in the *Metamorphoses*, XIII–XIV. In his radically truncated version of the *Aeneid*, the story of Dido, to cite just one example, is reduced to four lines. (For an account of how Ariosto may have been influenced by Ovid's shortened *Aeneid*, see Daniel Javitch, "The *Orlando Furioso* and Ovid's Revision of the *Aeneid*," *Modern Language Notes* 99:5 [1984], 1023–36.)

[31]In her paper "The Arraignment of Paridell: Historiography in *The Faerie Queene*.III.ix," delivered in San Francisco at the 1987 Modern Language Association Convention, Heather Dubrow interestingly analyzed Paridell's narrative to Britomart as a demonstration of the connection between sexual seduction and storytelling, as a "power relationship between storyteller and listener."

Moreover, like Paridell's Aeneas, entangled in "fatall errour," Brutus is portrayed as "wearie wandring" (48.7) and emerges as the founder of the new land only after "losse of many Britons bold" (50.2). Like Aeneas, Brutus is less a dynastic founder than a romance wanderer, whose integrity is further attenuated by thinly veiled accusations of parricide and bad leadership. Paridell concludes his attack on "auncient Troian blood" by offering praise of Britomart's "great Troynouant" in one moment, only to take it away in another by suggesting enigmatically that Troynouant knows no superior "except Cleopolis" (51.5)—the receding city not seen by Arthur, whose (infinitely deferred) arrival there is so crucial to the fulfillment of Tudor destiny. In the final analysis, however, the most outrageous irony of Paridell's antiprophetic redaction of the Troy story is its status as a distinctly finished narrative—one of the few completed stories in the entire *Faerie Queene*. Unlike the *Briton moniments*, which end "without full point," or Guyon's *Antiquitie of Faerie lond*, which "ne yet has ended," or Merlin's prophecy to Britomart, which "concludes" with Merlin's enigmatic and obsessional delay, "But yet the end is not," Paridell's narrative concludes unambiguously: "So ended Paridell" (51.9).

Paridell's cynical conflation of the *Troiana fortuna* is a vivid demonstration that the real enemy of imperial history may be slander, hence Spenser's anxious proliferation of characters like Ate, Enuie, Detraction, Sclaunder, and the Blatant Beast. Ate, in particular, is described as "fild with false rumors and seditious trouble" (4.1.28.3), posing a threat to imperial ideology that is especially resonant when we consider that Spenser also foregrounds this "mother of debate, / And all dissention" (19.1–2) as the discordant cause of the Trojan War itself. In the Garden of Proserpina in Mammon's Cave, Guyon sees a tree on which "here eke that famous golden Apple grew, / The which emongst the gods false Ate threw . . . / That many noble Greekes and Troians made to bleed" (2.7.55.4–5,9). In Book 4, the "darksome deluc" of Ate's cave is presented as a fetishistic "moniment" to the ravages of time and its toll on the vanity of imperial wishes:

> And all within the riuen walls were hung
>   With ragged monuments of times forepast,
>   All which the sad effects of discord sung:
>   There were rent robes, and broken scepters plast,
>   Altars defyl'd, and holy things defast,

Disshiuered speares, and shields ytorne in twaine,
Great cities ransackt, and stron castles rast,
Nations captiued, and huge armies slaine:
Of all which ruines there some relicks did remaine.

                                                        (1.21)

Among other things, then, Ate's cave serves as a monument to the
antiquated chivalry of the *Orlando furioso*, reducing the ferocity of its
narcissistic object-libido to "disshiuered speares, and shields ytorne
in twaine."[32] But most prominently displayed on Ate's "riuen walls"
is a necrophilic "memorie" of "sad Ilion," in particular: "on high
there hong / The golden Apple, cause of all their wrong, / For which
the three faire Goddesses did striue" (22.3–6).

In *The Faerie Queene*, the return of a Trojan repressed is not a
Priam, or a Hector, or a Polydorus as representative of Troy as the
forgotten origin of the *translatio imperii*, but rather Ate as the instiga-
tor of Troy's "tumultuous trouble"—as, indeed, the "origin" of an
"originary" Troy as little more than "factious deedes," a city (like the
Garden of Eden) lost because of a contentious apple. And perhaps
in Ate's gruesome museum of "euill wordes, and factious deedes"
(25.5), of "tumultuous trouble and contentious iarre" (25.8), one
could also hang the text of Paridell's contentious monument to
"times forepaste."

For Paridell and Ate, Troy is not the foundation of narratives of
imperial glory but merely the origin of "factious deedes" as the
(con)founder of narratives of empire.[33] For these two figures of
slander, Troy is no longer the elusive city not seen of an imperial
Imaginary, but rather a topos of obsolescence—and even death. For
that matter, this may be Spenser's realization, too—for by the conclusion of *The Faerie Queene*, the westering of empire rests finally
neither at Troynouant nor Cleopolis, but in tiny, provincial Ireland
on Arlo Hill as the locus of the trial of the seditious Mutabilitie.

---

[32]For a discussion of Ate's "Demon-Empire" as symbolic of the decline of chivalry,
see Richard Neuse, "Book vi as Conclusion to *The Faerie Queene*," *English Literary
History* 35 (1968), 329–53.
[33]None of which is to argue that Paridell himself is immune to the entanglements of
the *Troiana fortuna*. Much of his "gracious speach" is intended not for Britomart, but
for Malbecco's beautiful wife Hellenore. Paridell, like his ancestor Paris, recapitulates
the "origin" of the Trojan War all over again, abducting Hellenore (as his "Helen")
and thereby enacting his own repetition compulsion with Troy. Nor does Paridell's
pseudosophisticated distance from Troy allow him to escape the ravages of epic
death. In Book 5, the figure of Zele testifies to Mercilla that Duessa, after enlisting
Paridell's aid in rebelling against Mercilla, "did dryue" him to death (41.9).

"Who knows not Arlo-Hill?" (7.6.36), the poet challenges the reader, deliberately parodying Dido's "Quis Troiae nesciat urbem . . ." ("Who knows not Troy?") and daring the reader to question the decorum of his comparison between this unknown locus in Ireland and Troy as the memory-trace that structures all of dynastic epic.

In the final analysis, Paridell "knows" that, as the primal scene for epic, Troy is always traumatic, insofar as trauma always means that we are too early or too late for an essential encounter. Thus dynastic epic always waits for its retroactive memory-trace of Troy, perpetually caught within a *Nachträglichkeit* that constitutes the very temporal space of waiting—a waiting for Troy that can only lead to the death of its own heroes. As Forrester writes, "In the 'waiting for death' of the obsessional, there are two components: the waiting and the death. Yet these two themes may not be separable: the waiting may not simply be postponing: the very concept of time hollowed out by waiting may prepare the way for, or make possible, the idea of death."[34] Epic waiting, in particular, makes possible the idea of Troy—the search for which, in turn, leads epic to its proper path of death.

In the introduction to my book, I suggested that, for the new historicism, the subject of epic romance would have to be seen as dispersed within a field of sociocultural (that is, imperial) codes—a dispersal that necessarily renders psychoanalysis "belated." But if epic romance is the genre of the obsessional neurotic, then the new historicism by itself offers very little analytic capacity to understand the operations of the deadly narrative of narcissism that constitutes dynastic epic's search for Troy. Greenblatt's argument that the Renaissance "self" is defined solely through cultural and legal authority simply cannot apply to the waiting game of epic romance where obsessional deferrals themselves render belated the sociocultural determinations of the imperial subject. If Ariosto's Atlante is in fact using epic deferral to construct for his beloved ward Ruggiero a kind of reverse psychogenesis (a primal state before consciousness—before the cathexes of self-representation), then psychoanalysis can scarcely be viewed as belated. The psychic and temporal peculiarities of *festina lente* become the very essence of imperial ideology. Indeed, dynastic epic, not prepared to renounce the "symptom" of Troy, reveals that psyche renders history belated.

---

[34]*The Seductions of Psychoanalysis*, 174.

Frequently Cited
Secondary Sources

Borch-Jacobsen, Mikkel. *The Freudian Subject.* Trans. Catherine Porter. Stanford: Stanford University Press, 1988.

Brown, Norman O. *Life Against Death: The Psychoanalytic Meaning of History.* Middletown, Conn.: Wesleyan University Press, 1959.

Durling, Robert. *The Figure of the Poet in Renaissance Epic.* Cambridge: Harvard University Press, 1965.

Felman, Shoshana, ed. *Literature and Psychoanalysis: The Question of Reading: Otherwise.* Baltimore: Johns Hopkins University Press, 1982.

Ferguson, Margaret W., Maureen Quilligan, and Nancy J. Vickers, eds. *Rewriting the Renaissance: The Discourses of Sexual Difference in Early Modern Europe.* Chicago: University of Chicago Press, 1986.

Giamatti, A. Bartlett. *Exile and Change in Renaissance Literature.* New Haven: Yale University Press, 1984.

Greene, Thomas. *The Descent from Heaven: A Study in Epic Continuity.* New Haven: Yale University Press, 1963.

Johnson, Barbara. *The Critical Difference: Essays in the Rhetoric of Reading.* Baltimore: Johns Hopkins University Press, 1980.

Kerrigan, William, and Gordon Braden. *The Idea of the Renaissance.* Baltimore: Johns Hopkins University Press, 1989.

Kofman, Sarah. *The Enigma of Woman: Woman in Freud's Writings.* Trans. Catherine Porter. Ithaca: Cornell University Press, 1985.

Laplanche, Jean. *Life and Death in Psychoanalysis.* Trans. Jeffrey Mehlman. Baltimore: Johns Hopkins University Press, 1976.

Marcuse, Herbert. *Eros and Civilization: A Philosophical Inquiry into Freud.* Boston: Beacon Press, 1955.

Murrin, Michael. *The Allegorical Epic: Essays in Its Rise and Decline.* Chicago: University of Chicago Press, 1980.

Nohrnberg, James. *The Analogy of "The Faerie Queene."* Princeton: Princeton University Press, 1976.

Parker, Patricia, and David Quint, eds. *Literary Theory/Renaissance Texts*. Baltimore: Johns Hopkins University Press, 1986.

Smith, Joseph H., and William Kerrigan, eds. *Interpreting Lacan*. New Haven: Yale University Press, 1983.

Weber, Samuel. *The Legend of Freud*. Minneapolis: University of Minnesota Press, 1982.

Weinberg, Bernard. *A History of Literary Criticism in the Italian Renaissance*. 2 vols. Chicago: University of Chicago Press, 1961.

Index

Abraham, Nicolas, 215n
Aeneid (Virgil), 34, 36, 42–44, 87–88, 132;
 Achates, 69; Aeneas, 44, 46, 225–27,
 245–46, 249–50 (*see also* Troy: memory
 and); Anchises, 42–45, 60, 213, 245;
 Andromache, 59, 102; Arruns, 164n;
 Camilla, 164n; Chloreus, 164n;
 Creusa, 57, 59, 73; Deiphobus, 57;
 Dido, 34, 48, 55–56, 58, 60, 77, 79, 80,
 82, 95, 101, 214, 253; Diomedes, 62;
 Hector, 57, 59–60, 62, 77, 100–102,
 105–8, 110–11, 119, 124, 140, 185, 252;
 Helenus, 59; Misenus, 155n; Palinu-
 rus, 57; Panthus, 56, 71; Polydorus,
 57, 183, 252; Priam, 57, 62, 67, 77, 79–
 80, 99, 252; Troilus, 62; Turnus, 83–
 84, 86; Venus, 82, 151
Allen, Michael J. B., 151n
Althusser, Louis, 9, 15–16, 17n
Anderson, Judith H., 225n
androgyny, 112–19, 156–68, 170–72,
 180–81, 200–203, 210–11
Arctinus, 163
Ariosto, Ludovico. See *Orlando furioso*
Aristotle, 72, 134–35, 204
Ascoli, Albert, 86n, 87n, 88n, 92n, 93n,
 126n, 246n
Austin, R. G., 65, 72, 125n, 226n

Bakhtin, Mikhail, 29n
Barthes, Roland, 159, 202, 209n
Benson, Pamela Joseph, 193n
Berger, Harry, 223n, 238n, 239n

Bersani, Leo, 140n
Boiardo, Matteo, 27, 85n, 92, 101, 103.
 See also *Orlando innamorato*
Bonifazi, Neuro, 86n
Bono, Barbara J., 79n
Borch-Jacobsen, Mikkel, 87n, 110, 158–
 60, 167
Braden, Gordon, 2, 39n
Brand, C. P., 93, 111
Brenkman, John, 17n
Brooks, Peter, 21, 29n, 244
Brown, Norman O., 35n, 40
Burckhardt, Jacob, 1–3

Carne-Ross, D. S., 89n, 93
Carroll, David, 24n, 53n
Casey, Edward S., 18n
Cheney, Donald, 201n, 239n
Cixous, Hélène, 160n, 161n, 178, 179,
 181
Clayton, Jay, 29n, 30n
Cody, Richard, 152n
Comito, Terry, 240n
Croce, Benedetto, 92n
Culler, Jonathan, 91
Curtius, E. R., 41n, 72n

Damrosch, David, 42n, 44, 47n
Dante, 24n
Davis, Natalie Zemon, 8, 19
Davis, Robert Con, 29n
death, 75, 78–80, 156–66, 168, 172–73,
 180–81, 183–88, 239–53

Library of Congress Cataloging-in-Publication Data

Bellamy, Elizabeth J. (Elizabeth Jane)
  Translations of power : narcissism and the unconscious in epic history / Elizabeth J.
Bellamy.
      p.   cm.
  Includes bibliographical references and index.
  ISBN 0-8014-2698-7 (alk. paper). — ISBN 0-8014-9990-9 (pbk. :
alk. paper)
  1. Psychoanalysis in literature. 2. Narcissism in literature. 3. Subconsciousness
in literature. 4. Epic poetry—History and criticism. 5. European poetry—Renaissance, 1450–1600—History and criticism. I. Title.
PN56.P92B346   1992
809'93353—dc20   91-55549